Benny Goodman and the Swing Era

# Benny Goodman
# and
# the Swing Era

JAMES LINCOLN COLLIER

OXFORD UNIVERSITY PRESS

New York      Oxford

Oxford University Press

Oxford   New York   Toronto
Delhi   Bombay   Calcutta   Madras   Karachi
Petaling Jaya   Singapore   Hong Kong   Tokyo
Nairobi   Dar es Salaam   Cape Town
Melbourne   Auckland
and associated companies in
Berlin   Ibadan

First published in 1989 by Oxford University Press, Inc.,
200 Madison Avenue, New York, New York 10016
First issued as an Oxford University Press paperback, 1991

Oxford is a registered trademark of Oxford University Press

Library of Congress Cataloging-in-Publication Data
Collier, James Lincoln, 1928–
Benny Goodman and the Swing Era.
Bibliography: p.   Discography: p.   Includes index.
1. Goodman, Benny, 1909–
2. Jazz musicians—United States—Biography.
3. Jazz music—United States.
I. Title.
M422.G65C6   1989   781.65'092[B]   89–16030
ISBN 0-19-505278-1
ISBN 0-19-506776-2 (pbk.)

2 4 6 8 10 9 7 5 3 1
Printed in the United States of America

This book is for the musicians
I have played with for many years,
from whom I learned
much of what I know about jazz.

# Preface

For me, Benny Goodman was first. Like many kids of my generation, I was caught up in the popular music of the day when I was ten, and very quickly went on to become an avid fan of the big bands. By the time I was twelve or so I was increasingly being drawn to the best of them—Casa Loma, the Dorseys, Ellington, Basie, Harry James, Glenn Miller. But of them all, it was the Goodman band, and the sound of Goodman's clarinet, that gripped me the hardest. It was "King Porter Stomp," "Avalon," "The Wang Wang Blues" with Lou McGarity, "Six Flats Unfurnished" and all the rest of it, that I played unceasingly on my second-hand portable with those cactus needles.

By that time I was reading *Down Beat* and learning about people like Bix Beiderbecke, Jimmie Noone, King Oliver, and the other early heroes of jazz. It was a good era for exploring the older jazz, for that was the period when the first important reissue programs were bringing onto the market "albums" of seventy-eight recordings of the Armstrong Hot Fives, Bessie Smith, Bix and Tram, the Morton Red Hot Peppers, and Red Nichols groups with Teagarden. Quite by chance, I also discovered in the attic of a rented house we lived in for several years, four of the Original Dixieland Jass Band recordings. I began discovering the books, too. Our local library had Wilder Hobson's *American Jazz Music*. I found Winthrop Sargeant's *Jazz: Hot and Hybrid*, and of course Ramsey and Smith's *Jazzmen*. Then there were the "Esquire Jazz Books," Barry Ulanov's *Duke Ellington*, Louis Armstrong's *Swing That Music*, Hoagy Carmichael's *Star Dust Road*, and of course Goodman's *The Kingdom of Swing*. At fourteen I coaxed a family friend into taking me to Nick's and after that I began occasionally hearing the people I was reading about live, at least as much as I could afford at a time when kids worked for twenty-five cents an hour at after-school jobs. At sixteen I was jamming with a few sympathetic pals from the high school marching band in the band room at lunch hour. Between everything, by the time I graduated from high school I had, like thousands of other youngsters around the world, given myself the start of an education in jazz. I had come to know the importance of Armstrong and the New Orleans players; I could see that "Cottontail" was a better piece of music than "Tuxedo Junction"; I knew that Beiderbecke was a greater jazz musician than, say, Harry James. I had a lot of learning still to do: it was some time before I was able to grasp the frightening new bop that had suddenly been sprung on us. And of course ahead were Miles Davis, John Coltrane and Ornette Coleman. But, at least partly by chance, by the time I went off to college, where I fell in with some like-minded students and began playing for fraternity house parties, I had come to appreciate the great jazz musicians of the period, many of whom were still relatively young.

But Benny Goodman was first. It was his magical clarinet that began it. It has been, thus, a considerable pleasure for me to have had the opportunity to explore more systematically this music that meant so much to me in adolescence. I hope that pleasure will be evident in the book that follows.

As always, it could not have been written without the help of many people. I would like to thank Dan Morgenstern and his staff at the Institute for Jazz Studies at Rutgers; Harold Samuel and his staff at John Herrick Jackson Music Library at Yale; Curt Jerde, Bruce Raeburn and the staff at the Hogan Archive of Jazz at Tulane; and the staff of the Music Research Library at Lincoln Center, New York, who have been helpful in many ways. I would also like to thank John Bunch, Helen and Stanley Dance, Mannie Klein, Jimmy Maxwell, Carol Phillips, Mel Powell, Jess Stacy, Helen Ward, and Sid Weiss, who offered me their memories of Benny Goodman and his bands. James T. Maher not only spent many hours generously sharing with me his voluminous research into dance bands and the Goodman bands in particular, along with his own memories of Benny, but read the manuscript and gave me many useful comments and criticisms. The manuscript was also read by Robert Sparkman, who spent much time answering my questions about clarinet technique; and by John L. Fell, who in addition supplied me with many audio and video tapes I was otherwise unable to obtain. Ernest Lumer and Jerry Sciortino discussed Goodman's classical music with me. Finally, anybody who writes about Benny Goodman owes an enormous debt to D. Russell Connor, who has made a lifetime's work of tracking down the details of Goodman's recording and playing career. This research has resulted in three books, the last of which is called *Benny Goodman: Listen to His Legacy*. I have depended on it, with very rare exceptions, for discographic details.

Readers who want more information on Goodman's records than I can give even in a book as large as this will want to consult the Connor volume. Russ Connor also read the manuscript and offered me many valuable criticisms and suggestions. Last, as always, I am grateful to my editor, Sheldon Meyer, and his staff for their sensitive and efficient help in many things.

New York                                                              J. L. C.
February 1989

# Contents

Benny Goodman and the Swing Era

# 1
# The Family

One of the critical movements in America in the twentieth century has been the construction of the great entertainment machine which today lies at the center of the culture. Professional entertainment has, of course, existed in one form or another in most cultures at most times: we think of Greek theatre, the circuses of Rome, the minnesingers of medieval Europe, the minstrel shows of nineteenth-century America. But for most people, in most places, professional entertainment has been an occasional treat: the band of music at the weekly market, the mystery play put on at the holiday fair, the lecturer traveling a circuit. Before the twentieth century, professional entertainment was available regularly only in large cities; and only a small fraction of human beings lived in cities.

This was certainly the case in the nineteenth-century United States: as late as the 1880s, two-thirds of all Americans lived in small towns and on the surrounding farms.[1] Entertainment was confined to the local firemen's band, the choral society, occasional traveling lecturers and tent shows. In the nineteenth century most American entertainment, like much else, was homemade. People sang around the piano, played baseball, ice-skated, told ghost stories, played charades, word games, and in the less restrained circles, gambled at cards. The single form of professional entertainment that was widespread was the reading of books, newspapers and the magazines which proliferated in the latter part of the last century.

But beginning in the years around the turn of the century, there arose with an astonishing swiftness the enormous entertainment system which so dominates the culture today. The propelling events were multifarious, and the whole story is far too complex to deal with in detail here. Among the causes, however, were the great movement of the population to the cities, which created a convenient mass audience for shows, dances, concerts; the invention one after another of astonishing mechanical devices for propagating sights and sounds—the player piano, the record player, film, radio, television, audio and visual tape recording machines—and, perhaps most important, a sweeping transmutation of American attitudes, which in the span of thirty years, from 1890 to 1920, changed a Victorian ethic of gentility, hard work, and self-sacrifice to one of "individualism," which had self-interest at its heart.[2] This new ethic said that pleasure was a legitimate goal for human beings, and one source of pleasure was entertainment. Today, the majority of Americans spend more time being entertained than they do anything else, including working and sleeping.

Among the most significant forms of entertainment throughout the twentieth century has been popular music. There had been popular music before; there has probably always been popular music. But never has it been as ubiquitous as it became in this century. We are so accustomed to having music pouring at us incessantly in our supermarkets, offices, factories, on the streets, our homes and our automobiles, that we find it difficult to imagine a time when people might go days at a stretch without hearing any music at all, except for their own singing. The change was occasioned not just by the invention of mechanical, and then electronic, sound reproduction systems, but by an attitude which accepted music as a background to almost anything; indeed, "background music" is a special category in itself.

But it is not just the ubiquity of popular music that has made it so central to our culture, for various forms of music have been seen as shibboleths, battle cries, for the generation which took them up. In the 1920s jazz was seized upon by a young generation as symbolic of the new hedonistic spirit which their elders so decried, turning it into a standard to the point where the period became known as "the jazz age."[3] Forty years later another generation of the young made rock symbolic of a new hedonistic revolution, again to the dismay of their elders.

The music which came in between early jazz and rock was called "swing." In its "hotter" forms this music is seen today as part of the broad stream called jazz, but taken overall it was really a jazz-based dance music which was sufficiently compelling to stand on its own as concert music. Swing was the theme music for a generation of adolescents struggling into adulthood during the critical days of the Depression and World War II, from which the United States would emerge the dominant power in the world. Its audience was born between, let us say, the years of World War I and the early years of the Depression. It was a generation too young to have partaken of the ongoing rebellious festival enjoyed by their fathers and mothers in the 1920s and too old to have joined the rather similar party held by their children in the 1960s. It was a serious generation growing up in hard times and coming of age to face the most devastating war in man's history. This generation was political: It took up socialism, voted for reforms, fought to improve society and to upraise the downtrodden.

But like any generation of young people, it wanted to have fun, too. It was the generation which listened regularly to radio, saw the invention of talking films, formed the habit of going to the movies at least once a week, and brought to maturity serious film scholarship.

But more significant to this generation than the movies was swing. People of all ages went to the movies, but swing was theirs alone. Dancing to swing was central to their courtship style. Young people danced—at first the fox-trot, then the so-called jitterbug dances which arose in the mid- to late 1930s—in huge, often elaborate dance palaces, in hotel restaurants and ballrooms, in high school gyms and, perhaps most of all, in living rooms to swing music from radios and record players. By means of the new "portable" radios their music went with them everywhere: on woodland picnics, to beaches, summer houses, skating ponds, big city parks. These people not only danced to swing, they ate to it, drank to it, necked to it, talked to it, and frequently just listened to it. It was everywhere.

This was my generation. I am therefore perhaps biased when I say that the popular music of that time, swing, was better—more sophisticated, more genuinely musical—than virtually any popular music before or since. I am by no means contending that swing ought to be put on a level with nineteenth-century Italian opera, or the classical symphonies of Mozart and Haydn. Most of it was simplistic, and much of it was shallow. But judged as popular music, a music meant to provide light entertainment, it reached a level of musicality that few popular forms have aspired to. I will have more to say on this subject later on. Here I will only say that its king was Benny Goodman.

The term, the King of Swing, was fastened on Goodman by a press agent, but it was for once an accurate invention. Goodman was not the finest improviser of his day, although he was one of them; he did not invent swing music, although he was more responsible than anyone else for developing it out of its earlier forms; his was not at every moment the most popular dance band in the country, although it probably won more of the many rather unsystematic polls of bands than any other leader.

But Goodman was the one who captured the public imagination, and his grip on it was so strong that it lasted all of his life, long after the music had dropped out of the mainstream and he had anything new to say himself. When Goodman was almost seventy, the percipient jazz critic John McDonough said, "Goodman is the only bankable jazz star left who can pack a concert hall by himself. Basie would need a co-star. So would Herman, Kenton, maybe even Rich . . . but the Goodman mystique has not only survived, it's thrived."[4]

Benny Goodman came out of one of the millions of immigrant families that so colored American society of the late nineteenth century and after. We know unfortunately little about his family. They, and people like them, were usually too busy to keep diaries, carry on elaborate correspondences, heap up mementoes of holidays, births, deaths and other significant mileposts in their lives, as middle-class families do. Nor could they always afford the cameras and film to put together photo albums showing Pop holding the new baby, Sis in her graduation gown, for their descendants to leaf through on rainy days. The basic source for information on Goodman's family and his youth is his early autobiography, *The Kingdom of Swing*,[5] written in collaboration with the music critic Irving Kolodin.

Goodman's father, David Goodman, came from Warsaw at a period when it was under Russian domination. His mother, Dora, was from Kovno, today known as Kaunas, a city in central Lithuania which was for a period the provisional capital of the country. (I calculate, on the basis of the dates of her children's births, that she could not have been born before 1875 nor after 1881, with 1877 a likely date.) Both of Goodman's parents, thus, came from the Jewish ghettos of relatively large cities, not the small town *stetls* made famous in the musical *Fiddler on the Roof*. When they immigrated to the United States is not known, but the early 1880s had seen major pogroms and the so-called "May Laws" leveled against Jews by the Czarist government.[6] A flood of emigration followed, and it is probable that David and Dora were swept into the United States on this tide. By the early 1890s they were in Baltimore, where they met, married and produced first Lena and then two boys, Louis and Morris.

In about 1903 the family moved to Chicago, which was experiencing boom times. It is difficult to know exactly where the family lived and how David Goodman earned his living. The first Jews to immigrate to Chicago in numbers had been the German Jews, who eventually clustered in the Maxwell Street area. This group was, by the time the Goodmans arrived, relatively affluent, and they tended to be somewhat scornful of the East European "greenhorns" who began flooding into the city in the 1880s. By 1900 there were some 80,000 Jews in Chicago, of which 52,000 were from Eastern Europe. These European Jews settled in an area running "approximately from Canal westward almost to Damen Avenue, and from Polk Street south to the railroad tracks at about 16th Street."[7] The main commercial area for the district was the mile along Roosevelt Street from Kedzie Avenue to Crawford Avenue. There were a number of theatres along Roosevelt, in some of which Benny would eventually get his start in music.

It is probable that the Goodmans settled in this area when they first reached Chicago.

Through the alleys came a constant procession of peddlers in horse-drawn wagons, hawking their fruits and vegetables in sing-song fashion. Mingled among them were the milkmen and icemen. Occasionally fiddlers would play Jewish melodies in the yards, and housewives would throw them a few coins wrapped in paper. . . . In the evenings most people would sit on their front porches conversing with their families and neighbors as a procession of ice cream, candy, and waffle vendors passed.[8]

Goodman later remembered his father coming home with bags of apples and bananas bought from the peddlers' wagons on the way home from work. He would also, much later, have one of his biggest hits with a song based on an old Jewish melody, "And the Angels Sing."

David and Dora Goodman produced a large family, which was ulti-mately a blessing, but one that certainly did not make life easy for them as the children were coming along. Ida and Ethel were born shortly after the move to Chicago, and for a period thereafter the children arrived almost continually—Harry, Freddy, Mary and Benny. Thereafter the pace slowed, but there were three more boys born in the next ten years—Irving, Eugene and Jerome—making twelve children in all.

In everything written about David Goodman it has always been said that he was a tailor, and by 1917 he was listed as such in the Chicago City Directory.[9] Goodman's early publicists surely liked the picture of David as a master craftsman sitting cross-legged in a little shop turning out fine suits for gentlemen. In fact, Benny had clear memories of his father work-ing in the stockyards for at least part of his youth,[10] which would suggest that David did not work full time in the garment business until he had been in Chicago for some ten years, although he—and other members of the family—may have been doing piecework at home, sewing on pockets and the like. Eventually, however, he got work in a tailoring shop of some kind, not as a master craftsman, however, but as sweated labor probably working at a machine.[11] Finally when some of the children were beginning to make good incomes, David was able to get a job at a newsstand, which at least got him out of the sweatshops.

For twenty-five years Dora Goodman had at least one and usually two or three babies to take care of, and she could not contribute much, if any-thing, to the family income. By the time Benny was born, some of the older children were teenagers and were expected to get jobs and contribute to the family. It is difficult for us today, when even people officially below the poverty line can sometimes afford to dress well and own television sets, to understand how poor American working people were in that day. According to one study of immigrant families:

Up until World War I, working-class Americans . . . made up a majority of the nation's population. . . . A high degree of transience
diluted the effects of middle-class norms on working-class life. . . .
Most working class families moved frequently, seeking work and subsis-
tence wherever they could be found. Full-time year-round employment
was a rarity, and most working-class families depended on supplemen-
tary income from more than one wage earner . . . the families of
blacks, immigrants and the American-born working class, all accepted
the necessity of a cooperative family economy. . . . During economic
slumps, children might be their family's primary source of support.
Children's obligation to help support their family did not end with
adolescence. At times when economic stress was most acute, children
were expected to defer marriage, remain at home, and contribute to
the family's income. Young men or women generally worked for perhaps seven years before marrying and were frequently unable to establish households of their own until their early thirties.[12]

Louis, who was always called Charlie because there was another Louis
at a place where he worked, was apparently still living at home when he
was well into his twenties; and as we shall see, Benny's older sisters helped
to outfit him when he started to play professionally. And when Benny
himself began to make a lot of money, he took it for granted that he
should make a substantial contribution to the support of his mother and
younger brothers.

Benny Goodman, thus, grew up in dire poverty. New clothes were rare;
children lived in hand-me-downs that were repaired again and again and
worn until they were translucent; toys were few and those simple, like tops
and hoops; food was never abundant. Goodman said that breakfast for
the family was usually coffee and rolls—buying milk for a family of that
size was out of the question.[13] He even remembered times when there
was no food at all—none whatever.[14] When he was a little bit older, and
the family was a little bit better off, it was a great Sunday morning treat
for him to dash out of the house and buy a piece of Swiss cheese for his
breakfast.

Benny Goodman was born on May 30, 1909, and named Benjamin
David Goodman. He was one of four children who would seem to have
been born within four years. At his birth there were older siblings aged
about one, two, three, five and six, as well as three older ones in their
teens. Benny was lumped in with the rest, and it is as certain as we can be
about such things that his mother was nursing at least one other child
along with him. Dora Goodman must have been nursing almost continuously for fifteen years from the time the family arrived in Chicago in
1903. She was apparently an easy-going woman who took life as it came.

During these early years she was confined to the house for the bulk of the time, socializing mainly with her own children. She spoke broken English to the end of her life, and was illiterate.[15] She has been described as "a peasant." She had, Goodman said, gone to work when she was eight;[16] and for some forty years she was occupied with children. It is hardly to be expected that she could have acquired much education.

Goodman, thus, spent his early years in a crowd, and I think at least two of the personality characteristics he showed later in life can be traced to this crowded infancy and boyhood. For one thing, Benny does not seem to have been very close to his mother. Later in life he always saw that she lacked for nothing, and indeed helped to provide her with a life far beyond her early expectations; but he does not seem to have involved himself with her any more than he thought it was his duty to. Eventually, as he moved into a larger world, they became somewhat remote from one another. According to James T. Maher, a writer who came to know Goodman well in the last decades of his life, as a youth Goodman sensed that there was a better world out there, a world of people with polished manners, elegant clothes and expensive automobiles.[17] I will have more to say about this aspect of Goodman's personality later. My point here is that Dora Goodman did not fit with this picture of life Goodman would aspire to. People who knew Dora later, when Benny was beginning to earn a good deal of money as a free-lance musician, remember her with affection. She was, said Helen Ward, the first important singer with the Goodman band, "a living doll"; others found her warm-hearted and took her solecisms as amusing. Helen Ward quotes her as saying, "I love those sexual sofas."[18] But there is also no question that, once Goodman was moving up in the world, she was something of an embarrassment. He had been only one of many children: he would be dutiful, but no more.

For a second matter, being raised among a crowd of siblings in an environment where everything was in short supply, he must have found that he had to struggle to get his share of what little there was. This picture is of course conjectural: Goodman himself did not have any memory of these very early days. But it fits precisely with the Benny Goodman people knew as an adult—a suspicious man, always worried that he was about to be cheated and determined to hang onto what he had.

The person who was most important to Goodman as he was growing up was his father. David Goodman seems to have been almost saintly, a man willing to sacrifice himself in almost every way for his family. He labored at the most fearful jobs, twelve and fourteen hours a day, as was generally the rule for sweated labor at the time. He did the family shopping, scrambling and scrounging every day to find enough food for all those mouths. He took the children shopping for shoes and trousers when there was money for them, and he pressed them to educate themselves. In *The Kingdom of Swing* Goodman said:

> Pop was always trying to get us to study, so that we would get ahead in the world. He always envied people with book-learning and education. Whatever any of us have amounted to may be pretty much traced to him.[19]

And get ahead they did: by the time Benny was in school his teenaged sister Ida was working as a stenographer and Ethel was studying bookkeeping, both occupations which put them a substantial cut above the many immigrant girls who worked in sweatshops. Goodman's love and admiration for his father lasted all of his life. Maher said, "Toward the end of his life he began to talk about 'Pop.' It struck me that his father had always been very, very important to Benny."[20] Helen Ward, who knew Benny well through much of his adult life, said, "He reminisced about his Dad at times, and tears would come into his eyes. Dad encouraged them— a very kind man, very poor man. Dad wanted the kids to have everything."[21]

An image that stuck in Goodman's mind to the end of his life was the picture of his father coming home from the stockyards. According to Maher, Goodman told him:

> There was a period when Pop worked in the stockyards, shovelling lard in its unrefined state. He had these boots, and he'd come home at the end of the day exhausted, stinking to high heaven, and when he walked in it made me sick. I couldn't stand it. I couldn't stand the idea of Pop every day standing in that stuff, shovelling it around.[22]

Here lies one clue to Goodman's character. He had grown up seeing this man he so much admired working so hard at so debilitating and demeaning a job. He grew up determined to rescue himself—and his father—from this; and it was always a source of great regret to him that his father died before Benny was able to raise him completely out of the mire.

Despite the frictions inevitably created by poverty and overcrowding, the Goodman family had a great deal of solidarity. At one point, when Dora was lying in with one of her last children, some of the others were put out to foster homes where they could be temporarily cared for. Within twenty-four hours they had all run back home. Whatever the problems, there was a certain security there.[23]

This solidarity helps to explain why Benny, when he began to make money later on, always felt duty bound to help support the others when necessary. Benny was, in one way, close to his brothers, especially the ones near to him in age—Irving, Freddy, Harry—and the two younger ones, Gene and Jerome. But even though they might see a good deal of each other at times and know what each other was up to, there was also a certain animosity. The others were not above making hostile remarks about Benny to people, inspired partly by jealousy and partly by Benny's own tendency to aloofness. Over the years relations between Benny and some of his siblings grew increasingly strained, to the point where contact between them was fairly rare. It is not surprising, then, that Benny's favorite among them was his sister Ethel. The Goodman boys must be seen as allies rather than friends; but whatever Benny felt about the rest of them, for a long time after he was grown-up, he felt a certain loyalty and sense of duty toward them, which was an outgrowth of this early family solidarity.

During Goodman's early years the family moved frequently. It is difficult to trace these movements: Goodman himself did not remember all the places he had lived as a boy. The Chicago City Directories list several tailors named David Goodman, none of them living at the same address for very long. The houses were mostly three-story buildings, some of them the classic wooden workingmen's housing with back porches, where lines of wash were invariably strung, and outside stairs leading to the top floors. Others were brick, but essentially not much different. Not all such places had indoor toilets, or even running water; there might be outhouses in the backyards, and common pumps. Few of them had central heating; heat was supplied by coal or kerosene stoves of one kind or another, and there were times in the histories of most families when there was no money for fuel on a winter's night. Apartments were cramped and dark. The Goodmans sometimes lived in cellar apartments.[24] Privacy was non-existent: the huge family lived like puppies in a box, always on top of one another. Carol Phillips, a former editor of Vogue and Estée Lauder executive, who was Goodman's companion at the end of his life, said, "You had to create privacy in your head."[25]

By his early boyhood things had improved marginally for the family. The three older Goodman children, now in their twenties, had been working for some years. Ida may have married early, but at least Charlie (Louis) and Ethel remained at home to contribute their earnings. When Benny was eight the family moved to 1125 Francisco Avenue, into an apartment which he remembered as cramped and dark. However, it was only a short distance from Garfield Park. Harry, Freddy and Benny attended Sheppard Grammar School, just down the block, and the three of them, so close in age, ran together as a pack through much of their boyhoods.[26]

In about 1918 or 1919 a family from Boston moved into a nearby building. The father was working in the garment business, and Pop fell in with him. He quickly discovered that the boys in the new family, who were somewhat older than Benny, played musical instruments and earned an occasional dollar or two from playing.[27] At that time, few middle-class families would have approved of popular music as an ambition for their children. Their children might study the piano or voice with a view to developing a love of the finer things in life, but they would certainly not aim to be professional musicians, except for the rare genius heading for the concert stage. But to working-class people, a professional musician was several steps up the ladder from the sweatshops.

The popular music machine was already in place. The country had seen ten years of a huge boom in social dancing, with a concomitant demand for music, and competent musicians were earning what to sweated labor seemed handsome incomes. And it occurred to David Goodman, always keen to see his boys studying and getting ahead, that there might be a way for them to learn to play musical instruments.

# 2
# The Musical Apprentice

The decision made by David Goodman to see that some of his boys learn to play music was obviously momentous, not only for the family, but for the history of American music.

David Goodman was not an especially religious man, but he was an ethnic Jew, and inevitably he turned to the synagogue for help. He quickly discovered that the Kehelah Jacob Synagogue, about a mile and a half from the Francisco Avenue house, had a boys' band and offered some sort of instruction, along with musical instruments which could be rented cheaply.[1] The boys' band was a common institution of the time. The astonishing growth of the cities in the latter part of the nineteenth century and the early part of this one brought with it enormous social problems—the poverty such as the Goodmans endured, crime, prostitution, drunkenness and much else. From above, the immigrants particularly were seen by many as an unruly and dangerous mob.[2] Boys were likely to become criminals if left to themselves, so it was believed, and various schemes were introduced to thwart these tendencies. Music, it was thought, had a civilizing influence, and boys who were practicing trumpets and drums were not out shoplifting. All over the United States numberless boys' bands were started for the express purpose of giving these young males something worthwhile to do in their spare time. Louis Armstrong got his first musical training in such a band,[3] and Lionel Hampton, who would later be one of Goodman's stars, was playing in the *Chicago Defender's* Newsboy Band[4] at about the time Goodman joined the synagogue band. (The *Chicago Defender* was a famous black newspaper; many papers of the time formed bands made up of their newsboys.)

Actually, the practice was not quite as cynical as it might seem. It was an era of social experiment, when the social sciences were beginning to mature, and many of these experiments were tried in a genuine concern for the plight of the poor masses and in the hope of creating a better society.[5]

Pop took Harry, Freddy and Benny, who were at the appropriate ages, to the synagogue, where they were fitted out with instruments. The story, which has been told many times, goes that Harry was given a tuba because he was the biggest, Freddy a trumpet because he was next in size and Benny the clarinet, because he was the smallest. Benny insisted on the truth of the story, and it is certainly unlikely that at ten he would have been given a tuba to play.[6] But plenty of ten-year-olds have started on trumpets, drums, trombones, and the like; and it is probable that other factors, such as what instruments were available, and which ones the band needed, entered in.

It was, in any case, a lucky accident. Whether Goodman would have proven as masterful a trumpeter as he was a clarinetist we shall never know. Nonetheless, it seems to me that certain instruments suit some people better than others, especially in jazz. Every good jazz musician has an individual musical conception exhibited in a consistent set of preferences, or tastes, which jazz fans term his "style." A player like, say, Wild Bill Davison, a cornetist who inflects his music with a great many bends, twists and growls, would be severely handicapped playing a piano. A very busy player who thinks in terms of showers of notes, like saxophonist Charlie Parker, would not be able to express his ideas nearly so well on a trombone, which cannot be played as fast as a reed instrument. Similarly, a player like Duke Ellington, who tended to think harmonically, was better off with a piano rather than a wind instrument.

Benny Goodman proved to be a natural clarinet player. He thought in terms of cascades of notes, even at the fastest tempos, and he liked to inflect his line with growls and rasps, although this tendency decreased as time passed. The clarinet was a suitable instrument for expressing his musical ideas, and it is my guess that he would not have been the dominant player he became had he been given on that fateful day, let us say, a trombone, although certainly he would have been a fine musician on any instrument he attempted.

The bandmaster at the synagogue is known only as Boguslawski. His son Ziggy was a competent pianist and acted as contractor—that is, hiring agent—for a big local theatre, probably one of the ones on Roosevelt Street.[7] Boguslawski urged Pop to give the boys private lessons. This is a standard ploy: bandmasters of this kind frequently take on such jobs primarily in hopes of winnowing out private students. How much, or what, Benny learned from Boguslawski we do not know. A bandmaster must of course teach all the instruments; he is bound to know some better than others, and may in some cases do more harm than good. But apparently

Boguslawski at least did Goodman no harm, and may have given him the beginnings of a foundation.

The synagogue band collapsed from lack of money probably within a year. Pop was determined that the boys should continue their musical studies. He eventually discovered that the famous Hull House was forming a band, and he applied to it on behalf of his boys.[8]

Hull House was one of a group of so-called settlement houses which came into being around the turn of the century. Their primary function was to help acclimate newcomers to American society, and they gave courses in cooking and the domestic arts in general. But they were far more than simple cooking schools, for the leading spirits in the settlement house movement were social reformers, who saw the houses as social experiments designed to improve the masses spiritually as well as physically. Hull House was founded by Jane Addams and Ellen Gates Starr in 1889 in the former home of the wealthy Charles J. Hull. Addams was a feminist and reformer who believed that aesthetics were important to the spiritual development of people. Hull House offered classes in dance, sketching, drama and of course music. (The American premiere of John Galsworthy's *Justice* was given at Hull House; and Frank Lloyd Wright gave his famous lecture "The Art and Craft of the Machine" there.)[9]

The Hull House band had first been formed in 1907, but had been given up later, probably during the war. Sometime in 1921, or perhaps late 1920, when Goodman was eleven or twelve, the band was reactivated under the leadership of James V. Sylvester.[10] A complete set of new uniforms and new instruments was purchased, and Goodman says that it was as much the allure of the uniforms as the instruments that attracted him and his brothers to the band.[11]

The instrument that Goodman was given both in the early band and at Hull House was the Albert system clarinet, also known as the "simple" system as opposed to the Boehm system, which has somewhat more complex fingering in order to make it easy to play certain combinations of notes at high speeds. (Actually, the Boehm system clarinet was not devised by the famous instrument inventor Theobald Boehm but by the clarinetist Hyacinthe Klosé and the instrument-maker Louis Buffet in 1839. The misnomer came about because Klosé applied certain principles to the clarinet which Boehm had worked out for the flute. The Albert system was developed from an older Muller system in the 1840s by Mahillon and Albert.)[12] The Boehm system was widely used in symphony orchestras by the earlier part of this century, although the Albert system lingered until after World War II; but the Albert system continued to be preferred in marching bands and dance bands until well into the 1920s.

This was not simple conservativism. In designing various woodwinds

Boehm aimed for brilliance at the expense of a more "mellow" sound—
the trumpet as opposed to the cornet, for example—and the Albert system
had a certain richness (especially in the lower register) that many clarinet
players preferred. But after the mid-1920s, when recording and radio became common, clarinetists were frequently working with microphones,
where the brilliance of the Boehm was more effective, and the Albert system died out in jazz and dance orchestras, except with some of the older
New Orleans musicians, like Edmond Hall, and their followers.[13] Goodman remembered switching to the Boehm clarinet when he was about
sixteen. He said later, "There are certainly undisputed advantages to [the
Boehm] but I think it did lose something."[14]

The Hull House band played the usual repertory of marches, simple
overtures and tunes drawn from the standard American song bag. It gave
occasional concerts, and paraded on holidays. There exist photos of the
band resplendent in their semi-military uniforms at the time Benny was
in it, although it is difficult to be sure which one he was.

Goodman got some instruction from Sylvester, probably not individual
instruction, but as part of a group, when Sylvester would take the whole
clarinet section through exercises and rehearse them in the band's repertory.[15] Far more important to Benny at this time were the private lessons
he began to take from Franz Schoepp. Schoepp was no ordinary music
teacher. He tutored men from the Chicago Symphony, and long after his
death Woodwind Magazine referred to him as "the great Franz Schoepp."[16]
He was always, it appears, a man with a social conscience, because he had
black pupils as well as white, which was a rare, indeed shocking, practice
at the time. When Goodman was studying with Schoepp a fellow pupil
was Buster Bailey, later a star clarinetist with Fletcher Henderson; Schoepp
would sometimes have Goodman and Bailey play duets. Schoepp also
taught Jimmie Noone for a period; Noone would shortly be one of the
clarinetists around Chicago whom Goodman would listen to.

There exists a copy of the Carl Baerman exercise book from which
Goodman studied (although not the specific copy) which was given to
Goodman in about 1950 by one of Schoepp's grandsons. Goodman noted
inside that he began studying with Schoepp in 1919. "He was seventy years
old and I was ten. These studies went on intermittently for about two
years, and that was the extent of my formal music education. At this time,
despite my extreme youth, I was already making personal appearances
playing jazz, which was my first love, although this was obviously frowned
on by Mr. Schoepp."[17] There is a problem with this dating: In The
Kingdom of Swing Goodman implies that he was already in the Hull
House band when he started studying with Schoepp; but the Hull House
band was not reactivated until 1920 at the earliest. Goodman did not

make this notation until 1966, forty-five or so years after the fact, and I
tend to trust the early remembrance given in the biography.

Furthermore, there is the whole question of how Goodman came to be
accepted as a pupil by the great Franz Schoepp. Given Schoepp's social
conscience, it is likely that he had some connection with Hull House and
came across Goodman, or was told about him, there. It makes it clear, in
any case, that Benny was already, within a year or so after taking up the
clarinet, showing signs of his remarkable talent. It was a tremendous stroke
of luck. Schoepp provided Goodman with what musicians call "the foundation"—that is to say, a sound technique, in this case involving a proper
embouchure, correct fingering, the right way to tongue, breath, and all the
rest of it. In that day most jazz musicians were self-taught; and if they
had any instruction it was the minimal advice they got from a school
bandmaster, who may not have known much himself.

Learning to play a musical instrument requires incorporating into the
nervous system a group of automatic responses, many of them involving
minute movements of the muscles at very high speeds, all exactly coordinated. It is no use to simply tell a beginning musician how it is done; the
student has to be trained, that is to say, carefully watched over week to
week to make sure that he is not picking up bad habits. In jazz the self-
taught musicians were in many cases assiduously practicing mistakes. Louis
Armstrong began destroying his lip from the moment he first picked up a
brass instrument, and by the time he was in his early thirties he was having serious lip problems which dogged him for the rest of his life, and
eventually limited his ability to get around on his instrument.[18]

Benny Goodman, however, was studying with a man who may have
been the finest clarinet teacher in the United States of the time, and got
what was probably the best early training of any jazz musician of his generation. Just as important, he picked up an attitude toward musicianship
which had profound effects on his career, and lasted until the day he died.
That was that music must be taken seriously if anything was to be made
of it. Goodman came to believe in endless practice, of the daily playing
of scales and exercises. Throughout his life, long after he had made himself
into one of the most technically proficient players in jazz, Goodman continued to practice, generally more than the men in his own orchestras,
most of whom were not in his class as instrumentalists. He insisted upon
a lot of rehearsal, and he was always driving his men to the highest level
he could screw them up to.

About the time he started with the Hull House band, Goodman was
also getting his first exposure to jazz. The music had begun to seep out of
New Orleans by as early as 1910 or so, when it was still not fully formed.
Contrary to the prevailing myth, it went first to the West Coast, in par-

ticular San Francisco, where the famous Barbary Coast sin district offered it an ecological niche similar to the one it had grown up in at home. In 1915 and 1916 it was brought to Chicago by two loosely organized white bands, which played at various of Chicago's disreputable cabarets, including Schiller's Cafe in the South Side, which was raided by police, the Casino Gardens on North Clark, a gangster hang-out, and Freiberg's, the main dance hall of the notorious Levee district, then winding down. Within two or three years, black musicians began arriving from New Orleans, among them the ones that made up the shifting personnel of the seminal Original Creole Orchestra, which eventually became the great King Oliver band. When Goodman was still a boy jazz was beginning to become popular, especially in low clubs and dance halls; and by the time he went into the Hull House boys' band, it was a national fad, being picked up by musicians all over the United States.[19] Popular Mechanics said, "Now there are thousands of jazz orchestras in this country. Almost every town of 5,000 or more has one or more. Few vaudeville programs are complete without a jazz number."[20] This was dixieland jazz, in the main.

Goodman would not have heard any of the early New Orleans bands in Chicago; he was too young and they were working in clubs he would not have been permitted to enter at that time. His own story is that he first heard jazz in about 1921. The family had somehow gotten hold of a second-hand phonograph. Charlie (Louis) began bringing home records. Goodman was particularly taken by the band of clarinetist Ted Lewis. Lewis today is mentioned only with scorn by jazz writers, because of the considerable commercial taint to much of his music. But in the early days, when he was having his first success, his group was primarily a small dixieland jazz band modeled, as so many of them were, on the Original Dixieland Jass Band. It was not a bad band in terms of the time, despite the leader's tendency to impart a tremendous wobble to his notes. The Goodman boys were impressed by the group, and Benny very quickly learned how to play a fair imitation of Lewis.[21]

Goodman cannot have avoided hearing the records of the Original Dixieland Jass Band at this time. The group had burst into the American limelight in 1917 with its Victor records, and had quickly become exceedingly popular. By 1918 it was the highest paid dance band of its size in the United States,[22] and the model for all the musicians interested in the new hot music, except the relatively small number who were hearing other New Orleans bands. Eventually most of the young jazz musicians primarily turned to various black groups for models, but at the beginning the Original Dixieland Jass Band was the major influence. Goodman does not mention the Original Dixieland Jass Band in The Kingdom of Swing, probably because not long before the book was written Nick LaRocca, the group's dominant figure, began insisting that the group had invented jazz, a claim which jazz critics indignantly rejected, citing the accepted view that the music had been originally developed by blacks. In 1939, when the book was published, it was not a smart idea to speak well of the Original Dixieland Jass Band. But later on Goodman said that Larry Shields, the group's clarinetist, was one of his early models,[23] and he is known to have owned some of their records, which jazz writer Grover Sales, who has seen them, says were "played white."[24]

Goodman also said that he was hearing, at about the same time, a group called Bailey's Lucky Seven.[25] This was a name used for recording purposes by Gennett Records, with a personnel that shifted over the years but which at various times included some of the leading white New York jazz musicians, among them trumpeter Phil Napoleon, trombonists Charlie Panelli and Miff Mole, clarinetist Jimmy Lytell, pianist Frank Signorelli and banjoist Nick Lucas. The group began recording in 1921, with Doc Berendsohn on clarinet, and Goodman was hearing some of its earliest records.

Jazz, thus, was already widely popular around the United States by the time Goodman first became interested in music, and he was hearing it right from the moment he picked up a clarinet. It caught him early, and he grew up with it in his ears as it began to develop into its first maturity in 1926 and thereafter. Goodman was fourteen when the King Oliver band issued the first important jazz records by a black band, fifteen when Bix Beiderbecke was recording with the Wolverines, sixteen when Louis Armstrong began the critical Hot Five series, in his late teens when the Fletcher Henderson and Duke Ellington orchestras began to make important records. He was thus hearing the music as an impressionable youngster as it developed into its early classic period. And very quickly he decided that this was the kind of music he wanted to play.

He was hardly alone. All around him young people his own age were caught up in the new hot music. To these young players jazz was the most exciting thing in their lives. It was something wholly different from the marches, overtures, church music, popular songs and ragtime tunes that they were used to hearing. But the music had a significance for them which transcended the lilting rhythms and hot intonations themselves. There was a sense that there was a new spirit in the land, a new freedom of expression, to enjoy life, to live fully. This generation would escape from the Victorian gentility which, as they saw it, had suffocated their parents. They would dance, drink, have sex and enjoy themselves generally. Jazz fit the new mood precisely: it was openly emotional, rhythmic and spontaneous. For many the music was part of a crusade.[26] Benny Goodman was not by nature a crusader. His interest was mainly musical, and very quickly he began to try to play jazz. But he could hardly help feeling the new spirit.

Working out the details of the first stages in Goodman's musical career is difficult. He was not always clear about the dates for things, and the ones he gave do not always jibe with documentary sources. But the broad picture is clear enough. Probably in 1921 he was invited to perform his Ted Lewis imitation as part of an amateur night at the Central Park Theatre, in the Roosevelt Street commercial district. In *The Kingdom of Swing* he said that it was a "jazz night," a promotional scheme in vogue at the time, and that his brother Charlie was responsible for persuading the theatre owner to let Benny appear.[27] Freddy Goodman says that the connection came through Ziggy Boguslawski,[28] the son of the synagogue bandmaster, who was the contractor for the theatre. However it came about, Goodman played "When My Baby Smiles at Me," Lewis's most popular hit, and possibly other numbers. Not long afterwards the theatre owner was suddenly short an act, and sent for Benny to fill in, paying him five dollars, which was as much as a working man might make in a day.[29]

At about this time pianist Art Hodes, who would have a long career in jazz—there is a tape of him jamming on the blues with Goodman shortly before Benny's death—was playing in a group called the Marionettes for a dance at Hull House. (It was not felt by everybody that young people ought to be encouraged to do the modern dances. But Hull House explained that "the well-regulated dancing party not only offers a substitute to the public dance halls, but is obviously a wholesome exercise and affords an outlet for the natural high spirits of youth which have been repressed through the day. . . . Situations occasionally occur which call for the utmost adroitness, but on the whole the best of order and decency have been maintained.")[30] Jimmy Sylvester brought Goodman into the dance, and asked the group if Goodman could sit in. Hodes said, "I looked at this kid, with a head that seemed so outsized and even though his head was outsized, his ego was outsized, too. And he had such an assurance and just a tilt of the nose almost. . . . But he could play. But I wasn't impressed because—I says, yeah, you play nice. I didn't hear no great ideas."[31]

Hodes was about four years older than Goodman, which must have seemed like a considerable difference at the time. He went on to become something of a jazz purist who took strong stands against what he considered to be commercialism, and he bore a good deal of resentment against Goodman's later success. But there was probably some justice in his view of Benny. Even that early Goodman had a confidence in himself, which taken too far could transmute into arrogance. Freddy Goodman said that at that first public performance on a large theatre stage, Goodman was unfazed. "Benny was never nervous, really. And right then he was very pleased to be called on."[32]

At about this time Goodman also began doing what budding jazz musicians have done for generations in the apprenticeship process, that is, jamming in band rooms, basements, garages. The Hull House band frequently played at Sunday picnics given by a German Lutheran group. The boys would stuff themselves with hot dogs and potato salad, and then a group of six or seven of them would go into the woods and jam. The group was the standard dixieland band of cornet, trombone, clarinet, tuba and drums, with snare and bass drums being manned by two different boys.[33] At the moment the Hull House boys were under the influence of the New Orleans Rhythm Kings, which for a period was the primary model for aspiring jazz musicians of Chicago. The Rhythm Kings opened in Chicago in 1921 as the Friar's Society Orchestra, but it is unlikely that eleven- or twelve-year-old boys would have heard them in the mob-run club they worked in. However, the group made a set of eight recordings in the summer of 1922, and it is presumably these that the Hull House boys were attempting to imitate.

About the same time Jimmy Sylvester brought some of his better Hull House players into the 124th Regiment Field Artillery band, which he also ran. After rehearsals at the armory some of the Hull House boys would stay on to jam with some of the older professionals in the band. This time the model was the New York group, Bailey's Lucky Seven.[34]

The Goodman boys were now beginning to be paid occasionally to play, mainly at parades they would march in for one organization or another. They realized that there could be money in music—we must remember that very small sums, like a dollar or two, were important in the family's economy. They therefore organized a band with some friends and rehearsed Friday evenings at the homes of various members, playing from "stocks." Music publishers had come to realize that many of the small dance bands around the country lacked the skill to work out arrangements, and that if they wanted their songs played where they would be heard, they had to offer simple arrangements with a variety of parts which could be played by various combinations of instruments. Goodman says that they stuck to the arrangements for only a chorus or two, and then would improvise. He was, thus, in several different circumstances, playing—or attempting to play—a lot of hot jazz.[35]

The timing of the sequence of events which followed is again difficult to pin down. If the dates Goodman gives in *The Kingdom of Swing* and elsewhere are accurate, he must have started going to Harrison High in 1922, when he was thirteen. He quickly fell in with a group which included pianist Bill Grimm and drummer Harry Gale, both of whom would work professionally in music. These young musicians, in various combinations, began playing for the high school dances. And at some point Goodman was asked to join a loose cadre of young musicians known to jazz history as the Austin High Gang, which included drummer Dave Tough, tenor saxophonist Bud Freeman, then playing C-melody sax, cornetist Jimmy McPartland, clarinetist Frank Teschemacher, and others. (In fact only a nucleus of them actually went to Austin High—Freeman, McPartland and his brother Dick, a guitar player, and bassist Jim Lannigan.)

Who asked Goodman to join the group is a matter of dispute. Bud Freeman said, "When I was fifteen years old and had just got my first long pants suit, I went to a street dance. . . . There was a kid in the band playing clarinet; he was no more than thirteen years of age. He played the clarinet so beautifully—it was not to be believed. He had the technique of a master and a beautiful sound to go with it. His name was Benny Goodman. He was a very pleasant little guy, who hadn't the faintest idea of the extraordinary talent he possessed."[36] At about the same time Goodman met Jimmy McPartland, who had recently started playing professionally and was working at a club run by a mobster named Eddie Tancil in the notorious Chicago suburb of Cicero. According to McPartland, Tancil brought Goodman in to sit in. The tune was "Rose of the Rio Grande." "I mean the changes for those days were difficult. . . . This little monkey played about 16 choruses of 'Rose' and I just sat there with my mouth open." The Austin High group was at that moment playing weekly tea dances at the Columbus Park Refectory, and McPartland asked Goodman to sit in. Thereafter he began working regularly with various members of the Austin High gang.[37]

They were an interesting group. Tough, who went to Oak Park High in a well-to-do suburb, was a fancier of the arts and literature, and under his influence some of the others, especially Freeman, attempted to cultivate themselves. Tough was probably also responsible for bringing to the group a romanticism which has haunted jazz ever since—the sense that the jazz man or woman was the classic neglected artist, scorned by the mob and fated to be properly appreciated only after an early death. These young men tended to see themselves as lonely keepers of a sacred flame, which the biting winds of commercialism were attempting to blow out. There was a certain truth in this: Although jazz was popular in the United States at the moment, most of the people who danced and drank to it did not understand it well, and often confused commercial versions of it with what the young jazz musicians considered the real thing.

To some extent, though, this view was a romantic delusion. There were a lot of knowledgeable jazz fans around the United States, as would become clear later in the decade when some of the best jazz bands in the country, including those led by Louis Armstrong, Duke Ellington and Fletcher Henderson, achieved considerable successes. I have written elsewhere at length on the subject of the reception given to jazz by the American public.[38] I will only say here that it was a mixed picture, with a substantial part of the population indifferent or actually hostile to the music, another substantial portion enjoying it at a relatively superficial level, and a smaller, but by no means insignificant minority, loving and understanding it. The Austin High group was really too close to the situation and could not see the forest for the trees. They were constantly faced by people at the dances they played demanding this or that soupy hit song, by managers of clubs and chairmen of dance committees asking them to tone down the racket, and especially by the spectacle of the commercial leaders like Paul Whiteman, Paul Specht, Ted Lewis, and others making money by the bucket. They failed to take into account the equally important truth that a great deal of first-rate jazz was actually being absorbed by the American public, including the rough and untutored version they themselves were producing. But the attitude that jazz was—and is for that matter—neglected by Americans found its first fuel here.

Benny Goodman, however, was not of this persuasion. Although he loved the music, and throughout his life always played it, he was also a child of poverty who had had a certain realism rubbed into his skin almost from birth. The social system worked in a certain way, and you got from it what you could. As a consequence, although Goodman would work with various of the Austin High group throughout his life, he was never really a part of it. He brought to jazz not the sense of the doomed artist but of the professional who would do what was necessary to survive. The others remained wary of him, and when he became rich and famous later on, they had a certain resentment of his success. As we shall see, when a very young Mel Powell was asked by Goodman to join the band, the older musicians he had been playing jazz with, many of them connected one way or another to the Austin High group, accused him of selling out.

By 1923 Goodman was playing frequently at pick-up affairs like the Austin High tea dances and developing a reputation among the young white jazz musicians. Sometime early in the year he was heard at a dance by a young man named Charles Podolsky, who was called "Murph," a common nickname at the time for Jews. Murph Podolsky was booking small bands around Chicago, mainly at colleges and high schools. Podolsky offered Goodman some dates which required him to join the union. The union delegates must have been a little nonplussed when confronted with a thirteen-year-old, but Benny was clearly qualified, and he joined.[39]

Goodman was now, still not yet fourteen, a professional musician, fre-

quently working several nights a week until one or two in the morning.
His sister Ethel, who was working as a bookkeeper for a clothing firm,
arranged to have a tuxedo made for him, and she also helped him to buy
a new Martin clarinet. With his own earnings Goodman bought a saxophone. Today, when many people do not start their careers until they are
well into their twenties, it may seem odd that a boy as young as Benny
would be doing a man's work. In fact, at the time a high school education
was considered a luxury in working-class families, and it was not at all
unusual for a youngster to start working full-time.[40] At fourteen Goodman
was not merely making a man's salary, but was earning what was for then
big money. Jimmy McPartland said that during this period he and Benny
worked together frequently, and could make from eighty to a hundred
dollars a week.

With the booming demand for music rolling along, accomplished musicians like Goodman, who could read well and play hot jazz, had no trouble
finding work. By the spring of 1923 Goodman was so busy he clearly could
not continue to go to school. From Dave Tough he heard of a school
designed for young professionals, which opened at eleven-thirty in the
morning, and for a period he attended this school.[41] However, the pressure of work was still too much, and when he turned fourteen in May, and
was legally able to drop out of school, he did.

Now a full-time professional who did not have to get up in the morning,
he was better able to get out and explore the night life of Chicago, then
the jazz center of the world. The city's black population had been swelling
since early in the century, tripling from 1890 to 1910.[42] This black influx
drew along with it the black jazz musicians from New Orleans. Back home
they were working for a few dollars a night; in Chicago they could earn
fifty to a hundred dollars a week, when a working man would do well to
make twenty-five dollars a week. It should be realized that, although black
bandsmen did play at blacks-only clubs and dance halls, the primary audience for jazz in the North was white, because whites out-numbered
blacks by ten or more to one and they had more money to spend. By the
early 1920s the white New Orleans jazz groups, like the New Orleans
Rhythm Kings, were playing in gang-dominated clubs for white audiences;
blacks were playing mainly in "black-and-tans" on Chicago's South Side.
These cabarets, some of them very elegant, were ostensibly meant for black
customers, but in fact existed on the custom of large numbers of whites,
especially on weekends, when whites would usually out-number the blacks.
One contemporary account described one such place, an after-hours club
called the Pekin frequented by gangsters and show business people, where
King Oliver played at one time:

In came a mighty black man with two girls. A scarred white man entered with three girls, two young and painted, the other merely painted. Two well dressed youths hopped up the stairs with two timid girls. . . . Two fur-coated "high-yaller" girls romped up with a slender man. . . . At one o'clock the place was crowded. Meanwhile a syncopating colored man had been vamping cotton field blues on the piano. A brown girl sang. . . . All the tables were filled at two o'clock, black men with white girls, white men with yellow girls, all filled with the abandon brought about by illicit whiskey and liquor music.[43]

It is clearly the racial mixing, not the music, nor even the drinking, that the writer of the piece disapproves of, a fact which we must keep in mind when it comes time for Goodman to create his mixed band. But for young white jazz musicians, these places were a revelation. They quickly came to take the black musicians as their models, instead of the whites of the Original Dixieland Jass Band and the New Orleans Rhythm Kings, although the influence of some of the whites, especially clarinetist Leon Roppolo and bassist Steve Brown, remained strong. Now it was King Oliver, Louis Armstrong, Jimmie Noone, Earl Hines, the Dodds brothers, Jelly Roll Morton and others to whom they looked. For the most part, during the years that Goodman was starting to play professionally, these jazz heroes were working at black-and-tans like the Plantation, the Nest, the Apex, the Sunset, the Dreamland. The white jazz musicians would regularly visit these places. Earl Hines said,

Most of the clubs and hotels where the white musicians played closed between one and two o'clock, and they'd come down either to King Oliver at the Plantation or where we were [the Sunset]. Benny Goodman used to come with his clarinet in a sack. . . . We all got a kick out of listening to each other, and we all tried to learn. We sat around waiting to see if these [white] guys were actually going to come up with something new or different.[44]

Various sources report Goodman at the Dreamland, the Sunset and other places, but in fact Benny did not go around to hear the black players nearly as often as some of the Austin High group did. Bud Freeman said, "I lived at the Sunset where Louis Armstrong and Earl Hines were playing. Benny might go there once a month or something."[45] Jess Stacy, who was around Chicago at the time, said that Goodman was something of a loner, and did not run with the pack as a rule.[46]

This was undoubtedly true: Benny Goodman was never a glad-hander, a hail-fellow-well-met, the sort who wanted to rampage around town drinking and sitting in, as did so many of these burgeoning young jazz musicians. Although he certainly heard most of the great New Orleans pioneers around Chicago a number of times, his exposure to them was less in person than through recordings.

Over the years between 1923 and 1925, Goodman worked a series of more-or-less steady jobs at various cabarets and dance halls: Guyon's Paradise, The Green Mill Gardens, various lake resorts and other places.[47] One story that has appeared in virtually everything written about Goodman was his first meeting with Bix Beiderbecke. Bill Grimm, the pianist from Harrison High, had a band on one of the excursion boats which sailed out of Chicago. He was suddenly short a clarinetist and called Goodman, who got to the job early. He was on the bandstand when he heard someone shout, "Get off that stand and stop messin' round with those instruments." This was of course Bix, himself still a teenager and not known to anybody but musicians and jazz fans at a few Midwestern colleges.[48]

The music that Goodman was playing during this period was by no means all jazz. These small dance bands were required to play a great many ordinary pop tunes, waltzes and even polkas. But not many of these groups were flush with good readers, and perforce there was a great deal of playing by ear in them. Records of the Midway Gardens Orchestra perhaps a year before Goodman joined it reveal a band using rough head arrangements, a lot of jammed ensembles, frequent breaks, occasional solos and various more carefully worked out passages. It was rather eclectic, but more than anything, it was a jazz band on the model of the New Orleans Rhythm Kings. Indeed, three members of the rhythm section— Elmer Schoebel, Lew Black and Steve Brown—had been with the Rhythm Kings. The important point is that jazz, as it was understood by the public, was the popular music of the day, and dance bands were expected to play it. Musicians' ideas of it varied, but a great many of the thousands of small dance groups in the United States were essentially jazz bands, however rough and awkward.

Goodman joined the Midway Gardens Orchestra, under the leadership of Art Kassel, in 1925. The place was typical of the "casino gardens" or "concert gardens," dating back into the nineteenth century, which had become important social institutions for working people, particularly newly arrived immigrants. The Midway Gardens was in the South Side, where so many immigrants were living, but not in the famous Black Belt. It had a large indoor dance hall as well as an outdoor "garden" for dancing during the heat of summer. Many people came in couples, paying a modest admission fee, but it was acceptable for young women to come alone, which a lot of them did, looking for young men or just a good time.

The band at the Midway Gardens during Goodman's time also in-

cluded pianist Mel Stitzel, another former member of the New Orleans
Rhythm Kings; Danny Polo, a fine reed player; and the great New Orleans
bass player Steve Brown, who would be with the important Jean Goldkette Orchestra in a year or so. Probably in the spring of 1925 there came
into Midway Gardens a saxophonist named Gil Rodin, who was working
on the West Coast with a Chicago drummer named Ben Pollack, who had
also been with the New Orleans Rhythm Kings. Pollack had heard about
Goodman and asked Rodin to go hear him while on a trip East. Rodin
liked what he heard, and told Goodman he could have a job with Pollack
as soon as there was an opening. Goodman was excited; the money would
be good, and in those days the West Coast had a romantic aura com-
pounded of movie stars, eternal sunshine and grapefruit free for the picking. In August 1925, the call came, and Benny Goodman, now sixteen
years old, entrained for Los Angeles.[49]

By the time he boarded the train, Goodman had been playing the
clarinet for only six years. His development had been astonishing, even
in jazz where musicians tend to blossom young. He was not only an excellent professional who could read well and play difficult music, but he was
considered one of the best young jazz musicians in Chicago, a comer who
was surely going to make a mark. Furthermore, he was almost certainly the
leading earner in his family, making far more money than his father ever
had, and more than any of his siblings, some of them fifteen years older
than he was.

It was impossible for all this not to have had some effect on his emotional apparatus. He was, in a sense, a child star, a boy competing successfully against men—out-playing older musicians and out-earning most of
the adults around him. Furthermore, he was regularly spending a lot of
time in relatively sophisticated surroundings, mingling with show people,
gangsters, gamblers and the rich—part of what must have seemed a glam-
orous life to his family, who could not share it. Few people even much
older and wiser would in these circumstances resist the temptation to see
themselves as a little above other people. Bud Freeman said, "I don't know
what happened to Benny Goodman to make him so disliked. I only know
as a young man he was one of the finest men I'd ever known. . . ."[50] The
roots of what would eventually be seen as Goodman's arrogance may have
been put down here.

# 3

# The Rise of the American Dance Band

Benny Goodman was now in the business of playing music for dancing. These small orchestras of course played for other occasions—as accompaniment to acts, in theatres and at picnics and on excursion boats as general entertainment. But their primary function was to play for dancing, and their "books" of arrangements were built around popular songs of the day worked out to be played smoothly, with a light bounce, at moderate tempos—from about 60 beats a minute for a moody ballad to 150 for a fast fox-trot. There could be a great deal of jazz content, or very little, depending on the interests of the players and how the leader assessed the mood of the crowd.

Human beings have always danced, if we can trust the interpretations of prehistoric cave art and footprints of children in the Le Tuc d'Audoubert Cave in France.[1] However, in the decades just before Goodman's birth, "nice" people, that is to say the middle and upper classes, did not dance in public, but either at home, or in private parties in hotel ballrooms and assembly halls, to which only people of their own class would be invited. By 1900 this stricture was breaking down, and even the best people would dance in fashionable restaurants and ballrooms. George Baquet, a New Orleans musician who played with the famous Robichaux orchestra, said, "A typical set opened with a one-step, continued with a schottische, a mazurka rag, waltz and ended with a quadrille."[2]

Working people had always frequented public dance halls in part, at least, because their crowded tenement homes offered neither the music nor the space for dancing.[3] (We must remember that at the beginning of this century there was no radio and the phonograph was a rich man's toy. For most people there was no such thing as music reproduction: All music was live.) Even in Victorian times the public dance hall was a meeting place for young men and women of the working class. And sometime around 1910 there began to develop in such places a whole group of lively and exciting new dances.[4] The "sin towns" or vice districts which arose in American cities in the late nineteenth century—New York's Tenderloin, San Francisco's Barbary Coast, Chicago's Levee, New Orlean's Storyville and others—were important breeding grounds for the new dances. The Barbary Coast in particular has been singled out as a source for them. According to one contemporary San Francisco musician, the famous Texas Tommy "practically originated out of Purcell's,"[5] a Barbary Coast black-and-tan. In 1922 the New York Times said of the Barbary Coast that "Here the turkey trot, the bunny hug and the rest of the 'gutter dances' originated."[6] Show business people tended to hang around places like Purcell's, which were likely to be open after they had finished their own acts, and they frequently picked up ideas from them. Al Jolson brought a team of Purcell's Texas Tommy dancers to New York to work in his shows,[7] and others did the same. The Texas Tommy was danced with the couple side by side, clasping each other around the waist. They took a couple of long strides, then two or three little hops into the air, each time stamping a foot.[8] The so-called gutter dances were somewhat acrobatic, and according to Irene Castle, they all tended to be alike.

Very quickly after 1910 simplified versions of these dances spread through the American culture. They were easy to learn, rhythmic and allowed the couples to dance in as close an embrace as they wished. For this reason, and because there was a good deal of hip wriggling and leg kicking in them, church groups and guardians of the public purity inveighed against them. This hostility was ineffective and after about 1912 the opponents of the new dances began to give up. As we have seen, by the early twenties Hull House was promoting dancing as healthy for its young people.

The music for these dances had originally been ragtime and the syncopated songs being generated by black composers for the black theatre early in the century. It was quickly discovered that dotted rhythms were especially effective for the new dances, and it is not surprising, as Edward A. Berlin has pointed out in his study of ragtime, that at just about the same moment the amount of dotted rhythms in rags increased substantially.[9] But the new dixieland music was built around dotted rhythms, and it rapidly replaced ragtime and other music as the basis for the new dances, to the point where the word jazz was used interchangeably for both the music and the dances. And it is again no accident that the music and the dances appeared simultaneously in San Francisco in the years after 1910.

The bands playing for these dances were small. According to Ferde Grofé, about whom we shall hear more in a moment, the usual dance orchestra in the West in 1908 consisted of violin, cornet, piano and drums. Additions, in order of preference, were clarinet, trombone, flute and string bass. Rarely, however, were there more than four pieces. "The calibre of the players was quite low. The strict oom-pah of the pianist, the mellow tones of the cornetist, seldom played above G or A above the staff, with the other members following along in the same pattern, was quite monotonous to say the least."[10] As late as 1919, according to Bill Challis, later an important arranger with Jean Goldkette and Paul Whiteman, "The usual band at the time was a fiddle, a saxophone, no bass—piano, banjo, drums."[11]

By 1919, of course, following the popularity of the Original Dixieland Jass Band, there were hundreds of bands around the country using the dixieland instrumentation of cornet, trombone and clarinet over a rhythm section. But whatever the line-up, the music itself remained quite simple, in many cases primitive. Many of the musicians could not read: pianists and violinists usually could, and would be required to teach the new songs to the others, but there were plenty of working pianists who could not read very well, either. In general, the bands simply played the song through as many times as was necessary to make up a dance. Variety was provided by the structure of the songs themselves, which might be made up of a verse and a chorus which could be alternated, as was the case with most popular songs, or of three or four strains, as in marches and ragtime. The better musicians might work out little introductions or codas, but there was little more arranging than that.

It was not true that there was no such thing as arranged dance music before the appearance of the modern dance band. As James T. Maher, who has made a study of the matter, has pointed out, the very wealthy at their elegant balls might use orchestras with as many as thirty pieces which would necessarily be playing arranged music.[12] Similarly, the very popular New York orchestras of James Reese Europe and Ford Dabney—both black—were relatively large combinations, and while they did not use written music, they did work from "head," or memorized, arrangements that were somewhat more elaborate than those played by the standard three-to-five piece dance band. But into the World War I era, the vast bulk of dance music was unarranged, ground out by these small combinations.

That began to change in the mid-1910s. The story is difficult to untangle, but it is clear that three people are mainly responsible for the creation of the modern dance orchestra: Art Hickman, Ferde Grofé and Paul Whiteman.

The career of Art Hickman has been studied in some detail by Maher, and I am indebted to him for much of my information about him. Hickman was born and raised in Oakland, California, across the bay from San Francisco. He formed a dance team with his sister, taught himself to play drums, and could "pick" at the piano. (Actually, Hickman's most famous composition, "Rose Room," has a relatively complicated harmonic structure for that time, suggesting that he had some understanding of music theory; however, it is also possible that somebody else, perhaps even Grofé, devised the harmonic scheme for the tune.) In about 1912, Hickman was asked to substitute on the drums in a group led by pianist George Gould, which included banjoist Bert Kelly, who would lead an early jazz band. Hickman eventually emerged as leader of the group. "Soon all San Francisco was dancing to the 'Rose Room' fox-trot by Art Hickman."[13]

In 1913 the Hickman group was hired to go along with the San Francisco Seals, a minor league baseball team, to their training camp. A report discovered later by Peter Tamony, a San Francisco lexicographer, said:

> Everybody has come back to the old town full of the old "jazz" and they promise to knock the fans off their feet while they're playing [baseball]. . . . What is "jazz"? Why it's a little of the "old life," the "gin-i-ker" [ginger], the "pep," otherwise known as enthusiasm. A grain of "jazz" and you feel like going out and eating your way through Twin Peaks. . . . [The ballplayers] have trained on ragtime and "jazz". . . . The players are just brimming over with the old "Texas Tommy" stuff and there is a bit of "jazz" in everything they do.[14]

This is the first printed mention of jazz as applied to music so far discovered, and it was the Hickman band that got the title, although how much jazz in the New Orleans manner it actually played is hard to know.

This brings us to the question of Ferde Grofé. He is remembered, if he is remembered at all, as the author of some fairly light pieces of classical music which had a vogue in the 1920s and 1930s. The best known of these is his "Grand Canyon Suite," from which comes the lilting "On the Trail," still sometimes heard today. But Grofé's real importance to music was his role in creating the modern dance orchestra, out of which grew the bands of Fletcher Henderson, Benny Goodman, Duke Ellington and the rest. In 1927, Henry Osborne Osgood, an early authority on these bands, called Grofé "the father of modern jazz orchestration."[15] Another early writer said he was "the first to reduce jazz to note and score."[16] And as late as 1953 the International Musician, the house organ for the American Federation of Musicians, called him "Father of Instrumentation."[17]

The facts of Grofé's early life are difficult to ascertain, as neither he nor the few people who wrote about him are entirely reliable. But the general outline of his development is clear. He was born on the East Side of New York, between First and Second avenues, on March 27, 1892. It was an area filled with German immigrants struggling to make places for them-

selves.[18] His father was Emil von Grofé, a French Huguenot born in
Braunschweig, in central Germany, coincidentally the town where Till
Eulenspiegel was reputedly born. He was a comedian and baritone who,
according to one report, was with "the old, original Bostonians," a light
opera group. A grandfather, Bernhardt Bierlich, was solo cellist for the
Metropolitan Opera in the 1880s. An uncle, Julius Bierlich, was for a period concertmaster of the Los Angeles Symphony. His mother, who termed
herself Mme. Menasco von Grofé, played violin, viola and cello, and supported herself for at least some periods in her life by playing popular music in casino gardens.[19]

All of this sounds a good deal more elegant than it was in fact. The
"von" was probably an invention of Emil Grofé's, and "casino gardens"
were frequently disreputable places that operated indoors in bad weather.
Very early in Grofé's life his father either died or abandoned the family,
and his mother took the little boy to California, where her brother Julius was
working with the Los Angeles Symphony during the season and elsewhere
at other times. She began giving Ferde instruction in music at a very early
age. He told one interviewer that he began studying the piano at five,
composing at nine. He said, "Almost the first thing I remember is writing
notes."[20] Like many children of professional musicians, he grew up im-
mersed in music, but it was classical music.

Then, in about 1906, when he was fourteen, he ran away from home.
Once again the details are shadowy, but apparently he wandered around
California mining towns catching his living as an itinerant laborer. From
time to time he also played music for dances, probably on banjo and violin
as well as piano. He said, "We were in a mining town called Winthrop in
a gulch in Northern California . . . the only job I could get was playing
the piano in a sporting house. . . ."[21]

In 1909 he returned home and very quickly was brought into the Los
Angeles Symphony, playing the viola. This was not, however, a full-time
job, and he had also to work in popular music to eke out a living. According to various reports, in the years from 1909 to 1912 he worked in a jitney
dance hall in Ocean Park in Los Angeles called the Horse Shoe Pier and
at the Majestic Theatre in Los Angeles. By 1912, aged twenty, he was back
in San Francisco, playing tea dances, doing some sort of work for the music publisher Jerome Remick, and playing at night at the Thalia, Hippo-
drome, Casino, and Portola Louvre, all famous "dives" in the Barbary
Coast district.[22]

It was a critical moment to be there. The black New Orleans dixieland
musicians were by that time established in San Francisco, and the local
musicians were struggling to learn this exciting new music coming out of

the South. Sid LeProtti, a black San Franciscan who worked extensively on the Barbary Coast, said, "It was along about 1912 when we switched to the New Orleans type of instrumentation,"[23] and added that in the 1912–1920s period when he was playing at Purcell's, the music was "what you call Dixieland style today."[24]

Grofé was never really a jazz musician, but he began hearing the music in its earliest stages. In the years after 1912 he was probably the only musician anywhere who was at home in both jazz and classical music. He began to realize that dance music could be made a lot more interesting if it were to make use of some of the simpler devices on which symphonic music was built—contrapuntal lines, harmonies using standard voice-leading procedures and the like. He apparently put together a band of his own during this period, and by 1915 he had become very influential with San Francisco musicians. "After hours, musicians from all the nightclubs foregathered to hear Ferde improvise his jazz and to acclaim his original orchestrations. At that time Ferde used the huddle system. Each musician had his job cut out for him. Grofé jotted down each musical part."[25] (The huddle system simply meant that Grofé told each musician what to play, as the quarterback did for a football team at the time.)

At some point in the years after 1915 Grofé went to work for Art Hickman as pianist and arranger. Tom Stoddard, in his study of San Francisco jazz, says, "When Grofé left the Barbary Coast to play the piano with Hickman's band at the St. Francis Hotel, the two arranged music that was different and sparkling. Other orchestra leaders who played in San Francisco—Paul Whiteman, Rudy Seiger, and Paul Ash—become conspicuous exponents of this new music."[26] Another report, apparently based on an interview with Grofé, says that he "found time to play piano for afternoon teas with Art Hicman [sic] in the Rose Room of the St. Francis Hotel."[27]

From this scanty information it is difficult to know exactly what either Grofé or Hickman contributed to the creation of a dance band arrangement. However, there is good evidence that by 1916 or so Grofé was writing arrangements for the Hickman, and probably other, bands. These were the first modern dance-band arrangements.

A critical event occurred in 1918, when Hickman—or somebody—happened to hear a saxophone team in vaudeville. The saxophone had never been taken very seriously by American musicians to this time. A whole family of them had been created by Adolfe Sax in the 1840s, but the instrument was probably not brought to the United States until later. James T. Maher says that the famous bandleader Patrick Sarsfield Gilmore used a saxophone quartet in the 1870s, and that by the 1890s stock arrangements often included saxophone parts.[28] However, as late as 1920 the saxophone was seen primarily as a novelty instrument and was frequently found in vaudeville shows. The Six Brown Brothers had a successful saxophone act using the full saxophone family, and Rudy Wiedoeft became famous as a saxophone virtuoso with his records after 1918—the best-known saxophonist of the day.

The sax team Hickman heard was Clyde Doerr and Bert Ralton. Doerr had a degree in violin, and Ralton also had serious musical training, which put them well in advance of most men playing in dance bands.[29] Which of the saxophones they played we are not sure, but undoubtedly between them they played most of the whole family. We do not know what kind of act they had, either, but it certainly included some pieces with showy fast passages, and at least some passages arranged in two-part harmony.

It occurred to somebody—probably Hickman—that the team could be used effectively in a dance orchestra. He was undoubtedly struck in part by the novelty of the instrument which would make a striking visual effect. But it was also important that Hickman was working in swank hotels, where the music could not be the raucous jazz heard on the Barbary Coast. The saxophone could be played in a softer, more dulcet manner than the brass instruments most dance bands were using, and could act as an analogue to the string section in larger orchestras.

It is impossible, at this point, to discover exactly what arrangements Ferde Grofé made for Art Hickman. However, the style that the band developed, presumably under his guidance, was a rich and florid one, based primarily on the division of the orchestra in saxophone and brass sections, playing contrapuntal lines which at points merged into straight-forward harmony and then separated again. Solos were frequent, and by 1920, if not earlier, the soloists were occasionally embellishing the melody line with "jazzy" turns. In general, there was a great deal of motion in the music, with, at times, three different lines going at once, in addition to what the rhythm instruments were playing. These arrangements made the Hickman group the talk of San Francisco.

By 1919 Grofé had departed—one report has him working with a group led by John Tait.[30] In that year the Hickman band was brought to New York to play at the Biltmore Hotel at the "instigation" of Columbia Records, which wanted to record the group.[31] The group was an instant hit. The showman Florenz Ziegfeld quickly snatched it up and installed it in his Midnight Frolic on the roof of the New Amsterdam Theatre, where his Follies were playing down below. The idea was that you would see the Follies and then go up to the roof to eat a late supper and see another show. According to Robert Haring, Sr., who did some arranging for Hickman at about this time, "Everybody—all the players, and the arrangers,

THE RISE OF THE AMERICAN DANCE BAND

even the band leaders—just couldn't stop talking about him. . . . But what they talked about most was the saxophone playing. . . . Bert Ralton and Clyde Doerr . . . completely changed the way the New York musicians thought about the saxophone."[32]

Hitherto, the saxophone had been used primarily as a novelty instrument in vaudeville shows, or as a solo feature at band concerts. Rudy Wiedoeft usually displayed a lot of fast passages played staccato, for a rather brasslike effect. Doerr and Ralton also used a heavy-handed attack at times, but they employed a lot of legato work, more in the manner of strings than brass. They would play solo, in harmony or in counterpoint, with one playing tenor or C-melody and the other alto. The crucial point was that they were using the saxophone not as a novelty solo instrument, but integrating it into the orchestra; and from this moment the saxophone would be central to the American dance orchestra. Between 1919 and 1925 some 100,000 saxophones were sold in America.[33] And in 1923 Mills Music reported selling twice as much sheet music for saxophone solos as for piano solos.[34] The saxophone quickly came to be seen as *the* jazz instrument; popular literature was filled with references to "moaning saxophones," and illustrative material on jazz in magazines, on book jackets, and night club decorations invariably featured saxes. Almost two decades later *Orchestra World*, in a retrospective piece, said, "Clyde [Doerr] was the first man to introduce the modern style of saxophone playing in New York. . . ."[35]

Hickman, it appeared, was bound for national fame. But he soon became homesick for San Francisco, and took the group home, despite an offer from Ziegfeld of $2500 a week, a huge sum for the time. He returned for later stays with Ziegfeld, but because he would not exploit himself as he might have, his band soon dropped behind the others coming along in his wake. He died relatively young in the 1930s, by that time almost forgotten.

Doerr and Ralton were forgotten even quicker. Ralton left Hickman in 1921, and eventually landed in London running the Savoy Hotel's Havana Band, one of the best-known dance bands in England of the time. In 1927 he was on tour in South Africa, and was shot to death in a big game hunting accident.[36] Clyde Doerr also left Hickman in 1921, formed his own band, made solo saxophone recordings for Columbia, and eventually drifted into the radio studios.[37]

Meanwhile, back in San Francisco there was a young musician from Denver who, like Grofé, had had substantial classical training, and also liked jazz—Paul Whiteman. Whiteman's father was conductor of the Denver Symphony and head of music education for the Denver schools.

Whiteman was raised for a career in music, playing both violin and viola. He rebelled, however, and by 1915 he was in San Francisco, attracted by the Panama-Pacific Exposition, which was making work for musicians. By the end of the year he was playing with the San Francisco Symphony Orchestra and, like other musicians, playing popular music to make ends meet.[38]

Whiteman was something of a womanizer and a drinker, and spent a good deal of time on the Barbary Coast. Here he encountered jazz, and here he met Ferde Grofé and heard what he was doing with his orchestrations.[39] Whiteman was also aware of the great success that Hickman was having with his saxophone-based band. He resolved to take the same route, and asked Grofé to come in as pianist and primary arranger for his new group. Whiteman was never able to play jazz, and he did not do much of the arranging for his band. He was, however, intelligent, ambitious, had a good sense of the popular taste, and knew music. He promoted a good job in Los Angeles' Alexandria Hotel, where the band quickly became popular with movie people, and then moved on to the new Ambassador Hotel in Atlantic City, probably on the strength of Hickman's earlier success in New York: Abel Green, for decades an important show-business journalist, told Maher, "I think [Whiteman] will be the first to concede that he rode the crest of Art Hickman's pioneering."[40] Here again the orchestra proved popular. The Victor Phonograph Company signed it to provide competition to Columbia's Hickman and Ted Lewis bands. Almost from the first these Victor records were enormous successes. The coupling of "Japanese Sandman" and "Whispering" sold two and a half million copies, and "Three O'Clock in the Morning" sold three and a half million, one for every other phonograph in the country, an extraordinary sale for any period.[41] By 1923 or so, Whiteman was growing wealthy as leader of what would be one of the most important popular music organizations the United States has ever produced.

Whiteman is remembered for elephantine orchestras playing over-blown arrangements using cumbersome devices drawn from classical music. But the early groups on which he made his name were much more jazzlike in both conception and performance. The band that made his hit "Whispering" in 1920 had a classic dixieland instrumentation of trumpet, trombone, clarinet, piano, tuba, banjo and drums, and even by 1922, when he was on his way to fame and glory, the group was only three brass, two reeds, and a rhythm section. Initially the music was strongly based in dixieland. His very early "Wang, Wang Blues" was out-and-out dixieland, and in other pieces like the aforementioned "Whispering" there are passages of dixieland trombone. Frequently a clarinet player was turned loose on the last chorus of hot numbers to improvise over an arranged final chorus, a device Duke Ellington made much use of years later; White-man's first clarinetist, Gus Mueller, was a New Orleanian.

As the money flowed in, Whiteman was able to enlarge the orchestra, partly to give Grofé more room to maneuver, partly so he could reach for special effects which were always characteristic of his work, and partly out of sheer grandiosity. Now Grofé began to develop what would be the basic design for the big jazz band, and in time the swing band. How much, at this point, he and Whiteman were indebted to Hickman is an open ques-tion. However, it is clear that Whiteman began by modeling his group on the Hickman plan; and it is also clear that at least some of the devices Grofé brought to his Whiteman orchestrations had been used earlier by Hickman, although of course it was Grofé who provided them in the first instance. However much Whiteman brought to the dance band, he was unquestionably building on a foundation laid down by Art Hickman.

The principles for the modern dance arrangement were: (1) the divi-sion of the orchestra into sections, at first brass, reed and rhythm, and later with brass sometimes further split into trumpet and trombone sec-tions; (2) the playing off of the sections contrapuntally or in call-and-answer fashion; (3) the intermixing throughout of shorter or longer solos, mostly improvised jazz, but occasionally straight renditions of a melody; and (4) the playing of ensemble passages with the jazzlike feel of an im-provised solo.

All of these principles were at work in the early Whiteman band. The 1921 "Everybody Step" has the sax section essaying some swing. "Hot Lips," made in 1922, was a feature for trumpeter Henry Busse's fluttertone imitation of a growl. The phrases of this famous solo were answered with brief phrases from the saxophone sections. (The piece also contains a break on a whole-tone scale which would become a cliché of the day.) "Pack Up Your Sins," also from 1922, has answers to a trombone lead, a bass clarinet counterpoint to a brass line and the hot clarinet over the brasses at the end. "Way Down Yonder in New Orleans," cut the next year, has a good fairly straight trumpet solo, probably by Tommy Gott; "Nuthin' But," also from 1923, has swinging ensembles, especially on the last chorus; the 1924 "San" has good solos by clarinet, trombone and trum-pet. What Whiteman was up to was recognized early. One unidentified critic wrote, "Now the Whiteman idea is to take this melody and build in the gaps between its occurrence with counter melodies."[42]

Grofé and Whiteman did not build their music exclusively on these principles, which would become central to swing. They were, it must be said, much more imaginative in their reach than many of the swing ar-rangers who came later and worked the formula to death. Grofé and Whiteman were fishing around in classical music for all sorts of things, in part, of course, simply for effect, and in many of their arrangements these basic swing band devices are not present. But they were nonetheless major components of the music.

From the point of view of sheer jazz, the Whiteman band could not stand up to the best of the hot New Orleans bands, or their imitators, such as the Louisiana Five, the Original Memphis Five and others. But they were trying to do something critical to what came after—to create a large jazz orchestra working largely from written arrangements. Most later critics would say that they did not entirely succeed, and some would say that they did not succeed at all. But they had established the principle and the format out of which big band jazz would grow.

Whiteman's enormous success drew the other bands after him, instantly altering the whole nature of American popular music. By 1922 the New York Times would say, "For a year now the dance orchestras of New York have been modeling themselves on the Whiteman plan—which means playing to music arranged for orchestration."[43] Other leaders of course insisted that they had come before Whiteman, as in fact Hickman had. Paul Ash, to be one of the best-known dance bandleaders of the day, had been in San Francisco when Hickman was becoming famous there, and certainly knew about the new system as early as Whiteman did.[44] Paul Specht, who also had a very popular dance band at the time, claimed that he had invented "classical jazz" in 1915 when he was at the Lafayette Hotel in Lafayette, Indiana, home of Purdue University, and attracting celebrities like George Ade and James Whitcomb Reilly. Specht also claimed to have made the first radio broadcast by a dance band, on September 14, 1920, within weeks of the first formal broadcast.[45] However, he only enlarged his orchestra in 1919, when Hickman was already established and Whiteman was making his first efforts. In 1923 Vincent Lopez, another of the best-known leaders of the day, also enlarged his orchestra and converted to the Whiteman style. (Paul Ash, Rudy Weidoeft, and another West Coast bandleader were, like Whiteman, in service bands, and undoubtedly there was considerable exchange of ideas.)[46] But there is no doubt that Hickman and Grofé planted the first seed, which Whiteman, with a good deal of help from Grofé, then brought to fruit.

Whiteman quickly began claiming that he had invented something called "symphonic jazz," which combined jazz rhythms with loftier musical ideas taken from classic music. To prove it, in February 1924, he put on a now legendary concert at Aeolian Hall in New York. The concert opened with a dixieland piece as an example of the older, raucous jazz Whiteman said his new music was pushing aside, and closed with a piece by George Gershwin commissioned for the event, "Rhapsody in Blue," which Grofé had to orchestrate for the still inexperienced Gershwin. The concert was seriously reviewed by classical music critics, and the effect of this, and Whiteman's skill at publicity, was to give jazz a respectability which it had heretofore lacked.[47] Whiteman, it was said, "made a lady of jazz," and once he had opened the door to the mainstream, a great jumble of jazz rushed through.

A second effect of the success of the new dance music was the rise of the "name" band. Dancers now were beginning to recognize distinctions between bands, and to specify which ones they wanted to hire. By 1924 an entertainment paper, *The Clipper*, could speak of the "band and orchestra" craze, and said ". . . where in former years they were content to dance to any old tin band, today they are unusually particular in the sort of music they 'hoof' to."[48] The emergence of the name band had important effects on the music. In order for a group to stand out from the crowd, it had to develop an individual and quickly recognizable style. Leaders began reaching for trick effects, the introduction of curious or exotic bits of music, the use of novel instruments. As early as 1920, Art Hickman was occasionally using oboe, bass clarinet, and slide whistle in his arrangements. Whiteman brought in a cymbalom, a Hungarian stringed instrument played with padded mallets, featured a bass clarinet in "Everybody Step," and a slide whistle on the famous "Whispering," a device copied by King Oliver when he had Armstrong play a slide whistle chorus on "Buddy's Habit." Patches of "Oriental" or "Arabian" music were everywhere.

The use of odd musical effects and novelty instruments required a relatively high level of musicianship; furthermore, leaders wanted to be able to present beautifully played solos—smooth, brilliant trumpet choruses, breathtakingly fast clarinet passages, dulcet saxophone melodies. They began competing for the best musicians, frequently drawing into their orchestras men fully capable of holding chairs in major symphony orchestras. Inevitably, salaries were driven up to heights as breathtaking as the clarinet work. As early as 1922 *The Clipper*'s dance band reporter Abel Green wrote, "According to the men who are booking orchestras all over the country there is an acute shortage of Class A dance orchestras at the present time." And he added prophetically, "The craze for dance organizations is just beginning, according to indications."[49] Salaries went through the roof: seventy-five to three hundred dollars a week was the range for dance band musicians, with men in the top orchestras averaging a hundred dollars a week.[50] The best players, like Whiteman's star clarinetist, Ross Gorman, could make as much as $20,000 a year.[51] This, mind you, was at a time when a haircut cost less than fifty cents, an automobile three hundred dollars.

Through the 1920s there came into being the celebrated big-name band

leader. Many of them got rich; by the mid-1920s Paul Whiteman's personal income was above $400,000 a year. Whiteman was of course by far
the most successful of these musical showmen, but even more modestly
successful musicians like Jelly Roll Morton were able to sport around in
diamonds, expensive clothes and luxurious automobiles.

The final effect was to kill the small dixieland jazz band. Against the
ten- to twelve-piece orchestra playing flashy arrangements with well-oiled
precision, the improvising five-piece jazz band looked like mighty small
potatoes. By 1924, especially after the publicity which attended Whiteman's Aeolian Hall concert, it was clear that the dance band of the future
would be a big one playing some sort of arranged jazz. The dixieland jazz
band did not die out immediately. In fact, an apogee was reached in 1926
and 1927 when Louis Armstrong, Red Nichols, Jelly Roll Morton, Bix
Beiderbecke and others made some masterpieces of the genre. But the
form was by then moribund.

However, there remained a feeling in a substantial number of musicians
and jazz fans that the older music had something that the new dance music lacked. The point was made specifically by Olin Downes, the New
York Times classical music reviewer, in his report on the Aeolian Hall concert. He said that the opening dixieland piece, intended by Whiteman to
demonstrate the inadequacy of the old jazz, in fact made the opposite
point. It was, said Downes, "a gorgeous piece of impudence, much better
in its unbuttoned jocosity and Rabelaisian laughter than other and more
polite compositions that came later."[52] Carl Engel, a composer who was
head of the Library of Congress's music division, wrote in 1922 that jazz
found "its last and supreme glory in the skill for improvisation exhibited
by the performers,"[53] not in the playing of fancy arrangements. And Abbe
Niles, jazz critic for The Bookman, accused Whiteman of "throwing the
baby out with the bath."[54]

There remained an audience for hot dance music, and just as important,
a group of musicians around who wanted to play it. What happened next
was a movement from the two sides into the middle. On the one hand,
the former dixieland bands added saxophones and began to play from arrangements, either written out or "heads" worked up in rehearsal and
played from memory. In Chicago Louis Armstrong, who had made himself
famous recording in the dixieland style with his Hot Five, was by 1927
fronting the large Carroll Dickerson orchestra. In New York, Red Nichols
was building his "Five Pennies" into a ten-piece group. And King Oliver,
who in 1923 had made the quintessential dixieland records with his Creole
Jazz Band, had by 1926 changed the name to the Dixie Syncopators and
was playing arranged music.

On the other hand, bands which had formerly been playing polite dance music began to heat up their product. The Duke Ellington Orchestra, which had begun life playing dreamy "under conversation music," as they termed it, started to become a jazz band in 1924 under the influence of Bubber Miley and Sidney Bechet.[55] In the same year the Fletcher Henderson Orchestra did likewise after the example of Louis Armstrong, who spent a year with the group.[56] And by 1926 there existed a group of big dance bands capable of playing hot arrangements with improvised jazz solos by some of the best jazz musicians of the day. The best-known, and most influential, of these groups were the orchestras of Red Nichols (whose "Ida, Sweet as Apple Cider" was the first million-selling jazz record), Fletcher Henderson, Jean Goldkette, and Ben Pollack. Among them these groups had as soloists Bix Beiderbecke, Coleman Hawkins, Benny Goodman, Jack Teagarden, Jimmy Harrison, Rex Stewart, and others. These bands, of course, had to play a great deal of ordinary dance music, both on location and for records. But they could—and did—play a lot of boiling hot music as well.

Through the next few years, more and more bands joined the group. The Ellington band reached its first maturity in 1927; in the same year Don Redman left Henderson to take over the musical direction of McKinney's Cotton Pickers, turning it into an excellent hot dance band; also in 1927 Bennie Moten's Victor records began to give it a national following; the Casa Loma Orchestra started recording in 1929. Even Whiteman, seeing how things tended, decided to heat up his orchestra, and in 1927 raided the Goldkette Orchestra for its primary arranger, Bill Challis, and its best soloists, among them Beiderbecke.

One factor that needs to be taken account of is the publication in 1926 of Arthur Lange's *Arranging for the Modern Dance Orchestra*,[57] the first thing of its kind. Lange, who was born in 1889, and was publishing songs by the time he was in his twenties, went on to be an important arranger for dance bands and shows. In 1929 he became head of M.G.M.'s music department, where he wrote the music for a number of important movies. He also composed orchestra pieces, conducted, and eventually led the Santa Monica Civic Symphony.[58]

Lange was, thus, a very well schooled musician, and his text on dance band arranging shows it. Not only does it cover the usual rules of harmony, but it discusses such matters as tone coloration, balancing the orchestra and how to use brass and reed sections to support each other. His chapter on "Forms and Routines"—that is to say, the order of choruses, verses, modulations and the like—could stand as a rule book for many of the pieces that made Benny Goodman famous a decade later. He writes,

"The third chorus may be properly termed 'arranger's chorus' because, in this chorus, the arranger may take any liberty, and let his imagination take vent."[59] This would become a convention of swing band scoring.

Furthermore, Lange discusses in detail, giving many musical specimens, how brass and saxophone sections can be played off against each other. He gives examples of call-and-response, of building contrapuntal lines, of using muted trumpets to punctuate melody lines in the saxophone section. All of the major devices later employed by the big bands are given in *Arranging for the Modern Dance Orchestra.*

Lange can hardly be credited with inventing these ideas himself: most of his examples are drawn from published arrangements, probably mainly stocks, making it clear that these devices were already in widespread use. But by codifying these ideas, he was putting them in the air for people to grab. *Arranging for the Modern Dance Orchestra* was seized upon by arrangers all over the United States: it went through ten printings in the first year after its appearance.

This now brings us to the difficult question of the role played by the Fletcher Henderson Orchestra in the development of the swing band. It has always been said that the Henderson group of the late 1920s and early 1930s was the model for the swing bands of 1935 and after—by me, among others, when I took on faith the opinions of several leading jazz writers, a mistake I have not made subsequently. Stanley Dance, for example, said, ". . . it was in this band that the basic principles of the big jazz group— hot and swinging—were fashioned."[60] Gunther Schuller and Martin Williams, in the brochure to their Smithsonian Big Band Jazz collation said that "the fundamental style that the majority of the swing bands were using in the 1930s had been realized several years earlier in the orchestra of Fletcher Henderson."[61] And in a recent book, popular music historian Arnold Shaw referred to Henderson as "the creator of big band swing."[62]

A study of the records reveals nothing as clear-cut as this. The Henderson Orchestra was not the first big, hot dance band, but merely one of a group which emerged at about the same time. The Goldkette and Nichols orchestras were better-known and as much admired by musicians and dance band aficionados as was the Henderson Orchestra, and there is good testimony that the Goldkette Orchestra bested the Henderson group in a famous battle of the bands at Roseland in 1927.[63]

Furthermore, many of the other groups had cadres of soloists which could match Henderson's: Goldkette had Bix Beiderbecke, Frankie Trumbauer, Joe Venuti, and, at various times, Don Murray and Jimmy Dorsey; Ben Pollack had Benny Goodman, Jack Teagarden, Bud Freeman, and Jimmy McPartland; Red Nichols had, besides himself, at different points, Miff Mole, Jimmy Dorsey, Benny Goodman, and Teagarden.

Finally, it is simply not true, as has often been said, that Henderson's first musical director and arranger, Don Redman, devised the basic armamenture for the big-band arrangement. Redman started his professional career as musical factotum for one of Whiteman's chief rivals, the very commercial Paul Specht.[64] Redman was an excellent musician with conservatory training, and was entirely capable of analyzing what Grofé was doing with the Hickman and Whiteman orchestras. His early arrangements for Henderson show Grofé's influence, for they are, if anything, even more florid and busy than the Grofé pieces and employ the same sort of contrapuntalism that was the key to Grofé's work.

We have to see the Henderson band, then, not as the forerunner of the swing bands but as one of a group of big dance orchestras coming along at the same time which together acted as the model for what came later. It is worth bearing in mind, in this respect, that virtually all of the most important of the white swing bandleaders got their training in the Pollack and Nichols groups, including Benny Goodman, Glenn Miller, Jimmy Dorsey, Tommy Dorsey, and Artie Shaw.

None of this is to in any way denigrate the Henderson Orchestra. It was admired and respected by musicians and dance-band fans, and was certainly one of the most popular hot bands of the day. And because it outlasted most of the others, it had a larger role, over the long run, in jazz history than the other groups did, especially in the number of important soloists Henderson discovered and brought into the group over a fifteen-year stretch. But it is important to note that none of the musicians who developed the swing band reported that he looked to the Henderson band as a model. People like Goodman, Gene Krupa, Bunny Berigan and others who were in the swing band movement from the beginning were always quick to credit the black musicians they had been inspired by: that they did not name Henderson as the developer of the swing band is significant. Even John Hammond, one of Henderson's greatest supporters, did not make this claim.

To recapitulate what was a rather complex process, hot playing—that is to say, jazz—originated in New Orleans, primarily by blacks. The idea of the jazz-based dance band playing from arrangements was worked out by Grofé, Hickman and Whiteman. After the enormous success of Whiteman, the dixieland model was abandoned in favor of the Whiteman one. The bands moved toward the new model from two directions. Some, like the Henderson and Ellington bands, started life as commercial orchestras playing for a variety of functions, and began to heat up their music as they became aware of the virtues of New Orleans jazz. Others, like the Oliver and Nichols bands, began as dixieland bands and drew the jazz feeling along with them as they converted to the new mode.

One important by-product of this musical shift was the emergence of the improvised solo as the dominant jazz form. In dixieland solos were rare and generally worked out in advance. Louis Armstrong, over the course of his Hot Five series beginning in 1925, showed what could be done with a jazz solo. The Hickman-Whiteman formula already allowed for solos, and it was only a small step to turn the solo playing of a tune into an improvised jazz solo.

Ben Pollack was a classic product of this evolution. He had come into music playing hot jazz with the New Orleans men in the dixieland style. When he started leading his own dance band, he inevitably wanted it to be a hot one. And he hired Benny Goodman as much for his skill at improvising as for his ability to read the arrangements with ease. Thus, when Benny Goodman climbed aboard that train for California, the hot dance band which would be his main medium through his life was just then coalescing out of the elements which went into it. It was, in 1925, an invention that was no more than two years old.

# 4

# The Pollack Orchestra

Ben Pollack is a neglected and ultimately tragic figure who deserves a larger place in jazz history than he has been given. From the late 1920s into the early 1930s, his band was one of the three or four best big jazz bands in the United States. The band is mentioned only in passing in jazz histories (including my own) which usually devote a great deal of space to other bands of the period which were no better. There is no biographical study of Pollack, and the only discussion of his career at all—and that is brief—is contained in John Chilton's study of the Bob Crosby band, which grew out of the Pollack group.

Pollack was born in Chicago in 1903 to a middle-class family.[1] His father was a furrier and as was generally the case with the middle class, the family did not approve of a career in dance music for their son. But Pollack, taken by the new hot music that was blooming in Chicago when he was a teenager, took up the drums in high school and began working around Chicago with dance bands. He was not, at first, playing jazz. But very quickly he began sitting in with the New Orleans Rhythm Kings, who were just beginning to attract the attention of the young Chicago musicians. In time he was asked to substitute on a date for the band's drummer, Frank Snyder. The other men liked his playing so well they hired him to replace Snyder. This is substantial testimony to Pollack's ability to play jazz: The Rhythm Kings was the best white jazz band in the United States, although not very widely known outside of the circle of jazz musicians and fans. According to Pollack, only pianist Elmer Schoebel could read music, and the musicians spent most of their time at infrequent rehearsals squabbling over what notes each man was to play. The band worked from one in the morning until eight or nine, and it acquired a devoted following among the local jazz musicians, including Bix Beiderbecke, who came around frequently asking if he might sit in, usually requesting "Angry," a tune he was sure of.

While with the New Orleans Rhythm Kings Pollack became a first-rate drummer. He said:

> Showmanship was the order of the day, and besides a press roll, I worked in an afterbeat and a tadada. But one night an M.C. asked me to leave out all the fancy stuff when I played the show because it confused the act. So I just played rhythm and the guys were so amazed the easy way they could swing they [missing] more drumming like it. So I discovered the secret of solid drumming, that is, to feed rather than to overshadow—to send the other guys rather than play a million different beats.[2]

In speaking of Pollack later on, even those musicians who had differences with him insisted that he was a fine jazz drummer. Bill Challis, one of the most important arrangers of the period, said that he "was a great drummer, he really was."[3] Jimmy McPartland, who worked with him a great deal, said, "Oh, he was a good drummer."[4] According to Goodman, Pollack was the first drummer to consistently play four beats to the measure on the bass drum.[5]

Pollack recorded with the Rhythm Kings, and began to develop a reputation among musicians. Then, in 1924, his family, in an attempt to wean him away from the music business, offered him a three months' vacation on the West Coast. He took advantage of the trip, but instead of returning as scheduled, he joined a dance band led by Harry Bastin. He stayed with Bastin for eleven months, and returned to Chicago only when his family threatened to disown him. He agreed to go into the fur business, but after one day he fled for New York. There he got a wire that Bastin was ill; would he come back to the Coast and take over the band? He did, and immediately set about making it into a hot dance band. He brought in alto saxophonist Gil Rodin to help with the musical direction of the band. It has been pointed out that music directors were often more important to the swing bands than the putative leaders were, at least so far as the music was concerned. They frequently rehearsed the bands, and some of them were responsible for showing the men how to phrase and "blend" together. Many such music directors played major roles in shaping swing music—Rodin, with Pollack and the succeeding Bob Crosby band; Eddie Durham with a number of groups; and Gene Gifford with Casa Loma.

Like most leaders, Pollack had his own ideas about how he wanted the band to sound, but he lacked musical training, and inevitably he had to turn to somebody for help. Rodin was an unassuming man who was always well liked by musicians, and, although he was never a great jazz soloist, through his direction of the Bob Crosby band later on, he became an important figure in swing.

About the same time, Pollack brought in Fud Livingston, a reed player who was interested in learning the still relatively new art of dance-band arranging. He next added trombonist Glenn Miller, who wanted to play hot jazz and was also learning to arrange. And soon after, he hired Benny Goodman.

Goodman arrived in California wearing "short pants." Jazz literature is full of references to young musicians wearing short pants, or getting their first pair of long pants. In fact, the short pants referred to were knicker-bockers, or "knickers," pants which closed around the calf, much like the old golfing pants, which American boys of the day wore until they were in their mid-teens. Goodman was excited about being in California, ex-cited by the idea that he was playing in the Pollack orchestra. The group had no reptuation with the public as yet, but musicians knew about it. The ésprit in the band was high, for these young men—some of them still teenagers—felt that they were in the avant-garde.

The band was a success in California, but in January 1926, apparently because some of the easterners were homesick, Pollack took the band back to Chicago.[6] A few of the men preferred to stay in the West, among them the bass player, and Goodman was able to shoehorn his brother Harry, still playing tuba, into the band. Pollack, however, was aware of the string bass work of Steve Brown, who had been with the New Orleans Rhythm Kings and was now with the Jean Goldkette Orchestra, rapidly becoming known as "the Paul Whiteman of the West."

Brown is another neglected figure in jazz. A New Orleanian, he learned the new hot jazz as a teenager and quickly became the favored bass player for white groups. He came to Chicago in 1915 with his brother Tom's band and developed a reputation as one of the best bass players in jazz. He had a strong sound and used the bow a good deal to produce a power-ful beat. He was playing on all four beats of the measure, rather than just on one and three, as early as 1923, and by the time he was with the Jean Goldkette Orchestra in 1925 he was playing on four often. How much credit Brown can be given for moving the bass away from two-four into four-four is hard to determine; but because he was playing with leading bands during much of the 1920s, he was unquestionably the most influen-tial bass player of the period. Having played with Brown in the Rhythm Kings, Pollack knew the virtues of the bass over the tuba, and agreed to hire Harry Goodman if he would learn string bass, which he did, although he continued to play tuba for awhile.

The Pollack group had no reputation in Chicago, however, and had

trouble finding jobs. Goodman took a job in a theatre with a band led by
saxophonist Benny Kreuger but continued to work with Pollack whenever
the group had work. They got two weeks in Cincinnati at the famous
Castle Farms dance hall, but then were out of work again. Goodman went
back to Kreuger. Finally, Pollack got a chance at a job in the Southmoor
Hotel.[7] This was an important location and could make the band. The job
would pay $1050. The hotel people liked the band but, recognizing that it
was still unknown in Chicago, insisted on a big name for opening night.
Pollack got Paul Ash, at the time one of the most famous dance band
leaders in the United States, to appear. Ash agreed, but Pollack was somewhat astonished when he got a bill from Ash for $250 for a "personal ap-
pearance." The opening drew 900 people at five dollars each, and from
then on the course of the band was upwards.[8]

Goodman, however, nervous about the band's prospects, was reluctant
to leave Kreuger and did not rejoin immediately. Pollack was annoyed; he
had expected a certain loyalty to the attempt to play hot music in a big
dance band. But very quickly Goodman returned.

He had not been in the band long when he was struck by one of the
most devastating events of his life, one which would stay with him until
his death. By 1927 Benny, Harry and some of the others were doing well.
There was no need for David Goodman to work in sweatshops any longer,
and his children, grateful for what he had done for them for so many
years, arranged for him to take over a newsstand at the corner of California and Madison streets.[9] Benny did not even want him to work that
much. In a story which he frequently told, he went to Pop and said something to the effect that there was plenty of money coming in, it wasn't necessary for him to work any longer. Pop looked Benny in the eye and said,
"Benny, you take care of yourself, I'll take care of myself."

It was an unhappy choice. Not long afterwards, as he was stepping down
from a street car—according to one story—he was struck by a car. He
never regained consciousness, and died in the hospital the next day.[10] It
was a bitter blow to the family, and it haunted Benny to the end that his
beloved father had not lived to see the enormous success he, and through
him some of the others, made of themselves. It is, truly, a sad story. The
years that the immigrant David Goodman had sweated in the stockyards
and the garment lofts had paid off in a way he could never have possibly
imagined, and he never got that reward.

Benny, in any case, was now on the upward path. The Southmoor job
established the Pollack band. As word of it got around, Jean Goldkette
touted it to Roy Shields, a scout for Victor, which signed Pollack to a recording contract.[11] From the Southmoor the group went to the Rendez-
vous and then to the Blackhawk, two of Chicago's most famous clubs.

Jimmy McPartland, Goodman's old colleague from the Austin High gang, came in on trumpet. In 1924 McPartland had been chosen to replace Bix Beiderbecke in the Wolverines, a clear indication that he was considered one of the best young white jazz musicians in the Midwest. With Goodman and McPartland in the band Pollack had two soloists of the first rank, and in Glenn Miller, a competent arranger and—for the day—respectable jazz soloist. As a major jazz soloist with what was coming to be an important orchestra, Goodman was developing a personal reputation among musicians and the more dedicated followers of hot music, so much so that in the spring of 1927 the Melrose music publishing company issued a folio called *One Hundred Hundred Jazz Breaks by Benny Goodman*. In the same year Melrose issued two similar folios by Louis Armstrong. The procedure was to have the musician record on cylinders the required number of breaks or solos, in a number of different keys, and then have an expert transcriber take them off the cylinders. Presumably this was how it was done with the Goodman folio.

Probably early in 1928 Goodman left Pollack to work with Isham Jones, ostensibly because the pay was more.[12] Goodman and Pollack would have their disagreements in the future, and I suspect that there was some conflict of personality here. The Isham Jones band was a commercial dance band which could, however, play respectable jazz when called upon to do so. The band was exceedingly popular, especially in the Midwest, and Jones made a lot of money. When he decided to leave the band business in the 1930s, the men agreed to keep the group together, and it evolved into the Woody Herman band. But at the time, Goodman would not have been able to play as much jazz with Jones as he had with Pollack.

Then, in March 1928 Pollack got an offer to come to New York to play at the Little Club, another well-known location. Pollack jumped at the offer. Through the early 1920s Chicago had been the center of jazz: the New York musicians acknowledged that the "Western style" was more advanced, that is, hotter, than their music.

But the situation in Chicago was changing. During the twenties the city had been run as a wide-open town by Mayor "Big Bill" Thompson, in concord with the Al Capone and earlier gangs. But people had begun to find the casual murder of bystanders in gang wars less amusing than it had seemed at first, and a growing reform movement was closing down the night clubs. Chicago musicians were suffering, and through the years 1928 to 1930 there was a general exodus of many of the best jazz musicians to New York. From that time to the present, New York has been the jazz center of the United States.[13]

The chance to get to New York could not be passed up. Gil Rodin persuaded Goodman to return to the Pollack band, and they brought in Bud

Freeman, another of the old Austin High men, on tenor saxophone. The band now had McPartland and Al Harris on trumpets, Miller on trombone, Goodman and Rodin on altos and Freeman on tenor, and a rhythm section of Vic Briedis on piano, Dick Morgan on guitar, Harry on tuba, and of course Pollack.[14]

The Little Club job lasted for three months, and then the band began to scuffle. Eventually Pollack got a booking at the famous Million Dollar Pier in Atlantic City. And at this point Pollack brought in a man who had recently come to New York, trombonist Jack Teagarden, then in his early twenties. Teagarden had a great deal of quite varied playing experience behind him, but most of it had been done in the Southwest and he was unknown in New York. However, he had worked with Pee Wee Russell in Texas for a brief period, and had made contact with Russell in New York. Russell knew the Chicagoans, and began touting the trombonist to local musicians. The story of how Teagarden was introduced to the New Yorkers has been repeated many times, almost always differently by those who claimed to have been there. According to one account, Russell—or somebody—brought Teagarden into a jazz musicians' hangout called Plunket's. After Russell insisted to everybody that Teagarden was a phenomenon, the trombonist was forced to take out his horn. He played a couple of choruses of his specialty, "Diane," floored the people in the tavern, and almost immediately word of the newcomer began to circulate around New York musical circles.[15]

Who actually alerted Pollack to Teagarden is a matter of dispute. Bud Freeman said he first ran into Teagarden wearing a Norfolk suit and a button cap, playing at a club called Randy's, and brought him around to see Pollack.[16] Teagarden agreed that Freeman recommended him to Pollack.[17] Gil Rodin said it was him.[18] Pollack only said that "somebody mentioned" Teagarden to him. According to his story, he went around to

a dingy room where a trumpet player by the name of Johnny Byersdoffer [probably New Orleanian Johnny Bayersdorffer] was reading a paper under a gas jet. I couldn't believe it, but I said, "Hello, Johnny, I'm looking for some kid from Texas by the name of Teagarden that is supposed to play a lot of trombone." Johnny gestured to a small cot on the other side of the room and said, "That's him." "Can he read?" I said. "He's the best," Johnny replied. "Well I got a job for him," I said. Byersdoffer walked over to the cot and shook the prostrate form of the kid from Texas and said, "Jack, you got a job in Atlantic City tonight, get up." But he only grumbled, "Man, I just got here. I don't want to go nowhere." All the shaking from then on was useless, and Johnny said to me—"Don't pay any attention to what he said, Benny, he's knocked out!" Disgusted, I started to go, when Byersdoffer said, "Well, there goes your job with Benny Pollack." At the mention of my name, the kid jumped up from the cot and said, "Man, are you Benny Pollack? When do I leave?"[19]

The Atlantic City job was successful, but when it was over once again they were scuffling. Goodman was by this time getting known around New York, and he was usually able to pick up a certain amount of radio and recording work; but there were some tight moments. Finally Pollack got a job at the Park Central Hotel, a prestigious location, which would do for the band in New York what the Southmoor job had done for it in Chicago. They were not hurt by the fact that not long after they opened the famous gambler Arnold Rothstein was shot there. Pollack was required to use strings for the Park Central job, and the music tended to be relatively commercial dancing and dinner music, as was frequently the case in hotel ballrooms.[20] But it was an important job.

Then, late in the year Pollack was asked to bring the band into the pit of a new musical scored by Jimmy McHugh and Dorothy Fields for Fields' father, the producer Lew Fields.[21] The show was called *Hello, Daddy*, and opened on December 26, 1928. At this point Pollack decided to give up drumming and to conduct the band out front. He was moved to do so, apparently, because he felt that he would go unrecognized behind the drums, especially in the gloom of an orchestra pit. (Russ Connor suggests that he may simply have been too busy to concentrate on the drums now.)[22] Ray Bauduc, who would become one of the best-known drummers of the swing period, replaced him.

The musicians were now making extremely good money, about $500 a week for the stars, and additional fees for recordings, the Broadway show, and radio broadcasts, which might bring them up to $650. The less important musicians in the band were making $300 or so. This compares with $125–$150 good dance musicians around New York could make. According to Jimmy McPartland, "We were a top band and working, you know, plenty of work."[23]

Although many of these men, particularly Goodman, Teagarden, Freeman and McPartland, were well known in jazz circles, none of them had really ever been in the big time before. They were, furthermore, young— Goodman was not yet twenty—and apparently this sudden fame caused a rush of blood to their egos.

Pollack, for his side of it, was making even more money and had become a figure in popular music. The problem, essentially, was that the sidemen believed that they had contributed a great deal to the band's success. They felt that they were not merely employees, but key members of a team that had been coaxed into being by a joint effort. Pollack, however, thought it was his band, and that the men ought to be subject to the ordinary strictures of band discipline. It should be realized that in that less unruly day it was commonly accepted that leaders could dictate matters of dress and deportment, call rehearsals when they chose, hire and fire without explanation, and tolerate no backtalk from their employees. Pollack was not a martinet, compared with some of his fellow leaders, but he did want to enforce his rules. Jimmy McPartland said, "Bernie Foyer (the manager) wanted him to become a Rudy Vallee, you know, be a real bandleader style. Whereas he had been one of the guys before. . . . The manager wanted him to be a real hard, down-to-earth leader style, you know. And so all the guys got down on him. Everybody was mad at him."[24]

In his turn Pollack said, "Benny Goodman was getting in everybody's hair about this time, because he was getting good and took all the choruses," an accusation others have made.[25] Teagarden was "drinking on the job," and sometimes came to rehearsal so hungover it affected his playing, a complaint that was also probably justified.[26] Through 1928 and into 1929, however, the band held together. It was still working primarily at the Park Central, doubling at theatres from time to time, and making records and radio broadcasts. The money continued to flow in. But the frictions continued to worsen. Teagarden, Pollack said, had found a running mate in the band, and "had become very irresponsible."[27] Pollack fired the running mate, but not long afterwards, probably in September, matters came to a head. Pollack explained:

> I bawled out Jimmy McPartland for not wearing garters on the stage. He ignored me and it got to the point where he could not stand taking any bossing from me. He said I would be sorry as he was on the verge of quitting, and I told him to do me no favors and quit! He called me into his dressing room and said, "You will be sorry. Here's my two weeks' notice." Another voice pops up saying, "That goes for me too." That was Benny Goodman. I said it was all right with me as he was getting a little hard to handle.[28]

McPartland's version of the story, although different in some details, is essentially the same. Apparently he, Goodman, Gil Rodin, and Harry Goodman got into the habit of playing handball after work. For a period, when the band was in the Fox Theatre in Brooklyn, they would go onto the roof, where there was a convenient wall, and play between shows. In the course of this McPartland dirtied his shoes, which was not noticeable until he came out in front of the band to sing "Sugar." After the show Pollack blew up at McPartland and gave him his notice. "And Benny Goodman said, if you fire Jimmy you got my notice, too."[29] (McPartland, incidentally, said, that Goodman was a "very good handball player. He was a good athlete. He could beat all of us.") [30]

Pollack, of course, had no way of knowing it, but he had reached the peak of his career. From this point on he slid gradually downhill, a step at a time. The next incident occurred during an engagement at the Silver Slipper, a New York club. According to Pollack's story, Benny Goodman and Dick Morgan had gone to the Park Central management and offered them the Pollack band without Pollack. Wind of this got back to Pollack, and he managed to stop the deal behind the scenes without saying anything to those involved. But he was angry, and found an excuse to fire Harry Goodman. "Following that I managed to get rid of the mutineers, one by one, as I found it convenient, without disrupting my organization in one blow." [31]

McPartland also confirmed the basic story. "We all got together and had a big meeting and we started to rehearse on our own without Pollack." [32] McPartland does not say why nothing came of the effort, which suggests that Pollack's tale is correct.

Another source of annoyance to the men was the arrival of singer Doris Robbins. [33] Pollack and Robbins fell into an affair, as a consequence of which Pollack began to feature her more and more at the expense of the jazz numbers. He also began to turn down jobs which would not show her off to advantage, sometimes leaving the band without work. There were more firings, more defections. Ben Pollack had a wonderful instinct for talent, and he was always able to replace departing musicians with first-class jazz players, bringing in clarinetist Matty Matlock, trumpeter Yank Lawson and saxophonist Eddie Miller, all to be stars with the Bob Crosby band which succeeded the Pollack band. But a situation like this could not continue, and it did not. Near the end of 1934, when the band was in California, the musicians decided that it was all over. They agreed to see if they could form a cooperative band of their own, and one sad night the men came to Pollack's place one by one and left off their band books. They went en masse to New York, and after some struggle, reorganized the band. Eventually it was arranged to have Bing Crosby's brother Bob, a good singer, front the group, and as the Bob Crosby Orchestra it went on to become one of the most popular of the swing bands.

But by that time Ben Pollack was a minor figure in popular music. Through the second half of the 1930s he had a swing band which at times sounded like both the Goodman and the Crosby bands and he billed himself as "The Dean of Sophisticated Swing." He was still discovering fine musicians: Harry James, Irving Fazola, Dave Matthews and others. All of them, however, became famous with other leaders—James with Goodman,

Fazola with Crosby, Matthews with Harry James when James formed his own band.

Despite his first-rate sidemen, Pollack continued to slide out of sight, until by 1942 he was directing a touring band for comedian Chico Marx. He ran a booking agency for a time, dabbled in other musical odd jobs, but when the swing band boom ran wild over America, he was not part of it. And in 1971, a forgotten man of sixty-eight, he hanged himself.[34]

In retrospect we can see that the problem lay mostly with Pollack. It is true that Teagarden had a serious alcohol problem for much of his life, it is true that Goodman was difficult—it would not be the last time he got himself fired by a bandleader—and it is true that some of the others could be prickly and pugnacious. But the music business is shot through with people like this, and it is the function of a leader to deal with personality problems. Eddie Miller said, "Ben was basically a good guy, but when he stuck a cigar in his mouth it was a signal that he was about to undergo a change of personality, and we kept out of his way."[35] It was too bad—for Pollack tragic, in fact—that he could not manage these fractious personalities better, for with good management and a little luck Pollack might have played the role in igniting the swing era that the Goodman band did. Yank Lawson said, "As I saw it, Pollack's was the only white band playing jazz. There were jazz musicians in many other bands, Paul Whiteman's for instance, but they never played a number that was jazz from beginning to end."[36] Charlie Barnet, who never worked with the band, said, "With the exception of Ben Pollack's, most of the jazz was being played by black bands."[37] These assessments discount other bands such as Casa Loma and the Goldkette and Mal Hallett orchestras, which were capable of playing fine jazz. But these bands were playing a good deal of commercial dance music. Of course Pollack had to do much the same at places like the Park Central. But he had begun as a jazz musician, and he recorded a great deal of fine swing.

The band's real significance, however, may lie not so much in what it did, but what came out of it. For one thing, Benny Goodman became a figure of importance in jazz playing with the Pollack band. He did not yet have a large reputation among jazz fans, but he was recording occasionally under his own name; and by the time he left Pollack, he was well established in the music business as one of the best young reed players in New York, a man who could read his way through a difficult arrangement, and play brilliant hot choruses when asked.

The Pollack band also introduced Goodman to a couple of devices which would prove important to his later success. For one, Pollack would at times pull a small jazz band out of the dance band, to come down front and play some hot music. This small group usually consisted of Goodman,

McPartland and Teagarden with a rhythm section.[38] Despite the dominance of the big bands by the end of the 1920s, there remained an audience for the older dixieland style; and of course it gave the men a chance to play a little free-wheeling jazz, which Pollack himself enjoyed. This band-within-a-band, as the device came to be called, was obviously the precursor for a whole array of such bands in the swing period, beginning with Goodman's famous Trio.

A second stunt that Pollack liked to perform was to play duets with Goodman. Occasionally, after everybody had soloed on a tune, Pollack and Goodman would simply take off by themselves. Bill Challis heard them do it at both the Southmoor in Chicago and the Little Club in New York. He said, "My God . . . it was great."[39] This, of course, was a precursor to Goodman's most famous hit, "Sing, Sing, Sing."

What about the music, then? Ben Pollack, however much he loved jazz, was primarily interested in making a commercial success of himself on the order of Whiteman, Paul Ash and the others. He would let the band play as much jazz as it could, but that depended very much on whether it was at the Park Central or at a college dance, where it could play a lot of hot music. The majority of the records issued under the Pollack name are straightforward dance music, frequently with a vocal sung in the nasal tenor that was in vogue at the time. To be sure, on most of these records there is always a little jazz—a solo by one of the superb hot men Pollack always had in his orchestras, or a hot arranged passage. In some cases the amount of jazz in these putative commercial numbers was substantial: "My Kind of Love" has Teagarden playing obligatos behind Pollack's cornfed vocal, and a solo chorus split between Teagarden and Goodman. But the music during the Park Central period and after was preponderantly commercial, and in some cases, it was entirely so.

The group was recording mainly as Ben Pollack's Park Central Orchestra, but it was also doing a lot of recording under other names—some forty pseudonyms were used at one time or another, and in these other guises it was more a true jazz band. Recording as The Hotsy Totsy Gang, among others, the band generally played hotter, aiming for the jazz audience. For example, the band cut "Futuristic Rhythm" on December 24, 1928, as Ben Pollack and his Park Central Orchestra; three days later as Mills' Musical Clowns; on January 8 as Jimmy McHugh's Bostonians; and as the Hotsy Totsy Gang on January 14. The Park Central version, cut for Victor, is largely played as a straightforward dance arrangement with a vocal by Pollack; the jazz, aside from the somewhat jazzy section work, is confined to sixteen bars by Teagarden, and one eight-bar bridge by Goodman. The Hotsy Totsy Gang version, made for Brunswick, opens with a fairly tricky hot introduction, and proceeds directly to a solo on the melody by Goodman, backed with an obbligato by McPartland. Goodman plays back-up licks behind the vocal; there is a full chorus for the trumpet, with Goodman taking the bridge. Teagarden also solos on the bridge, and there is a hot tag to end it. This is distinctly a more jazzlike version than the Victor cut. Changes had to be made, of course, so that the various cuts of the song would not be identical. But it is also clear that Pollack was as a matter of policy keeping his own name for the commercial dance music, but was recording the group—or arranging for others to record it—for the jazz audience under pseudonyms, thus collecting as much of the market for the tune as he could.

To a considerable extent it was Pollack's commercial bent, rather than his somewhat heavy-handed leadership, that kept his men constantly in a state of rebellion. These men thought of themselves primarily as jazz players: McPartland had modeled his playing on that of Beiderbecke; Goodman had been initially influenced by the New Orlanians; Teagarden was virtually incapable of playing a note devoid of jazz inflection. The problem is illustrated by a contretemps that occurred around a recording session for the Cameo-Pathe group of labels in February 1929. Gil Rodin had become straw boss of the band, as he would be with the Crosby group. On this occasion he was ill, and for reasons unknown, Goodman took it upon himself to run the session.[40] School was out. The tunes were "It's Tight Like That" and "Four or Five Times." As we shall see in more detail later, in the previous June a small group recording under Goodman's name had as a lark begun deliberately playing an excruciatingly corny "jazz" piece based loosely on "St. Louis Blues." Much to the musicians' dismay, the recording director had been entranced by it, and insisted that they repeat the number for the microphones. It had been issued as "Shirt Tail Stomp" and sold well; and from time to time thereafter various Pollack groups had been required to turn out similar material.

At the session in question, "Four or Five Times" was to be one of these, but the musicians chose to play it straight. It is fascinating to hear Goodman struggling to play the parody he was supposed to be working, momentarily inserting appalling glissandos in the Ted Lewis manner, and then falling back into straight jazz phrasing.

Furthermore, it is my sense that the musicians had gotten drunk for the session, possibly deliberately, although in the case of some of these men no advance planning would have been required. Tempos, especially on "It's Tight Like That," are grindingly slow, the beat is leaden, and there is a certain amount of fumbling in the soloing, all characteristics of the playing of a band which has been drinking a lot.

The recording director was not amused, and refused to pay the men until the session was remade a month later, this time by chastened musicians playing the cornfed version as required.[41] The story is important, because it shows how committed to jazz Goodman, at bottom, really was. He would play straight dance music if he had to, but it was not what he wanted to do, and at times he had trouble accommodating himself to the commercial side of his business. There was a tough integrity in Goodman which frequently expressed itself in rebelliousness, and at times caused him trouble. It is difficult to think of Benny Goodman, one of the most popular musical figures of this century, a man who married into the American aristocracy, as a rebel; but there was at least an element of that in his character.

Ben Pollack was sufficiently rebellious to flee his father's fur business, but for all of that he was never musically very adventurous. His primary arrangers during the early period were Fud Livingston and Glenn Miller, although we have difficulty in being sure exactly who made which of the Pollack arrangements. Both were highly skilled arrangers, as well as competent jazz improvisers. Livingston would go on to have a career arranging for radio and the movies, and Miller would make a fortune with his own swing band playing music based on his own musical ideas. But neither was reaching out for advanced notions, as were Bill Challis with Goldkette and Whiteman, Henderson and Ellington with their own bands, or Ferde Grofé with various groups earlier. There are interesting arranged pieces, of course: "Waitin' for Katie" has a half chorus alternating Bixian passages written out for brass with four-bar solos by Glenn Miller. (Interestingly, Miller, who began as a follower of Miff Mole playing fast staccato passages in a clear, ringing tone, had fallen under the influence of Teagarden, and is playing in a legato manner with a cloudy tone and even a bit of a burry throat tone.) "Memphis Blues" is given an elaborate "symphonic" treatment which is interesting in spots, if not very jazzlike. (Black music was being written about as an art form at the time, and this sort of serious treatment of the blues, spirituals and the like was becoming a cliché. George Gershwin's "Porgy and Bess" reflected this attitude.)

But by and large the Pollack arrangements are at best straightforward, at times even pedestrian, frequently with the band galloping along together without any thought given to countermelodies or answering voices. Why, then, was the Pollack band so highly regarded at the time?

For one thing, it regularly featured some of the finest young players in jazz. Goodman and Teagarden would eventually be considered among the greatest players on their instruments in jazz; at least some would say that they were respectively the finest clarinetist and trombonist to play the music. Jimmy McPartland was not at that level, but he was a fine jazz improviser in the Beiderbecke tradition, one of the best jazz trumpeters of the time. Others who passed in and out of the band, like Fud Living-

ston and Bud Freeman, were more than competent jazz players. It is fair
to say that in the 1927–29 period the Pollack band offered an array of
soloists who could compete on an equal level with those of the Henderson
and Ellington bands of the same years.

For a second, the band could swing as hard as any band in jazz of the
day. I realize that it will be taken as heresy by some critics and fans to
class the Pollack group with Henderson, Ellington and others in respect to
the ability to swing. Fortunately, it is easy to make the comparison. In
February 1931, the Henderson band cut an arrangement by Benny Carter
of "Sweet and Hot." A month later the Pollack band cut a record of the
tune, using an arrangement which was very similar. (The Pollack men
may have adapted the Henderson arrangement, or both bands may have
been working from a stock.)

The Pollack men achieve an easy, relaxed swing that is somewhat different from the rhythmic feel of the Henderson group. By this time Dick
Morgan of the Pollack band was playing guitar, while Clarence Holiday
with Henderson was still playing banjo. Harry Goodman was frequently
playing on all four beats of the measure, while John Kirby with Henderson
was playing mainly on first and third beats, in the older way. The combination of the four-beat bass and the lighter guitar, with its more precise
attack, gave the Pollack rhythm section a steady flow, which contrasted
with the more rocking, two-beat feel of the Henderson group.

This lighter swing had not been developed by the Pollack men: It is
evident in the work of some of the great New Orleans pioneers, especially
Armstrong, Bechet and Jelly Roll Morton, who, from their very first records, were playing a type of swing which was different from that of even
their fellow New Orleanians. For example, Armstrong's first important
solo, on Oliver's "Froggie-Moore," is quite different in character from the
music around it, and jumps out of it like a patch of color in a black and
white picture. Paradoxically, the white Chicagoans in the Pollack band
had heard Armstrong and Morton earlier than the black New Yorkers in
the Henderson and Ellington bands, and some of them had inculcated
that swing into their playing. I am not saying that the Henderson band
did not swing; but it was a different kind of swing, a more rocking, intense,
perhaps heated kind of playing as against the lighter, more cheerful sound
of Pollack.

The Ben Pollack band was certainly not a greater jazz orchestra, over
the long term, than the Henderson or Ellington bands. For one thing, the
unimaginative quality of most of the group's arrangements could hardly
stand comparison with the best of Ellington or Henderson. For another,
these two bands at times played with an intensity lacking in the Pollack

band—the price, perhaps, which had to be paid for the easy swing the Pollack men got.

But for that brief moment at the end of the 1920s, the Ben Pollack band could hold its own with any other band in jazz. And perhaps most significantly, it would be the primary model for the band Benny Goodman would trigger the swing movement with.

# 5

# Influences on Goodman

Patterns of influence in a jazz style are hard to trace, and they are particularly difficult to decipher in the cases of the early players, where who got recorded when was a matter of chance, and the disciple may have started recording earlier than the master. For example, Goodman made his first important record in 1926; Frank Teschemacher did not record until the end of 1927, but he and Goodman had heard each other on location, and as a consequence it is hard to know what to make of certain similarities in their playing. It is also true that musicians are at times unaware of how much they may have been affected by some early listening experience; and if they are aware, they may not always be candid about it. But we can at least find some sources for Goodman's earliest ideas about how jazz clarinet should be played.

Goodman's first influence was certainly Ted Lewis, whose records he was hearing almost from the moment he began to play the clarinet. As we know, he was impressed by Lewis's playing, and was able to produce a fair imitation of the Lewis style, which was characterized by an enormous wobbling vibrato and not much else.

Jazz at this stage meant dixieland, the style that was spreading out from New Orleans. The basic format was the use of three horns playing contrapuntally over a rhythm section of two to four pieces. In general, the cornet supplied a melodic lead in the middle register. The trombone played connecting links between phrases after the manner of trombones in marching bands and provided fundamental harmonies, especially utilizing the tonic and fifth. The clarinet played a rising and falling line mainly of eighth notes in the middle register. At times it would harmonize the cornet melody, and at other times use less-regular figures in the upper register. The use of auxiliaries in constructing a line was common.

This system, however, although the dominant one, was not inevitable.

Groups using other combinations of instruments were frequently organized, and at times one of the other instruments, especially the clarinet, would come forward to play the lead. Indeed, in some cases the clarinet was seen as the lead instrument. But the basic formula of cornet playing the melody was the standard one and quickly became a fixed convention of the music.

The Ted Lewis group was, at this early stage, essentially a dixieland band. Lewis, however, was an Ohioan who had come to the music at second hand and did not really understand it. Goodman soon began hearing the New Orleans players who had helped to develop the music. The most prominent of these was Larry Shields, playing with the Original Dixieland Jass Band, one of the most famous dance bands in the country at the moment that Goodman was learning to play. Shields worked in the standard dixieland manner. He was particularly fond of starting phrases on a long high note which was often quite shrill, and fell off markedly in pitch until it broke into eighth notes cascading on down. This upper register shrilling was probably derived from the sound of fifes in the marching bands Americans heard so much of in the late nineteenth and early twentieth centuries; but it was used also to make the clarinet heard over the naturally louder brass instruments, especially out-of-doors where so much New Orleans jazz was played. In the middle register, however, Shields had the very beautiful liquid tone that has always been characteristic of New Orleans clarinet players. And, like most New Orleans wind players, Shields employed a very fast terminal vibrato.

The Original Dixieland Jass Band was the first jazz band to have national fame, and Goodman could hardly have avoided hearing Shields had he wanted to. He is known to have owned a number of Original Dixieland Jass Band records,[1] and in discussing his early influences much later he included Shields in a list of clarinetists from the early days whom he "liked."[2] The Shields influence was, really, inescapable, and touched almost all clarinetists of the day.

However, of all the early dixieland clarinetists, the one who influenced Goodman most was Bernard "Doc" Berendsohn, a musician so obscure that only a tiny handful of specialists in these early bands knew even his name, much less anything about him. His date and place of birth are unknown, but he was probably born around 1890. One source has him moving to New Orleans in 1899,[3] but does not say where he came from. His father, Adolph Berendsohn, was a drum major with Tosso's Band, which "at one time played all important functions in New Orleans."[4] Adolph may have earned his living as a druggist. There were at least two sons, Bernard and his older brother, Sigmund. Sigmund was also a druggist, and both of the boys worked at least for a period as stenographers.[5] Bernard, however, went on to study dentistry at Tulane, and by 1913 he was working in the profession, hence the nickname, Doc.[6]

However, both boys were far more interested in music than they were in anything else. Sigmund was a trombone player, and Doc began as a cornetist. Both, apparently, picked up the new hot music that was burgeoning around them when they were adolescent, and were playing around New Orleans by 1915 and perhaps earlier.

New Orleans pay scales were low, and most of the local musicians had to support themselves by working "day jobs," and playing when and how they could. One of the important reasons for the exodus of jazz musicians from New Orleans was that they could earn much more elsewhere. In 1916 Doc Berendsohn was invited to come to Chicago by drummer Johnny Stein, who had formed what became the Original Dixieland Jass Band, without Stein.[7] Berendsohn was at this point playing cornet. His brother Sigmund also came to Chicago at some unknown date and eventually worked with the Benson Orchestra of Chicago, one of the better-known dance bands of the day. He went on to play with the Ted Lewis Orchestra.

In 1919 Doc Berendsohn, now playing clarinet, was spending much of his time in New York, where he was working frequently with a group of musicians who became well known as the Original Memphis Five but who were recording under a number of names for different labels. They included cornetist Phil Napoleon, pianist Frank Signorelli, and trombonist Miff Mole. For a brief period in very early 1920s Doc Berendsohn was working and recording with this group, the one genuine New Orleanian among them. After that moment he drops out of the record. We know only that at the time of his death—the exact date of which is unknown— he was teaching at the well-known American School of Music in Chicago.[8]

In 1921 and 1922 Berendsohn made a number of records under the title of Bailey's Lucky Seven. This was a house name used by bandleader Sam Lanin for dozens of records cut in the early 1920s, drawing on the cadre of New York musicians who were playing the new jazz music. Berendsohn clearly impressed the New Yorkers both with his musicianship and for the fact that he was a New Orleanian. He came forward to take the lead in the ensemble in these records, playing what amounted to brief solos, far more than was the practise with these early dixieland bands.

As we have seen, when Goodman was still very much an apprentice musician, he jammed frequently with members of the 124th Regiment Field Artillery band. He said, " 'Bailey's Lucky Seven' was making quite a few records at that time, and we tried to copy them as closely as possible."[9] This is the only statement I can find in which Goodman admits trying to "copy" somebody, aside from the early imitations of Ted Lewis. Bailey's Lucky Seven used a number of clarinet players over the years, but an examination of the dates makes it virtually certain that the clarinetist Goodman was following was Doc Berendsohn.

This of itself need not mean much. Young musicians often take models early whom they shortly drop. It is only when we listen to Berendsohn that we can see how he may have influenced Goodman. He was, to begin with, a thoroughly schooled musician, as the fact that he later taught at the American School of Music would suggest. Indeed, he may well have been the most technically proficient of any of the early New Orleans jazz musicians, many of whom were self-taught, or largely so, and most of whom could not read music well, if at all.

For a second thing, his manner of playing was quite different from that of the much better-known New Orleans players like Shields, Johnny Dodds, Leon Roppolo and others whom Goodman was hearing during these early years. Berendsohn had a pure, almost flute-like sound entirely without the shrilling that even the best of these early New Orleans clarinet players evinced at times. For another, he was a much more precise player than the others, with a firmer attack and using far fewer slurs than they did. His terminal vibrato was less pronounced than was customary with New Orleans wind players, and he used a great many grace notes, and especially gruppettos, or "turns," drawn from his exercise book.

Overall, Berendsohn played in what is known as the "German" as opposed to the "French" style of clarinet playing. According to the authority Jack Brymer, the French school is "light and superbly expressive," and generally bright. The German school is "at the opposite extreme"—a "broader and more sweeping" style, which produces "a clarinet tone of considerable purity."[10]

It is difficult to pin Benny Goodman's playing to either of these schools. Nonetheless, he got his formal study from a man of German extraction, and he worked primarily from a German method book. And it seems to me that in his later work Goodman evinces marks of the Berendsohn style—the full, pure tone, the precision and the technical proficiency. Robert Sparkman, who has studied the Berendsohn records carefully, says, "It's easy to see how Goodman, who was studying with a classical teacher, would be struck by Doc's sound and his fine technique."[11]

Did Goodman know who he was listening to? Doc's brother Sigmund was playing with an important Chicago dance band, and may have told some of the men Goodman was jamming with about Doc and the records. It is also possible that some of them had heard Doc either on cornet or clarinet when he was working in Chicago a few years earlier. Yet it is equally possible that Benny did not know the name of the clarinetist he was hearing. In any case, he seems never to have mentioned him, except by inference.

This is hardly to say that Goodman formed his style on that of Berendsohn. He was listening to many other clarinetists at the time, and undoubtedly he absorbed something from many of them. But he was consciously studying Berendsohn's manner of playing before he heard Dodds, Roppolo and others who might have influenced him, and I am convinced that Doc was Goodman's first important model.

However, Benny was still an adolescent, hardly more than a boy, when he began to hear the better-known jazz clarinetists in Chicago. One of these was Johnny Dodds (the name is pronounced "Dots"), whom he presumably heard at Lincoln Gardens, where Dodds was playing with the King Oliver band that had Louis Armstrong on second cornet. By 1922 the young white musicians of Chicago had discovered the Oliver band and went to Lincoln Gardens regularly to hear it. In any case, it began to record early in 1923, and Goodman would certainly have heard these important records.

Dodds had come to Chicago in 1919 specifically to work with Oliver, and he went on to be the clarinet mainstay of the Armstrong Hot Five records which would strike jazz musicians with the force of a hammer. The early jazz writers considered Dodds the preeminent New Orleans clarinet player, in the case of some critics almost to the exclusion of anyone else. According to Goodman's brother Freddy, "Johnny Dodds was another clarinet player Benny really appreciated."[12]

Dodds, in the early days with the Oliver group, played in the typical dixieland style as exemplified by Shields. However, he was a more modest and four-square player. He used far fewer of the shrill high notes Shields liked to use, and his melodic line was frequently built on imitation—that is to say, parallel phrases set higher or lower. Dodds would often play four such phrases going up and a different set coming down. Dodds also attacked more firmly than Shields, and it seems to me that Goodman's attack more nearly resembles Dodds than any of the clarinet players of the time.

But however much Goodman took from these early players, especially Doc Berendsohn, he eventually came to prefer the work of two of the most influential of the pioneer clarinetists, Jimmie Noone and Leon Roppolo. Roppolo came to Chicago to work with his New Orleanian pals, cornetist Paul Mares and trombonist George Brunies, at the Friar's Society Inn, as part of the general influx of New Orleans jazz musicians. Friar's Inn was a gang-run speakeasy, typical of the illegal clubs burgeoning in the gang-run city after Prohibition. The group, originally the Friar's Society Orchestra, quickly changed its name to the New Orleans Rhythm Kings, and as such made the records which had so great an impact on the Austin High group. Roppolo was idolized by the young Chicagoans, who were in fact not much younger than he was. Unfortunately, he suffered increasingly from mental illness, and by 1925 was incarcerated in a mental institution, where he remained until his death in 1943. This fate made him a natural subject for romantic legend; there were stories of his throwing his clarinet in Lake Ponchartrain in a fit of despondency over his inability to play what he was hearing in his head.

Roppolo, inevitably, played in the standard New Orleans mode also reflected in Shields and Dodds. His attack and general four-square approach are reminiscent of Dodds, but he uses a lot of bent notes in the Shields manner, and there is at least one report that he consciously emulated Larry Shields. Goodman heard Roppolo in person only once, if that, as Roppolo left Chicago in about 1923.[13] But he heard the records, and declared much later that Roppolo "was one of my favorite players."[14] Roppolo frequently used figures based on alterations of notes a second or a third part, as did many jazz players of the time.

But Roppolo's career was truncated by his illness, and there is no knowing how he might have developed. Jimmie Noone, on the other hand, became a far more formidable player than Roppolo, and Goodman eventually paid him a good deal more attention. Noone was a Creole, and played with the relaxed manner and relatively even eighth notes and liquid tone that the Creoles favored. He began playing around Chicago in 1917 with various of the New Orleans bands, and eventually landed with Cook's Dreamland Orchestra, a big theatre band that employed many New Orleans jazz musicians to provide the hot touches audiences demanded. Initially, Noone played in the standard New Orleans style used by Dodds, Roppolo, Shields and others, as the records with Cook show. But in 1926 Noone took a small group featuring his own clarinet playing into a black-and-tan called the Nest, later the Apex Club, and when he recorded with this group in 1928 his style had changed dramatically. The fast terminal vibrato typical of New Orleans playing had been drastically pruned. More important, Noone is playing with a great deal more variety of phrase and intonation than was typical of the New Orleans players, who characteristically employed one of two patterns—long sequences of eighth notes replete with auxiliaries and imitation, and long bent notes, usually downwards. Noone of course did not entirely abandon these devices. The long, easy, eighth-note runs played with delicacy and a warbling, liquid tone are everywhere in his work. But there is much more: The low register legato phrases on "I Know That You Know," followed by a driving, sharply attacked, chorus; long, lazy, looping phrases in "Sweet Sue"; very simple direct statements of sharply attacked quarter notes at the end of "Four or Five Times."

Exactly how much Goodman was influenced by Noone is difficult to know. Goodman later on liked to play long passages in the low, chalumeau register of the clarinet, something at which Noone was a master. But Goodman's playing during this period is much closer to that of another clarinetist, Frank Teschemacher, than it is to Noone's. Teschemacher was one of the Austin High group, considered by many of them to be the leading figure in it. Clarinetist Pee Wee Russell once said, "If Tesch had lived, he would now be the greatest clarinet player on earth."[15] Unfortunately, Tesch was killed in an automobile accident in 1932.

Like so many others, Tesch started out under the influence of the New Orleanians, playing long strings of eighth notes and using a rapid terminal vibrato. But as his style developed, he began breaking up the eighth-note strings and his phrasing became quite unpredictable; it was this sudden, startling rush off into surprising directions that excited his fellow musicians. He used a lot of saw-toothed figures, especially downwards, off-beat "back-sliding" phrases and he frequently introduced an unaccented long note, swelling and widening the vibrato as it went. He tended more than most jazz players to use a substantial vibrato throughout a note.

But perhaps more than anything, what characterizes Teschemacher's playing is a tense, rough, almost twisted quality which expressed itself in short, stubby phrases, sudden bent notes and a very fast terminal vibrato. Benny Goodman was capable of very similar tense, driving playing.

The two men admired each other's playing, at least privately. According to Jess Stacy, who played for years in Goodman's big band, and was around Chicago in the late 1920s, "Benny Goodman was playing at the Southmoor Hotel with Ben Pollack, and Benny used to go over and stand behind a post and listen to [Teschemacher]. He didn't want to be seen listening to Teschemacher."[16] Conversely, Bud Freeman, who was close to both men, said of Teschemacher, "He idolized Benny Goodman, he was not influenced by Benny Goodman."[17]

There are differences, as well as similarities, in the two men's styles. Goodman was technically the more competent player. Teschemacher's intonation could fail him at times, and he did not have the speed that Goodman had. Teschemacher used much more equal "eighth" notes than Goodman did, whose eighths were markedly unequal. Goodman used little vibrato, except for a quick, brief terminal vibrato, as opposed to the broad vibrato Teschemacher liked to use. On the other hand, both liked to break up rhythmic patterns, leaping about at times erratically; both frequently employed long, sweeping notes in the upper register; both could be very fiery, intense, impatient players, as hot as anybody in jazz. It seems to me, finally, that the two men had a mutual influence on each other, encouraging one another by example, to form hot, strong styles.

By his later records Teschemacher was playing a smoother and technically much improved manner, and it is easy to agree with Pee Wee

Russell's assessment that had he lived he would have been a superb jazz musician. But by 1928, it seems to me, Goodman was a more interesting player than Teschemacher was, and it would have taken Tesch some doing to outdistance Benny.

Other clarinetists who Goodman was aware of during the 1920s were Jimmy Dorsey, Pee Wee Russell, Fud Livingston, Jimmy Lytell, Volly DeFaut and Don Murray. Of these Jimmy Dorsey was the most significant. Jimmy and his brother Tommy were gifted young musicians, both of whom played several instruments. By 1924 when they were barely out of their teens, they had developed major reputations as first-rate studio musicians. That year both began recording with the California Ramblers, a very popular dance band, and this association began to give them names with dance band aficionados. In 1926 Jimmy started to record with Red Nichols in various dixieland combinations generally known as Red Nichols and His Five Pennies. These groups frequently included trombonist Miff Mole and together the three quickly became the best known of the white jazz musicians of the moment. Through the Nichols records and others, Dorsey became the model for many young clarinetists, not only in the United States but in England and France as well. Among the people he influenced was Lester Young, who would become one of the greatest of all jazz musicians.[18] Eventually Jimmy and Tommy would form an orchestra together which would be very popular; and during the swing era each would have one of the four or five top bands.

During this early period, Dorsey used the long sequences of eighth notes characteristic of the New Orleans ensemble style, but he did not use the fast terminal vibrato tpyical of the genre. He tended to play in a more "legitimate" manner than some of the other jazz clarinetists, using fewer of the swoops and glissandos typical of jazz playing of the time. He was a somewhat more academic player, if we may use that term, than others of his peers, although he was capable of playing with considerable force.

Between 1926 and 1934 or so, Jimmy Dorsey was far better known to the general public than Goodman was. Although they worked together occasionally and actually roomed together for a brief period, they were direct competitors for much of their careers and Goodman never mentioned Dorsey in any of several discussions of clarinetists, but he could hardly have been unaware of him.

Pee Wee Russell, who became the darling of the dixieland buffs in the 1940s, had not yet in the 1920s developed the eccentric, raspy manner of playing for which he later became famous. At this time he was playing in a relatively calm, straightforward manner with a clean, facile style. He sounds as if he had been listening to Goodman. Fud Livingston, who would work with Goodman in the Ben Pollack band, was a technically precise player who phrased like Frank Teschemacher, but without as much drive. However, he played with a good deal of warmth. Livingston was a highly regarded studio musician of the time, but probably enjoyed more renown in the music business as an arranger for studio orchestras and the movie industry.

Among the best of this group was Voltaire "Volly" DeFaut, today almost totally forgotten except by specialists in the period. He began, like so many of the others, playing in the straightforward New Orleans style of Dodds and Roppolo, but by the spring of 1925, when he recorded with Jelly Roll Morton in a racially mixed trio that anticipated the later Goodman trios, he had developed a style like that of the later Noone, although we cannot be sure how the lines of influence ran. When he began to record a year later, DeFaut's playing also resembled Goodman's to an extent. Goodman expressly singled out DeFaut as one of the clarinetists he "liked" in the early days, but once again, due to the paucity of recorded evidence, it is impossible to tell who influenced whom, if there was any influence at all in either direction.

One other clarinet player Goodman was hearing a lot of, on records at least, was Don Murray, simply because Murray was recording frequently with Beiderbecke. Murray played a relaxed, easy line that for the most part rose and fell in the middle register, and in that respect resembled Bix's line. His tone was at times thin, and he lacked the drive of a Teschemacher, but he has been considered by many Beiderbecke fans the best of the clarinetists Bix worked with. It is unlikely that he had any marked influence on Goodman.

Finally, there was Jimmy Lytell, who made a large number of early records with the very popular Original Memphis Five, which recorded under that name and various pseudonyms. Lytell, whose real name was Sarrapede, also played with the Original Dixieland Jass Band for a period.[19] He modeled his style on that of Larry Shields, but there are differences: His shrill high notes do not fall off as Shields' did, his vibrato is less marked and altogether he played in a relatively more graceful and controlled style. Goodman may not have known much about Lytell, but he was bound to have heard him on records.

What becomes clear in all of this is that between 1924 and 1926 the style of jazz clarinet playing changed markedly. In 1924 all of those whose records we have—DeFaut, Noone, Dodds, Lytell, and others like Jimmy Hartwell with the Wolverines—were playing in the old New Orleans style, depending mainly on strings of eighth notes, interspersed with occasional long bent notes and furnished with a fast terminal vibrato. We can assume that this was true of the young Goodman, too.

By 1926 all of these men were playing a much more varied style, utiliz-

ing the full range of the instrument, with attendant variety of timbre and
a more complicated phrasing. In the case of Noone, the lessons with Franz
Schoepp undoubtedly played a role, for better technical mastery of the
instrument would have liberated him considerably from the confinement
of the New Orleans genre. But Schoepp could not have given anyone a
different conception of jazz playing.

The answer, I think, lies in Louis Armstrong's Hot Five records which
began to appear in the fall of 1925. Dixieland jazz, we remember, was an
ensemble music, with solos infrequent and usually worked out in advance.
(Actually, as testimony from members of the Original Dixieland Jass
Band makes clear, the ensembles were fairly well worked out, too.)[20] In
1924 Armstrong was brought to New York as a jazz specialist by Fletcher
Henderson. His main function with the orchestra was to play solos, and
he galvanized the New York men with his power, his swing and his beautifully sculpted lines. He returned to Chicago in the fall of 1925 to work
primarily as a soloist against a backdrop of other musicians; and as the
Hot Five series progressed, they more and more became showcases for
Armstrong, with the other musicians appearing as a support group. Armstrong was noted for the enormous variety of phrasing and mood. His
unconfined manner, which allowed him to range freely wherever his daring took him, astonished the other musicians. Nobody was immune, and
it is my belief that it was Armstrong, more than any of the clarinet players, who forced the clarinet out of the limits of the dixieland style.

Sorting out all of these cross lines of influences is difficult. Goodman
was affecting the other men as much as they were affecting him, and no
doubt all kinds of feedback were at work. However, we can certainly say
that Goodman began as a dixieland player in the Roppolo-Shields-Dodds-
Berendsohn mode. By 1926 when he made some home recordings on cylinders with some of the Chicago musicians, his playing was closer to that
of Teschemacher than anyone else's, although it does not follow that he
was modeling himself on Tesch. Noone may have had some influence,
especially in respect to low register playing, but otherwise Goodman never
really played in the Noone style. Like the others, Goodman broke away
from the dixieland style, either directly under Armstrong's spell, or more
indirectly absorbing the Armstrong style as it spread generally through
jazz. And finally, he may have drawn bits and pieces of things from Dorsey,
DeFaut and others. But of course there was also Benny Goodman. Every
masterful jazz musician brings something of himself to his playing, and
this was certainly true of him.

# 6

# The First Recordings

Benny Goodman's formal recording career, which would last almost sixty years, began in Chicago on September 14, 1926, when the Pollack band cut three sides for Victor. These first Pollack sides were never issued and have since disappeared. Sometime thereafter, probably in the early winter, Goodman and some others, among them Glenn Miller, made some home recordings at the house of trumpeter Earl Baker, a well-regarded Chicago player who worked with the Pollack band from time to time. Goodman is certainly audible on these sides, but because of the recording quality, and the brevity of Goodman's appearances, it is difficult to say much about them, except that Goodman is here in the "Teschemacher" mode which characterized his playing—and again I am not implying anything about lines of influence but saying merely that both men had somewhat similar approaches to the clarinet at this time.

Finally, on December 9 and 17, the Pollack band cut some sides for Victor which were issued. Goodman has solos on two of these, "Deed I Do" and "He's the Last Word." On the former, Goodman has sixteen measures, and we notice immediately a characteristic of his playing of this period—extreme dynamic shifts from note to note, for a sort of "beedle, beedle, beedle" effect. "He's the Last Word" is a typical light-hearted, undistinguished melody with a humorous lyric built around the catch phrase of the title; catch phrases were exceedingly common starting points for lyrics of the times, as for example, "Nice Work If You Can Get It," "Let's Do It," "My Heart Stood Still," "She's Funny That Way" and hundreds more. Goodman again has sixteen bars. His playing is somewhat shrill and incoherent, with the phrases tumbling out on top of each other half finished, never rounded off in some comprehensible way. It is exactly the work of an excitable young man—a seventeen-year-old boy, in fact, impetuous and heedless. Nonetheless, the solo again displays some of the characteristics which mark his work at this time. Right from the opening phrases we hear a tendency to play short, stubby notes, usually concluded with a very fast and brief terminal vibrato, as if he were giving them a quick twist in order to make them stand up on their own.

For another, Goodman is playing his putative eighth notes markedly unevenly. It is necessary to say a word about this. In most formal Western music—symphonies as well as popular songs—a beat (assuming 4/4 metre) is usually divided evenly into two eighth notes, a triplet of three equal notes, or some other equal division. Exceptions are the so-called dotted rhythm (the dotted eighth and sixteenth) which divides the beat into three parts to one; and a tied triplet, which divides the beat into two parts to one.

It is a major trait in jazz for players to eschew these formal divisions of the beat, using instead much less mathematically exact and often unquantifiable divisions. These ways of dividing the beat vary not only from player to player, but from moment to moment in a given solo. However, players tend to divide beats in a more or less consistent manner which becomes a central characteristic of their styles. Coleman Hawkins, for example, divided the beat into very unequal parts, while Dizzy Gillespie plays his "eighth notes" much more evenly. Nor is it only a matter of time. Accents created by a sharper attack, increased volume or other methods are also used to unbalance the weight of supposedly similar notes. This practice is so well grasped by jazz players that arrangers write jazz passages in conventional notation of eighth notes with the understanding that the musicians will "swing" the line by some system of accent or weighting which will turn them into unbalanced pairs. At times, especially in solos by people like Hawkins, this unbalancing will reach such extremes that the lighter notes become inaudible. Such notes are known in jazz as "ghost" notes. We know they are "there," because the shape of the phrase indicates that they were intended, and indeed were probably actually fingered. (Transcribers write ghost notes with parentheses around the note head.)

At this early stage of his career, Benny Goodman was dividing the beat in a markedly uneven fashion, and we notice a good many ghost notes in the "He's the Last Word" solo. We find one in the first bar of the solo (after the four-bar introduction to it) and more in the next several bars. Then, in bars eleven and twelve he plays a figure in which three different degrees of stress are applied. If written out the figure would consist of a quarter note followed by two eighths, but as played by Goodman they are given successively less weight, like Papa Bear, Momma Bear and the Baby Bear.

Benny Goodman would never be the great master of drama that Louis Armstrong was, nor the designer of bits of intricate clockwork, as was

Beiderbecke, but there is more rhythmic variety in his work, from measure
to measure, than in the playing of almost any jazz musician I can think
of. This characteristic was evident early, and it is these things—the varied
way of dividing the beat, the terse fragments interrupted by long, soaring
notes, the quick twist at the end of notes, that contributed to the enormous
swing which was always present in his work.

Goodman's next major solo was on "Waitin' for Katie," another un-
impressive tune with the humorous lyric that audiences of the day liked.
It is an excellent solo—his best to date—and a harbinger of what was to
come. After a brief introduction by the band, Goodman takes the entire
thirty-two bars of the opening chorus to himself, with only the rhythm
section for support. This was a format he would later make a huge success
of with his Trios and Quartets, and just as he would do in those later
records, he uses the melody as a point of departure. He plays it straight, as
much as any jazz musician is likely to do in any case, through most of the
first eight bars, probably on the instruction of either Pollack or the recording director, who would have insisted on a clear statement of the tune at the
opening of the record. Goodman plays in the middle register, as he would
again do in the Trios and Quartets, where he could play with good volume, firm control, and a fuller tone than he was likely to get higher up.

But keeping the sometimes rebellious Goodman to a melody was like
trying to catch a firefly in the dark: it winks and is gone. After six measures
Benny begins to wander off. There are ghost notes in bars six and seven,
and a typical shower of irregular eighth notes as the segment ends. At the
beginning of the second eight he makes another stab at playing the melody, but this time is able to keep on course only into the second measure,
when he turns out a brief figure followed by a longer one, running through
the fourth bar, which is made up of two quick phrases that reflect the first
one. In bars seven and eight there are more of those uneven pairs. At the
bridge Goodman returns to the melody, and he does so again at the beginning of the final eight measures.

This regular reporting back to the melody undoubtedly helped to give
this solo more coherence than is found in much of this youthful work. It
is, as a whole, a first-rate jazz solo, despite a squeak at the end, filled with
rhythmic variety, surprising phrases that are more musically related than
is often the case in his work, played with the warmth and clarity of tone
that would always be an important part of his attraction. At seventeen
Goodman was already capable of playing brilliant jazz in a style which was
even then instantly recognizable as his own. Jazz musicians typically mature at young ages: Billie Holiday was singing in her own manner when
she was eighteen or nineteen; Charlie Parker was beginning to work out
the style which would become bebop when he was twenty-two; Stan Getz

was a star with Woody Herman at twenty. But no major jazz musician was quite as precocious as Benny Goodman, who, at seventeen, was capable of playing a solo as individual, assured and well-constructed as "Waitin' for Katie."

During the time Goodman was with Pollack he made over thirty sides with the group that were issued as by the Pollack orchestra, and an almost equal number with the group under a variety of other names—the Whoopee Makers, the Hotsy Totsy Gang, Goody and His Good Timers, Dixie Daisies, Mills' Musical Clowns, the Lumberjacks, Jimmy McHugh's Bostonians, Sunny Clapp and his Band O'Sunshine, and others. Not only was the orchestra given different names for various sessions, but sometimes the same records were issued under different names and for different labels. This was standard practice. The idea was to slip the record into as many markets as possible. As we have seen, the Pollack name was generally reserved for the more commercial records which would, in theory at least, catch the largest audience, while the hotter versions were put out under other names.

Many of these recording sessions were organized by Irving Mills, a major music business entrepreneur of the time, who was involved with as many aspects of the business as he could make profitable. He started as a singer, joined his brother Jack in a music publishing business that was very successful, and formed a partnership with Duke Ellington whom, in 1928, he was pushing into fame and fortune. Mills' idea was to let four or five hands wash each other, using his own bands to record his own tunes, so that he could collect several slices of each pie. He wanted to get his tunes recorded in order to popularize them, and he found the Pollack group, and various of the Pollack men in different combinations, very useful. They were good readers and as reliable as any musicians of the time were likely to be. Perhaps more important, as they could improvise, they were capable of quickly pulling together head arrangements in the studio, thus saving Mills a good deal of trouble and expense.

Goodman solos on over half of these recordings. Few of the solos are up to the level of the one on "Waitin' for Katie." There is some tendency to shrillness, a fault common in jazz clarinet playing even today, and the lack of coherence in "He's the Last Word," is evident in many of these solos. Nonetheless, there is plenty of excellent jazz here. On "Buy, Buy for Baby," another theoretically humorous tune ("or maybe baby will bye-bye you") he plays a very hot solo, replete with stubby, sharply accented notes, mixed with ghost notes. Because Goodman was right from the beginning one of the finest technicians of jazz, it became customary to think of him as always playing in a fluid, graceful and perhaps slick manner. It is critical for us to realize that, however flawless and flowing a

line he could produce when he felt called upon to do so, he was essentially
a hot, driving musician.

A comparison with Pee Wee Russell is interesting. Goodman and Russell have been seen as antithetical stylists by most jazz critics and fans of
both men. Yet they have more in common than this view suggests. Pee
Wee Russell, at least during the period of his greatest fame as a dixielander
in the late 1930s and early forties period, was noted for his "tortured" or
"tormented" style, replete with wry growls, gurgles, wavering notes, and
the like—notes that were not essentially melodic, but meant to provide
color, set a mood, add drive or simply express a feeling as a cry or shout
does. There is a tendency for jazz writers, especially those equipped to
make technical analyses of the music, to concentrate on such matters as
harmony, melody and form in examining a work. And these things must
of course be discussed in any attempt to understand a piece of jazz. But
in fact, jazz musicians have rarely had much interest in formal architecture, and many famous solos at points lack coherence. Moreover, musicians
frequently are content to work from the same harmonic material night
after night for years, as did Lester Young, Louis Armstrong and, in fact,
Benny Goodman. I should guess that half of early jazz was built around
half a dozen seventh chords. We must therefore keep in mind that these
other considerations—the notes that provide color, drive and the like—are
not simply embellishments but essential elements in the cloth. The playing of Pee Wee Russell cannot be understood unless this idea is grasped.

It is also true of Goodman's work. Over the years this element would
gradually diminish in his playing, but it would never disappear altogether.
And interestingly enough, it is more apparent in Goodman's playing in
this early period than it is in Russell's work of the same time.

Goodman had trouble taking the later Russell seriously. In a story that
has been told by several people, Goodman in the 1940s was invited to give
a few classes in the clarinet at the Juilliard School. According to Sid Weiss,
Goodman's bassist off and on for a considerable period, "Some smartass student said, 'Mr. Goodman, what do you think about Pee Wee Russell?'
Goodman's reply, Weiss said, was, 'He's a great artist, but if you want to
play like him, don't practice.' "[1]

Yet in fact, Goodman was entirely capable of using the devices Russell
specialized in even at the time he was speaking at Juilliard. There is a recent record of excerpts from several 1941 broadcasts of the Goodman band
when drummer Sid Catlett was with it, of "Roll 'Em," one of Goodman's
famous swing numbers of the time. Goodman's solos are chockablock with
swoops, growls, slurs, shrieks and long microtonal patches. He cannot be
mistaken for Russell; but he is using many of the devices Russell was
famous for.

We hear this element in "Buy, Buy for Baby." The structure of the solo is crippled. Goodman picks up at the last eight measures of the chorus, playing as if he had started at the beginning of a chorus, with the full band playing the final eight. Somewhere eight bars were dropped out, possibly due to time limitations. The melody Goodman creates will not bear much extended analysis: it darts hither and thither like a dog loose in the woods smelling down faint trails and dead ends. But the solo is filled with those non-melodic tones—a downward, unstable slur in the second bar, a hanging unresolved note in the fourth bar, another unstable slur in the tenth, a quick, drop-off moan, once again left entirely unresolved, in the eleventh measure. This is not one of Goodman's great solos; coherence, after all, is usually better than its absence. But the solo has drive and verve, imparted in considerable measure by the bent and twisted notes.

During this period Goodman was recording outside of the Pollack band for various leaders and record producers. Soon after he arrived in New York he began to develop a reputation as one of the best young reed men in the city, and worked his way into that elite of "studio" musicians which has existed in the city since the early 1920s. In that day probably the bulk of popular music recordings were cut not by permanently organized groups but by pick-up bands put together for specific recording sessions. In some cases these would be for a leader like Red Nichols, who reconstituted orchestras as he needed them, picking from a cadre of men he knew. In other cases the session was made for a label's recording director, or an independent producer like Irving Mills, who picked the tunes and slapped whatever name on the record he chose, often a "house" name like The Hotsy Totsy Gang that Mills was using with Brunswick.

By 1928 Goodman was in demand for such sessions, and in his years with Pollack he was hired for about a dozen of them. Some of these were for Red Nichols, who was, by the late 1920s, perhaps the best known of the white jazz musicians, to the general public at least. He was recognized as a fine jazz musician by 1922 and went on to form his own groups, working a great deal in combination with Jimmy Dorsey, Miff Mole and pianist Art Schutt, sometimes as Miff Mole and His Molers, Red and Miff's Stompers, but mainly as Red Nichols' Five Pennies. Nichols was a very popular figure, especially on college campuses where there was ardent support for jazz and he commanded high fees for appearances.

Red Nichols has met an undeserved fate at the hands of jazz writers. He became well known to the public playing in a style that derived from that of Beiderbecke, before Bix had any following outside of a narrow circle of jazz musicians and jazz fans in the Midwest who had heard him at college dances or had bought the records of the group he was featured with, The Wolverines. Nichols' influence was particularly strong in Europe, where his records were among the first American jazz discs to be widely known. When it became apparent to jazz fans in 1928 or so that Nichols was the follower and Beiderbecke the creator of the style, Nichols was cast aside as a usurper who had gotten rich off the work of a greater man.

The charge was unfair. Both Nichols and Beiderbecke developed out of Nick LaRocca of the Original Dixieland Jass Band, and his immediate followers, especially Phil Napoleon of the Memphis Five. Nichols may well have come upon elements of the Beiderbecke style independently of Bix. He said, "Bix made a tremendous impression on me, and I'd be the last to deny that his playing influenced mine. But I didn't consciously imitate him. I had already evolved the 'style' identified with me in later years, and the same was true of Bix. We both derived our inspiration from many of the same sources."[2] Furthermore, Nichols was hardly the only trumpet player of the time emulating Beiderbecke. There was a whole school of them, including Jimmy McPartland, Sterling Bose, Andy Secrest, Stew Pletcher and many more, among them a number of black musicians. The black trumpeter Doc Cheatham said that at the time, "We all chased around trying to learn to play like Bix."[3] And the influence of Bix is quite evident in the Bennie Moten band of the late 1920s. It was hardly reasonable for the critics to pull Nichols down for imitating Bix, when they praised McPartland for doing precisely the same thing; but Nichols was becoming wealthy and celebrated, while McPartland was a relatively unknown sideman at the time, and of course it is always those who make popular successes who are attacked by the critics, as Goodman would discover.

In fact, in the years around 1926, Red Nichols was one of the best trumpet players in jazz, topped only by Armstrong, Beiderbecke and possibly one or two others. He had a fine technique and played cleanly with a bright tone. He used a quick terminal vibrato and an occasional pitch sag produced by half-valving, both devices emblematic of the Beiderbecke style; and he swung as much as anybody but the very best of the day, such as Armstrong and Bechet. Moreover, his primary playing companions Dorsey and Mole were both excellent jazz players. Mole was without doubt one of the very best trombonists of the time, equipped with a flawless technique that was the envy of other trombonists, and a clean sound. He became the model for countless trombone players trying to escape from the confines of the ponderous dixieland style with its incessant portamenti. Eventually Jack Teagarden, and then a group of black trombonists, especially Jimmy Harrison with Fletcher Henderson, playing a blues-inflected legato style, would eclipse the brisk staccato manner of Mole. It would not be until the arrival of J. J. Johnson and the bebop trombonists some twenty years later that the staccato style would return. But in the years following 1926, Mole, Nichols and Dorsey were at the forefront of jazz, and their influence was obvious everywhere.

By 1928, however, Jimmy Dorsey was occupied with the Dorsey Brothers band. Nichols, who was working constantly, needed other men to fill in, and he began turning to Goodman. From 1929 to 1933 Goodman made over four dozen records with various Nichols groups. Many of these were commercial dance numbers, but virtually all of them had excellent soloists, and most of them have at least some jazz interest. Especially in the latter days, the bands consisted of eight or ten musicians playing arrangements with jazz solos scattered throughout in what was by 1930 the established "big" band jazz style. But there are also a number of small six to eight piece groups playing in the older hot style. In general, even these small groups tend to be built around hot arrangements, though some cuts, like "Ballin' the Jack," made in April 1929, are pure dixieland, in the direct line of descent from the now moribund New Orleans style. These small Nichols groups were producing some of the finest hot music of the genre. Indeed, they are generally superior, overall, to the much more famous Beiderbecke dixieland sides made two or three years later, if we except the playing of Bix himself. Nichols' sidemen are as a group better than Bix's, the arrangements are better throughout, and the rhythm section swings harder. In particular, guitarist Carl Kress, who was free-lancing around New York, and plays on some of these sides, was in my view the best rhythm guitarist in jazz at the moment. Although the guitar had been favored by the black New Orleans jazz pioneers, in about 1918 it had been supplanted by the banjo which was still in vogue in the late 1920s. Kress was one of the first to show that the guitar, with his lighter, less jangling sound and sharper attack, could give the rhythm section a more precise and delicate beat. It is true that Django Reinhardt, who would become the most influential guitarist of the early swing period, was influenced at first by Eddie Lang, whose work Reinhardt knew through the popular Venuti-Lang sides. However, the Nichols records were well known in Europe from about the time Django was learning to play jazz, and it appears to me that Reinhardt's rhythm playing more nearly resembles Kress' than Lang's.

Not the least of the virtues of these sides was the presence of Benny Goodman. He solos on many of these records—Nichols was very generous about parceling out solos among his sidemen, often at the expense of his own solo time. Goodman plays a very typical solo on "Chinatown, My Chinatown." As he frequently does, he opens the solo with a statement, or paraphrase, of the melody, but once launched, quickly departs from it.

The solo is filled with the abrupt, somewhat jerky phrases which seem at times to be squirted randomly here and there, like a child playing with a hose, that were characteristic of his work in this period. Many of the notes are finished off with the sudden, brief terminal vibrato, and there are in bars eight and ten emphatic bent notes. It is all energy and motion, with little attempt to construct flowing melodies, the heedless playing of a very young man.

"Ballin' the Jack" is in the classic dixieland style with solos by Goodman, Mole, Nichols and a final hot "ride-out" ensemble which became customary with the dixieland bands during the revival of the style about a decade later. Nichols has an impressive solo. It opens with an interesting two-bar figure that is then amplified in a long, rolling phrase stretching over the next six measures. He employs as well deft, fast triplet figures, and creates altogether a first-rate jazz solo which would have been remembered as a classic had not Beiderbecke done the same thing better, and earlier.

Goodman's solo begins atypically, with an attempt to make a more organized melodic line than he usually struck for: a two-measure phrase beginning on the first beat of the first measure is repeated, but this time starting a beat earlier, to produce one of those metric shifts so beloved of jazz musicians of this period. The remainder of the solo is less well thought out, but is nonetheless filled with drive and spirit.

Of particular interest is the ride-out ending. Benny Goodman did not make many records in the dixieland style, and was certainly never associated with the school; during the dixieland revival his manner was seen as almost the antithesis of dixieland clarinet playing, which had Pee Wee Russell as its major exponent. But we remember that among Goodman's first influences were the dixielanders Larry Shields and Doc Berendsohn. Goodman's management of dixieland ensemble clarinet, however, is a far cry from that of the original New Orleanians, with their heavy dependence on strings of eighth notes interspersed with long, high falling wails. As in his solos, there is great rhythmic variety—here some repeated off-beat notes to give an effect of back-sliding, there a quick patch of rising and falling eighth notes, there a long downward slide. He is not so much creating counter-melodies as the New Orleans clarinetists did, but producing driving rhythms to propel the music along. Benny Goodman was always an intensely rhythmic player, and it shows here.

One more thing must be said about Goodman's association with Red Nichols. Ben Pollack demanded the usual band discipline from his men, but he was no stern authoritarian. Nichols, however, was. His father was an elder of the Mormon Church, conductor of the Ogden, Utah, Municipal Band, and he trained Red in accuracy and clean execution. Nichols later said, "I grew up in an atmosphere of musical discipline that has been a great help to me all of my life, and I never cease to be grateful to my father for it. It's one of the factors responsible for the precision with which I play. . . ."⁴ His manager George Tasker said, "Considered by many as one of the roughest taskmasters in the business, it wasn't unusual for him to call section rehearsals as well as full band rehearsals time after time to improve intonation, phrasing, and technique on material that the band had been playing for months."⁵ This was precisely the leadership style that Benny Goodman adopted right from the first. Goodman would no doubt have come to it on his own, because he was, like Nichols, a consummate musician who practiced endlessly, and tried constantly to perfect the details of musicianship which are critical to good performance. But in Nichols he had a model for these demanding methods.

Possibly the most famous of the studio sessions Goodman made in these years was one put together by Hoagy Carmichael to cut one of his tunes, "Rockin' Chair." He brought in Bix and the growl trumpeter Bubber Miley, who had recently been fired by Duke Ellington for unreliability. He also had both Goodman and Jimmy Dorsey on the session because, so the story goes, Carmichael was friendly with both and did not want to offend either.⁶ The main interest in "Rockin' Chair" is the marked contrast between Beiderbecke and Miley, the first a lyrical performer with a bell-like tone, the second a rough-spoken growl specialist. There is a clarinet obbligato behind the vocal, probably played by Goodman.

The reverse, a comic "rendering" of the old pornographic song, "Barnacle Bill the Sailor," was an inexplicable choice for a jazz date. It alternates humorous vocal passages to a march beat, and sudden uptempo jazz passages in which various members of the group solo. Goodman has one of these sixteen measure passages. None of the soloists seems to know exactly what to do with the very simple chord changes of the tune, which basically alternates between tonic and dominant chords. Improvising jazz musicians prefer chord changes which offer variety, but do not move too rapidly, except perhaps as a special challenge, as in John Coltrane's formidable piece, "Giant Steps." For example, the chords of the Rodgers and Hart standard, "You Took Advantage of Me," change every two beats, which, when taken relatively fast, pens the soloist up so that he finds himself worrying about making the changes instead of following out melodic ideas. On the other hand, a tune like "China Boy," which opens with four straight measures of F-major, often leaves the soloist stuck in F-major when he has exhausted what he had to say on the chord for the moment.

It seems to me that in "Barnacle Bill" the musicians were suffering from the latter problem. The solos by Beiderbecke, Goodman and Bud Freeman all start off at red heat and then peter out as they go along, as if the players were asking themselves, "What the hell do I do now?" Goodman, impelled forward by the sudden doubling of the tempo, flies into his solo in the squirt and swirl mode, using two long notes twisted like crullers for a very hot effect. But by the middle of the chorus he is beginning to sound a little puzzled and he ends limply on a tentative phrase which is not even well articulated, followed by another set of quarter notes thrown in to fill up the space because he could not think of anything else to say. The record is famous in jazz circles mainly for the curious juxtaposition of Bix and Bubber playing in diametrically opposed styles, who between them make a hash of the ride-out chorus of "Rockin' Chair"; and for Joe Venuti's slurred singing of the word "shithead" instead of "sailor" in the vocal refrain.

Also of interest are a pair of sessions made in late 1929 with Goodman as part of a backup group for singer James Melton, who would eventually become famous as a Metropolitan Opera star but who was at the moment an unknown struggling to be heard. The tunes, which include "The Shepherd's Serenade" and "The Sacred Flame," have nothing to do with jazz, and neither do Goodman's accompanying obbligatos and brief solos. But by 1929 Goodman was seen as an all-around musician, in demand for this kind of "legitimate" playing as well as for his dance work. Goodman's tone is full and rich, probably somewhat fuller than that of most symphonic players, but it is certainly a more legitimate sound than anybody but a handful of dance band musicians could have managed.

The most important of the free-lance records that Goodman made during this period, however, were those he made under his own name. The first of these were cut in Chicago in January 1928, using men drawn from the Pollack band, except for Pollack. Pollack was signed to Victor and of course couldn't record for anyone else; but I suspect that basically he felt that it was beneath him to work as a sideman for one of his own musicians. The session was issued as by Bennie [sic] Goodman's Boys with Jim and Glenn, and the tunes were "A Jazz Holiday," and Jelly Roll Morton's "Wolverine Blues." A second session using mainly the same Pollack men was cut in June 1928. The band was now called Bennie Goodman's Boys. The tunes were another Morton piece, "Jungle Blues"; an original attributed to Goodman and Glenn Miller called "Room 1411"; an interesting pop tune, "Blue (and Broken-hearted)"; and the infamous "Shirt Tail Stomp." The date was contracted by Walter Melrose, a Chicago music publisher, who was then in New York.[7] Melrose was publisher of Morton's music, as well as the Goodman One Hundred Jazz Breaks, and he undoubtedly selected the Morton tunes. (Melrose is also credited as co-composer of "A Jazz Holiday.")

What is interesting about these two sessions, the first of the many hundreds to follow under Goodman's leadership, was that he chose to make them jazz sessions. A more commercially minded leader would have seen this as an opportunity to get his name better known to the public and would have picked at least a couple of hit tunes featuring vocals. But Goodman thought of himself as a jazz musician and he saw these sessions as a chance to make jazz records.

"A Jazz Holiday" is an aimless tune served up in a clumsy arrangement, presumably by Glenn Miller. Goodman's solo is atypically tame, lacking the intensity—the sudden little swirls, the bent notes—that are found in his best work from the period. "Wolverine Blues" has been beloved of jazz musicians for decades. (The tune was originally known as "The Wolverines"; in the underworld slang of the day a wolverine was a male homosexual who specialized in young boys.) Like Nichols' "Ballin' the Jack," this is classic dixieland; the fact that record companies continued to issue this kind of music after the big bands had taken over indicates the strength the form still had. Of particular interest is Goodman's ensemble playing in the opening and closing choruses. Once again he has eschewed the long strings of even eighth notes of the early New Orleans clarinetists he modeled himself on at first, and is playing a much more varied line, which darts in and out of the cornet lead, appearing and disappearing like a cork bobbing in the waves. But a taste of New Orleans style remains in the vicious slurred notes in the last eight measures. It is, in these ensembles, amusing to hear Glenn Miller, who would become famous for the slick, precise playing of his big band, attempting to play rough dixieland trombone. At times he manages a good approximation of the tailgate style, but frequently his native good manners, coached by Miff Mole, break through.

The Morton piece, "Jungle Blues," is an interesting anomaly. It is twelve bars long and divided into three four-bar phrases in the standard blues fashion. As Jelly Roll Morton played it, the tune is really modal, the first modal piece of jazz that I know of, in that the whole chorus is played on the tonic chord. In Morton's hands it is a wonderful piece of music, and gets much of its effect from steadfast growling over the implacable march of the pedal bass.

The Goodman men, however, did not quite get the idea; or, more probably, the tug of the standard blues chords was too much for them to resist, and we find them implying them here and there; for example, McPartland in the fifth and sixth bars implies the usual sub-dominant, and Miller frequently touches on the standard dominant in the ninth and tenth bars.

For Goodman specialists this record has always been of interest mainly for the fact that Benny plays a trumpet solo. Years later Goodman denied that it was him, but Jimmy McPartland, who was on the date, remembered that it was. According to McPartland,[8] the Dorsey brothers had been recording down the hall and dropped in on the Goodman session. Tommy

Dorsey is supposed to have even contributed a little backing to one side. Mannie Klein, who had also been on the Dorsey session, dropped in as well. He was standing at the door holding his trumpet; while the pianist was soloing Goodman suddenly snatched the instrument out of his hand, and began to play where McPartland was due to solo. In fact, McPartland can be heard playing a note or two before Goodman interrupts. There is not much to be said for Goodman's trumpet playing: the solo is shaky, rough and unimaginative. But Goodman clearly has been practicing on the instrument a little, possibly after the model of Jimmy Dorsey, who could play brass instruments.

"Room 1411" is credited to Goodman and Miller. It is a nice, very simple tune, with a good swing to it, and it is surprising that it was never much played by other musicians, or in fact that Goodman himself never played it again. Goodman plays a fairly straight baritone saxophone chorus that nonetheless swings hard, and there is nice, hard-driven dixieland ensemble work with Goodman leaping in and out of the lead line.

Perhaps the most interesting of this set is "Blue," a pretty tune with chord changes that are somewhat out of the ordinary. Goodman has solos on both alto and baritone saxes on this one. The baritone solo opens the record and sticks close to the melody. But the alto chorus which closes the record is a jazz chorus. Goodman at this time was required to play alto in the Pollack sax section, and on a good many of his free-lance dates as well: the clarinet has never been much used in big band reed sections except occasionally in clarinet trios, a device Fletcher Henderson employed frequently, or as a single clarinet voiced with the saxes for color. Goodman, sitting in the Pollack saxophone section night after night, was undoubtedly playing more alto than clarinet. Yet he never developed into a more than adequate altoist. The primary problem, I think, was his tone, which had neither the dancing lightness of a Benny Carter nor the rich warmth of a Johnny Hodges. It was instead muted, a little clogged and his line never came alive with the sparkle of his clarinet line.

But this particular solo on "Blue" comes off better than most of his alto playing did. It is not typical Goodman. The fast terminal vibrato is curbed, the eighth notes are played relatively evenly and the line itself is a little better organized than Goodman's inventions of this period often were. In fact, the whole solo appears to me to have been in the mode of Bix Beiderbecke and his sidekick, C-melody saxophonist Frankie Trumbauer. I suspect that Goodman had Beiderbecke in mind. He knew Beiderbecke, and had worked with him occasionally from the time of those days on the Lake Michigan touring boats. Much later he would say, "I got as much kick out of listening to [Bix] play that as I ever did out of anybody else."[9] For example, the figure in bar three (counting from the beginning of the chorus after the introductory break), which seems to double back on itself, is an example of the sort of melody Beiderbecke would create; and the sudden, intense, abrupt figure at the "turnaround" in bars fifteen and sixteen is pure Bix.

But if "Blue" is possibly the best of this series, certainly the one that sold the best, and became a jazz legend, was "Shirt Tail Stomp." As we have seen, this was produced when the recording director heard the musicians kidding around on "St. Louis Blues" and demanded that they cut it. Goodman reverts to his Ted Lewis imitation and McPartland does a take off on Henry Busse, a mute and buzz tone specialist with Whiteman who had an enormous hit with "Hot Lips." Fud Livingston lows as early jazz saxophonists tended to do, and the trombonist—either Miller or Dorsey—moos as well.

None of these Bennie Goodman and His Boys records is a jazz masterpiece, but they all contain some excellent moments. Perhaps the best of them are the straightforward dixieland numbers like "Room 1411." This was the style which these men had come into jazz playing, and they were still thoroughly at home in it. They would not be able to play it much longer; popular taste was leaving it behind. But for the moment it still had its fans, and Goodman shows himself as good a dixieland player as any of the men more identified with the style who became relatively famous during the revival of the music in the 1940s and later. This session occasioned what was certainly the first review Goodman ever got, when R. D. Darrell wrote in *Phonograph Monthly Review*, "Bennie Goodman's Boys are very hot and yet interesting in *Jungle Blues* and *Room 1411* (4013). The piano and clarinet parts are particularly good."[10]

Goodman followed these sessions with a trio date, also made in Chicago, in June 1928. Goodman insisted to Russ Connor that this session came in early 1927, but Connor thinks otherwise, and he is supported by a mention of the sides from the session in *Phonograph Monthly Review* of November 1928. The tunes were the dixieland classic, "That's A Plenty," which Goodman undoubtedly knew from the New Orleans Rhythm Kings version, and "Clarinetitis," which is credited to Goodman. The idea of a clarinet trio was not new: Groups of this kind had been working in the honky tonks of New Orleans for two decades; Jelly Roll Morton made several trio and quartet records featuring the clarinet beginning in 1924; and Jimmie Noone was working around Chicago with a small group featuring his own clarinet. The reason for building these groups around a clarinet rather than some other horn was because of the greater facility of the clarinet, which allowed it to fill the considerable amount of empty space that the three minutes of record duration can seem to be to an improvising musician suddenly confronted with it. There are very few jazz performances in which one instrument is called upon to perform unceasingly for long periods, although there are some: Louis Armstrong's "Dear Old Southland"; Dickie Wells' "Dicky Wells' Blues"; Charlie Parker's "Ko-Ko"; and a number of things by the exceedingly loquacious John Coltrane. But the clarinet was well adapted to the stunt, and of course Goodman would make a number of masterpieces in the trio format.

The two other musicians on this date were local Chicagoans, drummer Bob Conselman and pianist Mel Stitzel, who had worked with the Rhythm Kings. Goodman, who was never shy in alloting himself solo space, takes all of the relatively short "Clarinetitis" to himself, and all but one piano chorus on "That's A Plenty." He uses a formula which he would repeat again and again with his later trios: An opening chorus with the melody played relatively straight; an improvised chorus; a solo or solos by other members of the group; a solo taken in the low register for contrast; and a hard-driven ride-out chorus.

"That's A Plenty" is by far the more successful of these two pieces. "Clarinetitis" is an incoherent tune and never really hangs together. Furthermore, the tempo drops slightly in the middle, then speeds up in the ride-out at the end. In both pieces Goodman is playing in his "Teschemacher" vein to a degree, using, particularly in the intense last choruses, a very marked terminal vibrato which gives his sound some of the wryness of Teschemacher's. The eighths are played relatively more evenly in the Teschemacher fashion, and there are a number of the saw-toothed patterns which Tesch frequently used. Once again, I am not implying that Goodman was following Teschemacher. The lines of influence are hard to follow, and it is safe to say only that at this period the styles of the two men bore certain similarities. In any case, "That's A Plenty" is hot clarinet playing at its very best; there were few musicians in jazz at this time who could have brought off a tour de force of this kind, and it is not surprising that R. D. Darrell praised it in Phonograph Monthly Review.

These records—the ones made with Pollack and the free-lance sessions—leave no doubt that as a young man still only in his late teens, Benny Goodman was already displaying an extraordinary musical talent. He was suffering from the incoherence which he would never wholly eliminate; but his playing was fiery, intense, technically superb, rhythmically daring and always swinging. He was already a masterful jazz musician.

# 7

# The Free Lance

When Benny Goodman left the Ben Pollack band, he found himself part of a floating cadre of free-lance musicians who were producing a considerable percentage of the commercial music for the United States through recordings and radio broadcasts. Some of these people would go on to become important figures in the swing movement of the next decade: Tommy and Jimmy Dorsey, Glenn Miller, Artie Shaw, Bunny Berigan, Gene Krupa, all became celebrated band leaders. Others of them would play roles as important sidemen with the swing bands, like tenor saxophonist Babe Russin, who had stints with Goodman and both Dorsey bands; Charlie and Jack Teagarden, both of whom were with Paul Whiteman for extended periods; Bud Freeman, hot tenor soloist with the Goodman and Tommy Dorsey bands; guitarist George Van Eps, who served with the Goodman and Freddy Martin bands; bassist Artie Bernstein, who played with Goodman and Dorsey as well; and Arthur Rollini, who was with several well-known bands.

Some of these men were good jazz musicians, some were not. What mattered most was the ability to sight-read anything, to play anything put before them and to show up on time in the tightly scheduled world of radio and recording studios. They also needed enough musicality to be able to quickly work out smooth-sounding arrangements for the singers they were called upon to back all the time. It is clear from listening to the records that in many instances the musicians, with some direction from the man who contracted the job—that is to say, actually hired the musicians at the behest of the record producer—cooked up accompaniments on the spot, which they could do in perhaps twenty minutes. The ability to play a good hot solo was a bonus: leaders needed to have a few men on these jobs who could play respectable jazz when necessary, but it was not necessary to fill the group exclusively with jazz men.

For the most part these men were not known to the public. Occasionally one or the other might get featured billing on a record as, for example, "The Charleston Chasers, under the direction of Bennie Goodman," instead of the more usual "Charleston Chasers." But in general they were anonymous.

The classic example of the studio man was Mannie Klein, who was always in demand and contracted a lot of jobs himself. Klein's story was a familiar one.[1] He was born in the Jewish ghetto of New York's Lower East Side. He grew up in a family of five children jammed into an apartment with no central heat and one toilet for all the families on a floor. Some of his older brothers played musical instruments, and one of them started Mannie on a bugle at about eight. By ten he was playing cornet, and copying parts from records, among them those of Phil Napoleon with the Memphis Five, and probably Nick LaRocca with the Original Dixieland Jass Band as well. He had a natural gift for music, rapidly becoming a proficient musician and dropping out of high school at sixteen to work as a professional. He developed a clean, light sound, could read anything at sight and could manage passable jazz choruses when necessary. His sweet, slightly plaintive cup mute solos were everywhere in the popular music of the time.

Assertive and clever, Klein quickly came to be an almost indispensable member of the New York studio world. He, and others like him, controlled a lot of work, and had to be dealt with circumspectly by other musicians, who frequently found it a good idea to hire him for their own jobs. There was, in this business, a great deal of pure back-scratching, which explains in part why the same names turn up again and again on these recording sessions.

But around the time that Goodman started to free-lance, the whole nature of the music business underwent a rapid change, with a new invention, radio, becoming the heart of show business. Radio and popular music established a symbiotic relationship right from the beginning. Even before the first regularly scheduled broadcasting station went on the air on November 2, 1920, radio amateurs were sometimes playing phonograph records over the air. By 1921 the country had "radio fever";[2] in 1922 alone seventy-six new stations were authorized.[3] "In this pre-network era, in which hundreds of stations were mounting their own programs—eked out by phonograph and player piano on low powered stations—extraordinary numbers of musicians were involved."[4]

At first the musicians gave their services in exchange for the publicity they supposed they were getting, but by 1924 the musicians' unions were getting worried, and started demanding payment. This the stations could afford, because they had begun selling advertising to local business. In September 1926 the National Broadcasting System was incorporated, and began using A.T. & T.'s network of telephone lines to connect stations all over the country into two vast radio "chains," as the term then was. Five million homes now had radios.[5] A third network, called the Columbia Broadcasting System, was created in 1927. Its first program consisted of dance music played by a band led by Don Voorhees, who would hire Goodman frequently in the next decade. The second program featured a jazz band, the famous orchestra of Red Nichols.[6] "The programs NBC and CBS sent throughout the United States in 1928 and 1929 were still largely musical. Many were concerts, although dance music—it was called 'jazz' now—was on the increase."[7] After 1930, especially with the success of two whites in blackface—or black voice, to be exact—in a show called Amos 'n' Andy, comedy and then drama came to occupy more and more airtime. But music remained a staple, an almost sine qua non of radio. It made people like Bing Crosby and Kate Smith famous, and it would soon play a critical role in the careers of Benny Goodman and the swing bands to come.

But radio almost single-handedly killed much of the rest of show business. The main contributing factor was the Depression, which began after the stock-market crash in November 1929, and deepened year after year into the middle of the 1930s. Record sales fell from upwards of 150 million copies annually during the 1920s to about six million in the early 1930s, a drop so catastrophic that scores of record companies collapsed, with only Victor and Columbia surviving, and then just barely.[8] (Decca, which would become one of the Big Three, was formed in 1934.)

Radio, coupled with the Depression, also cut dramatically into business at nightclubs and dance halls. Cabarets all over the United States snapped shut, and in November 1930 Variety carried the headline "Dance Halls All Starving." The story said that it was "the worst season they have experienced since the war."[9]

But the radio industry was booming. It was intensely competitive, had money to pay for the best entertainers and, as a consequence, it attracted musicians as bees to the apple blossom. Very quickly it became the basic source of Benny Goodman's income. He of course made a lot of records, and played occasional dance jobs, many of them on college campuses where students still had a little money to spend. But he spent far more time broadcasting rather than recording; indeed, the term "studio musician" derives not from the recording studios but from the radio studios.

Much of the music heard on radio was broadcast directly from locations, that is to say, the remaining cabarets, hotels, and dance halls: it was Duke Ellington's broadcasts from the Cotton Club, not his records, that made him nationally known.[10] But a great deal of music was made by orchestras of all sorts gathered in the studios specifically to provide fifteen minutes or half an hour of musical entertainment. These shows were in the main live, although the practice of making "electrical transcriptions" of music by one orchestra or another, which could be sold to smaller stations as program material, was growing.

These studio groups ranged from solo pianists, or even somebody playing a musical saw, to orchestras of twenty or thirty musicians working from elaborate arrangements. In general, these larger orchestras were run by leaders who were hired by the networks or the advertisers to produce musical shows which might run for a half hour several times a week, sometimes even daily. Some of the best known leaders at the time Goodman was free-lancing were the aforementioned Voorhees, violinist David Rubinoff, Frank Black, Gus Haenschen, Andre Kostelanetz, and Al Goodman (no relation to Benny). These people had to produce an enormous amount of music each week. Today it might take a popular group months to put together forty minutes of music for an LP album; at that time a Voorhees or a Rubinoff might be responsible for turning out three or four hours of top quality popular music each week. In order to do this they were heavily dependent on a growing body of arrangers and that cadre of first-rank musicians who could knock off an errorless show after a relatively brief rehearsal. This Benny Goodman could do, and for the first few years after he left Pollack he made a lot of money, for the time, from radio.

He was also hanging out at Plunkett's, a legendary musicians' speakeasy of the period. It was located at 205½ West 53rd Street, under the elevated railway, and was listed in the telephone book as the Trombone Club, because of the number of trombonists who always seemed to be in the place. According to Herb Sanford, a musician and radio producer who was around at the time, "Plunkett's was General Headquarters. When a conductor or contractor wanted a certain musician for a radio or recording date, the direct line of communication was Plunkett's call board, which occupied a prominent position near the front door. It was covered with messages; the phone rang constantly."[11] Drinking was endemic among these young musicians. According to Artie Shaw, they were "almost without exception hard-drinking, fast-living, wild-eyed young guys living out their crazy, boozey, frantic lives. . . ."[12] This, then, was the world of the free-lance musician Goodman found himself in.

However, on leaving Pollack, Goodman's first job was not in radio but in a show band. According to McPartland, "I happened to hear of a job at the Paramount Theatre that they needed a saxophone and clarinet player and I called up Benny right away." The leader, McPartland said, was David Rubinoff.[13] Goodman said the leader was Eddie Paul, and that Glenn Miller was in the band. The job paid $175 a week, which was good money, but it called for four to six shows a day of commercial music.[14] Goodman hung onto the job for about two months, until he was asked to join a band Red Nichols was taking into the Hollywood Restaurant, one of the "first

big popular-priced girl show places on Broadway."[15] Goodman had to take
a pay cut to go with Nichols, but the music was better, the pace less grinding, and he would be freer to take studio work. The next month Nichols
took the band into the pit for a Gershwin show called *Strike Up the
Band*, which opened in January 1930. The band included Babe Russin,
Miller and Gene Krupa. Goodman had been living in Jackson Heights, but
at some point during this period he took an apartment with Jimmy Dorsey
on West 58th Street, probably to be nearer to the radio and recording studios scattered around Manhattan.

Goodman was well situated with the Nichols band. It was popular, with
a considerable following among the college crowd and the younger dance-
band fans. Indeed, for Goodman the situation was ideal, because of the
freedom it gave him to take outside work. But he chose to abandon it.
The cause was the cabal against Pollack designed to take Pollack's band
away from him and install it at the Park Central. Goodman gave Nichols
his notice in order to make this move, and Jimmy Dorsey replaced him.
When the deal fell through Goodman was out of work. He picked up
what studio work he could, and at the end of January he got a call from
Don Voorhees to join a pit band for a projected show called *The Nine-
fifteen Revue*. The show opened on February 11, closed on February 17
and Goodman was once again out of work. Fortunately Voorhees was using
the band for his radio shows, and this was enough to keep Goodman eating.[16]

Some time that spring Goodman left the 58th Street apartment and
moved in with Charlie Teagarden in a three- or four-room apartment. He
continued to free-lance. It is possible that by summer he had rejoined the
Nichols band in the pit of *Strike Up the Band*, because he recorded with
Nichols early in July, but we cannot be certain of that.

We suspect, however, that he did go back with Nichols, because in July
he moved his mother and her two youngest children, Gene and Jerome, to
New York.[17] It seems unlikely that he would have done this had he not
been sure that he could support them all. That fall he moved them all out
to Jackson Heights, where they would continue to live for many years.

Jackson Heights was a pleasant family neighborhood in Queens, an easy
subway trip to Manhattan where most of Benny's work was. Bunny Berigan
and Glenn Miller also lived in the neighborhood. But Benny continued to
live in midtown Manhattan, going out to see the family for Sunday dinner.
He was now running with "a Yale dropout and playboy named 'Whiskey'
Smith,"[18] and seeing less of the musicians who had constituted his primary
social group for years. Precisely what had happened is not clear, but Goodman has said that he was not very happy at this juncture in his life. It has
been reported that he and Smith had been doing a good deal of partying.
He continued to free-lance, playing for Voorhees' *Maxwell House* show, a

decreasing number of record dates and whatever else came along. Once he was asked to put together a band to play at Williams College. He chose Beiderbecke and Tommy Dorsey, among others, for the job. Dorsey was under the impression that Williams was somewhere near New Haven, in southern Connecticut, and that he and Bix could take an afternoon train up from New York. In fact, Williams is in western Massachusetts. When they discovered their error it was too late to get to Williams by train, so they chartered an airplane, an unusual expedient for the day. Unfortunately there had been a recent snow. The plane could not land anywhere near Williamstown and had to put down in Springfield, where there was a regular airport. They had to take a cab some fifty miles from Springfield to Williamstown. Making matters worse was the fact that Beiderbecke was drinking heavily and passed out on the bandstand. There is a story, probably apocryphal, that when Bix collapsed Goodman picked up his cornet and finished off his chorus. Goodman remembered, "Bix sprawled out like a broken puppet," and realized that he was not likely to live much longer, which proved to be the case.[19]

In the fall of 1930 Nichols was asked to form a pit band for another Gershwin show, *Girl Crazy*, and he hired Goodman. The band included many of his old group: Jack and Charlie Teagarden, Larry Binyon, Glenn Miller and Gene Krupa. It was once again a good job, because it allowed ample time for the men to free-lance during the day. Benny was making something like $350 to $400 with everything; but again he spoiled things. Probably sometime in late April or early May, he had a fight with Nichols. According to his own story, during an intermission of the show he began fooling around on the clarinet, playing deliberately in the old Ted Lewis manner.[20] Another report says that he did it during the actual performance, which seems more likely in view of what happened.[21] Nichols reprimanded him, and the other members of the band began to kid him about the incident. Goodman was embarrassed and unhappy. He told Nichols, "You know I was just kidding," or something to that effect, which might have been acceptable, but then he added: "You know how I sound when I'm kiddin'? Well that's how you sound all the time."[22] That was more than Nichols needed to take, and Goodman was either fired or quit, to be replaced again by Jimmy Dorsey when his two weeks' notice was up.

Not long after, Goodman had a similar problem with one of the major radio band leaders, probably Voorhees, whom Goodman left in September 1931. He then moved to another show with a coffee sponsor, *The Chase and Sanborn Hour*, with an orchestra led by Dave Rubinoff. There had been, thus, a succession of problems with major leaders—Pollack, Nichols and Voorhees. He had broken off relationships with his old friends, the jazz musicians who were his natural allies and best appreciated his talents. He said:

> I guess I was in kind of a bad groove mentally at the time, with not much desire other than to make money, keep the place going for my mother and the kids, and have as much fun as possible. . . . I sort of broke away from the fellows I had been with since I came to New York. . . .[23]

However, I think there was more to this than simply a bad mental "groove." Goodman seems at this time to have been depressed, surly, and generally hostile. We can only guess at the cause, but I suggest that it had to do with the fact that he was no longer the child star he had once been. At twelve he had excited adults with his gifts; at fourteen he was a professional and an important contributor to his family's income; at seventeen he offered to support his father in retirement; at eighteen he had a book of his "jazz breaks" published; at nineteen he was a star with one of the country's most important dance bands.

Now, in his early twenties, he was scuffling, just another one of several dozen top-flight New York professionals, unknown to the public, who were grinding out commercial music for the mass entertainment market. He was not going anywhere, and the applause was growing distant.

The charge most frequently leveled at Goodman was that he was arrogant, egotistical, had "a swelled head." Nothing is ever that simple, but Goodman does seem to have developed a sense by this time that he was special, that his own needs were always the primary concern. Or to frame it the other way around, throughout his life he frequently failed to show any concern for the people around him who were—or should have been—important to him. He was constantly hurting people by making remarks the effects of which he seems to have been totally unaware. Bud Freeman, who knew him from youth into old age, said, "Benny lives in an egomaniacal shell that prevents him from—well, I think of instead of being a part of the world, he thinks of himself as being apart from the world. . . . Benny's world is built around Benny."[24]

In part this had to do with his deep concentration on music, which characterized him all of his life. When he was thinking about music the rest of the world disappeared, including the people in it and he could speak to them as if they were trees. This sort of concentration is common in artists who have to become narrowly focused if they are to produce their best work. But with Goodman it went beyond his work. As a leader he exhibited an almost pathological insensitivity to the feelings of the men who worked for him. He was not always like this. He could, when the mood was on him, be cordial and actually quite funny, possessed of a real, rather wry sense of humor. But the mood was not always on him.

There is a story that has been told about Goodman by many people who claim to have witnessed it. In Lionel Hampton's version they were in a dining car on a train during a tour. Goodman ordered bacon and eggs. When the dish came, he picked up the ketchup bottle and shook it over the eggs. The cap was loose, and fell into the eggs. Instead of picking it off, as anyone else would have done, Goodman calmly ate all around it, until the ketchup top and the bit of egg under it were left alone on the plate.[25] The story is too improbable to have been made up, and something like it must have happened. It reveals a man who was so deeply engrossed in what was going on inside himself that he was anesthetized to the outside world. Mel Powell's wife, the actress Martha Scott, who knew Benny well at one period, would say that at such moments, "somebody pulls the plug out."[26]

Not long after the fight with Nichols, Goodman became contractor and straw boss for a band backing a singer named Russ Columbo. In hiring the men, many of whom he had worked with for years, drank with at Plunkett's and gone up to Harlem to jam with at the after hours clubs, he drove a hard bargain on salaries.[27] These men naturally resented Goodman's attitude. Whose side was he on, anyway? Goodman apparently had no awareness of how they might feel about it.

And I think that it was this trait in Goodman's personality that caused him trouble with Pollack, Voorhees, Nichols and others: he was, to a degree, unconnected to the outside world and had little sense of how actions of his might impinge upon it. He saw himself always from within, and not how anybody else might see him.

# 8

# Enter John Hammond

No matter how difficult Goodman was coming to be seen, he was nonetheless one of the best free-lance musicians in New York, a fine technician who could read anything and play wonderful hot solos. He continued to get work. In the fall he took a band into the pit of a show called *Free for All*, which lasted for two weeks.[1] He continued to get radio work from Rubinoff, Johnny Green and Al Goodman. Then in the spring of 1932 he was asked to organize the band for Russ Columbo, who was becoming one of the best-known "crooners" of the time.[2] He was billed as "N.B.C.'s Romeo of Song," and was seen as a rival to Bing Crosby.

For the Columbo band Goodman picked some of the men he had worked with for some time, among them McPartland, Krupa, Babe Russin, his brother Harry and a Chicago pianist, Joe Sullivan.[3] The band broke in at the Waldorf-Astoria Hotel without Goodman, for reasons that are not clear. Then on Sunday, May 15, it went into the Woodmansten Inn, on Pelham Parkway, on the northeastern edge of the city near the wealthy suburbs of Westchester County.[4] This time Goodman was with the band, playing saxophone and taking the clarinet solos. It was an important experience for Goodman. He was not merely a contractor responsible for hiring the men but actually in charge of the on-stand operation of the band, setting tempos, calling solos, raising and lowering the volume as necessary. He was now, in the real sense of the word, a bandleader.

The actual management of a band requires a good deal of skill and a certain amount of intuition. Audiences are always different, and a leader has to quickly get a sense of what each particular one wants—fast numbers, slow ones, ballads, hot pieces. He has to vary tempos, key signatures, and the character of the pieces. He must realize which men, or whole sections, of the orchestra are in good fettle and which are having off-nights, and play to their strengths. All of this takes experience; you cannot simply lay out a program beforehand, but must improvise. Goodman eventually became adept at this kind of band management, and he began to learn it at the Woodmansten.

It was, however, a thoroughly commercial band. Shortly after it opened John Hammond, about whom we shall hear more shortly, went up to the Woodmansten to hear it. He reported:

> We devotees of improvisation in "jazz" were all excited when we heard that Benny Goodman had organized a band in which were to be featured Babe Rusin [sic] on tenor; Joe Sullivan, piano; Gene Kruppa [sic], drums; Harry Goodman, bass; Max Ceppos, violin, and others, good, but less important.
>
> Last night I journeyed in the rain out to Woodmansten Inn, where the band is playing under the direction of that irrepressible crooner, Russ Columbo.
>
> Mr. Goodman, I fear, has forgotten all about the fact that there are actually individual human beings in the band. The result is painful, and the band is merely another smooth and soporific dance combination.
>
> Poor Kruppa does his best to keep up his spirits, but he is allowed by Goodman only the use of brushes. Even the elegant piano playing of Sullivan the leader tries to conventionalize.[5]

This was John Hammond's first contact with Goodman, but he did not introduce himself to Goodman at that time. That would come later.

The Woodmansten Inn job lasted through the summer. That fall the band played some theatre dates, but Goodman was not with it. He continued to do radio work, but his recording work had fallen off disastrously. In 1931 he was on over seventy dates and perhaps others we do not know about. In 1932 he was on only three. What happened?

In part the problem was the combined assault of radio and the Depression on the record industry, which was almost completely bankrupt. It is not true, as most jazz writers have insisted, that the recording of "authentic jazz records for the American market in the black years from 1930 to 1934 was zero,"[6] as anyone who cares to thumb through a standard discography can discover for himself. The numbers of records issued was certainly reduced, but the industry was by no means dead, and it appears likely that Goodman's difficulties in getting recording dates were mainly of his own making. He admitted as much: "I got to be known as a difficult guy to handle in some circles, which cut me out of jobs."[7] As a consequence, his income fell from three or four hundred dollars a week down to two hundred, and as 1932 passed into 1933, it fell further. This was not at all a bad income, comparatively speaking. Millions of American families were getting by on twenty-five dollars a week in the Depression, and black families in the rural South were earning far less than that. Nonetheless, Goodman was supporting a lot of people. He was the sole support of his mother and the two younger boys, Gene and Jerome; and he was probably contributing to the support of some of the others, although it is impossible to know for certain precisely how the money was spent.

Goodman felt the strain. He had accepted the responsibility of taking care of the family, and he would not let them down. But neither was he able to improve his ability to deal with people more successfully. Thus matters went through the spring and summer of 1933. There was a recording date in January, one in June, another in July, one in September. Goodman stayed solvent mainly through the radio shows. But these, too, were growing harder to get. By that fall, according to the not-always-reliable John Hammond, Goodman was down to a single radio show, playing "fourth sax"[8] in one of Al Goodman's orchestras. Goodman was still one of the finest studio musicians in New York, and in all probability he would have survived. But his life was about to take a sudden turn; and the catalyst was Hammond.

John Hammond would prove to be one of the most significant, and among the most interesting, figures in all of jazz history. Over a long life in music he would promote the careers of some of the most important people in twentieth-century music, among them Billie Holiday, Count Basie, Lester Young, Teddy Wilson, Benny Carter, Fletcher Henderson, Bob Dylan, Bruce Springsteen and of course Benny Goodman. Hammond has been credited with "discovering" these and other important musicians. That was not always the case: Teddy Wilson had made a reputation among musicians in the Midwest, and had worked with Louis Armstrong before Hammond began to record him; Benny Carter had been a featured soloist with Fletcher Henderson; Springsteen was brought to Hammond's office by his manager. But Hammond had remarkable sense for talent; and while he made mistakes, he was more often right than wrong and, when he was convinced he had found somebody who could be important, he would throw himself headlong into promoting his or her career.

Hammond's influence on jazz history, however, was not always appreciated by those involved at the time, and it is certainly true that he was meddlesome, tactless, arrogant and, when his self-righteousness was ablaze, insensitive to anything but the imperious demands of his own crusades. But he was the instigator of more first-rate jazz records than anybody but the leading jazz musicians themselves.

Hammond was born into a classic "society" family.[9] His grandfather Hammond had been a Union general during the Civil War, and his mother was the great-granddaughter of Cornelius Vanderbilt. Mrs. Hammond was not entirely typical of her social class: she was deeply religious and, as Hammond himself said in his rather unrevealing autobiography, had a "compulsion to save the world."[10] She was the very model of the eccentric reformer, and devoted her enormous energy to her causes all her life. Her son would do much the same.

Hammond, born in 1910, and thus almost Goodman's age, was expected to follow his father's course through private school, Yale, possibly law school and then a job in the power structure where he would in gentlemanly fashion make a lot of money and influence the capitalist system for the good.

He did, instead, just the opposite. He became interested in jazz at the age of twelve when, on a visit to London, he heard a pianist named Arthur Schutt, later to work with the early Red Nichols groups, performing with a visiting American band.[11] He went to Hotchkiss, a New England boarding school, and began collecting jazz records and reading whatever he could find on the subject, among them the reviews of jazz and dance recordings by R. D. Darrell in *Phonograph Monthly Review*. He began corresponding with Darrell, and the two became friends. Hammond does not mention Darrell in his autobiography, but Darrell was espousing the cause of black musicians at the same time that Hammond was, and undoubtedly had some role in shaping Hammond's taste.[12]

But Hammond was a man with an abiding faith in his own opinions and by 1927, when he was seventeen, he was visiting Harlem clubs and theatres to hear black blues singers and jazz musicians. Hammond said, "I went to every theater and club in Harlem and was usually the only white person there,"[13] leaving the impression that it was strange and daring for a white person to visit these jazz venues. In fact, by 1927 there existed in Harlem a huge entertainment business built around white audiences from "downtown." Hundreds of whites came up every night, among them many intellectuals, artists and wealthy "slummers" from Hammond's own social class. In 1926 Carl Van Vechten published a novel about Harlem called *Nigger Heaven*.[14] The book was widely read, and it is impossible that Hammond did not know of it. Van Vechten has received scornful notices in the jazz press for over fifty years, as a dilettante who capitalized on the vogue for black entertainment of the time. To the contrary, Van Vechten's father was one of the founders of the well-known Piney Woods School for blacks, and Carl grew up playing with black children.[15] His interest in black music was genuine, and in 1925 he wrote an excellent series of pieces on black music for the prestigious magazine *Vanity Fair*.[16]

Later on Hammond referred to Van Vechten's work as "drivel,"[17] and it is clear that he was simply jealous of Van Vechten, who had not only taken up the cause of black music and blacks in general before Hammond did but had actually pointed the way for Hammond through his writing, especially *Nigger Heaven* and the *Vanity Fair* pieces, which he is likely to have seen.

All of this is very important to the way jazz has been perceived. Hammond was, throughout his life, a vigorous advocate of black causes—a member of the NAACP, fighter to break down racial barriers in the music business, writer of dozens of fiery pieces on the subject—and this is all greatly to his credit. On the other hand, it was, for reasons we can only guess at, critically important for him to believe that he was the first, if not the only, white to support blacks in their struggle for equality. This was of course simple nonsense: there is a tradition of white support for black rights which antedates the writing of the American Constitution. This need to believe that he was the black person's greatest champion led him to see racism under every bush, and to exaggerate his own role in discovering black jazz in Harlem and elsewhere. But it must be said that, if he were not the first to see the virtues of black jazz musicians, he was certainly among the most important of those espousing their cause.

Hammond dutifully entered Yale in 1930, but his interests lay elsewhere, and he dropped out in his sophomore year to pursue his interest in jazz. At some point during this period he became the jazz correspondent for an English record magazine called *The Gramophone*. Not long afterwards, in 1931, during a trip to London, he switched to *The Melody Maker*, the English musicians' trade paper. He now had some sort of official status in the world of jazz, and he began pursuing his hobby with enormous energy and a powerful will. He must have been a strange figure in the Harlem black-and-tans he frequented. Tall and slim, wearing his hair in a crew cut, as he would all of his life, and drinking mainly lemonade, he stood out like a beacon among the assorted gamblers, pimps, white sports out on the town and of course jazz musicians who hung around in these places.

Hammond set for himself the goal of finding unappreciated jazz musicians and seeing to it that they got recorded, a hard task at a time when the recording industry was rushing full-tilt into the pit dug by the Depression and radio. On his twenty-first birthday he came into an inheritance, moved into Greenwich Village, and began throwing his weight—and his money—around, buying drinks for musicians and paying for recording sessions for his favorites. His income was "not princely," but it did amount to $12,000 a year,[18] the sort of money that a major executive might make at the time. He did not have to work, and because he had no expensive tastes, he could afford to support his various jazz projects.

John Hammond was a curious mix. He had acquired from his mother a certain moral tone. He did not drink, was shy with girls, and was in some ways rather unbending. But he was also a rebel who had walked away from

the power and riches that would have automatically come to him, in order
to consort with jazz musicians, and, even more horrifying to people of his
social class, black jazz musicians, in a twilight world of dives and dance
halls where drink, drugs and prostitution were a part of the environment.

He very soon began to establish himself as a force in the jazz world. He
was, as he admitted later, "Violent in my opinions, tactless, and scornful
of the commercial music business,"[19] all of which he could afford to be,
where many others could not. He read everything appearing in the press on
both jazz and politics—he was notorious for sitting in front of a bandstand
all evening going through a stack of magazines. He wrote incessantly, with
a slap-dash verve that gave scant heed to such journalistic niceties as conflict of interest and the checking of fact. He gave the famous Lester Young
"Shoe Shine Swing" a wildly enthusiastic review without informing his
readers that he had produced the record;[20] he printed, without checking,
the false story that Bessie Smith had been refused admittance to a white
hospital after an automobile accident and had bled to death as a consequence;[21] and he, more than anyone else, was responsible for creating the
myth that jazz was scorned by Americans and had to be discovered as a
serious music by more prescient Europeans.[22]

In his defense it must be said that Hammond was not alone in these
practices. During the 1930s and 1940s the jazz writing profession was a
morass of conflict of interest. Some of the critics were producing records,
writing songs and arrangements, putting on concerts, working for recording
companies and even playing in dance bands. These people were deeply
enmeshed in friendships, loyalties, business alliances and sexual relationships—many of which continue today—with musicians and music-industry
people, and their credibility as journalists was irreparably damaged. It is
true, of course, that the industry papers like Down Beat and Metronome
did not pay their writers enough to insure their journalistic purity, and they
were forced to take other work. But in fact notions of journalistic ethics
entered few minds. In the main, jazz writers of this period saw themselves
as crusaders for the music, or proselytizers for this or that musician or style
of playing. They did not see themselves as journalists so much as fighters
at the barricades.

Hammond was only following the accepted practice in using his columns
and reviews to push his favorites. He appeared in any magazine that would
take his material—Down Beat, The Brooklyn Eagle, The Nation, Tempo,
Chicago News, New Masses, and European jazz magazines like The
Melody Maker and Jazz Hot. He was not writing about jazz alone: He
wrote two excellent pieces for The Nation on the trial of the Scottsboro
Boys, some young black men falsely accused of raping two white women,

which the left had taken up as a cause,[23] and he frequently used his jazz columns to inveigh against anti-union practices in the music industry.[24]

But jazz was his main business, and he used his money and his access to the press to reshape the world of jazz to match his own vision. He handed out praise and blame in the most violent terms. Players he did not like "stunk" and players he did were geniuses. Otis Ferguson, possibly the best jazz writer of the 1930s, said in a profile of Hammond for a magazine, "His idea of giving a musician a hint is to hit him in the face with a shovel."[25]

He went everywhere, knew everyone. Music critic Irving Kolodin, who would collaborate with Goodman on *The Kingdom of Swing*, said that he "provided a visual counterpoint to the music with his violent jittering from the first note to the last. . . . An ear-to-ear-grin, a slap of the hand in the thigh, a bobbing from right to left showed a pleasure that . . . [more inhibited] folk merely expressed by a pounding of the palms."[26] Ferguson said, "His head juts forward at you, slightly lowered as if to charge, but belying any seeming truculence by the open heartiness of his greeting. He is either spilling over with enthusiasm (Isn't it *swell*?) or only partly concealing his disgust (It's a *crime*, it stinks)."[27]

By the mid-1930s his opinions were being taken seriously by a great many people. Kolodin said, "John really doesn't realize how people follow him. Maybe they don't write exactly what he does about somebody, but if John writes that Joe Doakes stinks, the next month you read everywhere: 'Stink is the word for Joe Doakes.' "[28] As his power increased, musicians became afraid of him, and they tended to do what he wanted them to do. For example, he found the Basie band in Kansas City, and saw to it that it was brought to New York, where it could be promoted. But he was also ruthless in getting Basie to revamp the band, replacing many of the original men with musicians Hammond thought better of. Hammond himself said that it "nearly broke Basie's heart" when he had to fire a man to take on one of Hammond's discoveries.[29]

By 1939 Hammond was the informal musical director of Cafe Society, an interracial nightclub featuring jazz and social comedy with a strong left-wing tone. At one point he decided he wanted Basie's trombonist Benny Morton in the Cafe Society house band. He told the putative owner Barney Josephson to make the change. Josephson replied that he could not afford to pay Morton what Basie was paying him. Hammond told him not to worry about it, just pay Morton the usual fee. Not until much later did Josephson learn that Hammond had been making up the rest of Morton's salary out of his own pocket.[30] Jimmy Hamilton claims that Hammond had him fired from the Cafe Society band run by Teddy Wilson in order to bring in Edmond Hall, a clarinetist with a much harder, driving style than the more lyrical Hamilton manner.[31] (One ironic consequence was that in 1942 when Barney Bigard left Duke Ellington, it was Hamilton who was available, not Hall, who was Ellington's first choice.) Teddy Wilson, who Hammond promoted with great zeal, said, "He never liked my big band, and so he offered me a job, a steady year round job as a band leader at the Cafe Society, but I would have to take his men, his personnel. . . . He wouldn't take the men out of my big band."[32] When he put Wilson in charge of a series of records he was making for Columbia, many of them featuring Billie Holiday, it was Hammond, not Wilson or Holiday, who picked the sidemen. Between his access to the media and his control of a certain number of jobs, by the late 1930s Hammond was the most powerful man in jazz. (Two people who he was never able to control were Duke Ellington and Louis Armstrong, both of whom had strong-minded managers with gangland connections and were not about to let Hammond muscle in. It is no accident that Hammond was intensely critical of the music of both of these men, assuring his readers that they had sold out to the evil forces of commerce.)

Such was his importance during this period that several magazine profiles were written about him. Otis Ferguson did a story on him for *Society Rag* in 1938;[33] Kolodin did one for *Harper's* in 1939, in which he said, "To his credit is the almost single-handed creation of a vogue for the type of music known as swing";[34] and in 1943 *Newsweek* said that ". . . on swing music he is an authority whose word is unquestioned."[35] It became a standing joke among jazz people that if you mentioned a record to Hammond he would reply, "Yes, I was personally in the studio when it was made."

By the late 1940s, when the swing band movement was fading and bop was rising in the jazz world, Hammond's power was lessening. Yet he continued to work in various posts in the record business, and years later he would play a critical role in promoting the careers of two of the biggest pop stars of the rock era, Bob Dylan and Bruce Springsteen. Just prior to his death he was, although very ill, still eager to keep abreast of the music business he had devoted his life to.

John Hammond came from great wealth and a social position in the society that allowed him great advantages that other people did not have. F. Scott Fitzgerald once wrote something about the rich being "different" from the rest of us. Ernest Hemingway is reported to have responded, "Yes, they have more money." But in fact, Fitzgerald, and not Hemingway, was right, if by rich we mean not the newly risen, but people with "old" money. Such people, although they would deny it, almost unconsciously believe that they are better than other people—more intelligent, more far-sighted, more capable of discerning the right thing in a given circumstance. Despite his rebellious nature, John Hammond was all of this: his espousal of the causes of underdogs—blacks, union workers, unappreciated jazz musicians—was built on his sense of himself as the lord of the manor coming down to show the serfs how to do things right. This was the way he was raised, and this he could not help, and it explains why he felt that he had a duty to revamp the Basie band, choose Wilson's sidemen or throw Jimmy Hamilton out of work.

But this same upbringing gave Hammond courage, the willingness to put his full weight behind what he believed in. Furthermore, his taste in jazz was excellent: Edmond Hall was a better jazz musician than Jimmy Hamilton; the men he picked for the Columbia sessions included some of the greatest musicians of the time; and the men he required Basie to hire were indeed better than the ones they replaced. It is true, as Hammond undoubtedly knew, that leaders pick sidemen for a lot of non-musical reasons—price, old friendships, favors owed and such. Hammond could be more impartial than could, say, Basie, with old loyalties stretching back ten years to Kansas City. However heavy-handed, indeed ruthless, he was, he almost always made the right choices. Without his management the careers of Basie, Holiday, Teddy Wilson, Fletcher Henderson and many others would not have been nearly as productive as they were, and the history of jazz would have been different.

In the summer of 1933 Hammond made an extended trip to England, ostensibly to renew his acquaintanceship with the British jazz world. During the course of the trip he was introduced to Sir Louis Sterling, president of the English Columbia Gramophone Company. He wrote:

> Sir Louis decided that with American Columbia in bankruptcy it was important for him to have an American who could record jazz for the English market. Through him I made a deal with English Columbia and Parlophone for a number of record sides for the English market, enough for a year's supply.[36]

Hammond's statement is disingenuous. He had been trying for a year or two to break into the American record business as a producer of jazz records, with little success. Hammond later would ascribe this to the fact that Americans had no interest in jazz, and that the companies were therefore not recording the music. As I have said, this was not the case. Between 1930 and 1934 perhaps a thousand jazz sides were issued, many of them today revered classics, although it must be said that 1933 was a particularly bad year for the recording of jazz. In 1933 Hammond was, as he said, "tactless and scornful of the commercial music business"—a young, brash opinionated rich man's son with very little experience who was barging through record company offices demanding a hearing for obscure musicians whose records were unlikely to have sold well even in good times. With the record industry virtually bankrupt, no company executive was likely to give Hammond expensive studio time to record a music that to many seemed to have had its day; and that, not a lack of interest in jazz, was why Hammond had trouble getting recording contracts in 1933.

The real story is this. In April of that year, the English musician and jazz writer Patrick "Spike" Hughes came to the United States to record some of his compositions with a black jazz orchestra. His contact in New York was Hammond, who organized a group for the recording session.[37] It undoubtedly occurred to Hammond that if Hughes could record serious jazz for the English market, he might be able to as well. And it is my sense that Hammond went to London in July of that year expressly to seek a contract to produce jazz records. Given his family background and his connections in the music business, he would have had no trouble managing introductions to people like Louis Sterling: among other things, his sister Alice was married to a Tory M.P.

There is no direct evidence for this scenario; but John Hammond was aggressive, willful and determined, and it is not believable that he met Sterling merely by chance, or that it was Sterling's idea to record jazz for the tiny English jazz market of the day. Whatever the case, Hammond returned with a commitment to make for English Columbia eight sides by the Fletcher Henderson orchestra, eight by Benny Carter's big band, four sides by a Goodman group and four more by a sextet led by Joe Venuti. He would also make a group of sides with some of these musicians and others for Parlophone, which would eventually become an important jazz label.[38] Hammond was making arrangements for a lot of musicians who knew nothing about it, some of whom did not even know who he was. It was typical of Hammond to operate this way, making commitments with the faith that he could somehow cajole people into doing what he wanted them to do.

This English contract put Hammond in the record business. Why he decided to record Goodman is difficult to know. Hammond had a strong predilection for black musicians over white ones. He did not believe that black musicians were necessarily better jazz musicians than whites, although he certainly felt that on balance there were more great black jazz musicians than white ones. His view was more that a lot of great jazz musicians were being neglected because they were black. And it is certainly true that when Hammond was learning about jazz in the late 1920s white musicians like Nichols, Beiderbecke, Mole, Eddie Lang, Adrian Rollini and others were getting more attention, and making more money, than equally good black ones. But Hammond did not believe, as some later jazz writers would, that only blacks could play good jazz. He wanted Goodman because he respected his playing. And it is also my guess that he wanted a Goodman band because he hoped to record a racially mixed group in order to puncture the racial barrier that existed in the music business. This desire would, of course, eventually have major consequences for both Goodman and the music business as a whole.

According to Hammond's own story, on the very night of his return from England he raced up to the Onyx Club on Fifty-second Street in search of Goodman. (However, dates of the recording sessions suggest it was later.) The Onyx was a speakeasy from Prohibition days run by a jazz fan named Joe Helbock. Helbock had put in a piano so musicians could come in and jam, and the place had gradually evolved into a jazz musicians' hang-out. When Prohibition officially ended in 1933, Helbock could operate openly, and he put in small jazz groups. Other former speakeasies on the block, seeing his success, put in trios and quartets of their own, and very quickly the block was transformed into the famous "Fifty-second Street" of jazz legend, now labeled Swing Street, although the Swing is long gone from there.

Goodman, like other musicians, frequented the place, and at ten-thirty he walked in, so the story goes. Hammond introduced himself and announced that he had a contract with Columbia to record four sides with a Goodman group. Benny replied to the effect that Hammond was a "goddam liar": he had recently spoken to Ben Selvin, now Columbia's recording director, who had told him that Columbia was bankrupt, or nearly so, and couldn't record him. Hammond quickly responded that he was talking about English Columbia, and that there was a chance that the records would also be released in the United States, as the domestic company would not have to pay for the recording session, but only a royalty on sales.[89]

Goodman agreed. He may have second thoughts. As it should be clear, John Hammond had a strong wish to control the musicians he worked with. He would not usually ask them with whom they wanted to play and what sort of music they wanted to play, but would make these decisions himself, choosing men he particularly admired or wanted to juxtapose, selecting the type of music to be played and making a stream of suggestions as the session proceeded. The final product would be as much his as the musicians'.

It was standard practice for a record producer to be firmly in command of record sessions. He generally picked the tunes, whether there would be a vocal, and perhaps had some say about tempos. But his motives were almost always commercial. Hammond's concern was artistic, and many times throughout a long and very successful recording career, he antagonized musicians. Duke Ellington actually left a record company to get away from Hammond's meddling.[40]

It was not surprising, therefore, Hammond had a clear idea of what he wanted the Goodman session to be: a mixed band using no arrangements and featuring a lot of soloing with jammed ensembles. He suggested the black saxophonists Coleman Hawkins and Benny Carter; and a white rhythm section of Gene Krupa on drums, pianist Joe Sullivan (who had been part of the Chicago group), and Dick McDonough, a highly regarded guitarist who was in demand for recordings; and bassist Artie Bernstein, a friend whom Hammond had played with in a string quartet.

Goodman was appalled by the scheme. It would not be a good idea for him to record with blacks, because the idea of racially mixed groups was offensive to many of the powers in the music industry. He was not sure, in any case, that a major record company would let him do it. He proposed instead that Hammond hear a group with whom he had been rehearsing. It is standard practice for musicians with not much work to organize fairly formal "rehearsal orchestras," ranging from small jazz groups to large symphony orchestras, which meet on a regular basis as a form of practice, to act as a showcase for their talents, and not incidentally, a chance to play music. Goodman's group was made up of studio musicians, including a drummer today known only as "Happy," who worked regularly with the highly commercial Meyer Davis groups.[41] Hammond went to a rehearsal at the Gotham Studios in the Grand Central Palace Building. As he suspected it would be, the group was entirely too commercial. "Benny's ideas and mine were almost diametrically opposed. . . . Benny had the idea that real improvised jazz was uncommercial and that you had to have a compromise in order to sell records."[42]

Goodman could hardly be blamed for believing this. The philosophy in the music industry was still that the public wanted only sweet, romantic music. But Hammond had no intention of recording anything of this kind and furthermore had a commission to record jazz for English Columbia. In the end, he and Goodman worked out a compromise.[43] Hammond got the rhythm section he wanted, which was an excellent one; however, there would be no blacks in the band. Both Hammond and Goodman wanted Jack Teagarden, but he and Krupa were both with Mal Hallett in Boston. Both wanted Bunny Berigan, but they knew that Teagarden would insist on his brother Charlie being included. Goodman wanted to use Mannie Klein as the other trumpet, in part because Klein was an excellent studio musician and in part because Klein controlled a lot of work. He also chose Art Karle to play saxophone. Hammond wanted one of the four tunes to be a blues. Goodman, on the other hand, wanted to record at least some commercial pop tunes, for safety's sake, and he picked out two recent

numbers, "Ain'tcha Glad," and Harold Arlen's "I Gotta Right to Sing
the Blues." The fourth tune was an original called "Dr. Heckle and Mr.
Jibe," written by Dick McDonough.

The Hallett band was based in New England, so Hammond telephoned
to Boston to arrange to get Krupa and Teagarden to come down for the
session. Teagarden was willing, but Krupa, bruised by his experience with
the Russ Columbo group, in which Goodman had insisted that he work
only with brushes, said he would never work for Goodman again, one of
the poorest predictions to come from a profession not notable for the
accuracy of its prophesies. Hammond thereupon took a train to Boston to
change Krupa's mind, which he did. The whole affair was typical of Hammond's unwillingness to compromise, or, if you prefer, his bull-headedness.
He could have found a perfectly adequate drummer in New York, but he
wanted Krupa, and he not only was able to talk him into making the date,
but actually badgered the record company into paying the travel expenses
for Krupa and Teagarden. It was a great deal of effort to put into what
another record producer might have seen as a rather casual and unimportant record date. But it was Hammond's first recording session of consequence, and for an inexperienced young man, he managed to gain a
substantial amount of control over the proceedings.

He did not have absolute control, however. Goodman, once again worried about commercial questions, did not want the band to simply go into
the studio and jam, and he got Artie Schutt, Hammond's first love on
piano, to arrange the pop tunes, in order to give the music the sound of a
standard dance band. Once they were in the studio, however, the arrangements turned out to be pedestrian, which Goodman himself realized, and
a substantial amount of time was wasted in revamping them, with the
result that only two numbers were cut at the session. Hammond then persuaded the company to allow him a second session, which once again required paying Krupa and Teagarden's transportation down from Boston.
The group went back into the studio the following week. Joe Sullivan was
unavailable, so the piano was played by Frankie Froeba, who had a higher
reputation among jazz musicians at the time than he does today.

In the end, the records, Hammond said, "were not what I had hoped for,
but not bad, either."[44] They were, in any case, good enough to interest Ben
Selvin. He decided to issue "Ain'tcha Glad" in the United States. He was
not sure that "I Gotta Right to Sing the Blues," with Teagarden's vocal,
was a strong enough coupling (in fact, the song would become part of
Teagarden's basic repertory), and wanted to issue "Ain'tcha Glad" with
another cut he had in the can, Clyde McCoy's "Sugar Blues." McCoy's
specialty was playing spurious jazz into a plunger mute, and Hammond
was horrified that this wholly meritricious piece of music would be coupled

to his jazz record. He produced some "well-placed screams"[45] and managed to get "I Gotta Right to Sing the Blues" as the B side of the record.

Taken as a whole, these four cuts are not among the classics of jazz. But they all contain excellent moments. For one, they feature Teagarden, who sings and plays trombone solos on all of them in the brilliant manner that had already established him as the leading trombonist in jazz, and would eventually give him an enduring reputation as one of the master jazz musicians of the twentieth century. He plays a superb coda break at the end of "Ain'tcha Glad," which sounds tossed off but which is technically very adroit, the sort of thing he was doing that frightened the other trombone players around the country. It contains a so-called lip-trill, a device Teagarden was the first jazz trombonist to employ, which involves the very rapid alternation of adjoining harmonics, or "lip positions." He also plays an excellent solo in the straight mute on "Dr. Heckle and Mr. Jibe," and on "Texas Tea Party" (the jammed blues that Hammond wanted) he sings a typical set of his blues choruses with the usual reference to marijuana: "Mamo, Mamo, Mamo, Mamo, where did you hide my tea?"

Goodman, surprisingly, takes a back seat to Teagarden. He plays a good, rather straight opening chorus on "Ain'tcha Glad," which is backed by some unfortunate muted twitterings by the trumpets, probably from the Schutt arrangement. He also plays a fine blues chorus on "Texas Tea Party." Goodman often managed, on the very simple structure of the blues, to play solos that were somewhat more melodically whole than was usual with him. He deftly answers a rising figure in the first measure with a variation of itself in the second, and then contrasts them with a figure that falls through the third and fourth measures. In the succeeding two bars he uses a simple repetitive figure drawn from Louis Armstrong's "West End Blues," a solo which was by that time embedded in the head of every jazz musician in the country. And it seems to me that the rest of the solo, which has a slightly plaintive quality, owes something to Armstrong's manner as well, as for example the descending figure in measures seven and eight with its suggestions of blue notes. Yet it is emphatically Goodman all the way.

Also of interest on this record is the introduction—by Goodman and guitarist McDonough alone—which consists of gracefully intertwined lines with the timbre of low register clarinet and single string guitar making a very pretty contrast. McDonough, who died unfortunately young five years later, was playing a modern melodic style built on the work of Eddie Lang and George Van Eps that was totally different from the playing of the black blues guitarists of the South who were quite popular among rural blacks and those recently emigrated to the big cities of the North. From the blues style would come the Chicago blues of the 1950s that contributed to rock; from the more modern style, whose principal exponents at the moment were McDonough and Carl Kress, would come the whole modern school of jazz guitarists from Allan Reuss, Goodman's principal guitarist with his early swing bands, through Barney Kessell to Bucky Pizzarelli, George Barnes and a host of others. This tasteful little passage foreshadows a great deal of guitar playing to come.

Characterizing these four cuts, aside from first-rate solos by some of the best jazz musicians of the time, is a light-hearted, infectious spirit. These records do not have the weight of some greater jazz cuts, like the afore-mentioned "West End Blues," nor the fire of, say, the Billy Banks Rhythm-makers sides or some of the sides Goodman himself would make a few years later. But the easy swing of them is very appealing, and it would be one of the trademarks of Goodman's work through the period of his greatest fame.

What was important at the time, however, was that the coupling of "Ain'tcha Glad" and "I Gotta Right to Sing the Blues" was a modest hit, selling, according to Hammond, 5,000 copies, which in those parlous times was a good sale.[46] Who exactly bought the records is impossible to know. However, it is probable that the primary market for them was "a sizeable group of incipient Hammonds in the colleges and preparatory schools," as one knowledgeable observer put it.[47] Colleges had always, right from the beginning, offered a welcome to jazz. The Original Dixieland Jass Band was playing fraternity dances as early as 1918, and Beiderbecke was something of a fixture at Indiana University, Northwestern and, after he came to New York, Princeton. By the mid-1920s there were clutches of jazz fans on many college campuses, people of some discrimination who knew who played what solos.[48] The college market would be crucial to Goodman's later success, and it seems likely that he began to establish at least a small reputation with students with these records.

Most important of all, the sales of these records, however modest, en-couraged Ben Selvin to let Hammond record Goodman again, this time directly for American Columbia. Hammond, who never lacked for self-confidence to begin with, was now driving himself like a peg into the record business with the energy and force that characterized everything he did. He could now truthfully say that he had made profitable records. Within two months of his return from England he had produced fourteen record sessions, using some of the most important jazz musicians of the day, among them Teddy Wilson, Coleman Hawkins, Bessie Smith, Joe Venuti, the Fletcher Henderson orchestra and of course Goodman and Teagarden. He also managed to put together two racially mixed sessions, the Bessie Smith date on which Goodman played, and another with a group issued as The Chocolate Dandies, a somewhat ironic title in view of the fact that three of the musicians on it were white.

Hammond's next session with Goodman was also racially mixed, in that it included a new Hammond discovery, Billie Holiday. Hammond is sometimes given credit for "discovering" people whom he had actually been tipped off to by other people, but John Chilton, in his biography of Holiday, credits Hammond with this discovery, and it is certain, in any case, that he was responsible for promoting her career and getting her recorded.[49]

It was not terribly unusual for a white group to back a black singer. A vocalist did not "mix" with the band, but stood somewhat apart, and was thus more acceptable than a black musician who sat side by side with whites. As early as 1928 Ivie Anderson, to be a star with Duke Ellington, was the featured singer with the white Anson Weeks Orchestra.[50]

But this time the band, which was otherwise the group from the "Ain'tcha Glad" session, included black trumpeter Shirley Clay in place of Mannie Klein. Clay was a good jazz musician, but there was no reason to use him in place of Klein; it was all part of Hammond's campaign to integrate the music industry.

It took two sessions to get an acceptable coupling of Holiday cuts. At the first session the band backed Ethel Waters, already a star, for two numbers, and then accompanied Holiday on "Your Mother's Son-in-law." At the second session a week later they produced "Riffin' the Scotch" as well as a number on which Teagarden sang. The Holiday pieces are mainly notable for being her first appearance on records. The arrangements are rather disjointed, and Goodman's solos are not among his best. Teagarden plays excellent solos on both cuts. As he did in the earlier Hammond sessions, Goodman gives Teagarden more solo space than he takes for himself. This was in part out of Goodman's respect for Teagarden's jazz playing, but I think it also may have been that Goodman was made a little nervous by his role as bandleader, and did not want the added burden of being the principal soloist on the date. This may also explain why such solos as he takes are relatively unadorned.

By the end of 1933 the musical partnership formed by Goodman and Hammond had drifted into a friendship. Hammond had a certain liking for Jews, akin to his interest in blacks. He had seen the extent to which Jews were discriminated against by the social group he had grown up in, and by this time his "two best friends, Edgar Siskin and Artie Bernstein, were Jews."[51] Undoubtedly Hammond's rebelliousness played a role in socializing with Jews and blacks. There was also a less attractive self-congratulatory element in it. But Benny Goodman was, besides being Jewish, a brilliant jazz musician, and it is not surprising that Hammond would choose to cultivate him, just as he had the black jazz musicians he admired, like Fletcher Henderson and Benny Carter.

What Goodman felt about the relationship is difficult to know. Goodman was an ill-educated boy from the ghetto. In the past when he had performed at the homes of people like the Hammonds, he would have been told to come in through the back door, and to spend his intermissions in the kitchen. Hammond was hardly typical of his social class, but he nonetheless had the manner. Goodman must have found him fairly exotic, but at the same time would have been flattered by the interest of this very rich man's son in him. Furthermore, it is the belief of James T. Maher that Benny Goodman right from early in life had aspirations to climb up out of the lard heap his father had sweated in.[52] As we will see, he eventually learned to dress, to carry himself and even talk like one of the American upper class. He undoubtedly recognized that Hammond provided him with both a link to this class and with a model on which he could form his own behavior. One consequence of the respect mingled with a shrewd opportunism through which he viewed Hammond was that he would, for some time, accept guidance from Hammond that did not really suit his own somewhat arrogant nature.

# 9

# The Free-Lance Recordings

Between the time Benny Goodman left Ben Pollack in August or September of 1929, and April 1934, when he took his own band into Billy Rose's Music Hall, he cut almost 500 records under dozens of different names for almost every label in the rapidly contracting record industry; and there may have been other sessions which Goodman collectors have not yet unearthed. However, a substantial proportion of these records, possibly as much as half, were made under the direction of Ben Selvin. Selvin was a violinist who had run a commercial dance band at the Moulin Rouge, a well-known New York restaurant, from 1917 into 1924, by which time Prohibition was killing off the big, old-fashioned restaurants of the pre-war period. He then turned to leading recording bands, and by 1928 he had cut over three thousand records.[1]

During this time he was also leading broadcasting orchestras of various types. By the time he started using Goodman in 1929 he had become an executive at Columbia, and eventually, as we have seen, recording director for the company. He was thoroughly commercial, and of the some 250 records Goodman made for him only about fifty have even brief solo passages by Goodman. But Selvin, like everybody in the music business at the time, knew that even if, as was thought, Americans were in the mood for dreamy music, they still wanted it spiced with a certain amount of jazz. He found that a man like Goodman, who not only could read well and play with facility but could turn out a first-class hot chorus at a signal, was very valuable.

Selvin, of course, was not the only recording director whose instincts were primarily commercial. Other leaders were using Goodman as Selvin was, to sit in the saxophone section reading the arrangements and playing brief bits of solo, or "fills," behind a singer. Goodman is audible, in one way or another, on about 60 percent of these records, but in most cases his appearances outside of the saxophone section are brief—usually a four-

or eight-bar solo passage, or some low register noodling behind a vocalist. Out of the roughly 130 recording dates Goodman made during this period, not more than about fifteen could be construed as jazz sessions, a good indication of what the record companies had concluded about the salability of jazz as the Depression deepened. Among the jazz dates were a session with Beiderbecke, a few with Red Nichols, some with Goodman's early idol Ted Lewis and featuring Fats Waller, two with Joe Venuti, and a sprinkling of others with leaders like Red Norvo and Adrian Rollini, both of whom had minor reputations with the dance-band public. Finally, there was a session arranged by John Hammond for Bessie Smith, on which Goodman plays mainly in the ensemble passages.

A few sessions were issued under the name of Benny Goodman and His Orchestra, but this does not mean that Goodman was in charge of the sessions. He does not solo on many of them, and for the most part they are as commercial as the ones issued under Selvin's name. There was little rhyme or reason to it. The record companies would frequently issue various cuts from one session under different names; at times a session might go out under four or five different names. Although a well-known band like Whiteman's or Ben Bernie's could sell on its own name, in probably the majority of instances it was the tune that was the selling point, and the name of the band was unimportant. The companies used dozens of pseudo-nyms, some of them "house" names, others invented at the moment; the name "Benny Goodman and His Orchestra" was in this sense as much a pseudonym as "Roy Carrol and His Sands Point Orchestra," where "Roy Carrol" was in fact vocalist Dick Robertson, who made hundreds of records during this period.

During this free-lance period Goodman probably made more actual jazz records with Red Nichols than with any other leader. Nichols had made his first reputation as a jazz musician playing in a dixieland band, and his followers expected a good deal of jazz from him. Nichols liked to use the best white jazz men around—Goodman, the Teagarden brothers, Jimmy Dorsey, Gene Krupa, Dick McDonough. He frequently used Goodman instead of Dorsey, despite the fact that Dorsey was an old sidekick from the days of his first success, and he gave Benny a lot of solos. Goodman solos on some 70 percent of the almost forty records he made with Nichols during his free-lance period.

Two solos of particular interest are the ones he made on "Carolina in the Morning" and "On Revival Day." They were cut in August and September of 1930, and show Goodman playing in two very different styles. In "On Revival Day" he uses a very fast, fluid, graceful style in, for the most part, a pure tone. (I am referring to the B master.) It is the kind of solo that later listeners would think of as a "typical" Benny Goodman solo, built around eighth notes, filled with bubbling rising and falling passages as in bars five, six and seven. There are, in this relatively long solo, two or three long, high notes which slur downwards in the fashion he learned from the dixieland players as a boy, but they are infrequent. Taken as a whole, it is what we would think of as "pure Goodman."

The "Carolina in the Morning" solo is an entirely different beast. The song is another one of those pieces with harmonies that change every two beats for much of its length, forcing the players to various expedients to construct a meaningful line. One approach to handling this kind of problem is to find one or two notes which fit fairly well with a group of successive chord changes, which usually can be done if the harmony is at all logical. However, this in turn forces the player to exploit as much as possible the notes he is limited to. Red Nichols' solo preceding Goodman's is uncharacteristically spare. It begins in a relatively busy fashion as, over the first half, Nichols makes an effort to outline the shape of the harmony. But by the second half his imagination is exhausted; in bars seventeen through twenty he builds his line around the fifth varied by a sudden hot octave rip; the next four bars are built around the sixth, while the harmonies shift underneath it; and so it goes throughout the rest of the chorus.

Goodman deals with the problem by vesting his line with a great deal of "hot" intonation. He plays virtually the entire chorus in a raspy tone, with the notes choked off abruptly at the end. At moments he ceases using the notes for melodic purposes at all, and instead squirts them around the room like bursts of gunfire. In bars nine and ten, for example, he plays just four raspy, twisted, slurred notes, and in bars twenty-four through twenty-seven he does something similar. This is the very reverse of graceful fluidity; and when we listen to Goodman's records of this period we find that this very hot, twisted, growling style is more typical of his playing than the lyrical, legato, technically exact manner we think of as the Goodman style.

Surprisingly, from the viewpoint of pure jazz, the sessions with Ted Lewis, the ultimate of commercial leaders, are among the hottest Goodman made at this time. Lewis, as we have seen, originally led a fairly honorable dixieland band, and had a taste for jazz, despite his own wobbling clarinet style. After he became famous he kept in his band for years two of the best white dixielanders, cornetist Muggsy Spanier and trombonist George Brunies, and he would from time to time bring other hot players into the recording studios, among them first-rate clarinetists like Jimmy Dorsey, Don Murray and Tony Parenti, presumably in the hope that audiences would think it was his clarinet work.

Goodman made nineteen cuts with Lewis, all of them in 1931 and 1932. The most famous, certainly, are a set of four recorded on two successive days in March 1931, which include Fats Waller. It is typical of the confusion that beset the music industry at the time that this very commercial leader would occasionally turn out some very good hot jazz. Nobody was really sure whether the music of the 1920s was dead or alive. Lewis sings "Egyptian-Ella," a novelty tune cast in a supposed Arabic mode, in which Goodman plays a solo intended to give the effect of a snake-charmer's flute. Waller sings the other three, two of which are blues. Goodman noodles behind Waller's "Dallas Blues" vocal, and plays again on the ensemble ride-out, a blazing hot blues in long metre driven by Spanier's cornet in the style he derived from Paul Mares and Joe Oliver. Louis Armstrong had cut the tune fifteen months before, and Spanier pays his obeisance to Satch in bar five of the opening chorus and at the end of the record.

On "Royal Garden Blues" Goodman plays an atypical chorus. He was not much given to repeating figures but tended always to rush forward into something new. In this case, however, he plays a two-measure figure to open his solos and then repeats it. Again, Goodman characteristically divides his beat into two quite uneven portions. Over the first four bars, he plays a sequence of relatively even and somewhat truncated eighth notes, which give the music a curiously deliberate feeling, as if he were walking on stilts. Again there is a hot dixieland ride-out with Goodman playing the long falling slurs he liked to use on these occasions. It is worth noting that trombonist George Brunies plays an ensemble line in the opening chorus which is very close to the one he would use in the 1940s on the Commodore Record version of the same tune. The original New Orleans pioneers, as has often been pointed out, were embellishers, rather than improvisors; once they had worked out a good ensemble part, or even a solo, for a given piece, they tended to play it more or less the same way each time. The people who followed the New Orleanians into jazz put the idea of improvising at the heart of jazz, but even so in these records, Goodman continues to use ensemble slurs taken directly from the old formula.

Perhaps Goodman's best playing on the Lewis-Waller sides is on "I'm Crazy 'Bout My Baby." It is an infectious tune, with a typically clever lyric by Andy Razaf, Waller's usual composing partner, who has never had the recognition he deserved as a gifted writer of pop song lyrics. After Waller sings in his jovial manner, Goodman plays sixteen measures of a typically happy, light-hearted chorus, paraphrasing the melody as he would often do in the records that made him famous later on. Jazz musicians, like everybody else, have their own favorites among popular tunes, and when they are given one to play they are likely to make steady reference to it. This is the case here; and Goodman's easy manner complements Waller's merry vocal so well that it seems a shame these two musicians were barred from working together by circumstances, among them the racism of the period. Both of them were able to make enormous popular successes while playing superb jazz, a stunt that only the greatest jazz musicians, such as Armstrong and Ellington, have been able to bring off. Lesser ones had either, like Harry James, to compromise their jazz work to become widely popular; or like Muggsy Spanier, refused to compromise and never became widely popular. But in the jazz playing of the masters there is the expression of a deep inner spirit which gives life to the music and attracts millions of people. It is, probably, a sense listeners have they are in contact with the core of another human being, which they do not feel with a lesser player. Goodman and Waller were two of these masters; the combination was felicitous.

Two other sides Goodman made with Ted Lewis are worth mentioning. On "Headin' for Better Times," Goodman plays his imitation of Lewis which he had played on his first public appearance—possibly at Lewis' instructions. "Dip Your Brush in the Sunshine" has long been a favorite of Goodman collectors. The song has one of the optimistic lyrics that Lewis recited, rather than sang, the point being that we are always painting our own picture of life and therefore ought to paint it in sunshine rather than cloudy gray. Goodman has a whole, very hot chorus over which Lewis keeps exhorting him to "paint it, Benny, paint it . . . paint it blue, Benny, sky blue, Benny." He does the same thing over Spanier's equally hot chorus. It is like fingernails scratching along a blackboard.

The Bix Beiderbecke date also has a story connected to it. Just as Hoagy Carmichael had brought redundant musicians to the "Rockin' Chair" session because he was loathe to offend anyone, so Beiderbecke brought Goodman, Jimmy Dorsey and Pee Wee Russell into the studio. (Russell had been Bix's roommate and drinking companion years before.)[2] In "Deep Down South" Goodman plays the four-bar modulation between the vocal and Bix's solo, as well as the following bridge; neither bit of music is exceptional. He does not solo on any of the other cuts: the clarinet solo on "I'll Be a Friend with Pleasure," which makes an unprepared modulation from F into D-flat, is by Jimmy Dorsey.

Another leader for whom Goodman did a certain amount of jazz recording was Adrian Rollini. He is a strange and somewhat misty figure in jazz history. A musical prodigy as a child, he gave a Chopin piano recital at four, and by fourteen he was leading his own band in New York, playing both piano and xylophone. In his late teens he joined the California Ramblers, one of the most popular dance bands of the 1920s, which included a number of good jazz musicians and could play hot.[3] Based in New York, despite the name, it recorded prolifically and was influential with young dance-band musicians. A good many of its records were issued in England in the twenties, and as a consequence Rollini came to be seen there as one of the leading American jazz musicians. He spent two years in England working with Fred Elizalde, leader of the first European band of consequence to play jazz with any success.[4]

Although he specialized in xylophone and bass saxophone, he also played hot fountain pen and "goofus." Despite this addiction to odd instruments, Rollini was a fine jazz musician. He was not inventive, but he swung as hard as any of the early white players, as for example in his brief chorus on Beiderbecke's "A Good Man Is Hard to Find." Furthermore, in those days when saxophone technique was only being developed, he was possibly the most technically proficient jazz man on saxophone, playing his ponderous instrument with facility and good intonation. He was much admired by musicians of the 1920s, and quite influential—Coleman Hawkins even bought a bass saxophone to play in the Fletcher Henderson orchestra on Rollini's example.[5] Even today he must be considered one of the few masters of that rarely used instrument.

Given his obvious musical talent and feeling for jazz, it is surprising that he has not earned a bigger place in the history of the music. The trouble may have been that he never took either himself or the music seriously. Unlike Benny Goodman, he was not driven to practice incessantly, nor impelled to build a successful band, although he did lead his own groups from time to time. He insisted on playing instruments which were as much a hindrance as a help in playing jazz; had he developed himself as a clarinetist or an alto saxophonist he might be today remembered as one of the finest jazz men of the period.

Goodman made three record sessions with bands led by Rollini, which at one time or another included a number of the New York studio musicians who would eventually work in Goodman's bands, Bunny Berigan, Mannie Klein, and Rollini's brother Art, who played tenor saxophone. Goodman solos on several of these records, but they were basically commercial sessions, despite the presence of important jazz men.

Among the best-known sessions Goodman made with these pick-up recording bands in this period is a 1931 session which was issued as Eddie Lang–Joe Venuti and Their All Star Orchestra. It included, besides Lang and Venuti, the Teagarden brothers, Goodman and pianist Frank Signorelli, who had been an early jazz star with the Memphis Five. These are purely jazz records. Venuti and guitarist Lang had formed a musical partnership in the late 1920s, recording in duets, trios and other combinations. They became popular, and their fans expected a good deal of jazz from them, which gave them a little more leeway in recording what they wanted. The four cuts from this session are mainly strings of solos with jammed ride-out endings. Charlie Teagarden, who could be somewhat slick at moments, does some of his best recorded work here, especially his strong chorus on "After You've Gone." Brother Jack is excellent as always despite a late entry on "Farewell Blues." Taken as a whole these are excellent jazz.

Goodman solos on all of them, and it is interesting how varied his playing is. On "Someday Sweetheart," which is taken quite slow, he plays an immaculately conceived and executed cadenza to introduce the record, and then takes a solo which to a degree reflects the same symphonic approach. He plays a long line which keeps rolling upwards and downwards, and is filled with atypical trills and sixteenth-note passages which give an out-of-tempo effect. He is in quite a different mood on "Farewell Blues," in which he plays sixteen measures in the low register and sixteen higher up. In the low register he plays his eighth notes quite evenly, a departure from his normal manner, and it was this kind of playing that reminded listeners of Jimmie Noone. The school of Creole clarinet that Noone came out of employed much more even eighths than was customary in jazz, and its members liked playing long runs of them in the chalumeau register.

Goodman is in yet another mood on "Beale Street Blues." As I have said, a man's musical personality may differ markedly from the person people know. Benny Goodman could be heavy-handed and arrogant with people, but he was rarely like that in his playing. In this cut he plays accompanying fills both to Charlie Teagarden's lead line in the opening chorus and to Jack Teagarden's vocal. He inserts his notes unobtrusively, placing them exactly where they belong. Frequently it is just a single held note that sags or falls off, and then steps gracefully aside in a brief downward run that disappears behind the main line. He is working in the clarinet style developed by the dixielanders, but in his hands it is far more subtle and delicate.

There was another session with Venuti which was issued as Joe Venuti and His Blue Six. The four cuts included another version of "Sweet Lorraine," taken in an unusual uptempo after the standard slow opening chorus, and a version of the famous King Oliver "Dippermouth Blues." Goodman makes a few passes at the standard clarinet solo created for the tune by Johnny Dodds, but it is far more Goodman than Dodds. Goodman rarely played somebody else's famous chorus on anything, although he did refer to the Noone version of "I Know That You Know" on his own cut. He may have been unwilling to go to the bother of learning them, or he may simply have refused to walk where another man had trod first. But he does play snatches of the Dodds chorus, enough in any case to tell us that he knew it. Probably his best work from this session was on "Doin' the Uptown Lowdown," a piece in a minor key. In bars ten through twelve he uses similar figures to create an interesting, if brief metric shift, and after

Bud Freeman's solo on the bridge he plays a series of descending slurs, an example of his purely hot phraseology.

Another session worth mentioning is a set of two cuts Goodman made with Red Norvo in 1933. Norvo, who would have a long association with Goodman, had studied piano as a child, but switched to xylophone which he was playing on the vaudeville circuit by the time he was an adolescent. The xylophone was seen as a novelty instrument appropriate for a vaudeville act, but not of much use in a jazz band. Norvo, however, proved that he could swing on the instrument and gradually worked his way into jazz. In time he added marimba and then vibraphone, both related instruments.

The session with Goodman was the second of two which offered Norvo as a soloist with a minimal accompaniment. The pieces were exceedingly unusual for the time. The group consists of Norvo, Dick McDonough, Artie Bernstein and Goodman playing bass clarinet, one of the earliest examples of a jazz band without either piano or drums. The tunes are the Bix Beiderbecke piano composition "In a Mist," written when Bix was under the influence of the French impressionist composers, and a Norvo composition, "Dance of the Octopus." These are not entirely jazz pieces. Parts of them are out of tempo, and on the whole they are impressionistic, owing more to Beiderbecke's rambling piano style than to, say, his much more direct cornet style. The pieces have to be seen as part of an introspective strain in jazz, which includes the four Beiderbecke compositions, such Ellington pieces as "Mood Indigo," several Norvo works from this period and a group of compositions by Reginald Foresythe Goodman would record in a year or so. These pieces share an interest in "advanced" harmonies, less usual forms, and the avoidance of certain central traits of jazz like the non-diatonic tones such as the blue notes, and a propulsive beat. Because these pieces lack these characteristics this strain in jazz has never developed a significant following. But the pieces remain interesting, and although Goodman is confined in the main to a written line, it is a chance for fans to hear him on the bass clarinet.

Finally, there is a famous session with Bessie Smith, which was organized by John Hammond. Bessie had not recorded for over two years, because the blues boom of the 1920s seemed to have ended with the Depression. Hammond had been listening to Smith from early adolescence, and was determined to revive her career. He brought a racially mixed all-star band into the studio, which included Goodman, Teagarden, Chu Berry, who would become one of the leading saxophonists of the 1930s, and trumpeter Frankie Newton. Goodman is inaudible on three of the four cuts, and some people question whether he was in the studio the whole time; but it is possible to make out two clarinet notes peeking through a brush pile of sound on the last chorus on "Gimme a Pigfoot," one of the most powerful vocals in the entire history of jazz.

Considering the fact that jazz was supposed to have run its course and was now seen as a relic of the 1920s, it is surprising how much pure improvised jazz there is on these records, most of which were made with commercial intent.

Nonetheless, however much Goodman liked playing in small jazz bands, he knew that any future he might have lay in the bigger, band-playing arranged music. Over his free-lance years he made a number of sessions on which he was leader, and the records produced at them moved him toward the big dance band which would bring him his great success.

A session of particular interest is a date made on February 9, 1931, at which were cut versions of "Basin Street Blues" and "Beale Street Blues," which were issued as the "Charleston Chasers Under the Direction of Bennie Goodman." Goodman said later that these sessions were the first in which "I put across something like a style of my own."[6]

It is difficult to know what he meant. Glenn Miller provided the arrangement, and was responsible for cooking up, possibly with Teagarden's help, a verse for "Basin Street Blues" which has since become part of the tune. Otherwise the side consists of a sequence of solos, including a vocal by Teagarden, with minimal accompaniment. "Beale Street Blues" is primarily a vocal feature for Teagarden. It also has a minimal arrangement, in which Goodman plays only some accompanying interpolations in the vocal. These two performances are, in the main, jammed and hardly figure as precursors to the kind of big band music that would in a few years make Goodman famous.

He does, however, play interesting solos in "Basin Street Blues." The second of these is on the familiar main theme of the song, which is not a blues, but an ordinary sixteen-measure pop song; but the first is a true blues. There was no particular reason for inserting a blues chorus into the record; Goodman probably did it because that was what Louis Armstrong did with his version of the record made over two years earlier, a supposition given weight by the fact that in the Goodman version pianist Artie Schutt plays brief interludes, as Earl Hines had done on the Armstrong cut.

But it is also true that Goodman could have given the blues chorus to another player. The fact is that Benny Goodman liked playing the blues. Later, with his famous Trios, Quartets and other small groups, when he could work with whatever material he chose, he played a good many blues. And of course some of his greatest hits, like "Roll 'Em" and "Bugle Call Rag," were basically blues. Once again Goodman plays on the blues a more carefully worked out solo than is usually his way. It is a stop-time chorus, with the band hitting the first three beats of each measure, a device that had become familiar to jazz players from its use behind Johnny Dodds' famous chorus on King Oliver's "Dippermouth Blues." Goodman plays the entire chorus with a rasp or growl. He begins with a two-measure descending figure, which he repeats almost exactly, and repeats again a fifth lower to match the chord change. The solo then becomes more typically disjunctive, but it is a strong passionate blues, which ends on a long, touching falling note. In the work of the best jazz players there is always variety—variety of rhythmic patterns, of approach, of mood. Goodman was capable of the easy light-hearted playing he exhibited, for example, in the Lewis "I'm Crazy 'Bout My Baby," but he was also able to play dense, impassioned blues like this.

There followed a number of sessions which were issued as by Benny Goodman and His Orchestra and in some cases under other titles as well, but these were strictly commercial sessions made under the direction of record producers. They do not reflect Goodman's own ideas about music, and many of them do not have clarinet solos. These are not really "Goodman" groups.

Then came the first Hammond session, in which Goodman did have a good deal of control over the music. With the success of these, Selvin was willing to record Goodman again. There followed the Ethel Waters–Billie Holiday session also produced by Hammond, and then sessions in December 1933, February and May 1934, as well as some radio transcription dates. How much Hammond had to do with any of these recording sessions is difficult to know. He lists himself as producer of them in his autobiography, and he was undoubtedly in the studio when they were made. Teddy Wilson, whom Hammond was promoting at the time, was on the May 1934 session, but that may have simply been because Goodman admired Wilson's playing a great deal.

Particularly interesting is "Tappin' the Barrel," made in December 1933. The song is a cheerful novelty apparently celebrating the end of Prohibition and is sung by Teagarden. What matters, however, is the arrangement: this cut sounds like the Benny Goodman band which would go on to become famous a year and a half later. Many of the devices that appear repeatedly in Goodman scores after 1935 are here. The arrangement opens with a rather busy eight-measure introduction very much like dozens of others Goodman would use. For the first four measures of the tune tenor saxophonist Art Karle plays the melody—reading it—and his line is answered by brass punctuation; then Goodman picks up the melody and plays it fairly straight. The formula is repeated for the second eight bars, the full band plays the bridge and then the opening formula is repeated to round out the first eight. Again and again later on Goodman would do precisely this, that is trade fours with one or another section of the band. The call-and-response between tenor and brass, too, would be ever-present in Goodman's music.

This opening chorus is followed by a long, sixteen-measure interlude to make the modulation from F to E-flat for Teagarden's vocal. Yet again, long modulations of this kind are very common in Goodman's famous groups. Following the vocal Goodman solos for sixteen measures, Teagarden plays the bridge, and the whole band sweeps in for the last eight measures, once more a formula for final choruses that would appear on Goodman's records many times. There is, finally, a typical Goodman coda involving his solo clarinet and the band.

The records that Goodman had had some hand in shaping previously are far more casual pieces, frequently using head arrangements pulled together in the studio, as in the case of "Beale Street Blues," or simply jammed for the most part, as with "Texas Tea Party." "Tappin' the Barrel" is a carefully thought-out, well-written arrangement, played by a band that has obviously been rehearsed with some care. Unhappily, we know nothing of how this came about—who made the arrangement, what instructions Goodman gave him or what went on in the studio. It sounds like the sort of arrangement Lyle "Spud" Murphy, who wrote many important pieces for Goodman in the days of his first success, liked to work out. Murphy, it seems to me, wrote rather ornate passages like the introduction and interlude in this piece, but this guess is questioned by James T. Maher.[7]

The February 1934 session was a little different. It was put together by Hammond to feature the great black tenor saxophonist Coleman Hawkins, who had been for a decade one of the stars of the Fletcher Henderson Orchestra which Hammond so admired. By this moment Hawkins was the dominant saxophonist in jazz. He had arranged to leave the United States to work in Europe, where he would remain until 1939, and it is probable that Hammond wanted to record him before he left.[8] Hawkins has long solos, and Mildred Bailey, another musician whom Hammond was pushing, sings three of the four cuts. Hammond's predilection for improvising jam bands is evident, for the arrangements are in the main sketchy, and most of the space is devoted to solos. Hawkins, it seems to me, was not at his best at this session.

However, the cuts from the May 1934 session return to the more carefully worked out manner of "Tappin' the Barrel." The arrangements are not quite as satisfying, but they are in the new mold. Among other things, Goodman is using far fewer of the growls and twisted notes than he customarily did. I think this was a matter of policy. Goodman was always conscious of what he thought audiences could take, tending to err on the conservative side, if anything, and he undoubtedly felt that a smoother, lighter style would be more acceptable. These records were going out under his name.

It is clear, in any case, that by the end of 1933 Goodman was beginning to have some ideas about what kind of music he wanted to play, and this inevitably would lead him to thinking about having a band of his own. He was now about to walk out on the springboard from which he would jump into the swing era.

# 10
# Goodman Forms a Band

Like most musicians, Benny Goodman had occasionally toyed with the idea of putting together his own band. Since the rise of the "name" band in the aftermath of the success of the Hickman and Whiteman bands, it had become possible for a leader of a popular band to grow rich and famous; and even leaders who were less well known, like Pollack or Nichols, could earn substantial incomes. Moreover, a leader could work out his own ideas to express his musical yearnings.

By 1934 Goodman had other, personal reasons for thinking about putting together a band of his own. He was now aware that he was marked down as difficult in the studios, and the work had fallen off considerably. According to his own story, by 1934 he was down to one forty-dollar-a-week radio[1] show and perhaps a recording session a month. Goodman was not a particularly reflective man, but he may have come to understand that he was not temperamentally well-suited to taking orders from other leaders, and would be better off as his own boss.

He had already tested the waters, first with the Russ Columbo band and then with the Hammond recording sessions. The music business was in a bad way, but it was clear enough that it was still possible to do well with the right kind of band. Paul Whiteman was still making a lot of money, although he was considered by young people to have fallen behind the times. The black bands led by Louis Armstrong, Duke Ellington and Fletcher Henderson were eminently successful, broadcasting and recording regularly, and even making a few movies. The Ben Pollack Orchestra, despite its travails, was a going concern; Tommy and Jimmy Dorsey had formed the Dorsey Brothers Orchestra, which was beginning to make a mark; and the Casa Loma Orchestra was firmly established, especially with the college students who constituted an important segment of the dance-band audience.

The Casa Loma group in particular was showing Goodman a way he might go. The group had sprung from the Jean Goldkette organization in

Detroit in the late 1920s.[2] Eventually the members formed it into a cooperative, with decisions made mutually and profits shared evenly. Saxophonist Glen Gray was the musical director, but the key member was Gene Gifford, who wrote many of the band's best arrangements. It was managed by
a smart Irishman, Francis "Cork" O'Keefe, who had begun booking bands,
especially on college campuses, during the early 1920s and was becoming a
force in the music business. The Casa Loma Orchestra played a judicious
mix of sentimental ballads and uptempo swingers, featuring solos by some
competent improvisers, like trombonist Pee Wee Hunt, trumpeter Sonny
Dunham, and clarinetist Clarence Hutchinrider (who is still working in
jazz at this writing). By 1933 the band was working regularly at the Glen
Island Casino, a famous dance pavilion on an island in Long Island Sound
off a wealthy part of Westchester County, just east of the city and within
easy reach of the many colleges and private schools in the area—Yale, Columbia, Fordham and more. The band broadcast from Glen Island and
elsewhere frequently, and by the 1933–34 winter of Benny Goodman's dis-
content, it was also being featured on the Camel Caravan, the most important radio showcase for a dance band.[3] It played a lot of sentimental dance
music, but it could play first-rate hot numbers, like Gifford's "Casa Loma
Stomp," when it set out to do so.

Thus, despite what appeared to be a Depression with no bottom to it, it
was possible for a good dance band to thrive. This, then, was the situation
in early 1934 when the Pollack band, with Harry Goodman on bass, came
back to New York to open a new mob-owned club called the Casino de
Paree on Fifty-fourth Street.[4] The club was managed by an entrepreneur
named Billy Rose, who would have a long career in the entertainment business. Harry began hearing gossip around the club that Rose was going to
open a similar supper club in an empty theatre nearby, which would be
called Billy Rose's Music Hall. He reported all of this to Benny, and the
question arose: Should Benny put together a band to audition for the new
club?

When it came down to it, he really had little choice. He was rapidly
coming to a dead end in the New York music business. He had, it was true,
a standing offer from Paul Whiteman for a long-term contract at a good
salary,[5] but the job would force him to travel, playing a good many one-
nighters. Moreover, he would be spending his time primarily sitting in
Whiteman's saxophone section, and playing only brief solos two or three
times a night. At about this time Jack Teagarden accepted a five-year contract from Whiteman, which he came to regret. Teagarden was a far more
tractable man than Goodman, and Benny may have sensed that he would
very quickly begin to chafe under Whiteman's baton and get himself in
trouble.

In the end, he decided to put together a band to audition for Rose. What role John Hammond played in all of this is hard to determine. His own story of how Goodman got the Billy Rose job differs considerably from the one told by others, including Goodman himself. He said he offered to help Goodman find musicians which, knowing Hammond, was undoubtedly true, and he claims to have found bassist Hank Weyland working in a Chinese restaurant.[6] But many of the musicians Goodman took on were studio players, not the hot men Hammond would have been drawn to, and it does not seem likely that Hammond was important in organizing this first band.

As soon as Goodman began talking about the possibility of the band, word began to circulate among musicians. Benny was by this time a figure of consequence in the New York music world, a young man recognized as both a brilliant jazz improviser and a highly regarded instrumentalist who had already made a number of records under his own name. The band, it seemed clear, would play a lot of hot music; and if it succeeded, it would be something worthwhile being in on. As a consequence, as soon as Goodman went into rehearsal, musicians came around to audition.[7] Over the time he was rehearsing the band the personnel shifted as Goodman replaced men with better ones, or as they became disenchanted for one reason or another and left. Through pianist Oscar Levant, whom Goodman knew from the studios, an introduction to Rose was managed.[8] Eventually Goodman auditioned twice for Rose with different line-ups. The last audition, however, included a young female singer named Helen Ward, who already had developed a small name and who auditioned with Benny as a favor to him.

The salary Goodman was offering was not large and the prospects for the band were uncertain. As a consequence Goodman could not command many of the top New York musicians. It is some testimony to the interest the group aroused that he got as many good musicians as he did. One of these was guitarist George Van Eps, younger brother of the famous Fred Van Eps, a celebrated banjo player who had made best-selling duets with the famous Sylvester "Vess" Osman in the early days of ragtime. Two other top calibre players were trombonists Jack Lacey and Red Ballard. Lacey was considered possibly the finest studio trombonist in New York, who could also play good jazz. Ballard, who would be with the Goodman band for years, rarely soloed. (Ballard later on said, "I always got along fine with Benny—the only sideman who did, maybe.")[9] Ballard was also a fine jazz musician, but he never recorded any jazz solos with Goodman. Other men who worked in this first band were two studio trumpet players, Russ Case and Sammy Shapiro, who as Sammy Spear would become well known as director of the band for The Jackie Gleason Show. (One report says that

Shapiro replaced Eddie Wade.)[10] The third trumpeter was Jerry Neary, who according to trumpeter Pee Wee Erwin, who came into the band later, was "a pretty darned good trumpet man"[11] but refused to play solos, except the answers in Goodman's closing theme, "Good-bye." The saxophonists were alto Hymie Schertzer, who would become one of the finest lead alto players of the swing era but who was hired by Goodman because he could also play violin; Adrian Rollini's brother Art, who would be Goodman's principal tenor soloist for five years, and Ben Kanter. The rhythm section was Hank Weyland, who would soon be replaced by Harry Goodman, Van Eps, pianist Claude Thornhill, who would have an important swing band ten years later, and a sequence of drummers, none of whom stayed long. Hammond later referred to it as "a thoroughly undistinguished band,"[12] and it is certainly true that it lacked top quality jazz soloists. On the other hand, Van Eps, Lacey, Ballard, Schertzer and Rollini were excellent studio musicians and if not brilliant jazz improvisers, certainly competent. Finally, as it eventually worked out, a very beautiful young woman named Ann Graham, who worked in the show at the Music Hall, did the vocals with the band. This personnel, however, began to change almost immediately, and was considerably different by the time the group left the Music Hall.

Through the spring Goodman waited nervously to hear from Rose, and finally, after the second audition, at which Helen Ward helped out, the band was hired. By this time Goodman had become convinced that he had to have his own band, and he was excited about getting the job. It was a fresh start after the unhappy years of his free-lancing.

The Billy Rose Music Hall was housed in the old Manhattan Theatre, the floor of which had been leveled to allow for tables and dancing. It was to be a supper club with a charge of two dollars and fifty cents for dinner and the show. According to Goodman, the show included a lot of out-of-work vaudeville acts that Rose could get cheaply—tumblers, fire-eaters, trained dogs and the like.[13] There were to be two bands, alternating, but at the first rehearsal it was decided that the other band, led by the songwriter Harold Arlen's brother Jerry, would play the show and Goodman would play for dancing. (One report says that the Goodman band had trouble playing the music for the show, but I find this difficult to believe.)

The band opened at the Music Hall on June 21 "with a fairly good crowd."[14] Rose, who knew the uses of publicity, had generated a lot of press for the club, and it proved to be successful. He was also able to arrange for a radio wire which broadcast the Goodman band at seven o'clock several evenings a week.

Nobody connected with this band has much good to say for it. Among other things, there was no budget for arrangements, which had to be paid for out of Goodman's own pocket. He said, "Our numbers, except for the few arrangements we could afford, were made up as we went along and consisted of improvised solos by various members, with the rhythm section behind the soloists."[15] (Actually it was probably not quite as bad as that; experienced musicians should be able to work out instantaneously chords and background riffs to play behind soloists, which they would usually rather do than sit all night holding their instruments, and these backgrounds, played night after night, often grow into fairly full "head" arrangements. It is my assumption that the band developed a number of such heads.) Rose had little interest in jazz, which forced the band into a more commercial vein than was perhaps necessary.

The band worked from seven in the evening until three in the morning, a very hard night, although in those days hours of this kind were more usual than they are today. Unfortunately, the radio program was played at the beginning of the evening, when the musicians were "cold" and often out of tune over the air.[16] The pay was bad, too, about fifty dollars a week[17]— according to Art Rollini, "the lowest salary I ever worked for."[18] (Rose was paying $850 for the band; the sidemen earned $600 of that, and Goodman was probably spending another hundred a week on arrangements. There would have been other expenses, of course. Goodman says he lost money most weeks, and survived on his savings, which is probably true.)[19]

But no matter how bad the conditions, and how undistinguished the music, Goodman, at twenty-three, was now a real bandleader working in an important New York club. He had been leading bands sporadically since the first recording dates under his own name in the late twenties, but now he was getting a full dose of it, night after night. It was an important experience. As should already be clear, he never did learn how to handle well the people who worked for him, always creating around himself a miasma of bad feelings. But he did become adept at picking numbers, mixing tempos and keys, and presenting the music as well as he could; he laid the base for that at the Music Hall.

Goodman was still involved with Columbia, and recorded for the label with the Music Hall band twice, once that summer and again in the fall. One of these pieces was a version of "The World Is Waiting for the Sunrise," called "Music Hall Rag" on the recording, a tune Goodman would play thousands of times in his career. Art Rollini said, "Every night he would play 'The World Is Waiting for the Sunrise,' and he played it brilliantly every time. On the Columbia recording he played poorly compared to the way he played on the job."[20]

Unfortunately for Goodman, some time probably in late August or September, Billy Rose went to Europe. The club's management changed, and the Goodman band was abruptly fired. According to Hammond the real story was that Rose had a quarrel with the mobsters who had backed him, lost the club, and decided to get out of New York until the matter cooled down.[21] It is a credible tale, but the truth will probably never be known. Whatever the case, Goodman was out of work again. But Hammond, energetic as ever, had come up with a new scheme. This was to take a racially mixed band of jazz stars abroad for a European tour, under the auspices of Jack Hylton, an English bandleader who also had his own booking organization, the theory being that a mixed band would be acceptable abroad. Goodman was to front the band, and the personnel would include trumpeters Doc Cheatham, Charlie Teagarden and Red Allen; trombonists Teagarden and J. C. Higginbotham; saxophonists Benny Carter and Chu Berry; and a rhythm section of Teddy Wilson, Hank Weyland, Gene Krupa and guitarist Lawrence Lucie. It would have been an extraordinary band, without question, but at the last minute the deal suddenly collapsed, to the considerable disappointment of Hammond and the musicians involved.[22]

What happened was this. Back in the early 1920s, when the new dance music of Hickman and Whiteman was aborning, there was a good deal of demand in Europe for American musicians who could play it. One American musician on his return from four and a half years abroad in 1923 said, "European musicians are absolutely unable to grasp the underlying principles of American dance music."[23] The consequence was that a great many Americans went to Europe, especially England, to work, and were followed over by touring bands: Whiteman and Specht in 1923, Vincent Lopez in 1925, and later on Gus Arnheim, Hal Kemp, Ben Pollack, Isham Jones, the California Ramblers, George Olsen, Abe Lyman, Fred Waring and others. British musicians, understandably, were angry, and the union leaned on the Ministry of Labor to bar American musicians. By 1924 American musicians were being ordered out of France,[24] and a little later the German musicians brought pressure to bear.[25] By 1925 American bands were virtually barred from England. Paul Specht, at the moment an important leader, had been booking bands in London. He announced that "London and other English cities were closed to engagements by American bands,"[26] and began fighting back. In 1927 an American musician named Al Payne was deported from England. Payne insisted that there were a thousand foreign musicians working in the United States, as opposed to fifty Americans playing in London.[27] At this point Congress threatened to take action; the American government intervened, and the British ban was loosened, at least somewhat. Over the next few years there was an intermittent and acrimonious debate between American and British sides, and the American union made efforts to ban British bands from the United States. The shoe was now on the other foot. In 1935 Jack Hylton said, "In the last seven or eight years the goose has allowed between forty and fifty complete American orchestras to play in England, but the gander has not yet allowed even one to play [in the United States]."[28] Al Payne responded that the English open door was in fact mostly closed. Whatever the truth, in 1935 the British Ministry of Labor barred American musicians from working in London completely, except as vaudeville acts working from a stage, rather than in hotels and ballrooms. The ban stayed in effect until well after World War II. Neither side behaved very well in the situation, but the Americans could justly say that the British had cast the first stone. In any case, in 1934 Jack Hylton must have realized that he would get himself in considerable trouble with English musicians if he sponsored an American band, and so he withdrew from the project under whatever pretext he could find.

Goodman had now lost two jobs, one before it had even started, and he was tempted to give up and either sign with Whiteman or see if he could resurrect his free-lance career. For the moment, however, he stuck it out, booking the band where he could around New York for occasional dance dates. And then came what everybody who has tried to succeed in the entertainment business prays for: "the big break."

Sometime previously, while Goodman was still at Rose's Music Hall, the National Biscuit Company, a huge concern which produced a wide variety of baked goods, decided to introduce a new party cracker called Ritz. The idea may have been worked out by the company's advertising agency, Mc-Cann-Erickson in conjunction with N.B.C. (the radio chain) chief John Royal.[29] N.B.C. was having trouble selling advertising for Saturday night, because advertisers were convinced that nobody was home then listening to their radios. Royal and the McCann-Erickson people cooked up the idea of a three-hour Saturday night "dance party" which might convince people to gather in living rooms, where they would presumably eat a lot of Ritz Crackers, instead of going to the movies. The show would be called *Let's Dance*, and use a "sweet" band, a hot band and a Latin band. A studio violinist named Murray Kellner, with whom Goodman had occasionally worked, was asked to pull together the sweet band. (Eventually his name for the show was changed to Kel Murray partly because his real name sounded Jewish, partly in hopes listeners would confuse it with Ken Murray, the name of an entertainer popular at the time.) The Latin spot was won by the Xavier Cugat band, and the show made Cugat the best known Latin bandleader of the swing era. That left the hot band.

Precisely what happened has been given differently by nearly everybody who was involved. However, the whole story has been carefully researched by James T. Maher, who used to listen to the show as a young man.[30] According to Maher, the key figure was Josef Bonime, McCann-Erickson's music director. Bonime had used Goodman frequently as a free lancer, and respected his musicianship. He was also aware that Goodman was leading a band at the Music Hall. "We were looking for a band with rhythmic bite," Bonime told Maher. He then went to Dorothy Barstow, who was head of radio for McCann-Erickson, and asked her to go to hear the band with him and his wife. He then warned Goodman that he was bringing Barstow in, as it happened, on the last night of the band's stay, October 17, 1934.

Goodman laid out a set of ten or twelve of their best numbers. When Bonime, his wife, and Dorothy Barstow walked in, he immediately called for this carefully selected set. When it was exhausted, the musicians downed instruments and walked off the stand, as if finished. Either Bonime understood what the game was, or the party took the bait, for they shortly left, and the musicians climbed back onto the bandstand and started to play their usual patched together pieces.

Meanwhile, out on the street, Bonime asked Barstow if he could bring the Goodman band in to audition. She replied simply, "Why not?" She said years later, "I was young, I was willing to take chances." The audition for the bands was held in a large room in the N.B.C. offices in Radio City. Bonime, Barstow and others involved in the decision listened to them, along with some young employees of the client and the network, who would represent the popular taste. The bands played in studios, and the music was piped into an audition room where the informal jury danced on a carpeted floor. The Goodman band won the hot band contest by one vote.

Much later John Hammond insisted that there was more to the story than that. He wrote, "How Benny got the job must remain a mystery, because of the libel laws."[31] The implication was that somebody had been paid off. Maher, who knew both Goodman and Hammond well, does not believe the story. The amount of money that might have been involved would not have been enough to tempt high-paid executives. Goodman, Kellner and others angrily denied the accusation to Maher.[32]

Goodman and the bandsmen were ecstatic. Goodman later said, "If anyone were to ask what was the biggest thing that has ever happened to me, landing a place on that show was it."[33] The opportunity to be heard nationwide on a major show over three hours could—with luck—give the band national celebrity at a stroke. Truthfully, in this century few unknown popular musical groups have been offered a similar opportunity. The show was scheduled to begin in early December, giving Goodman a month in which to prepare.

In everything that has been written about the *Let's Dance* show it has always been said that each of the three bands played for an hour, with the Goodman band coming on last to do the hot numbers when the older people had gone to bed and the younger folks were still up dancing. Maher's research, however, makes it clear that the show was divided into half-hour segments each of which included all three bands, except at moments when the Cugat band had to rush off to the Waldorf-Astoria twice each night to play half-hour sets, complicating the logistics considerably. They were complicated even more by the fact that in the spring when daylight saving time—not universal then—started, the bands had to stay in the studios for a total of five hours to match up with the patchwork of time zones across the country.

Besides the potential fame the show offered, there were exceedingly handsome salaries for those Depression days. Goodman was to get about $250, and the sidemen about $125 for the show and the rehearsals. More important, there was an allowance of $250 for arrangements.[34] A three-hour radio show required a lot of music, most of which had to be new each week. At about thirty-five to fifty dollars a piece, Goodman could now buy six or seven new arrangements a week. Not only would this improve the quality of the music going out over the air every Saturday night, but it would allow him to build up his still very slim book at no cost to himself.

The band began to rehearse and inevitably there were more personnel changes. Just then the Pollack band ended its run at the Casino de Paree and disbanded, and Harry Goodman, Gil Rodin and trumpeter Charlie Spivak, who would have a popular band during the swing era, joined Goodman. Spivak shortly had words with Goodman, and he and Rodin quit to join a new Pollack band. Ruby Weinstein was now playing first trumpet and Stan King was on drums. Most important, Helen Ward began to sing with the band regularly. She was just eighteen but had been working as a professional singer for two or three years.[35] Her father played the piano by ear, and she learned to play piano and to sing. As it happened, her mother played bridge with a woman who had a musical nephew named Burton Lane, who would write "Everything I Have Is Yours," "How About You?" and many other standards. The two young people were introduced and began working as a piano-vocal duet. Ward then got work singing with various bands, among them those of Nye Mayhew, Rubinoff and Enrique Madriguera. For a period she also appeared on a regular radio show sponsored by United Cigar. By the time of the *Let's Dance* show she was better known in popular music circles than Goodman was, and she was doing him a favor when she helped him at auditions. But Goodman now had a plum to offer, and she was glad to join the band. Among other things, it was not full time, and she could continue to work with Madriguera much of the time.

Helen Ward was very important to Goodman's first success. According to George Simon she had "a warm, sinuous jazz beat, and her body moved in a very sexy manner."[36] Goodman's core audience would be male college and high school students. Many of them developed crushes on Ward—she was, after all, their own age—and when she eventually left Goodman to marry there was a lot of wailing and gnashing of teeth on college campuses. She was not a great popular singer like, let us say, Ella Fitzgerald; her intonation failed her at times and her vibrato was broader than it needed to have been. But she had one of those natural voices that were just coming into popular music, and she sounded very fresh. In the 1920s there was a tendency to use more or less trained voices, especially somewhat fruity tenors. Bing Crosby, however, sounded like a nice young fellow singing with his pals over a beer, and he made himself a fortune. Similarly, Helen Ward sounded like the girl next door singing as she walked home from school. The manner of this new "unaffected" style was very direct and personal. It was as if each member of the audience was sitting in a darkened living room with the singer, and when Helen Ward sang "You're a Heavenly Thing," tens of thousands of college men believed her.

The *Let's Dance* show was broadcast from N.B.C.'s Studio 8H, the largest one it had, before a live audience. The idea was to make the broadcast as much like a hotel ballroom job as possible. The musicians dressed in tuxedos, and for Goodman's segment there were tap dancers, who "drove Benny crazy," because their time was poor. At moments Helen Ward got up and danced with the various "boy" singers who appeared on the show. There were rhumba dancers during Cugat's segments of the show. The studio seated about 1,500 people, who came and went, so that perhaps 3,000 saw portions of the show each Saturday night. Because the show ran on so late, a lot of musicians fell into the habit of dropping in after their own jobs were finished for the evening. Music business people were very much aware of the band, and curious to see if it would succeed. There was a certain heady sense that what Goodman was doing might prove important.

The *Let's Dance* show was a success, drawing a sufficiently large audience to satisfy the sponsors. The Goodman band, however, almost got fired quite early in the show's run. Harrison King McCann, head of the advertising agency, found the Goodman band too loud and jazzy and for the first three weeks complained to Joe Bonime about it. Bonime, however, was committed to Goodman, and he stuck with the band, fending McCann off by telling him he was too busy to find another band at the moment; eventually McCann accepted Goodman.

Almost from the beginning of *Let's Dance* Goodman evidenced a characteristic that would be with him through his career. That was a restless, almost compulsive, hiring and firing of musicians. Fairly quickly he replaced Stan King with Gene Krupa. King was, during the late 1920s and early thirties, one of the busiest studio drummers in New York. He was hired at one time or another by many of the best-known leaders of the day, among them Jean Goldkette, Paul Whiteman, Red Nichols, Roger Wolfe Kahn, the Dorsey Brothers, and later on, Jack Teagarden. King was a solid drummer when it came to keeping time, which Krupa was not, but it is clear from the recordings that he failed to swing. He divided the beat relatively evenly, and played with very little accent. He used the brushes a lot, with which he produced a flat "pat" rather than a sharp sting. The result was that he seemed to be simply tapping out the beat, instead of driving the band. Leaders used him endlessly on hundreds of hastily thrown together records, where reliability counted the most; but when they wanted a band to swing they turned to a drummer like Krupa, who played with more fire. King was understandably bitter about finding himself in rehearsal bands and then being left behind when they became successful. But that was a choice leaders were making.

Also fairly early in the show's run Goodman let Ben Kanter go and brought in Toots Mondello. Mondello was considered the finest lead alto[37] in the music business, a reputation he would have for many years as he trundled in and out of the band. Goodman also replaced Ruby Weinstein with Bunny Berigan, who was developing into one of the finest trumpet players in jazz.

George Van Eps also left, but this was his own decision. He knew that the band would eventually go on the road, which he did not want to do, and he began grooming a student of his named Allan Reuss, who was driving a laundry truck, to take the job. Reuss soon began playing whatever club dates the band picked up, and finally replaced Van Eps on the radio show near the very end. As a student of Van Eps, Reuss descended from a princely line of guitarists and was schooled in a tradition of hard swinging. He went on to be, in my view, one of the finest of the big band guitarists, who can be ranked with such great rhythm players of the period as Basie's Freddie Green, Waller's Al Casey, and his contemporaries Dick McDonough and Carl Kress. Moreover, Reuss, who was getting formal training under Van Eps, was harmonically more sophisticated than some of the self-taught guitarists in jazz. As will become clear, I feel that Krupa tended to have a heavy beat, and was, furthermore, no believer in metronomically exact time. Harry Goodman, too, was never considered a master bass player, and it is my opinion that Reuss was crucial in giving the Goodman band its romping swing. James T. Maher once said something to Goodman to the effect that he had not realized how important Reuss had been until he was gone. Goodman's response was, "Neither did we."[38]

This steady changing of personnel, then, was not always Goodman's doing. Musicians came and went for a variety of reasons. But Goodman was always reshuffling the deck, and as a consequence it is difficult to be certain about exactly who was in the band at many moments during the run of

*Let's Dance.* At one time or another the trumpets included Berigan, Jerry Neary, Sammy Shapiro, Ralph Muzzillo, Nate Kazebier and Pee Wee Erwin. On at least one, and probably more, occasions, Mannie Klein, who was in the Kel Murray band, hastily replaced Berigan during the course of the show when Berigan passed out from drink.[39]

As important as people like Reuss, Berigan and other musicians were to Goodman's early success, it is clear that a critical role was played by the arrangers. Unlike bandleaders such as Duke Ellington and Glenn Miller, Benny Goodman did not have much grounding in theory, and could not really arrange for his own band. He counted on buying arrangements from other people. But he had a good sense about what he wanted, and which arrangers could give it to him. In these early days, when he was building the band, he used a good many arrangers including Fud Livingston, Dean Kincaide, Jimmy Mundy, Fletcher Henderson and his brother Horace, Jiggs Noble, Edgar Sampson, Joe Lippman, Artie Schutt, Benny Carter, Spud Murphy and a few others.[40] However, most of these people contributed only one or two arrangements, although some of them, like Edgar Sampson and Jimmy Mundy, would go on to be important to Goodman later on.

In the 1934–35 period when Goodman was finding a style for the band, and it had its first fame, the bulk of the arrangements were written by Fletcher Henderson and Spud Murphy. In everything that has been written about the Goodman band, Henderson has been presented as the key figure, who single-handedly shaped the band's style. This, once again, was a view Hammond propagandized for later on. But the matter is not that simple. For one thing, the band's first hit record, a coupling of "Hunkadola" and "The Dixieland Band" for Victor, was written by Dean Kincaide. For another, some of Goodman's most memorable pieces from the time were written by others: "Always" and "Dear Old Southland" by Horace Henderson, his opening theme "Let's Dance" by George Bassman and his closing theme "Good-bye" by Gordon Jenkins, "Madhouse" by Jimmy Mundy, and "Stompin' at the Savoy," which was in the band's book at this time but not recorded until later, by Edgar Sampson.

Most significant, Spud Murphy wrote at least fifty arrangements for *Let's Dance,* and taken together, probably wrote at least a third of the band's arrangements for this critical period. Many of these were the pedestrian dance tunes with vocals that the band had to have, such as the forgotten "I Was Lucky" and "If the Moon Turns Green." But he also wrote some wonderful swing arrangements, like "Get Happy," "Restless," "Limehouse Blues," "Darktown Strutters' Ball" and a brilliant version of "Anything Goes," with a chorus for trumpets composed in the manner of a Bunny Berigan solo. I will discuss these records in detail somewhat later.

For the moment it is only important to realize that Murphy was as significant as Fletcher Henderson in establishing the Goodman band.

Lyle "Spud" Murphy had an interesting background. According to Pee
Wee Erwin, he had been shipped over to the United States by his aristo-
cratic family at the time of World War I, when he would have been about
six, to be raised by a Mormon family, where he also acquired the name he
was known by.[41] He became a tenor saxophone player, but had a fine ear,
and as a teenager was taking arrangements off records.[42] By the early 1930s
he was in demand as an arranger in New York, and eventually became one
of the busiest arrangers of the swing era, writing over a hundred charts for
Casa Loma, in addition to the ones he did for Goodman and others. Erwin
said, "Fletcher Henderson's arrangements were becoming the identifying
trademark of Benny's band, but Spud's were the backbone."[43]

But the role of Fletcher Henderson in helping to form the Goodman
style should not be minimized. Henderson wrote some of Goodman's most
important pieces, among them "King Porter Stomp," "Sometimes I'm
Happy," "Down South Camp Meeting" and "Wrappin' It Up," and he
went on writing for Goodman off and on for years. His classic arrangements
are almost as essential a part of the Goodman sound as Goodman's clarinet.

Fletcher Henderson was an unassertive man who drifted into a major role
in American popular music almost by mistake.[44] He was born to a middle-
class family in Georgia, studied classical piano as a youth, and went on to
college where he majored in chemistry. He came to New York in 1920,
ostensibly to find work as a chemist. This, however, was next to impossible
for a black man in that day, although probably had Henderson been a more
forceful man he might have found an opening he would have squeezed
through somehow. Instead he drifted into the music business, began leading bands and by the late 1920s had one of the leading American dance
bands. Initially, out of a strange lassitude often remarked on by his sidemen, he left the musical direction of the band to others, principally Don
Redman. But after Redman left he was more and more forced to write for
his own band. He turned out to have a gift for writing swing band arrangements. According to Dicky Wells, who played trombone with the band in
the 1930s, "Fletcher had a way of writing so that the notes just seemed to
float along casually. He didn't write too high—there wasn't any screaming—but his music used to make you feel bright inside."[45]

In particular, Henderson's arrangements were very spare, with a good
deal of open space, and two or three notes where another arranger might
write seven or eight. And it is my suspicion that the very laid-back quality
which hampered Henderson's career as a bandleader was the key to his
success as an arranger. The writing of a busy arrangement at a fast tempo
might involve the setting down of 5,000 notes, a time-consuming chore

which for the most part is not a "creative" experience, but simple drudgery. Drudgery was not Henderson's favorite mode; instead of writing a complex counter melody, Henderson might back the saxophones with muted brass that licked at the beat here and there, just enough to propel the saxes forward. The trick, of course, was in knowing where to put the notes. This turned out to be something that Henderson had an instinct for.

In 1934 Fletcher Henderson was having hard times with his orchestra, which in time actually fell apart. John Hammond was of course close to Henderson and knew he needed money. He suggested to Goodman that he buy some arrangements from Henderson.[46] Goodman respected the Henderson band, which had been famous for almost ten years, and was happy to find a source of ready-made arrangements. Henderson not only began writing new pieces for Goodman but sold him some of his band's own arrangements, including "Down South Camp Meeting" and "Wrappin' It Up."

Goodman discovered Jimmy Mundy and Edgar Sampson apparently through Red Norvo and his wife Mildred Bailey. The Norvos lived out in Jackson Heights near the Goodman apartment, and Benny had fallen into the habit of dropping in on them to listen to records, jam and eat—Mildred loved to cook. In turn, the Norvos started coming around to hear the *Let's Dance* show, and it was apparently Mildred who urged Benny to find more interesting arrangements than some of the straightforward commercial ones he was using, and suggested that he listen to people like Sampson, who was writing for Chick Webb, and Mundy, who was writing for Earl Hines.[47] These men would over the years contribute important pieces to the Goodman book: Mundy brought in the nucleus around which "Sing, Sing, Sing" developed, and Sampson wrote "Don't Be That Way" and "Stompin' at the Savoy." But Goodman's initial success was built primarily on the writing of Fletcher Henderson and Spud Murphy. Both men were utilizing the devices which had become standard in dance bands: playing off sections against each other, mixing in solos and generally moving the music around the band. They are distinguished primarily because Murphy wrote arrangements that were busier than the usual spare Henderson pieces. Henderson also tended more to use one section to answer, or punctuate, the line of another, and wrote fewer actual contrapuntal lines than Murphy did. In general Murphy was writing a little more "symphonically" than Henderson was, probably under the influence of Ferde Grofé and Bill Challis. But too much should not be made of these differences, for many of their arrangements could have come from the pen of either one.

Over the course of *Let's Dance* Goodman was steadily improving the band—bringing in better musicians, finding excellent arrangers, rehearsing regularly. What sort of impact the band was having across the country nobody was sure of. But it was beginning to get ecstatic reviews in the jazz press. *Down Beat* said:

> Benny's performance is magnificent, the band is the smoothest and fastest thing heard yet and the soloists are not to be improved upon.[48]

*Metronome*, not yet really the jazz periodical it would become, but still covering commercial music said:

> Benny Goodman and his *Let's Dance* band are a great medicine . . . a truly great outfit—fine arrangers, and musicians who are together all the time—they phrase together, they bite together, they swing together.[49]

During the course of the *Let's Dance* show the orchestra recorded twice for Columbia, in January and February 1935. Among the records it made was "The Dixieland Band," arranged by Deane Kincaide and sung by Helen Ward. The record began to sell fairly briskly, especially on the West Coast, where it was apparently being played on the air by some disc jockeys. But it was clear that if the band's potential was to be realized, it had to have good management. Goodman went to Music Corporation of America, the famous M.C.A. that played so large a role in American popular music; but M.C.A. was interested in commercial music and decided against taking Goodman on.

Then Goodman got a lucky break. Sometime probably in February or March, M.C.A. hired a young violin player from Philadelphia named Willard Alexander to help book bands. Alexander had had his own band at the University of Pennsylvania and had had some experience as a booker. He was a man with a genuine interest in hot music, and as a young musician himself, was sympathetic to the other young musicians around him. He said, "When Casa Loma started making it, M.C.A. decided it ought to have a band like that too. I'd heard Benny on records and so I sent for him and we signed him even though I never felt that Jules [Stein, head of M.C.A.] and Bill [Goodheart of the New York office] really wanted him."[50]

Alexander, in a sense, had gone out on a limb, and his determination to make the Goodman band succeed was critically important. The world of commercial music in the United States has always had a taint of the underworld, in part at least because music usually came along with wine and song in the questionable dance halls and cabarets where musicians were often forced to work. Much of the time musicians took it for granted that they would be cheated by dance hall and cabaret managers, would be expected to pay bribes and kick-backs, would be ordered around like busboys. A leader absolutely had to have the backing of strong management which could shoehorn him into good locations and see that he got paid. Even a hood running a jitney dance hall had to be careful in his dealings with important agencies who could shut him off from the talent he needed to run his business if they did not like the way he conducted himself. In Alexander and M.C.A. Goodman now had the necessary strong management.

Alexander's first move was to sign Goodman with Victor. Eli Oberstein was attempting to rebuild the company after the disastrous years of the early Depression, and was looking for good bands. Casa Loma and the Dorsey Brothers band (which ultimately became the Jimmy Dorsey band) had recently signed with the brand new Decca company, an aggressive label pricing records at thirty-five cents against the standard seventy-five cents. Decca was making money with these bands appealing to youth, and Victor wanted to get into the business. Goodman was really the closest thing around. Victor immediately rerecorded the band's only hit, "The Dixieland Band," backed by another Kincaide score, "Hunkadola." A second session produced Murphy's "Restless," Horace Henderson's "Always" and Fletcher's "You're a Heavenly Thing," a bright, bouncy pop tune sung by Helen Ward. The third Victor session included Horace's "Dear Old Southland" and Fletcher's "Blue Skies." Most of these arrangements, cut at the very beginning of Goodman's association with Victor, became standards for him, things that he would play not merely for years but for decades. Either through luck or intuition Goodman had got the band off to an excellent start.

The band was playing whatever club dates and one-nighters Alexander could arrange. Among these were a series of dates opposite Chick Webb at the Savoy Ballroom—"battles of the bands" were common during the period. This was the situation in May 1935, when the National Biscuit Company was struck by its employees.[51] The company saw no point in advertising goods they could not produce and closed down the *Let's Dance* show after the twenty-sixth broadcast on May 25. This was a serious blow to Goodman, who had little other work for the band, and would not be able to keep it together if he could not pay the musicians.

Creating a swing band of some fifteen people is not just a matter of gathering musicians and handing out the scores. To make this kind of coordinated music it is necessary to rehearse each piece carefully and play it for a period of time in order to establish nuances of phrasing, dynamics, tone color and the like. Everywhere in big band jazz playing are little devices, many of which are not written, or even not possible to write, like brief fall-offs, half-valvings, momentary pitch sags, variations in attack and much more, which can only be coordinated over time. In swing these little details are often critical, for it is they, more than the broad outlines of the melody, that produce the heat, the pulse, the fire in the music. The details can be attended to only when the arrangement is so well understood that it is practically memorized. Only then can the musicians play with the confidence and verve that brings the music to life.

Furthermore, the people in such a band come to know each other's strengths and weaknesses, so they can lean on this person at one moment, compensate for his deficiencies at another. This is especially true for a leader, who cannot treat his men as automatons, parts in a machine, but must play to their strengths. Over the months of the Music Hall and the *Let's Dance* show, Goodman had created an orchestra, despite the changes in personnel, which had developed a book of about 150 numbers it could take out any time and play with accuracy and zest. Dispersing this carefully drilled team would have been disastrous, and might well have discouraged Goodman from trying again for some time.

Willard Alexander, now desperate, booked the band into the Hotel Roosevelt. The location had been the home of Guy Lombardo, playing soft and syrupy music. The Goodman band had been created to play hot music, or at least a swinging version of dance music. The band was not trained to play the kind of music the Roosevelt wanted, and Goodman, moreover, admits that he got a little stubborn about bending to the requirements of the job. The first night waiters went around holding their ears and the band was given its two-week notice immediately.[52]

The band should not have been booked into the Roosevelt, as Alexander was willing to admit. But as he said later, at the time he had nothing else for the group, and he would have booked the band "into the Holland Tunnel if there'd been a date."[53]

This chain of events was discouraging, to say the least. The radio program, which had seemed so promising at the outset, had apparently done little or nothing for the band's reputation, and the failure at the Roosevelt would not encourage other New York hotels to hire the group. But there was one hopeful sign: the records were selling well enough to encourage Victor to keep recording them. On July 1 the band cut two more of its enduring classics, "Sometimes I'm Happy" and "King Porter Stomp," both arranged by Fletcher Henderson. Furthermore, Alexander remained determined to make the band succeed. He knew from his own experience that there was a potential audience for the band on college campuses at the least; it was a question of awakening them to the band. He would not give up.

Just about the moment when *Let's Dance* was ending, there occurred a now-legendary party at the home of Mildred and Red Norvo that had a substantial effect on Goodman's career, and in fact, the course of jazz. Among the guests at the party in question were Goodman, Hammond,

Teddy Wilson, and Mildred's cousin Carl Bellinger, an amateur drummer. Goodman and Wilson began to jam, and Bellinger joined them, playing with whisk brooms on a suitcase, a common substitute for drums in those days. The music electrified the other guests, and inevitably people began saying that the group ought to be recorded.[54] Who actually decided to make the first Trio records is difficult to know. Hammond in his autobiography lists himself as producer of these as well as other of the early Victor sessions, and it certainly would have been to his taste to record such a group. But it is not really clear who was responsible for getting the records made. However, Hammond had signed Wilson to a Brunswick contract, in order to make under his leadership a series of all-star records which would eventually be seen as jazz classics. He arranged a swap: Wilson would be allowed to record with Goodman on Victor if Goodman would appear on an equal number of Wilson's Brunswick sides.[55] The Wilson sides were cut on July 2, 1935; they featured Billie Holiday and included two of her most memorable numbers, "What a Little Moonlight Can Do" and "Miss Brown to You," both classics of jazz.

The chance to play with the Trio was a substantial blessing for Teddy Wilson, and would in a few years make him the most famous piano player in jazz. Goodman had another view of the swap, however. He was a bandleader, and he did not fancy the idea of working as a sideman for somebody else for an insignificant amount of money. He slipped out before the last side, "Sunbonnet Sue," was cut. Wilson and Hammond were not pleased, but Wilson could not afford to balk at the chance to record with Goodman. At the first Trio session the tunes were "After You've Gone," "Body and Soul," "Who?" and "Someday Sweetheart," all safe standards with proven longevity.

The idea of a trio of this type was hardly new. The so-called "stink" bands in the New Orleans honky-tonks were usually one to four pieces in size, and frequently employed one horn in front of a rhythm section. The New Orleans clarinetist Johnny Dodds recorded in duets and trios in Chicago in the 1920s. Goodman himself had made the trio record of "Clarinetitis" and "That's A Plenty." In fact there is a report that Goodman had played with a trio on Let's Dance.[56] But none of these groups had the impact of the Goodman Trios and succeeding Quartets, Quintets and the rest. Over the next few years these small groups would become increasingly important to the success of the Goodman band, selling as many as 50,000 copies each.[57] As the swing movement boomed, other leaders offered small groups in imitation of Goodman's, not only recording with them but bringing them down front once or twice an evening to play jazz specialties: Woody Herman's Woodchoppers, Tommy Dorsey's Clambake Seven, Bob Crosby's Bobcats and others. As a further consequence, the success of these groups suggested to record company executives that there was an audience out there somewhere for unadulterated jazz, and this led the major record companies, timidly at first, to begin offering small doses of hot jazz to the public.

Perhaps more important, it encouraged a handful of jazz lovers to start their own tiny record companies devoted solely to jazz, beginning with Milt Gabler's Commodore Records in 1938. Through the 1930s and 1940s these small record companies sprung up in increasing numbers, and it is they, more than the majors, who recorded the great body of classic small group jazz from the period—scores of cuts featuring Lester Young, Coleman Hawkins, Roy Eldridge, Charlie Parker and many more. Certainly part of Goodman's significance to the history of jazz was his proving to the intensely commercial music industry that jazz continued to have a wide audience in the United States.

# 11
# The First Victor Records

Between the moment Benny Goodman formed his band for the Music Hall and the end of the long trip across the country to California, the band made sixteen sides for Columbia, sixteen and four Trio cuts for Victor, and a series of fifty-one cuts of transcriptions meant for radio broadcast which were issued as The Rhythmakers, or Rhythm Makers Orchestra. (There were also two cuts with an abbreviated band issued as Harry Rosenthal and His Orchestra.) In addition, in recent years airchecks of some of the *Let's Dance* shows have been issued on LP. In general, the band depended far more on the arrangements than it did on hot soloing for its effect. This was broadly true of the bands Goodman was competing with, the Casa Loma and Dorsey Brothers orchestras, important foundation stones on which the swing movement was built. In general, these groups saw the band, not the hot soloists, as the main point, and they took great pains to play the arrangements with precision and panache.

Goodman, in particular, wanted good jazz players for his leads—that is to say, first trumpet, first trombone and first alto—so that they could swing the sections. Jimmy Maxwell, who played lead trumpet for Goodman later, pointed out that the Henderson and Ellington bands of the period often used rather stiff first trumpets—Russell Smith and Arthur Whetsol respectively—and the sections at times suffered accordingly.[1]

Virtually all the solos in the Goodman band from the period under discussion were played by Art Rollini, Jack Lacey, Bunny Berigan, when he was present, and of course Goodman. Solos comprise, as a rule, no more than a quarter of each cut, although there are exceptions, particularly in the arrangements written by Fletcher Henderson. Goodman takes more solo time than the others, but not by much; on some of these recordings he gives Berigan long solos and takes little or none himself. Goodman has always been accused of hogging the solos, and it is true that as time went on the sound of his clarinet tended to dominate the music. But he could be very generous with solos when he had somebody in the band he particularly admired: Teagarden, Berigan, Harry James, Vido Musso, and in the small groups Teddy Wilson, Charlie Christian and Cootie Williams.

In this early Victor band only Berigan, besides Goodman himself, was a master jazz improviser. Art Rollini has never been considered an important jazz musician, although he was certainly competent. But Goodman liked him and kept him in the band for five years, making him one of the longest serving musicians Goodman ever had. At the time tenor saxophone players were almost universally under the influence of Coleman Hawkins, who played with a forceful driving style clothed in a big, somewhat hoarse sound. Goodman's later tenor stars, Vido Musso and Georgie Auld, were in this mold. Rollini, however, was one of the few well-known tenor saxophonists of the time to use a smooth, light sound with an easy, almost effortlessly flowing line. This approach followed an older tradition of dance-band saxophone dating back to Wiedoeft, Doerr, Ralton and its principle exponent when Art Rollini was young, Frankie Trumbauer. It was akin to the approach taken by Lester Young, and it is worth noting that Goodman became a great admirer of Young. Despite the fact that Goodman generally wanted forceful players in his band, his own saxophone playing was always mellifluous, and it is not surprising that all three of these men—Goodman, Young and Rollini—were impressed by Trumbauer. And this explains why Goodman kept Rollini for so long: he liked Rollini's sound. Rollini was in no way the jazz musician that Young was, and his tone cannot be confused with Young's; but his light, easy attitude suited Goodman, and he should not be, as he has been, entirely dismissed as a jazz musician.

Jack Lacey is even less well regarded than Rollini. However, he was at the time considered one of the finest studio trombonists in the business, a man who could read anything, who had a wonderful, smooth, bright sound, an impressive high register, and an ability to move effortlessly from note to note that only the greatest technicians of the time, like Dorsey and Jack Jenney, could equal. He plays straight solos on "Blue Moon," "Cokey" and a version of "Star Dust" done for *Let's Dance* (quite different from the one later recorded for Victor) which displays his flawless playing. It is my view that Lacey was possibly the finest of all trombonists of the period at exposing an unadorned melody. His tone is pure and clean, but a little richer than Dorsey's, and his playing is technically virtually perfect.

In his jazz playing Lacey used the legato approach coming into fashion in the late 1920s in response to the heavy-handed playing of the dixielanders, and the staccato playing of Miff Mole, which all the white musicians emulated in the 1920s. Jack Teagarden was the principal model for this legato style and his influence is recognizable in Lacey's playing. He tends to use a lot of quarter and even half notes, instead of depending on eighth notes as most jazz musicians do, although he was certainly capable of playing the faster runs. His best-known solo with Goodman is on "Always." Teagarden was sitting next to him in the band at the time, having been brought in for this recording session only, and that may have been why he played a more vigorous solo than he usually does. Teagarden used a slurring style in which the notes were largely "half-tongued"—that is to say, not completely separated from each other, but given a soft accent rather than a clean break. Lacey carried this procedure further, so that there is no break at all in his sound for long stretches, as for example across bars three, four and five on "Always." His debt to Teagarden is also evident in figures he uses in measures three and across measures fourteen and fifteen, where he employs brief phrases that are virtually hallmarks of Teagarden's playing. Lacey lacked the enormous swing that is everywhere in Teagarden's work, and the abundant confidence that Teagarden had, but he was technically Teagarden's equal, and he was as good as anyone in the business at simply exposing a melody. Lacey is one of those players more admired by other musicians than by the fans, and he was able to pick and choose his work, even at the bottom of the Depression.

But whatever the virtues of the soloists, for the Goodman band what really counted was the precise, deft playing of bright, sparkling arrangements. These qualities are evident in the Goodman band right from the beginning. In "Crazy Rhythm," available only as an aircheck from *Let's Dance*, there is constant movement between saxophones, brass and occasional brief solos, with rarely eight bars, and usually not more than four, passing without a change in texture, density or approach. Countervoices are common. A brief figure by unison saxes behind the vocal is used again in the next chorus as an answering voice. In the first bridge in "Anything Goes," available as an aircheck, and the reissues of the Rhythmakers transcriptions, the saxophones behind the lead in the trombone play a figure which has an entirely different rhythmic feel from the rest of the piece, suggesting 2/4 against the 4/4 in the melody line. Particularly felicitous in this piece is the chorus following the vocal, which is worked out to capture the feel of an improvised jazz chorus. This, in fact, came to be a convention of swing music, so that the chorus after the vocal was frequently referred to as the "arranger's" chorus. In this case, arranger Spud Murphy has scored the chorus to resemble a Bunny Berigan solo. There was a precedent for this: Bill Challis, with Goldkette and later with Paul Whiteman, sometimes wrote music for the trumpet section in the manner of a Beiderbecke solo. In this "Anything Goes" chorus we can hear very typical Berigan figures in measures two and three, five and six, and eleven and twelve, with other bits and pieces sticking out here and there. It is a very fine example of this kind of thing. Ward sings the tune with warmth, and it is surprising that Goodman never saw fit to record it.

Nonetheless, despite the felicities in pieces like "Anything Goes" and "Crazy Rhythm," this early band was still trying to find its way. Between August 1934 and February 1935, it cut sixteen sides for Columbia. There was another title, "Stars," which was recorded under Goodman's name with a pick-up group which was never issued. Six of the Columbia pieces are very ordinary arrangements of pop songs that could have been produced by any number of competent dance orchestras. The two arranged by Benny Carter, who would go on to have a distinguished career as an arranger, lack the polish of his later work. None of these arrangements has much of the interplay of sections that would be the key to the Victor records to come shortly. There are fewer solos than there would be, in part because his early band did not have the collection of first-rate soloists that would come. Even Goodman takes less solo space than he would.

A forgotten soloist worth giving his due is the trumpeter who plays the famous King Oliver "Dippermouth Blues" chorus on "Nitwit Serenade," and perhaps other solos on "Down Home Rag" and "Bugle Call Rag." He is under the influence of Berigan, and possibly Armstrong either directly or through Berigan. I have not been able to find any definite identification for him, but suspect that he might be Jerry Neary, who according to reports was a good jazz player. Another obscure sideman from the period was vocalist Ann Graham, who sang regularly with the band at the Music Hall but made only one record, "It Happens to the Best of Friends." She has been, I think, too much maligned. On the basis of this single vocal chorus it is clear that she is not in a class with Helen Ward, but she is not any worse than a lot of singers who came and went throughout the swing era.

In general, these Columbia recordings are not typical of what we would think of as the Goodman style. "Nitwit Serenade," written by Will Hudson, is a reworking of the much better-known "White Heat" which Hudson had written for Jimmie Lunceford a few months before. The piece is built around the interplay of brass and reeds which would be basic to the Goodman style, and to swing in general, but the phrases are much briefer and simpler than would be customary. In the Victor classics of the period, like "You Can't Pull the Wool Over My Eyes," the interplay tends to be contrapuntal, and consists of sequences of somewhat different figures. That is to say, the trumpets play figures A, B, C, and are answered by reed figures X, Y, Z. In Hudson's "Nitwit Serenade" the brass and reed riffs are simply repeated to give us A, X, A, X, and so forth.

Another atypical hot piece is "Cokey," a strange novelty arrangement which is quite imaginative but certainly not the sort of thing anyone would associate with the famous Goodman band to come. It is notable for fairly extensive soloing by Ballard on a snatch of pretty melody and a short clarinet passage which I suspect is not played by Goodman, as unlikely as that may be. (However, Goodman does play a typical solo earlier in the record.)

Yet another oddity from the Columbia dates is "Down Home Rag," which utilizes a clarinet choir in places but is arranged so that, especially in the opening chorus, it sounds like the James Reese Europe ragtime version made in 1913, which was even then an ancient piece of music. It is difficult to understand why Goodman would have recorded something so dated.

Of these sixteen Columbias only three really suggest the band to come. One of these is "Music Hall Rag," really a disguised version of "The World Is Waiting for the Sunrise," which Goodman was playing virtually every night at the Music Hall as a showcase for his high-speed clarinet playing. The arrangement is minimal, probably a head. It is taken at above 350 beats a minute, a terrifying pace. The other soloists, even pianist Frankie Froeba, play it at half-time. Goodman, however, flies through it with aplomb, and it was exhibitions like this that left other musicians sitting in the dust with their mouths open. Goodman would go on using the tune as a showcase for the rest of his life, usually playing it at tempos that would extend even excellent pianists.

A second one is the first version of "Bugle Call Rag." It is essentially the same arrangement that became famous later on, except that there is an opening chorus based on the original tune, which is omitted in the later version. There are good solos by Lacey and the trumpeter I believe to be Jerry Neary, and the whole thing is played by the band with the kind of drive that Goodman wanted, and usually got, from his men.

Finally there is "Night Wind," a bluesy popular song with a rather dramatic key change at the bridge, sung by Helen Ward. It is taken at a moderately quick tempo, and is written with more imagination and a better jazz feel than most of the other pops Goodman was recording at this time. It opens with one of the rare alto solos in the whole Goodman canon, followed by a passage for unison trombones supported by reeds, and there are other nice bits of writing. This recording of "Night Wind" prefigures the swinging treatment of pop songs that would be so important to the success of the Goodman Orchestra.

But surprisingly, the biggest hit that Goodman had from the Columbia sides was none of these but another atypical one, "The Dixieland Band," a rather mindless Bernard Hanigen–Johnny Mercer novelty about a band which cannot swing until it dies, goes to Heaven and has Gabriel take over the trumpet part. A good deal of it has the "dixieland" quality that would prove very successful for the Bob Crosby Orchestra in a few years. Only in the chorus after the vocal is there something of the later Goodman style, with riffs and interplay of brass and reeds.

It must be borne in mind that the first eight of these Columbia cuts were made before *Let's Dance*, with its budget for arrangements. At the Music Hall Goodman was scrambling for whatever scores he could get and was in no position to give anybody instructions. He was still feeling his way toward what he wanted his band to be like. Like a lot of people, Goodman apparently was not always clear about what he wanted until he heard it. Some bandleaders, for example, would hire inexperienced people, and work with them until they had made them the kind of players they wanted: Duke Ellington and Artie Shaw operated this way. Goodman, however, would rather replace the person than explain to him what he wanted and keep after him until he got it. Sid Weiss, who worked for both Goodman and Shaw, said, "Artie would hire talented musicians who were kind of rough, and he would train them. Where Benny, he'd hire Cootie Williams, Jimmy Maxwell, top of the line, Ziggy, Harry James, Toots Mondello, Hymie Schertzer, some really heavyweight guys. They could all sit down and play the book as if they'd rehearsed it for a year. But that was the difference between Artie and Benny."[2]

It was certainly true that Goodman always tried to hire the best players, not merely the great soloists like Berigan and Wilson, but the finest lead men as well, like Mondello and Lacey. Later on he would employ a host of major jazz musicians, among them Zoot Sims, Stan Getz, Wardell Gray, Sid Catlett, Cootie Williams, Lou McGarity, Red Norvo, Charlie Shavers, George Duvivier, Charlie Christian and many others. It is probably true that Benny Goodman at one time or another over a fifty-year career as a bandleader hired more great jazz musicians than anyone else, even including Ellington and Basie.

Benny's philosophy, thus, was not to form his musicians but to get them ready-made. And when he did give instruction it was frequently more baffling than useful. He once complained to Peggy Lee about her "phrasing." Peggy could not figure out what he meant and, disturbed, asked Harry James about it. James advised her to tell Benny she understood and would follow his instructions, and then to sing as she always did. She did as James suggested, and Goodman seemed satisfied.[3]

Goodman appears to have dealt with his arrangers in the same way. He did not give them much instruction; but if he was not satisfied with the arrangement he would either amend it, or simply not use it very often, if at all. Using this trial and error method it would inevitably take Goodman time to work his way to the style he wanted the band to have. But this does not really explain why he recorded "Sing a Happy Song" or "Down

Home Rag," when he had "Crazy Rhythm" and "Anything Goes" in the book. The answer undoubtedly lies in the fact that Columbia felt safer recording the pop tunes rather than the hot numbers.

During the time that Goodman was at the Music Hall, and even later, he continued to free-lance when and where he could, simply because he needed the money. He played at least one weekly radio show, using a borrowed tenor, and he recorded for other leaders from time to time. One of the most interesting sessions that Goodman made during this period was under the leadership of Reginald Foresythe, a pianist and composer from the West Indies, who was perhaps better known in London musical circles than he was in the United States. Foresythe was trying to write music that drew elements from both jazz and classical music. As such he was part of a long tradition in jazz, which dated back to the efforts by Paul Whiteman to create "symphonic jazz," and would continue through the work of Claude Thornhill, Boyd Raeburn, Stan Kenton and even Goodman himself with pieces like "Bach Goes to Town." Indeed, the first piano solo in Foresythe's "Lullaby" anticipates Thornhill's "Snowfall."

Foresythe was known to the New York jazz musicians, who admired him because he was better schooled in music than most of them were. In January 1935, he made a set of four of his compositions for Columbia, using a nine-piece band built around a nucleus drawn from Goodman's Let's Dance orchestra, with the composer at the piano. As in many similar works, the influence of Igor Stravinsky is evident; the harmonies are more dissonant than was customary in dance bands of the period, and perhaps 75 percent of the music is not jazz—that is, was not meant to swing. From moment to moment, however, the swing suddenly breaks out. It seems to me that in these small, confined and wholly unpretentious pieces Foresythe makes a better marriage of jazz and classical music than happened in other more imposing efforts. They are small, at times delicate and charming. Of them all I think the most successful is "The Greener the Grass," which is built around a very pretty melody stated first by a clarinet duet. (Johnny Mince, later a highly regarded big band soloist, is the other clarinetist.) Here and there are spots of jazz, and the piece ends on an abrupt modulation to the final chord, perhaps meant to suggest that the grass on the other side may prove to be a surprise. According to Russ Connor, Gene Krupa, who was on the date, remembered it "with great clarity and relish. Krupa recalled that he, Benny and the other musicians on the date had always admired 'Reggie' Foresythe, and given a chance to do some of his things on record, they all leapt at it."[4] These pieces deserve to be heard more often than they have been.

There were, in this period, a few other sessions, some of them fairly commercial. One of the most interesting was a set under Jack Teagarden's name. By the early 1930s Teagarden had established himself as having commercial potential with his lazy, untutored singing. It is surprising, in view of the fact that Goodman had worked closely with him in the Pollack band and had made him first choice for his own dates, that Teagarden used Goodman only on two of a half-dozen sessions when Goodman might have been available. On some of these cuts Goodman again demonstrates his abilities as an accompanist to a vocalist, something Teagarden seems to have recognized himself, for on several of his vocals Benny does the backing. On "Your Guess Is Just as Good as Mine," Goodman inserts his notes into Teagarden's line with delicacy and restraint, playing enough to keep the music moving, but never interfering. A casual listener might not even remember that Goodman had played; his absence would have been more noticeable than his presence.

There was also one more session with Adrian Rollini. Goodman has several solos. Particularly interesting is his sixteen bars on "Davenport Blues." In the fourth bar there is a long fall-off from the sixth. Fall-offs of this kind were usually made from the fifth, minor third, or blue third (which are not the same thing); the choice of the sixth adds a poignant touch.

These scattered free-lance sessions are insignificant compared with what was to come. In April 1935 Goodman began the long Victor series which would become the core of his musical legacy. Within weeks he had cut some of his most enduring standards—"Blue Skies," "Always," "Dear Old Southland," "King Porter Stomp," "Sometimes I'm Happy" and the first of the Trio sides. "Blue Skies," one of Fletcher Henderson's classics, opens with staccato trumpets over the rhythm section, a device that allows a lot of air into the music and lets the sound of the rhythm section come through clearly. The saxophones play the first four bars of the bridge, followed by trombones for four bars, after which the saxophones return to finish out the chorus. There are no answers, no accompaniment anywhere, except by the rhythm section.

The next chorus opens with the trumpets in straight mutes, supported by the saxophones, which punctuate in the open spaces. Arthur Rollini plays the bridge and the last eight measures again with minimal support. The next sixteen bars are given to Berigan, who plays an awkward figure in bars nine and ten that sounds suspiciously as if he were playing wrong notes; the bridge goes to the saxes with brass punctuation, and the full band plays the last eight measures. The final chorus opens with Goodman and the band trading fours; the bridge is played by unison saxophones, and the last eight bars by unison trombones, with band punctuation. It is really a very spare arrangement, with almost a third of it given to solos, and another sixteen bars in unison, which is a lot simpler to write than harmonized parts. As I have suggested, I believe that Fletcher Henderson's dilatory habits led him to write in this spare manner, which was a considerable contrast to that of his own first arranger, Don Redman, who wrote heavy, bristling, very busy scores. But I think it is also true that Henderson knew how effective these simple arrangements were, and therefore saw no reason to write more complex ones.

Furthermore, as is clear in "Dear Old Southland," Henderson's brother Horace was writing in much the same mode. Once again we hear a good deal more soloing than was customary with the band. As James T. Maher has pointed out, some of these arrangements were originally written for Henderson's band, which generally made a greater display of the soloists.[5] The main theme is only sixteen measures long, with a sixteen-measure interlude in minor, played only once. Goodman opens the number with a full sixteen-bar chorus and solos again at the end. There are other solos by Art Rollini, pianist Frankie Froeba and Jack Lacey. The choruses for the band are sparse, but the phrases are carefully syncopated, almost always beginning on the second half of a beat, to give the effect of a hot solo. The Henderson brothers clearly shared a musical philosophy which valued simplicity, lightness and ease over the much more complex writing of Redman, Duke Ellington or some of Goodman's other arrangers.

"You're a Heavenly Thing," recorded in April 1935, is the only record date made by the Goodman band which included Jack Teagarden. Goodman would have loved to have had him, for with himself, Berigan and Teagarden, he would have had an array of soloists that would have matched that of any band. But Teagarden had accepted the safety of a long-term contract with Whiteman, and by the time it was up he was ready to lead his own group. He never played with the Goodman band regularly, but was brought in for this session, replacing Red Ballard, probably simply because he was available. He plays a typical solo on this record, but just plays with the section on the other sides made at this session. In fact, Jack Lacey has the long solo on "Always," and it appears that Goodman was for once tactful enough not to give all the trombone solos to the outsider. (The solo, much to Lacey's annoyance, has often been credited to Teagarden, but it is clearly Lacey's.)

As we shall see, within six months of Goodman's signing the Victor contract, he had sprung loose the swing band movement. Both the Columbia and Victor records, and the Let's Dance show contributed to his catching up a youthful audience and turning them into loyal fans. The question remains: Why did it happen first to Goodman and not to any of his better established competitors?

To begin with, the moment was right, for his direct competitors, that is to say, bands which could play a hot version of dance music, were in disarray. Because of the leader's inability to manage a band well, the Henderson

Orchestra was about to fall apart.[6] The Dorsey Brothers, after getting off to a good start at the Glen Island Casino, broke down when Jimmy and Tommy had a fight on the bandstand there, and would record again under Jimmy Dorsey's leadership only after Goodman had established his band.[7] The Pollack band was in trouble, and would be in a hiatus until it reformed as the Bob Crosby Orchestra.[8] Duke Ellington, whose band in the early thirties was one of the most famous in the country, was going through a period of intense mourning for his mother.[9] Ellington was just going through the motions, and was beginning to be seen by college students as out-of-date, a left-over from a previous era: Marshall Stearns, head of the Yale Hot Club, complained in Down Beat about what he saw as stale jungle music.[10] Again, Louis Armstrong, who had emerged as a popular bandleader in 1930 and 1931, spent most of his time between mid-1932 and the beginning of 1935 in Europe, recording very little.[11] He would not rebuild his reputation until 1936. Only the Casa Loma Orchestra, whose success had inspired M.C.A. to sign Goodman, was offering serious competition to Goodman as a hot dance band.

Goodman, thus, was filling a void. A few years earlier there had been Pollack, Henderson, McKinney's Cotton Pickers, Goldkette, Ellington, the Coon-Sanders Nighthawks and others: now most of the hot dance bands that had appeared in the mid- to late 1920s were gone.

But it was not just luck that gave Goodman his first success. The band was giving its audience something it wanted, too. An important factor was the presence of a "girl" singer. (In the swing era it was considered flattering to refer to people of whatever ages as "the boys in the band" or the "girls at the club," even when the boys were bald and the girls were henna-rinsed. Band singers, no matter how old, were invariably called the boy singer or the girl singer.) The idea of carrying a girl singer was not new. Whiteman had signed Mildred Bailey in 1929, and Ward herself had been working with Enrique Madriguera before she joined Goodman. But it was not usual. The early dance bands, if they had a singer at all permanently attached to them, preferred males. Duke Ellington did not take on a female vocalist until 1931, when the band was already celebrated nationally. Fletcher Henderson never really had an important female vocalist as part of his group. The Casa Loma Orchestra featured Jack Richmond and then Kenny Sargeant. The Dorsey Brothers were featuring Bob Crosby before the breakup. Whiteman's primary singer was Bing Crosby. Of course all of these bands occasionally backed female vocalists in the recording studios, but there was no real association.

But the heart of the audience for the swing bands would be high school and college males. It is hardly surprising that they welcomed a pretty, young female vocalist. Helen Ward was featured frequently on *Let's Dance*, sang on almost half of the Columbia series, on six of the early Victors, and, as was customary, sat beside the band down front on location between numbers. She was an important part of the band's sound, and a significant contributor to its success.

For a second thing, the Goodman band was playing more interesting arrangements than were most of the other bands around, leaving aside Ellington, who was a special case. The Dorsey Brothers Orchestra was, for its hot numbers, playing in an arranged dixieland style, as for example "Eccentric" or "Dippermouth Blues," a style which would prove to be more successful with the Crosby band a year or two later. It also used a lot of novelty numbers, like "Fidgety," which is rhythmically very limp. The Casa Loma Orchestra had an excellent arranger in Gene Gifford, who wrote many of the band's most important pieces; his "San Sue Strut" and "Casa Loma Stomp" are first-rate swing numbers and were hits four years before Goodman opened at the Music Hall. But Casa Loma also gave its public a lot of stiff arrangements of sentimental ballads meant for dancing. Fletcher Henderson always had a lot of excellent arrangements, some of which Goodman bought for *Let's Dance*. But by and large the lesser black bands were using scores that were no more imaginative than those of an ordinary white dance band. Claude Hopkins' arrangements, for example, are rather flat and uninspired.

But Goodman, blessed with the *Let's Dance* budget, was able—indeed required by his employers—to hire the best writers he could, and right from the start his band was playing from scores that would come to be seen as classics of the genre—pieces that were always musically interesting, not merely in the melody line, but in details, as for example the accompaniment to the saxophones on the last eight bars of the first chorus of "Blue Skies," or the saxophone accompaniment to the lead in the muted trumpets in the chorus that follows.

Furthermore, Goodman was getting interesting arrangements not only for the swingers, but on many of the pop tunes he recorded. John Hammond always insisted that the Goodman band became successful in good measure because he persuaded Benny to let Henderson treat the pop songs as he treated the more jazzlike pieces.[12] As we have seen, credit for this should not go entirely to either Hammond or Henderson, but I agree that playing the popular songs with a jazz-like feel gave the band's whole output, or a large part of it in any case, a rhythmic pulse that other groups did not have. For example "Restless," an undistinguished and long forgotten tune sung by Helen Ward, is nonetheless made melodically interesting at the outset by arranger Spud Murphy, by giving the saxophones a variation

on the melody itself; rarely does Murphy let more than four bars go by
without introducing some sort of change in texture, timbre or orchestral
color.

Another factor was Goodman's own great musicality, which made him
insist on good intonation, well-coordinated section work, and attention to
details of dynamics and breathing which are so important to musical performance. Jazz fans have always liked to believe that polishing a band to a
high shine causes it to lose spontaneity, and it is true that Duke Ellington
sometimes wrote "sloppy" on his scores, or got musicians drunk before record sessions in order to keep them loose.[13] But musicians in general do not
accept this idea. The point is that if a piece is sufficiently well rehearsed, so
that it is almost memorized, the players can come to it relaxed enough to
make it swing without sacrificing precision. It is when a piece is under-
rehearsed and the players are struggling just to find the right notes, that
the performance is likely to be tense. It is simply true that a musical statement which is accurately played is more readily comprehended than one
which is not. Goodman had men in his band who could play a piece com-
petently at sight, and be comfortable with it after a brief rehearsal, but he
also rehearsed his band as much as possible before recording a tune.

Goodman practiced incessantly himself—he practiced the day he died—
and he expected everyone else to bring the same dedication to music that
he did. (Needless to say, few people did.) Lionel Hampton said, "Benny
was a real fanatic about rehearsals and arrangements. If some idea hit him,
he would call a rehearsal at seven o'clock in the morning."[14] Jimmy Maxwell said,

> When they had a new tune Goodman would take a whole rehearsal
> on it, three hours. Rehearsed twice a week, even when they were play-
> ing theatres, they might rehearse between shows. They'd play the tune
> through two or three times for notes. Benny would edit. They'd mark
> the parts, then go over the phrasing section by section. There was no
> idea of the lead phrasing the stuff—Goodman did that. Then he'd
> have them work on it without the rhythm section. "If you can't play
> without the rhythm section, you can't play."[15]

According to Jess Stacy, "When I played with Goodman he was always hell
on intonation. That band had to be perfectly in tune. I was hitting A's all
the time. I got that habit when I came to the Crosby band, and they said,
'Jess, if you don't quit hitting those A's, you can take your six years' notice.'"[16]

A third factor which contributed substantially to the effect of the band
was the strength of the rhythm section. Harry Goodman has never been
considered a powerful jazz bassist, but he played the right notes and kept

good time; Jess Stacy was one of the hardest swinging band pianists of the entire swing era; Gene Krupa, despite his lack of subtlety and his tendency to rush, was an intense, hard-driving drummer who never coasted; and Allan Reuss was as good as any band guitarist of the period. Stacy, for example, rather than playing the customary stride, comped with both hands at once to power the band along with a steady flow of chords; and Reuss accented on two and four, which not many rhythm guitarists of the time did. Furthermore, these men stayed together right through the whole period of the band's early success, coming to know what to expect of each other and how to coordinate themselves in a way that rhythm sections casually thrown together for a recording session or a club date cannot do. The Goodman rhythm team was far better than the rather pallid Dorsey Brothers section, despite the presence there of a good drummer in Ray McKinley; better than the good Casa Loma section, which had an excellent drummer in Tony Briglia; better than that of Ellington, which suffered from what has been termed drummer Sonny Greer's "slushy" playing, although Ellington himself was a fine rhythm pianist and usually had excellent bassists. The quality of the Goodman rhythm section was recognized by musicians. Cootie Williams, when he left Ellington in 1940 to join Goodman, was drawn in part by the fact that the band had "terrific rhythm . . . that was the main thing. The band had a terrific beat."[17]

The beat, however, was not entirely due to the rhythm section. Goodman, who understood swing as well as anybody, recognized quite early that the sections—indeed individual players—ought to be able to swing without help from the rhythm section. He told the musicians, "The rhythm section is not there to drag you through the piece. They're another section punctuating your notes."[18]

Many people have objected—and did at the time—to Goodman's being labeled "The King of Swing." (Actually Gene Krupa was first given the title by a publicist for Slingerland drums, who used it in an advertisement featuring Krupa.) But in truth Goodman was intensely concerned with "swing." He chose to play arrangements "with an awful lot of in-between the beats syncopations," and he worked very hard to make sure the band was swinging, not just on the uptempo numbers where it might be expected, but on the softer, popular dance tunes as well. In 1935 the Goodman band did, I think, swing harder than any of its competitors, and that certainly helped to draw the young following its success was built on.

It was, moreover, a specific kind of swing. This is a subject that is terribly difficult to talk about. Even musicians who worked with Goodman for many years have trouble describing what it is that makes one way of swinging different from another. The term most often used is that the Goodman band played "on top of the beat." There was a sense that the band was al-

ways "charging ahead." John Bunch said, "Benny seemed to want a really
tight—I hate to use the word tense—but a really exciting feeling, particularly at the faster tempos. I guess you'd call that on top of the beat."[19] Sid
Weiss, who as a bass player was perforce concerned with the question, said,
"Benny was always playing on top of the beat. It is almost an anticipation,
but it doesn't come before the beat, that wouldn't happen."[20] Weiss went
on to make the comparison with the Basie band. He said, "All I can think
is, [Basie was] stressing something that's after the top of the beat."[21] Mel
Powell made the same comparison. With Basie, "They always seem to me
to be back of the beat. They'd wait until the last minute. You'd think
they'd missed the train and then they'd land. Benny's band would not wait
until the last minute."[22]

Powell also made a comparison to Billie Holiday, who was one of the
great masters of stretching and condensing figures to the point where the
notes did not seem to relate to the underlying ground beat at all.

> Now with Billie, her sense of where [the beat] was must have been im-
> peccable, because she could go anywhere. And I often thought, many
> years later, I'd hate to have to transcribe that. Twelve against seven-
> teen or something. She was the one I'd always beat my foot with, just
> make sure I knew [where the beat was]. I'd stay very steady. She could
> throw you off. Teddy Wilson told me, "I got to count when I play
> with Billie." Now Benny doesn't do that. She's real rubato. Benny
> does not play that way.[23]

Jimmy Maxwell also made the comparison with Basie, saying that the
Basie band was behind the beat, the Goodman band a little bit ahead.
"You were always on the edge of falling, like running down a hill. Lionel
[Hampton] was always pushing the beat. Harry [James] played on top of
the beat, so did Ziggy."[24]

Precisely what this means, however, nobody is really sure. Despite the
great advances that have been made in the ability of computers to analyze
sound, nobody has yet devised a system for making fine measurements of
"the beat" produced by a band, or even a given instrumentalist. Even the
best jazz musicians cannot say precisely what it means to "push the beat,"
to play "ahead" or "behind" it. They do not want to admit that players—
who might be themselves—are actually enunciating notes fractionally off
the beat in some manner. But they do admit that something like "playing
on top of the beat" or "laying back" does occur, and it is difficult to think
of what else might be going on except for fractional anticipations or delays
in playing the notes. If this is the case, we must assume that the Goodman
band tended to hit just ahead of the beat at least at times. The effect was

a rushing excitement. Powell described it as "Playing hard. Gritted teeth playing. No laying back. Gritted teeth, hard, driving. No lollygagging."[25]

Benny Goodman, then, was a driven, indeed obsessed musician, to whom nothing less than perfection was good enough. He fought to get the best arrangements and the best players he could afford; he drove the band hard; and it is therefore not surprising that he was able to beat out the competition. And furthermore he worked himself even harder than he worked the men.

It is my opinion that Benny Goodman was the finest jazz clarinetist that we have ever had. Not everybody agrees. Even at the moment when Goodman was at the peak of his fame there were those who preferred his chief competitor, Artie Shaw. Today critics from various schools would cite Frank Teschemacher, Jimmie Noone, Pee Wee Russell, Edmond Hall, Barney Bigard, Buddy DeFranco, George Lewis, Johnny Dodds, or contemporary clarinetists like Bob Wilber, Kenny Davern, Jimmy Giuffre, Eddie Daniels as "the best."

But there can be no denying that Goodman was a brilliant clarinetist—a great technician who played with fire and propulsive drive. Musicians, especially those who worked for him, whatever they may have felt about his personality, admired him extravagantly, and some were simply in awe of his skills. Not one of the scores of musicians whose comments on Goodman I have heard or read while researching this book had anything but the highest praise for his playing, and that includes people who worked with him at the end of his career as well as at the beginning. John Bunch pointed out that Goodman was constantly accenting on the second half of the beat. "That's a very exciting thing to do. That's very hard to play. Benny could do it. He could do it to perfection. He was absolutely brilliant at that sort of thing. He could do it at extremely fast tempos right in between the beats. Not many guys can do that, if any. He'd just eat those fast tempos up like nothing."[26]

Mel Powell said that Goodman "was one of the most incredible players the field has ever known. . . . It wasn't just that his own improvisation was marvelous, the spirit, the verve, the vitality, even humor he played with, but the sheer technical mastery. He played that thing like it was a yo-yo. . . . The only thing comparable from a technical point of view would be [Art] Tatum."[27] Sid Weiss said, "To me, some of the best moments of my life were playing with Benny."[28] Jimmy Maxwell said, "He was totally in command of everything. He was always a heavy practicer. He practiced all the time. He had ideas on how everything should be done in the band—bass, everything. Nobody argued with him, everybody had great respect for him."[29]

Goodman, then, was a very exciting player, who worked hard, never let down and was always trying to give audiences the best he could. John Bunch once said to Goodman that there seemed to be something about the clarinet that made people listen. Goodman replied, "That's not right. It's not the clarinet. It doesn't matter what instrument it is. You've got to make them listen."[30]

It is a very telling anecdote. According to James T. Maher, Goodman "was obsessed about the clarinet—its evolution, physically, mechanically."[31] When Goodman was playing music—and a good deal of the time when he wasn't—he was totally concentrated. He was always trying to play as well as he could: there were to be no letdowns. As is frequently the case, the seemingly effortless playing was produced by a lot of hard work. Goodman's clarinet playing, then, was an important part of the appeal the band had for the young public it was courting.

Yet beyond all of these things, beyond the first-class arrangements, beyond the attention to detail, beyond the swing, beyond the excellent soloists and Goodman's own playing, there was something else in the music that many other bands lacked, or perhaps did not produce with the same consistency. That was a happy lilt, a joyousness, an exciting, almost sexual lift. Of course, Goodman did occasionally play solemn pieces, as for example his melancholy closing theme, "Good-bye," blues numbers with the small groups and pensive ballads like "Star Dust" and "Body and Soul." But by far the majority of his pieces, at whatever tempo, were alive with optimism and good cheer. It is an interesting truth that the ostensible personality of a jazz musician is not always reflected in his music. Louis Armstrong was a clown on stage, and with people he was for the most part relentlessly cheerful; but some of his finest works, like "West End Blues," "It's Tight Like This," "Star Dust" and others, express a very solemn view of life. Similarly, the reserved, polished Duke Ellington liked best to play strong, earthy, even brutal pieces like "Ko-Ko," "Black and Tan Fantasy" or "Mainstem."

For all that has been said about Benny Goodman's dark side, he had his cheerful moments. John Bunch said that Goodman did not spend much time with the musicians off the bandstand. "But it did happen and he could be delightful, absolutely delightful. He'd tell jokes and he'd laugh so hard you'd think he was going to get sick. I've seen him do that, turn right around and be the funniest guy. He could tell a good joke, too."[32] John McDonough said that Goodman had "a mischievous good humor, often punctuated with a dry, sophisticated wit. Often no one seems to enjoy it more than Goodman himself."[33]

But this cheerful Goodman only peered out occasionally. More typically he was self-absorbed, moody, irritable. He had periods in his life when he suffered from depression, and it appears that at some point he had some alcohol problems. Yet his music was characteristically happy, swinging, full of good cheer. It seems, then, when we look at Goodman and similar cases, where the music contrasts sharply with the exhibited personality, that we are dealing with people who can express certain aspects of their natures only in their music. What does not come out in their lives comes out in their art.

Whatever the case, it is clear enough that possibly the single most important element in the music that made Benny Goodman a central figure in twentieth-century music is that joyous lilt that was always there. How could a generation of young people, coming of age in a parlous hour, when there were breadlines in American cities, and fascism and the threat of war abroad, not have been attracted to this music?

When it was all together—the lilting optimism, the clever arrangements, young soloists, Goodman's own playing—it made the band sound fresh and new. The music it made was different from the hot stuff of the 1920s—by no means entirely different, but different enough to sound to audiences modern and up-to-date. This was the new music, and young people wanted to follow it where it was going.

Finally, it must be said that this was Benny Goodman's band. Whatever contributions were made by Hammond, the arrangers, the musicians, Willard Alexander and others, it was Goodman's vision, Goodman's ideas about music, Goodman's intense dedication, Goodman's energy and drive that pulled together all the elements to make a unified, consistent, and exciting sound. Benny Goodman needed a lot of help from others; but without him it would not have happened.

# 12

# Making It at the Palomar

Despite the problems occasioned by the ending of *Let's Dance,* Goodman decided to struggle on, and the musicians were prepared to support him. This was a band of very young men. None of them was yet thirty, and many of them, like Nate Kazebier and Art Rollini, were still in their early twenties. Although they all understood how difficult the music business was, the optimism of youth told them that they would be exceptions. Morale was high. They were playing a lot of good music, the sort of music they had come into the business to play, and they had the feeling that all they needed was that one break—or rather, a second break, as the radio show had not, apparently, made the band famous.

But they needed to work, and so in the spring of 1935 Willard Alexander set up a national tour which would take the band across the country, ending at a huge new Los Angeles dance hall called the Palomar. This was an incentive to keep going. The pay would not be good, but at least it was work, and California still had a mystical appeal—a land of endless sunshine filled with suntanned maidens as accessible as the grapefruit that could be picked up in the front yard.

Some of the men, however, did not want to leave New York. Toots Mondello had all the studio work he could handle for far more money than Goodman could pay, and after the band's brief engagement at the Stanley Theatre in Pittsburgh, he left. Goodman auditioned a clarinet and saxophone player named Bill DePew at the theatre, and hired him, saying of his clarinet playing, "He sounds like me."[1] George Van Eps had similar reasons for staying in New York, and Allan Reuss came into the band on a full-time basis. The trumpet section, which would always be more in flux than the other sections, was revamped. Pee Wee Erwin left to join a band put together by Glenn Miller for the English composer and bandleader Ray Noble. The Noble band had solid financial backing, a booking at the new Rainbow Roof on top of the R.C.A. Building in Rockefeller Center, was playing a radio show called *The Coty Hour*, and looked like a safer bet than Goodman's did.[2] Both Nate Kazebier and Ralph Muzzillo, who had been in and out of the band, came back; and most important, so did Bunny Berigan.

There was yet one more change, a critical one. John Hammond had long been dissasitfied with Frankie Froeba who, he would claim, "rushed."[3] He had heard from Helen Oakley Dance (a young jazz writer) of a pianist working in Chicago named Jess Stacy.

Jess Stacy was born in 1904, and was therefore a little older than most of the men in the Goodman band. His interest in music was awakened when he was about ten and heard a woman in a neighboring house playing "St. Louis Blues" and other popular tunes of the time on the piano.[4] Not long after, Stacy's mother took in an orphaned girl named Jeanette Mc-Combs. The girl had inherited a piano, which she brought along. She was taking lessons, and after she finished practicing Jess would run to the piano and play the exercises he had heard. At this point his mother decided he should have lessons, but, like many young musicians, he rebelled and continued to work things out himself. "I had good teachers, but I wasn't inested at the time."

In 1918, when he was about fourteen, the family moved to Cape Girardeau, Missouri, a Mississippi River town at the southern end of the state. He began hearing the bands on the famous riverboats as they came through. He heard Louis Armstrong, Baby and Johnny Dodds and Henry "Red" Allen on the boats, although at the time he was not aware to whom he was listening. He was also hearing the seminal records of the Original Dixieland Jass Band. "I worked in a music store in Cape Giradeau. I used to sweep out the store to the Dixieland Jass Band." Not long after, he joined a little group called the Agony Four, made up of saxophone, violin, piano and drums, a very common dance combination at the time. The group played dances around the neighborhood, and very quickly Stacy became a sufficiently competent musician to start working on the riverboats himself. In addition to playing piano with the dance band, he also played the boat's calliope, a huge "organ" of steam whistles which could be heard for miles and was used to warn people of the imminent arrival of the boat. Stacy got five dollars extra to work the calliope. "The view was fine and from time to time you got a face full of cinders from the stacks. What's more, the keys on the darn thing were of copper, and after awhile they got plenty hot from all that steam."[5]

Stacy played the riverboats and generally gigged around from about 1921 to 1924, when he joined a territory orchestra led by Joe Kayser and ended up in Chicago. This was the time when Armstrong, Oliver, Noone, the Dodds and other New Orleans jazz pioneers were working in the South

Side black-and-tans. Stacy said he "lived" at the Sunset, and he quoted Eddie Condon as saying, "You could take a trumpet out of its case at 35th and Calumet, and it'd blow by itself."[6] To support himself, Stacy worked wherever he could. "I worked for all the gangsters around there, in little clubs, speakeasies." Among these clubs was the Midway Gardens, where Goodman had worked.

He was absorbing influences from all around him. According to Bud Freeman, Jess was "very much influenced by Bix [Beiderbecke], very strongly influenced by Bix, played all the Bix compositions, you know, 'In a Mist,' 'Candlelights.' "[7] He was also influenced by Earl Hines, as were most piano players of the times, and to a lesser extent by Art Tatum. "We were good friends. We'd talk a lot. He'd say, 'I'll have a touch.' A touch was a triple scotch and an ale chaser. He was a hell of a nice guy. I told him, 'You can do anything with your hands.' He said, 'Jess, I worked my head off. I studied hard. It didn't come easy.' "[8] According to Stacy, Tatum had a way of playing scales with his thumb and first two fingers, instead of all five as is customary, although he was adept at the standard method, too; the point was that by using only the stronger digits he could play a more even run. They called it, Stacy said, "the bowling ball technique," because only the thumb and first two fingers are used to grasp a bowling ball. "He could do anything with his hands."[9]

But Hines, clearly, was Stacy's first influence. Teddy Wilson once pointed out that "Hines came along before microphones and so he played with great strength and power. He spread his right hand out to an octave so that he got his whole hand behind his fingers. James P. Johnson did the same thing, and I've seen him play so hard the piano actually bounced."[10]

Hines, in particular, "rocked" the octave in his right hand to produce a tremolo effect. This not only increased the volume but allowed him to reproduce on the piano a version of the fast terminal vibrato that was a characteristic of the style of New Orleans horn players he was working with. Stacy adopted a somewhat similar device; but instead of rocking his hand to produce the tremolo on the octave, he would hit the octave as Hines did with thumb and little finger, and then play a trill on the interval of a second or third with the first two fingers inside the octave.

A second important characteristic of Stacy's style was a pronounced use of accent, or dynamics, throughout his work, either on alternate notes, or more generally through the line, so that the music seems always to be coming and going. Stacy also divided the beat quite unevenly. These devices imparted to his work a tremendous swing. He was in my view one of the hardest swinging pianists in jazz.

In his first years in Chicago Stacy did well, earning perhaps a hundred dollars a week as a rule, but by 1935, as the Depression seemed to run on endlessly, he was working at a large but very seedy cellar club called the Subway for twenty-one dollars a week.[11] Helen Oakley, by this time a leading member of the Hot Club of Chicago, was writing for *Down Beat* and the new French publication, *Jazz Hot*. She wrote pieces about Stacy for *Jazz Hot*, and either through these, or via personal contact with Oakley, Hammond found out about Stacy.[12] Hammond claims that he went to Chicago to hear Stacy and persuaded him to come East, but Stacy said that Goodman telephoned him at the Subway and asked him to audition.[13] It would hardly have taken much persuading, in any case, to get Jess to leave a twenty-one-dollar-a-week job in a dive to join a band that was beginning to be nationally known.

By the time Stacy got to New York, Teddy Wilson was on piano for the Goodman Trio. The group was not playing on locations but only in the recording studio, for the idea of presenting a mixed group in public was not yet generally acceptable. Goodman, however, had no intention of putting Jess into the Trio in Wilson's place. He may have felt that such a move would have been seen by Wilson, Hammond and others as racist; but the more important consideration, from Goodman's viewpoint, was that he was entranced by Wilson's playing, as he always would be. I will discuss Wilson's contribution to the Trio shortly; but it was obvious from the very beginning that Wilson had great sensitivity and the ability to coordinate musically with Goodman in a way that would be hard for anyone else to follow.

In public Wilson and Stacy always had kind things to say about each other. Otis Ferguson, who wrote several pieces about the band in the late thirties, quoted Stacy as saying, "Anybody I *really* admire, it's that little old Wilson," and Wilson saying of Stacy, "Only wish I could work a band like that."[14] But there was always a certain tension between them. His long stay with Goodman made Stacy well known to the jazz fraternity and dance-band fans; but he had also to watch Wilson become a jazz star and the model for pianists around the world through his work with the Trio and Quartet. He also was kept aware of the fact that Goodman preferred Wilson.

The band that was about to make jazz history, thus, consisted of Kazebier, Berigan and Muzzillo on trumpets; Ballard and Lacey, trombones; Schertzer, DePew, Rollini and Dick Clark, saxophones; a rhythm section of Stacy, Krupa, Reuss and Harry Goodman; and of course Goodman and Helen Ward. It was an excellent band: Berigan, Goodman, Stacy and Reuss were among the finest players on their respective instruments in jazz at the moment; Kazebier, Lacey and Rollini were more than competent jazz improvisers; and the others were solid professionals with a lot of experience behind them, despite their youth. It had now been over a year since Goodman first organized the band. Aside from Goodman himself, only four of the men who had opened at the Music Hall were still with the band. In most cases the replacements were superior to the original men. The band, furthermore, now had a fairly large book which included some first-rate numbers turned out by some of the best arrangers in the business. It had had a considerable amount of playing time, which had given them a chance to polish the arrangements. They were ready for whatever lay ahead.

Paradoxically, it is the most famous member of the rhythm section that there are questions about. Gene Krupa was a very likeable man, serious about his music, and he always got a good press from the jazz writers. Later on, despite the fact that many writers were urging jazz musicians to get rid of the dopester image the music had earned, they supported Krupa at the time of his infamous "drug bust" in 1943. Nonetheless, they have in the main been somewhat uncertain about his abilities as a supporting drummer. In part this was due to the immense popularity developed by his showy drum solos—jazz writers of the 1930s and 1940s tended to be suspicious of popularity in jazz musicians, when so many of the good ones, like Jimmie Noone and Johnny Dodds, were working in obscurity. But in the main it was a question of Krupa's musical taste.

Krupa was influenced directly by the New Orleans drummers he was hearing in Chicago, especially Zutty Singleton and Baby Dodds, whom Krupa frequently cited as his first influences.[15] New Orleans drumming style had evolved out of the marching bands, in which a large bass drum and a snare were played by two people. The school of military drums on which this style was based called for a long booming sound from the bass drum, and plenty of noisy rattling in the snares, to carry for distances over a lot of hard-blown brass. Dodds and Singleton, in the Chicago days, used big bass drums and played mainly on the snare with sticks. True to this tradition, Krupa got a great, hollow boom out of his bass drum, and he worked primarily on the snare rather than on the cymbals as many other jazz drummers, like Walter Johnson with Fletcher Henderson, were beginning to do in the early 1930s. He was, furthermore, a "punchy" drummer, constantly giving the snare a good stiff bang for frequent accents, rather than providing a subtler steady flow, as, say, Dave Tough would do.

There was, furthermore, a question about Krupa's ability, or perhaps willingness, to keep time. Bassist Sid Weiss, who was with Goodman for a long time later on, said that Krupa frequently disregarded the beat Goodman counted off, and set his own tempo.[16] Jess Stacy said, "Krupa, you had to hold him back, too. I had the bass going down there. I played rhythm piano. . . . He'd go faster, perpetual motion or something. There'd be no end to it."[17] Krupa himself admitted that he did not believe in a strict "metronomic tempo."[18]

The problem of "time" is something that jazz musicians discuss end-lessly. Some believe that nobody has actually to state the beat if it is clear in everybody's head—that is to say, the rhythm section can be "pushing" or anticipating the beat, or conversely "laying behind" it. Others say that may be all right in theory, but in practice it is necessary for at least some-body to be playing exact time. Yet again, some musicians feel that there is no harm in a band's gradually speeding up, so long as it happens almost imperceptibly and feels natural to everybody. But on the whole, most im-provising jazz musicians like a beat which is exact as possible and stated explicitly. It is hard work for some members of a group, as was the case with Stacy, to have to constantly fight another player's beat.

Yet Gene Krupa was, with all his faults, a strong, somewhat rough and dramatic drummer and it was players like these Goodman preferred. When he was once asked who his favorite drummer was, he replied, "Gene Krupa, without a doubt."[19] Goodman also would pick a crude saxophonist like Vido Musso, who had trouble reading music—indeed reading English—and sometimes played incorrect chord changes, over a subtler player. Good-man, himself a hot player, was drawn to others of the same kind. Further-more, Goodman undoubtedly liked the punchy way that Krupa played, and he may also have been unaware of Krupa's deficiencies in other re-spects. Although John Hammond pushed Goodman to use Krupa, Good-man had hired him for the Russ Columbo band before he met Hammond, and continued to hire him for many years afterwards. Goodman once told James T. Maher, "The one thing about Gene, I always knew where I was."[20] Jazz musicians live in fear of getting lost, and in particular of losing track of the "down beat"—that is, where each measure begins. This can result in his "turning the beat around" so that he is a beat away from everybody else, raising havoc with the metric system of the music. A less direct drummer, playing complicated figures, can confuse a soloist and cause him to lose track of the down beat. Krupa's strong punchy style left little doubt as to where the down beat was. He was, Maher said, Good-man's "safety net."[21] In the end, Krupa played a major role in making the Benny Goodman Orchestra famous.

At the moment, however, it did not seem to be an immediate prospect. In the mythology of jazz, the trip by the Goodman band across the United States in 1935 was an unmitigated disaster. In fact, it was not nearly as horrendous as has usually been said. At the Stanley Theatre in Pittsburgh, for example, some of the kids danced in the aisles,[22] anticipating the uproar at the Paramount Theatre in New York by two years. In Milwaukee, ac-cording to Helen Oakley's report in Down Beat, "There was good atten-dance and the place was filled with musicians who had come up from Chicago and numerous other nearby towns."[23] Jess Stacy said, "Sweet's in

Oakland was packed. Salt Lake City wasn't too bad, but not like Oakland."[24] Russ Connor says that some of the dates "were mildly successful, some were not."[25]

The major problem seemed to have come at Elitch's Gardens, in Denver. Elitch's was a so-called taxi, or jitney dance hall, where patrons paid so much for each dance. There had been a boom in such places beginning in about 1910. Some of these dance halls were reasonably respectable, but many were not, and some were fronts for brothels. There was eventually a civic movement to put them down.[26] By 1935 the day of the taxi dance hall had passed, and Elitch's was residue from another age.

The problem was that as the patron was charged for each dance, the numbers had to be as short as possible, and usually did not last as long as a minute, compared with the two to three minutes of a standard dance piece. Furthermore, bands in taxi dance halls were supposed to play a mix of music, including waltzes and rhumbas, as well as the pop songs that were the heart of any dance band's repertory. The Goodman band, however, had been developed as the hot band over the six months of the *Let's Dance* show. Although the book did include current pop songs, on *Let's Dance* the Kel Murray Orchestra had been playing the pops, with Goodman playing many standards and special numbers. It simply did not have a book appropriate to a taxi dance hall. It should not have been booked into Elitch's, but once again Willard Alexander had taken what he could get.

The result was that the Elitch Garden's management gave Goodman his notice immediately.[27] Goodman was in despair. There had been the failure at the Roosevelt, the spotty success of the tour to this point and now a repetition of the Roosevelt disaster. He was ready to disband. He called Willard Alexander in New York. Willard bucked him up, and some of the bandsmen urged him to stick it out. Jess Stacy said, "Benny, get over the mountains first and see what happens."[28] In the end Goodman had a talk with the management, and it was decided that if they cut the numbers down in length, and played a lot of waltzes, they could get through the job. Goodman then divided the band in half. Helen Ward played piano in one small group with Berigan on trumpet and played a lot of waltzes.[29] They survived the two weeks.

From Denver they went directly to the Coast. Again the band's reception was mixed: A good crowd at McFadden's Ballroom in San Francisco, poor audiences at Pismo Beach, an enthusiastic, packed hall at Sweet's in Oakland. And so, not knowing what to expect, they headed for Los Angeles, where they would open at the new and prestigious Palomar on August 21.

The Palomar was the old Rainbo [sic] Gardens at Vermont and Second which had been elaborately redecorated. It offered a substantial menu in addition to drinks and dancing. Once again stories of this by now legendary engagement vary. Art Rollini said that the crowd was only moderately good on opening night but grew during the week.[30] However, other sources insist that when the band arrived that night they found a crowd of eager customers lined up around the block. Unbelieving, they went in and set up. The most generally accepted story, which Goodman gave in *The Kingdom of Swing*, is that he started the evening playing the milder arrangements of pop tunes he had come to believe people wanted. When the response to these numbers was tepid, he said something like, "The hell with it, if we're going to sink we may as well go down swinging," and broke out "King Porter Stomp." The number was greeted with an enormous roar, and from that moment on there was no looking back.[31]

Other reports are different. One said, "The place filled slowly but steadily that night . . . Benny's boys, who had been rather listless at the start, suddenly discovered that at last they were playing for an audience that had awakened to the feel of the music. They came to life and let go. And the dancers became aware of the fact that something was happening."[32] Jack Lacey insisted that Berigan, who was sick of the road and planning to leave the band in any case, got tired of the pop tunes, and began demanding to play the hotter numbers, especially those he had solos on. "He yells out to Benny, 'Let's cut this shit, let's get out 'Bugle Call Rag,' " or words to that effect.[33]

The details, then, are not certain, but it is clear enough that there was an audience for what would come to be called "swing" on the West Coast. How did this come about?

Over the twentieth century in the United States every generation of young people has sought out, and nourished, some sort of strongly rhythmic, usually fairly simple kind of music which they not only danced to but simply listened to for the sheer pleasure in it. Ragtime rose in about 1900, jazz spread rapidly through the country after 1917, swing emerged in the early to mid-1930s, rock appeared in the 1950s, and there have been various modifications of rock over the years since.

At two points in this continuum there were gaps. One was in the years between 1946, when the swing band boom suddenly collapsed, and the mid-1950s, when Bill Haley and Elvis Presley brought forward something new. During these ten years or so popular music consisted mainly of romantic ballads sung by attractive young men and women, among them Eddie Fisher, Jo Stafford, Patti Page, Vic Damone and others. This music, however, failed to satisfy the thirst for hotter rhythms that existed in many adolescents. In their searches across the radio dial for something stronger, they came upon a music that had been created out of a combination of jazz and the blues for an audience of urban blacks, called rhythm and blues. The astute Sam Phillips at Sun Records in Memphis, noticing this phenomenon, said that if he could find a white youth who could play rhythm and blues he would make a fortune. Shortly he came across Elvis Presley, although it was Victor, rather than Sun, that made the fortune.

The other gap in the continuum was briefer, and came in the early 1930s. As we have seen, the arrival of the Depression in 1930 markedly reduced that amount of 1920s hot music being recorded and played on the air. But young people wanted something with "rhythmic bite," as Josef Bonime put it. They continued to buy the records of Fletcher Henderson and Duke Ellington, and in 1930 they discovered a new black band led by a trumpet player named Louis Armstrong. In 1931 Armstrong's records sold 100,000 copies, a huge number for the time, a substantial percentage of them on college campuses.[34] When the Casa Loma band emerged, playing a mix of easy dance tunes and fast riff numbers, it rapidly become popular with the young, again especially on college campuses.

It was not, then, that Goodman had created a demand for swing. The demand for something along those lines was already there and already, to an extent, being fed. What happened was that Goodman's version of the music suited the youthful taste more exactly than did that of his competitors. Goodman was half a generation younger than Ellington, Henderson, Goldkette, Whiteman, Armstrong and other well-known leaders of dance bands who had developed their musical styles to suit the tastes of audiences of the 1920s. In 1935 Goodman was twenty-six, only a few years older than the college students who were following the music.

This audience of swing fans did not suddenly appear on the West Coast. There had been indications on the trip out, in places like Pittsburgh and Milwaukee, that there was interest in the Goodman band in spots around the country. But this interest first manifested itself in force during the Palomar stay. According to Goodman, the West Coast office of M.C.A. wired the home office that the opening had been "sensational."[35] The engagement, originally scheduled for a month, stretched to two.

Why, then, did it happen on the West Coast? According to researches by James T. Maher, sales of Goodman's last Columbia records, particularly "The Dixieland Band," had been especially good in the West.[36] Willard Alexander said also that these early records were being played on the West Coast by local radio stations.[37] Even in this early stage of radio's development disk jockeys were beginning to play a powerful role in the popular music business. Down Beat was referring to Al Jarvis, for years the best known of the West Coast jockeys, as the "famed record commentator."[38] It was records, as much as the Let's Dance show, which had built interest in the Goodman band over the year before the Palomar opening.

In any case, the huge success of the Palomar opening was news, at least in jazz circles. *Down Beat* ran a story on Goodman in every issue for months afterwards, many of them on the front page. There was other publicity, and a lot of word of mouth among musicians and dance-band fans. Record sales were good, and back in New York Willard Alexander was getting phone calls from hotels and dance halls asking about the band. Goodman had come into the Palomar feeling that he might well be, like Frederic Remington's famous Indian, staring out into the sun setting over the Pacific, with no place further to go. When he left California it was clear that he had a chance of making a real success. The band was not yet famous; but at least it had made a start.

There were again changes of personnel. Bunny Berigan left. He was drinking heavily. According to Art Rollini, "He would play great until about 11 p.m., and after that he was impossible." The generally told story is that Berigan was tired of the road and wanted to return to New York. However, Rollini said that Goodman finally had to fire him. If this is true, it would have been very painful for Goodman.[39] Bud Freeman told a story about Bunny sprawled in his chair passed out during the *Let's Dance* show, and somebody asking Benny why he kept him in the band. Goodman replied, "But he can *play*."[40] Irving Goodman, who was in Berigan's own band for three years, said, "There haven't been many guys who could electrify Benny, but Bunny was certainly one of them."[41] James T. Maher said that Goodman "absolutely adored Berigan as a musician, but this crazy Irishman was a hell of a problem to him."[42] John Hammond said that Bunny "was a funny guy: unhappy when he worked for somebody else, uncomfortable when he was his own boss."[43]

Whether Bunny quit or was fired, he shipped his trumpet to one of the important contractors in New York so that the man would know he would soon be available, went home to Fox Lake for a week's rest, and thence to New York. He played the studios for awhile, made two unsuccessful attempts to lead his own band, with stints with Tommy Dorsey sandwiched in between, and finally died in May 1942, of the effects of chronic alcoholism. It was a life almost as short and tragic as that of Bix Beiderbecke. He was, however, one of the finest trumpet players of the 1930s—a great, blowsy, romantic player with a full rich sound through the whole range of the instrument. Not even Louis Armstrong could play with such authority in the risky lower register.

Berigan has never really been given his due by jazz critics. He was certainly the equal as a jazz improviser of Ellington's Cootie Williams and Basie's Buck Clayton, both of whom have been written about extensively, and he was without doubt superior to a number of his contemporaries, like Hot Lips Page, Rex Stewart, Charlie Shavers and others who are generally better known to jazz fans. Benny Goodman knew how good Berigan was, and according to Jimmy Maxwell, was giving his wife a weekly pay check during Berigan's last days, when he was having trouble functioning.[44]

Paradoxically, according to several people close to the situation, Berigan thoroughly disliked Goodman.[45] Part of it was undoubtedly the disdain the wounded often feel for the aggressively successful. But most of it had to do with personality differences. Goodman was a hard man to work for. Teddy Wilson said that he was "a very strict taskmaster."[46] Mel Powell said he was a "tough guy."[47] Berigan was just the reverse. Irving Goodman said, "As a leader, he was great to work for. The whole band would do anything he wanted. It was a real happy family. His attitude was so great, too. Like when we played the boondocks, when it didn't really count, Bunny never let up. He always gave everything he'd got. Another thing, he never acted like he was anything special. . . . Besides being a nice person, sweet and lovable, Bunny was a musical giant."[48] There was little chance that a man like Berigan could have warmed to Benny Goodman, who was intolerant of sloppiness and unprofessionalism on the stand. It is too bad, because Berigan, for the brief period he was in the band, gave it so much. He played not only all of the trumpet solos but 70 percent of the lead as well. He is present on only eleven of the band's recordings, but he has solos on nine of them, a clear indication of how much Goodman valued him. In some cases Goodman gave him more solo space than he took for himself. "King Porter Stomp," in particular, is almost a feature for Bunny. He has the famous eight-measure introduction and the sixteen measures which follow. This muted solo became a standard part of the piece, which later trumpeters were expected to emulate. He also has an additional sixteen measures later on in the record.

However, perhaps Berigan's best-known solo with Goodman is on "Sometimes I'm Happy," a pensive Vincent Youmans ballad which has remained popular with jazz musicians. Berigan opens his solo with a moody, three-note figure in the lower register, which he then repeats an octave higher, a figure which became so embedded in the ears of trumpet players of the era that they had to struggle to avoid using it in their own solos on the tune. Bunny then skyrockets into the top of his range in a manner that was characteristic of him, and wends his way slowly downwards over four bars. He lingers in the middle register for a few bars, playing some very loose rhythmic figures in bars twelve and thirteen, and then once again goes up to the top and works his way down to a conclusion. It is a classic Berigan performance, the sort of thing that made him one of the heroes of the time to jazz fans.

But by the end of September 1935, Bunny was gone, and when the band reached Chicago, Harry Geller came into the section. Nate Kazebier, who could sound like Bunny, and later Pee Wee Erwin took on the trumpet solos.

A second change was the departure of Jack Lacey, who, with his immaculate technique, could make a lot of money playing studio work. According to James T. Maher,[49] Lacey and Berigan had agreed to make the trip west, and had roomed together during the tour. Lacey had not planned to stay on beyond the summer because of the amount of work available to him when the fall radio season started. (It is possible that Berigan also had not planned to stay, either.) In any case, Goodman had hired trombonist Joe Harris as a singer when the band was in Denver, suggesting that Benny knew that Lacey meant to leave and wanted Harris waiting in the wings.

# 13
# Finally, Success

The Goodman band left the Palomar in October 1935. It played a few club dates, and then headed for Chicago to play the Urban Room of the Congress Hotel. The Urban Room was an important location for a band to appear in, but it was not notably a jazz room. However, during the previous summer an attack of amoebic dysentery had struck guests at several Chicago hotels, including the Congress, and business had fallen off drastically.[1] The manager, Irving Kaufman, was desperately looking for novelties which would draw a crowd. The Goodman band was seen as something new and different. The *Chicago Tribune* story on the opening said, "Benny Goodman will introduce his 'swing' band at the Urban Room."[2] This is the first use of the word swing in this sense I have come across. The term, however, was in use among musicians for some time before. Indeed, as early as 1917 a professor of English literature at Columbia University spoke of the "swing"[3] of jazz rhythms. Cootie Williams claimed to have invented the phrase "It don't mean a thing if it ain't got that swing," which Duke Ellington used as a song title in 1932.[4] Who decided to call Goodman's a swing band is not known, but it was undoubtedly a publicity man's coinage.

Goodman was excited by coming back to his home town with his own band to play at a prestigious location. Crowds were good from the start. A lot of the success of the Urban Room engagement was due to the interest taken in the band by members of the Chicago Rhythm Club. The central figure of this group was a wealthy young Princeton graduate named Edwin "Squirrel" Ashcraft III.[5] He had been one of a group of jazz buffs at Princeton in the 1920s who had frequently brought Bix and other New York musicians out to play club dances. He was a fairly proficient pianist, and he had made his home in Chicago a kind of private jazz club, where he would frequently invite local musicians in for a party and to jam. Eventually these sessions had been formalized into a club.

One of the main forces in the club was Helen Oakley. She was from a wealthy Toronto family, and it was fairly daring at the time for a young woman of her social class to take an apartment of her own in a distant city.[6] It was Oakley who suggested to Ashcraft that they form the Rhythm Club, which was modeled on the Hot Clubs developing in England. Many of the members were wealthy society people who routinely went to places like the Urban Room to drink and dance; they felt quite at home there, and they began encouraging their friends to come out to hear Goodman regularly.

Because these people were wealthy and well-connected they were able to get done the things they wanted to do more easily than others might. Early in the fall of 1935, when Goodman was still on the West Coast, they had put on a dance featuring a jazz band led by Jimmy McPartland and including trombonist Floyd O'Brien and drummer George Wettling.[7] It had proven successful, and the club decided to put on another one, this time featuring Goodman. The hotel agreed to let the club have the Urban Room for a Sunday afternoon dance—these, after all, were important people—with the proceeds to go to the local musicians' union, a ploy to get around the fact that the band would not be paid. Oakley said she had to "battle" with Goodman to do it, but finally persuaded him that the publicity the affair would generate would make it worth while to play for nothing.[8]

The dance took place on the afternoon of Sunday, December 8, 1935. Although billed as a tea dance, the crowd was so large that most of the dance floor was covered with tables, and the few people who had the temerity to dance were booed from the floor.[9] It was, really, a jazz or "swing" concert. The audience of some eight hundred was built around the Rhythm Club— "Squirrel Ashcraft's friends," Helen Oakley said. "It was Chicago society."[10]

The affair was a huge success. *Down Beat* reported, "A crowd of society debs, musicians, bookers etc. were so enthralled with the music of Benny Goodman's band, at the first rhythm concert, that it positively preferred to listen and watch."[11] The success of this concert encouraged Oakley, Ashcraft and the others to try another one. This one was held on March 8, 1936, and featured the Fletcher Henderson band, which was appearing in Chicago at the moment. *Down Beat* said, "Harlem's sons of swing lifted their horns to the cool sophisticated ceiling of the swanky Urban Room and poured out their melodic heat and Afric cadenzas to some 800 enthusiastic, stomping, applauding white folks."[12] (The implication that it was unusual for a black band to play for white audiences, or at a good hotel, is nonsense. Henderson himself had broken the color line at the Congress Hotel in 1927, and his primary audience had always been white.[13])

It is important to note that at the Henderson concert Goodman and Krupa came in and jammed with a small group drawn from the Henderson

band, among them trumpeter Roy Eldridge and tenor saxophonist Chu
Berry, two of the most highly regarded jazz musicians of the day. This,
Goodman said in *The Kingdom of Swing*, was "the first time, probably,
that white and colored musicians had played together for a paying audience
in America."[14] This mixed jam session was probably Helen Oakley's doing.
She said much later that the Ashcraft people were mainly interested in the
Chicago whites they had heard as youngsters, like Beiderbecke, and members of the Austin High group, while she, like Hammond, was mainly interested in black bands. Not long after, when she had a chance to work
with either the Goodman or Ellington organizations, she chose the latter.[15]
The mixing occasioned no public concern, and it immediately occurred to
someone to bring Teddy Wilson out from New York and present the Trio
in a live performance.

Whose idea it was is open to question. Credit has usually been given to
Hammond, but Hammond says it was Squirrel Ashcraft's idea,[16] and Helen
Oakley said it was hers. She said to Goodman, "If I get Irving Kaufman to
present it, then you do it, you put him in as intermission. You present the
band, the band plays the first half or whatever, then you bring on the Trio,
right onto the floor. . . . I got in touch with Teddy, I paid his fare. . . .
He figured and I figured that all it took was this once and then he'd have a
job. Teddy didn't get paid for the gig, since it was a benefit."[17] I am in-
clined to believe Helen Oakley's version. She was on the spot, was interested in black musicians and was assertive about getting things done.

By this time the Trio records were selling well, and the success of these
purely jazz cuts had encouraged Goodman to put together a little jazz
group called the Jam Dandies, which came out once or twice a night and
jammed. Personnel were probably Goodman, Kazebier, Dick Clark, Joe
Harris and the rhythm section.[18] The group had been well received, but
presenting a mixed group was another matter, and Goodman was not at all
happy about the idea.

This concert with the Trio has always been written about as the first
public appearance of a mixed group in the United States. In fact, mixed
bands were not rare in the United States. The first of the famous riverboat
bands consisted of Emil Flindt, a white violinist who wrote the hit song,
"The Waltz You Saved for Me," and Fate Marable, a black pianist.[19]
(Flindt became a footnote to jazz history a second time when, in the early
1940s, he had a very young Lee Konitz in his band.)[20] Willie "The Lion"
Smith reported hearing mixed bands on Hudson River cruise boats in the
1890s,[21] and some light-skinned Creoles, like Achille Baquet, moved easily
back and forth between white and black bands. White musicians had been
sitting in with black bands from the early days of jazz, and Benny Carter,
who was doing a lot of arranging for white bands, sat in with the Charlie

Barnet Orchestra in 1934.[22] It is also probable that in the western mining towns, where there was a good deal of racial mixing, there occasionally were mixed bands. And there had always been a lot of whites sitting in with blacks in the big-city black-and-tans.

But presenting a mixed group in a major hotel was quite a different matter from using one on a riverboat or in a mining camp saloon. Goodman was reluctant. Unlike some of the musicians of the time, he was not affected by racial prejudice. He said, "I can thank my parents for that, and thank my environment at that time. When I studied with my old clarinet teacher in Chicago [Schoepp] a Negro [Buster Bailey] followed me into the room, and we played duets together or something like that, you know."[23] But he had a new band that was a long way from having established itself. According to Oakley, "Benny hemmed and hawed, he wasn't at all sure it would go down."[24]

It was not really fair of Oakley and whoever else was involved to push Goodman on this point: They had nothing to lose, but it could cost Goodman his band if there proved to be a public uproar about it. Besides, he was playing the dance almost as a favor to Oakley and Ashcraft. Why should he be asked to jeopardize his future for it? But Helen was persuasive, and Goodman, to his credit, agreed to take the chance. *Down Beat* in its April issue reported, "Negotiations are under way to have Teddy Wilson, famous colored pianist," at the next Rhythm Club concert.[25]

In the end, it was all anti-climactic. Nobody cared what color Wilson was, and almost immediately the Trio was incorporated into the band's performance, coming on two or three times a night to play as a separate group. The consequences were enormous, but they were not apparent immediately. Reaction in the music business was that Goodman might get away with racial mixing in the Trio, but it would be quite a different thing to introduce blacks into the main body of the band. It did not happen immediately, but when it happened it came about in the most offhand way, with Goodman using Lionel Hampton on drums briefly in March of 1938 when Krupa left the band; Hampton occasionally filled in on drums with Goodman thereafter. A month or two later Charlie Barnet added black trumpeter Frankie Newton to his group; and in 1939 Fletcher Henderson played with both the small groups and the big band for a relatively brief period. Through the late 1930s and the 1940s white bandleaders increasingly brought black musicians into their groups, and by 1950 big jazz bands were racially mixed more often than not.

However, Goodman's experiment with racial mixing was not entirely without problems. According to Jimmy Maxwell, in 1940 when Goodman had Sid Catlett, John Simmons, Cootie Williams and Charlie Christian in the band, the manager of the Hotel New Yorker told Goodman, "I don't want these black guys coming through the lobby and through the restaurant. Have them go through the kitchen." Goodman was by then a star, and he said he would quit the job first. The manager then said to tell all the musicians to go through the kitchen. Goodman once more refused, and the matter was dropped.[26] Again, at the Dallas Exposition in 1937, a professor at the University of Texas who knew Wilson sent a bottle of champagne backstage, and then attempted to go back himself to have a drink of it with Wilson. A local cop threw him out. The next day the Dallas police chief sent for Lionel Hampton, who was now with the group, and told him he was in charge around there, and "If you have the slightest trouble at all, you come and let me know, because I'm the baddest man here."[27]

There were other problems. The producer of the *Camel Caravan* show, which the band was playing in 1936 and 1937, suggested to Goodman that he drop Hampton and Wilson because there had been letters of protest. Goodman of course refused.[28] But on the whole, the incidents were remarkably few, considering how worried everybody had been at the outset. Goodman said,

> We were pretty adamant about it. We were quite fortunate, too, you might say, in the sense that we were successful. And we certainly didn't compromise about that, anymore than we did about a lot of other things. I must say that we would tell promoters, or whatever it might be, if we were going into a territory that we knew was against this kind of procedure—we'd tell 'em in advance that that's what it was. We didn't want to give 'em any surprises. And if they didn't want it, we'd go someplace else.[29]

Wilson himself said,

> Oh it was a tremendous success. As a matter of fact, it was an asset, racial mixing. The interest in the United States was tremendous, and the public was so for the thing that not one negative voice in any audience did we ever get. Just tremendous enthusiasm. This interracial thing was just wonderful . . . the cooperation was good in the band. We were like brothers, the whole outfit. . . . There were southerners in it, Harry James from Texas and Dave Matthews from Oklahoma, and there were Jews and Christians and Lionel Hampton and I represented the Negroes in the band. . . . Everybody was a dedicated musician, we believed in what we were doing, socially and musically. But it was very different from Jackie Robinson having to fight the guys on the team and the fans and so on, insulting players on the field, giving them a hard time. The jazz fans were like they were just hungry for this sort of thing.[30]

Wilson probably exaggerates the upwelling of good feeling that the racial mixing produced. There were plenty of Americans, especially in the South, who did not like it. But the dance-band fans had for years been fox-trotting to the music of black orchestras in ballrooms and dance halls, and it did not seem to matter to them whether they heard Cootie Williams with Duke Ellington or with Goodman. In retrospect, it seems that Americans would have accepted mixed bands much earlier. Black and white actors had been appearing together in movies for some time. If they accepted that, surely they would have accepted the sight of a black musician in a white band.

Yet Wilson and Hampton could not, in the late 1930s, stay at white hotels. Wilson said,

> It's hard to call that a problem because it was the norm of the day. We didn't challenge the norm. . . . If we'd had to make a battle of that in every town on one-night stands, you couldn't ever get to work, making an issue of that. So Lionel and I generally would drive our cars and go into the Negro district of town and go to a Negro hotel. . . . We went along with the tide the way it was because we had opened up a door already, a giant crack.[31]

Wilson gives much of the credit for integrating the band to John Hammond: "He was the driving force behind the scenes of forming the Goodman Trio and putting me on an equal basis with Krupa in public—away from the recording studio. But in public, right out in the open, he pushed and pressured Goodman to add me on as a regular member of the band."[32]

However, Wilson made this statement years later, when he had come to loathe Goodman. At a television special salute to Hammond late in his life, at which Goodman also appeared, Leonard Feather said something to Wilson about them "rolling out the red carpet for Benny." Wilson replied, "It should be hot coals."[33] Benny deserves more credit than Wilson was willing to give him. It was Benny, not Hammond, after all, who had something to lose by taking a chance on the mixed group. Jimmy Maxwell, who grew up knowing blacks and was very sympathetic to their cause, pointed out that despite the fact that Goodman was always eager to make as much money as he could, he "cut off almost half the country"[34] (i.e., the South) to take in Wilson. Lionel Hampton said, "As far as I'm concerned, what he did in those days—and they were hard days in 1937—made it possible for Negroes to have their chance in baseball and other fields."[35]

Goodman's bringing of blacks into his orchestra did not alone lead to opening the doors to blacks in sports and elsewhere; there were many forces in the society impelling it toward integration. But it did show that

Americans would accept racial mixing more easily than anyone had suspected.

A second consequence of the public presentation of the Trio was to give
Teddy Wilson a prominence in popular music that only a few other blacks,
like Louis Armstrong, attained during that time. Ellington, Lunceford and
Basie were seen by the dance-band public primarily as "bandleaders," not
great jazz musicians. But Wilson was a sideman, an improvising jazz musician like Berigan, Krupa and Musso. As the swing band boom erupted in
the years following Wilson's accession to the Trio, he became famous
among swing fans. This would not have happened to him had he been
left in the obscurity of records. To be sure, it was the records which young
musicians of the time studied; but it was those several thousand appearances in theatres and ballrooms across the country with the Goodman Trio
and Quartet, before audiences of millions of Americans, that made him famous. How could people help liking this slim, good-looking, young black,
who conducted himself with a quiet demeanor and gentlemanly bearing?

Like a number of other young blacks who migrated into jazz at the time,
among them Duke Ellington, Claude Hopkins and Fletcher Henderson,
Teddy Wilson came from the upper margins of black society.[36] His father
graduated from Wesleyan College, one of the small, highly regarded colleges in New England that as a matter of conscience took in a few blacks.
He eventually moved to Austin, Texas, where he was dean of men at Sam
Houston College. Teddy's mother taught in the elementary grades there,
and Wilson was born in Austin in 1912. In about 1915 his father got a job
teaching English at the noted Tuskegee Institute, and Teddy grew up in
Greenwood, Alabama, near the Tuskegee campus. His father also led the
school choir—". . . with that school, music study was just sort of taken
for granted."[37] He was given piano lessons as a matter of course. These
were not jazz lessons but the routine classical studies that many children
got. Later, in high school, he played the violin, the clarinet and oboe in
various musical groups, and piano in the dance orchestra. "But the classical
foundation, and having learned to read, stood me in good stead."[38]

In most middle-class black homes jazz, and especially the blues, were
frowned upon as the music of rough working people. The Wilsons apparently were an exception, for there is a report that there were records by the
blues singers Mamie and Trixie Smith, Waller, Beiderbecke, Lang, Hines
and Armstrong in the home. By slowing down the record-player turntable,
he studied carefully the styles of both Hines and Waller.

His father died in 1926, and his mother took the family to Detroit, where
she had a sister, for the summer. Teddy graduated from high school in 1928,
spent a year as a music major at Talladega College, and in June 1929, went
to Detroit to live with his aunt. He began hearing important jazz musicians

of the time at the Greystone Ballroom, among them Jimmie Noone, Fletcher Henderson and McKinney's Cotton Pickers, a Detroit-based band. And he started gigging around the city, playing club dates. He worked briefly with Speed Webb, and then accepted a steady job in Toledo.

Toledo was the home base of Art Tatum. Wilson got to know him, and they would travel around to after-hours clubs together. "As long as we could stay up and physically play the piano we would take turns, and that was a very important point in my life, because Art Tatum was a tremendous influence on me as a jazz pianist, because back in school I had had all the recordings of Earl Hines and the early Fats Waller solos. . . ." Tatum, as he had been with Jess Stacy, was generous with his secrets. "He'd slow it right down, and let me stand behind his shoulder, and he would show me exactly what he did." "Art Tatum's feeling at the keyboard did not require very high volumes. He would build his intensity by making his harmonies much more complete. . . . In my own playing too I keep with a narrow range. . . . I use a finger technique inspired by listening to Tatum, and I combine that with the melodic idea and touch of Hines' octave playing and, since I can stretch the 10th in the left hand, I use the stride bass I got from Fats Waller."[39] Thus, both of Goodman's first important pianists had been tutored by Tatum.

In 1931 Wilson shifted his base to Chicago. He played briefly with one of Louis Armstrong's bands; but more important, he happened to get a job working with the Eddie Moore band that subbed in the Grand Terrace for Hines, when the Hines band was on the road. John Hammond, who had a powerful radio in his car and was constantly searching the dial for unknown bands, heard the group and was impressed by the pianist. Hammond was, at that point, helping Benny Carter to get a dance band going. He urged Carter to bring Wilson into his band, a request Carter was not in a position to refuse in any case. Hammond paid for Wilson to come to New York.[40] The Carter band was not successful, but Hammond began to use Wilson on the famous Brunswick series, and then came the celebrated party at the Norvo house that led to the formation of the Goodman Trio.

Wilson's mentors had all come out of the stride style of piano playing, a direct descendent of ragtime, in which a strong bass made up of alternations of single notes, octaves, or tenths and full chords keep up a relentless, driving rhythm, over which the right hand plays repeated "pianistic" figures—figures that are not so much song-like melodies but worked out to fall neatly under the five fingers of the hand. Waller was trained in this style and played it all his life. Hines, too, originated as a stride player, but developed a muscular, aggressive style in which the stride bass was constantly interrupted, and the right-hand figures suddenly gave way to jagged running phrases, often in octaves with a terminal tremolo. Tatum had founded his style on Waller's—his opening chorus of his 1933 "Tea for Two" could have been played by Waller except for a brief key change in the twentieth measure. But he very quickly established his own method, a rich, baroque style built on dense harmonies, fleeting shifts into distant keys, long wiry runs and a good deal more rubato than is customary in jazz playing.

Wilson concocted his style out of a blend of ingredients taken from these men. He occasionally played the ordinary stride bass Waller would have used, mostly when he was accompanying a soloist. Perhaps two-thirds of the time he played something else in the bass—single notes, tenths, octaves, riff-like figures, even leaving an occasional beat untended here and there. In the very slow "The Man I Love," done by the Goodman Quartet in 1937, he plays almost fugal figures in the bass.

This highly varied line owes something to the jagged, interrupted stride of Hines, but it is far less forceful. As we have seen, Hines began his career in a day before electric amplification and so had to hammer at the piano to make it sound over the band. The Wilson bass is more a "comping," or "accompanying" bass, supplying punctuation and harmonic suggestion, rather than a driving rhythm, although Wilson could certainly play with rhythmic drive when it was called for.

Wilson's right hand owed more to Tatum than to Hines. A substantial proportion of his figures are descending runs. In general, although hardly always, Wilson starts his phrases up the keyboard and comes down. Rising figures are likely to be tenths or octaves, usually sparser phrases whose purpose is mainly rhythmic. At fast tempos the runs are often fairly even eighth notes, but at slow tempos, as for example his solo on the bridge to the first chorus of the Goodman Trio "Body and Soul" of 1935, he uses triplets, sixteenths and less definable patterns, often somewhat rubato.

As a whole it is a light, feathery style perfectly suited to playing in small groups like the Trios and Quartets. Wilson had an excellent technique and in his solos he could be appropriately busy, filling in the chinks and crannies in order to keep the music moving. But when backing Goodman or Hampton, both busy players, he played more sparsely, his light bass and relatively simple right hand unobtrusively complementing the soloist. He was, in any case, being supported by Gene Krupa, a forceful drummer, and he did not need to pound out a heavy rhythm.

Wilson's playing, however, was not as simple as it might appear to a casual listening. His son Ted, a drummer and music teacher, said, "He always had a definite, clear melodic line going on top and a powerful but controlled rhythm line on the bottom. Between top and bottom, however, there was so much going on—harmonic colorations and continually inventive countermelodies."[41]

However, it was undoubtedly the surface sparkle and simplicity, with its light, polished swing, that so appealed to the fans. The early Goodman Trios and Quartets are filled with a merry dash, a happy chasing hither and yon which was enormously exciting, and Wilson was a major contributor to this effect. His popularity soared quickly, and by the mid-1930s he was the major model for young pianists all over the United States. Tatum and Hines were playing in a heavier style which lacked the dash of Wilson's more effervescent manner. Fats Waller had his own radio show, made movies and was the best known of all the jazz pianists of the time. All of these men had followings; but Wilson was the one who captured the young pianists—for one thing, his style seemed easy to imitate—and by 1940 almost all the pianists in jazz were playing in his manner. And it was on the Wilson style that Bud Powell and other beboppers based the bop treatment of the piano.

Taken all together, the Congress Hotel engagement was a great success. *Time* mentioned the Rhythm Club affair in a piece on popular music.[42] In March the band picked up a radio show sponsored by the Elgin Watch Company. In May the band won *Down Beat's* "All-time Swing Band" poll.[43] The Congress booking, originally scheduled for a month, continued for six. Finally, in May the band went to New York, where it played one-nighters, recorded and made radio broadcasts.

There were additional personnel changes. Joe Harris left to go back to the West Coast to work at the M.G.M. studios. He was replaced by Murray McEachern, who would have a long career with the swing bands and later with the movie studios. A second addition was Gordon "Chris" Griffin, the first of the men who would form what would be considered the classic Goodman trumpet section. Griffin had worked with some of the early swing bands, but he thought of himself primarily as a jazz musician. Goodman, however, saw him as a section man, and during his three-year tenure with the band he played few solos. Arranger Jimmy Mundy, who had been working in Chicago with Earl Hines, began writing for Goodman full time.[44] The long engagement at the Congress had required Goodman to beef up his book. Mundy would be the band's principal arranger through 1936 and 1937, and would continue to make important contributions for several years thereafter. Among his early hits for the band were "House Hop," "Madhouse" and "Swingtime in the Rockies."

By the early summer of 1936 it was clear that the Goodman band was a resounding success. It had been an extraordinary twelve months, beginning with the ending of the *Let's Dance* show, the unnerving failure at the Roosevelt, the ups and downs of the trip west, capped by the dismal reception at Elitch's, and then suddenly the roaring success at the Palomar and the Congress. The band was now "hot" in the show-business sense. Willard

Alexander signed it to make a movie called *The Big Broadcast of 1937*, and it replaced the Casa Loma Orchestra on the *Camel Caravan*, an important and popular radio program. According to Russ Connor, at the beginning the show was an hour long, with Goodman and the Nat Shilkret Orchestra sharing the time.[45] The *Camel Caravan* was listened to by most dance-band fans religiously. Goodman stayed with it for some time, and it was important in building his celebrity.

The balloon was now ascending, and morale in the band was high. Symptomatic was the fact that while they were at the Congress, Tommy Dorsey had called Art Rollini in Chicago and offered him a job for the same money Goodman was paying him, with a promise to give him more solo space. Rollini turned the job down: "Why go to the number three band when I was already playing with the number one?"[46]

In July the band climbed onto a train and began to work its way west with a series of one-nighters, heading for the Coast, where it would make the movie and double at the Palomar. They traveled this time by Pullman; Goodman had a drawing room, Helen Ward her own compartment. The force of events was now beginning to isolate Benny from the other men. Goodman had never been particularly close to the others, always a bit of a loner. But now he was becoming celebrated, and while the other musicians, especially Helen Ward, were also gaining some celebrity among dance-band fans, it was Goodman who mattered. He was now making enough money to allow him to hire whomever he wanted for the most part. He could do what he pleased, and when they reached the Coast it pleased him to fire Dick Clark. Clark is not remembered in jazz history as a master musician, but he was a good section player and a competent improviser. He had, furthermore, stuck it out with Goodman through the hard days. Unfortunately, Clark was prematurely bald. Goodman wanted his band looking as if it was filled with enthusiastic young men, and in Salt Lake City he told Art Rollini, "When we get to California, I'm going to get rid of the bald-headed son of a bitch."[47] There may, of course, have been more to it than that. But Goodman clearly had taken a dislike to Clark, quite possibly for no very good reason, as he often did, and in California he gave Clark his notice. Years later Clark said, "I've no ill-will toward Benny."[48] But it could not have been very pleasant for him to watch the band he had helped from the early days rise into massive celebrity with him on the sidelines.

A second man to leave was Nate Kazebier. Exactly what happened is not clear, but he and Goodman had words over something, and Kaz quit in the middle of the movie shooting. Mannie Klein, who had moved to Los Angeles to work in the movie studios, temporarily filled in.

The band went into the Palomar at three times the fee it had been paid only a year earlier—*Orchestra World* reported that Goodman's "astounding rise in the world . . . has made him one of the key money-makers for MCA."[49] It also began rehearsing for the movie, and then doing the actual shooting, which required the men to get up at five in the morning after having played at the Palomar until one o'clock at night. They were exhausted much of the time, and according to Pee Wee Erwin, Goodman was only paying them scale for the work, even though he collected $50,000 for the movie stint. (Erwin said that base pay was $125 a week, with records and radio broadcasts bringing total income to perhaps $250. Erwin thought this was low, which perhaps it was for musicians in a band as successful as this, but it compares well with Depression salaries—at the time the median income for professionals was under $2,000 a year.)[50]

Goodman now had to find permanent replacements for Clark and Kazebier. As it happened, a band led by Gil Evans, who would become one of jazz's most celebrated composers, was working at a club in Balboa Beach, with Stan Kenton on piano. Art Rollini claims that he was the first of the Goodman men to hear the band and was impressed by a saxophonist named Vido Musso, who had a "huge tone" and played with fire.[51] He told Benny about Musso, and Benny told him to bring Musso in. Vido turned up for the last set at the Palomar shortly afterwards. Goodman did not ask him to sight-read an arrangement, but called for "Honeysuckle Rose" and turned Musso loose on a lengthy solo. He hired Musso then and there.

Unfortunately, Benny neglected to ask Musso if he could read music. Vido had been born in Italy and had come to the United States at about the age of seven. Like many immigrants, he was badly educated in most things, including music. His malapropisms circulated through the music world. He talked about seeing a boat "drown," and about having a boil "glanced, and the doc put some easy tape on it."[52]

Goodman, still unaware of Musso's deficiencies, asked Rollini to go over the tenor book with him:

> I met Vido the next afternoon at one and, with two tenors, we turned to the first number in the book, "Minnie the Moocher's Wedding Day." Vido struggled. He couldn't read. We went over and over it, but with the highly syncopated charts he was lost. I said, "OK, Vido, let's go to the next number." I forget at the moment what it was, but it was the same struggle. Our one hour was over.
>
> At two o'clock the band came in to rehearse. Vido struggled and Benny looked at me. I just stared back at him. Benny nodded his head knowingly. Vido sweated that night out and finally made his famous remark: "It's not the *notes* that bother me, it's them damn *restes*."[53]

Musso was correct. Highly syncopated music is filled with "restes," to allow for phrases to begin on second beats of measures, notes to be played after the beat, and the like. It is impossible to read this kind of music a note at a time; musicians must recognize whole patterns at least a bar in length, and know how each pattern is played. Musso was reading the notes one at a time, constantly trying to count each rest as it came along, a hopeless job. But Goodman stuck with Musso, and Vido persevered, woodshedding the book after the job. Eventually he learned the book and became a passable reader.

Musso was an interesting choice. Goodman was a perfectionist, demanding good intonation, clean attack and, what is most difficult of all in a swing band, the careful coordination of each section so that the details of dynamics, delay, vibrato and the like were played the same way. Goodman was, furthermore, impatient with players he considered to be inadequate, and as time went on, fired them more and more quickly, sometimes after only a single night's trial. Yet he hired Musso on first hearing, and kept him on when Musso was making a hash of the arrangements night after night. But Musso was a very hot, passionate improviser who played heedlessly, with power and drive, the kind of playing Goodman was drawn to. Furthermore, the "kids" who constituted the bulk of his audience wanted strong meat, and in this Goodman was lucky, because that was what he wanted, too. In Musso he had found such a man, a tenor player far more forceful than Clark or Rollini, who played with a smooth, legato style with a light tone.

A second arrival was a musician cast in the same mold, Lionel Hampton, whose image even today is of a man pounding fast passages on the vibraphone, his face covered with sweat.[54] Hampton came from a musical family. His father, Charles Hampton, who was killed in action in World War I, was a singer and pianist. His uncle, Richard Morgan, although not a musician himself, liked to surround himself with them, and eventually became the consort of Bessie Smith.

> My uncle bought me everything. Silk shirts, the finest clothes, my first marimba, my first set of drums—it had a light in it. . . . He was crazy about piano players, but all the musicians used to love to come to his place because they could meet all the chicks there, and my uncle would give them all the whiskey they could drink, and all the chitterlins they could eat. I used to dream of joining Ma Rainey's band. . . .[55]

Hampton, thus, was brought up in the heart of Chicago's South Side at the time it was boiling with the new hot music. Hampton played with a fife-and-drum band and learned the rudiments. He then played in the famous *Chicago Defender's* Newsboy Band, led by the equally famous Major N. Clark Smith, who had a hand in teaching many of the young black jazz musicians coming out of Chicago at this time, and later. Hampton listened especially to Jimmy Bertrand, a locally celebrated show-band drummer who played at the Vendome Theatre with the Erskine Tate Orchestra. Bertrand played chimes and xylophone and indulged in showy displays, and he made a mark on Hampton, who always had a penchant for showy effects.

At fourteen Hampton went on the road, eventually landing in Los Angeles with the Les Hite band. He gigged around, working for Hite and various leaders and finally went with Hite into Frank Sebastian's Cotton Club, the best-known cabaret on the West Coast, which attracted movie stars, gamblers, mobsters and young swells with money. The band also included trombonist Lawrence Brown, shortly to become a star with Duke Ellington.

In 1930 Louis Armstrong came to Sebastian's to front the Hite band for several months. By this time Hampton had got a set of orchestra bells, which he occasionally played with Armstrong. At one point Armstrong and the Hite band went into a studio to record. They noticed a vibraharp, then a rare instrument, in a corner. Armstrong asked Hampton if he could play it. Hamp said that it was basically the same as the orchestra bells and he played brief passages on some of the records with Armstrong.

By 1936 Hampton was working at a rough sailors' joint with sawdust on the floor, called the Paradise Night Club, on Sixth and Main.[56] He was now an all-around showman, playing vibes, drums, singing and leaping around. Who precisely discovered Hampton there is moot. Pee Wee Erwin said that he and Hymie Schertzer frequently went out after the Palomar job in search of food, and stumbled into the Paradise one night.[57] John Hammond simply said that he "found" Hampton at the Paradise.[58] Art Rollini said that "a few of us went down to the Paradise Club" to hear Hampton.[59] However, Jimmy Maxwell said that he and some others from the Gil Evans band, where Rollini found Musso, knew about the Hampton group and used to sit in from time to time.[60] Hammond had come out to the West Coast for the Palomar opening, and to scout bands. He went to hear the Gil Evans band and was told about Hampton by Maxwell and some others, which led him to the Paradise. Hampton said only that "One night I heard all this clarinet playing, looked around, and there was Benny Goodman."[61]

The truth is probably that the local musicians had known about Hampton for some time. After all, he had spent a winter backing the great Louis Armstrong, and had recorded with him. Word about Hampton would have filtered back to Goodman, Hammond and the musicians in the band. When word goes out about a wonderful musician playing at such and such a place, few musicians can rest until they have gone to see for themselves whether the word is correct or, as is so often the case, the result of too much local enthusiasm. Inevitably the Goodman musicians would have been drawn to the Paradise.

In any case, Goodman came in and jammed with Hampton for several hours into the early morning and then, according to Hampton, Goodman brought Wilson and Krupa in to try Hampton with the Trio.[62] He was pleased with the result, and asked Hampton to join them on an upcoming record date. The result was the first Benny Goodman Quartet record, "Moonglow," one of the classics from the period. At a second session the group recorded three more sides which have also become famous: "Dinah," "Exactly Like You" and "Vibraphone Blues," the last two of which Hampton sang. But these were just special record dates; Goodman did not bring Hampton into the Palomar, but continued to work there with the original Trio.

In September the band went back East for a series of dates which included the famous Steel Pier in Atlantic City, and others around New England, ending with what would be a long engagement at the Madhattan Room of the Hotel Pennsylvania, in New York. It was symptomatic of the sudden rise of swing music: not much more than a year before the band had been summarily dismissed from a similar hotel for playing too loud.

There were again personnel changes, principally in the trumpet section. During the months from the end of the Congress Hotel job to the opening at the Pennsylvania Hotel, Pee Wee Erwin, Nate Kazebier, Zeke Zarchey, Herb Geller, Mannie Klein and Sterling Bose, a New Orleans musician of the dixieland school, had been in the section. While the band was at the Steel Pier, somebody happened to hear the house band, led by Alex Bartha, and was struck by a powerful trumpet player in the group. Who first noticed Ziggy Elman is again moot. Art Rollini said it was his wife, Ena, who heard Elman playing not only trumpet but vibes, piano and baritone saxophone with Bartha. According to this story, Elman sat in and played at a rehearsal for a *Camel Caravan* show, "and Benny hired him on the spot, paying off Sterling Bose."[63] Other sources say that Bose was ill, and Goodman was looking for a replacement in any case.[64]

Elman was born Harry Finkelman in Philadelphia and raised in Atlantic City. He was a natural musician. He studied violin as a boy, and was appointed concert master of his school orchestra. He went on to learn trumpet, trombone, clarinet, the saxophones and piano, and developed an out-going personality. George Simon called him "a colorful, enthusiastic, cigar-smoking extrovert,"[65] and Otis Ferguson remarked on "that eight-inch cigar permanently in his teeth and talking the current obscene jargon of the day in that noisy gangster's voice of his."[66] By the time he was eighteen he was working with Bartha.

Ziggy Elman was a powerful player who not only could play fine lead trumpet but could tear off those hard-driving jazz solos Goodman so liked. Elman also, apparently, had learned trumpet on his own and had developed a homebrewed technique which, as is often the case with self-taught trumpeters, required a good deal of pressure in the upper register. Elman went on to become one of the stars of the Goodman Orchestra.

Four months later, there joined an even more significant trumpet player, one of the heroes of the swing band era. That, of course, was Harry James, next to Gene Krupa the most important sideman Goodman ever had. James[67] was born in Albany, Georgia, in 1916 to a show business family. His father was director and trumpet soloist with the orchestra for the Mighty Haag Circus, and his mother was a trapeze artist. Harry grew up breathing music. He was playing drums by the age of four, trumpet by eight. By nine he was working in his father's orchestra, and at twelve he was leading one of the circus bands.

Eventually the family gave up the circus and settled in Beaumont, Texas, presumably in order to raise the children in a more normal environment. As a teenager James gigged around Texas in the Galveston and Dallas areas. At some point he was heard by Ben Pollack, who was now struggling to get in on the swing band movement he had played so important a role in getting started. James went with Pollack in 1935. By 1936 the band was an all-star group which included James, Glenn Miller, Charlie Spivak, Irving Fazola, Freddie Slack and Dave Matthews, all of whom went on to become swing-band stars. According to one report,[68] Irving Goodman heard James with the Pollack band and told Benny about him. And in January 1937, while the band was at the Madhattan Room, James joined. After James joined, Art Rollini told Goodman that he had jammed with James after hours when they were at the Congress in Chicago. "Why didn't you tell me he was so great?" Benny demanded. "I just didn't want to see another man go," Rollini said.[69]

The famous Goodman trumpet section, possibly the most acclaimed trumpet section of the swing-band era, was now in place. There is no question but that the acclaim was justified. Jimmy Maxwell said that in most swing bands the first trumpet played lead, the second was the hot man, and the third was "an alcoholic or somebody's relative."[70] But in this trumpet section all three men could read, execute and play first-rate jazz solos. Elman and James did most of the soloing on records, but on location they frequently swapped the books around, so that any of them might solo or play lead at one time or another. It is only necessary to listen to the first chorus of "Don't Be That Way" to see the excellence of this team—the accuracy of the punctuation behind the saxes, the subtle dynamics of the bridge, the attention to details of attack and length of notes. I think that in particular James added a verve, a spirit, evident in subtle twists he applied to notes, mainly through half-valving, that lifted the section up, and with it, the whole band. But all three trumpeters were important to the sum effect.

In November, 1936, Lionel Hampton joined the band as a full-time member. Hampton's wife Gladys was a successful modiste, having worked for famous movie stars like Joan Crawford and Rosalind Russell, and it would cost her a career to come east. Nonetheless, Hampton said that he would not go without her. Goodman offered plane tickets, but instead Hampton hooked a little trailer to his car, loaded his drum set and vibes into the trailer, and drove to New York.[71] He would prove a valuable addition because he could sing and could play drums when Goodman had fired one drummer but had not yet found another he liked.

Finally, in about December, Helen Ward left in order to marry her second husband, Albert Marx. She had been with the band for only two years, but they were a critical two years. She had been important to the band's success, and it is her name, more than any other vocalist, which comes to mind when we think of the Goodman group. But in fact, she was not with the band when it was at the height of its fame in the years from 1937 into the early 1940s. How Goodman felt about her is suggested by the fact that he had trouble finding another singer who satisfied him. There came into the band a string of singers who stayed only briefly—Margaret McCrae, Frances Hunt, Peg LaCentra, Betty Van, some of whom never recorded with the orchestra. Not until August of the next year would Goodman find somebody he would stick with, Martha Tilton.

Sometime that winter of the Hotel Pennsylvania engagement, Willard Alexander booked the Goodman Orchestra into the Paramount Theatre in the Times Square area of New York. The opening was scheduled for March 3, with the band continuing to play at the Madhattan Room after the last of the five daily theatre shows. The band would share the bill with a Claudette Colbert film called *Maid of Salem*, which has found its niche in the history of American popular culture through that association. Neither Goodman, Alexander, the theatre management nor the people in the band expected anything particular from the Paramount job. The band had had some good audiences in theatres, and some poor ones. To everybody concerned it was just another job which would bring in some extra money, and cause the musicians to lose a lot of sleep. Among other things, there was still the *Camel Caravan* to rehearse and play on Tuesdays.

The musicians arrived at the theatre at seven in the morning opening day to play a rehearsal. They were astonished to discover hundreds of people, most of them students, lined up at the box office, waiting for it to open. One report later said that there had been six or seven hundred fans in front of the theatre an hour before sunrise, most of them "high school kids from the Bronx and Brooklyn and Staten Island," who were dancing, shouting and lighting fires. "Fans were multiplying by the minute, pouring up out of the Times Square subway exits like bees from a smoked hive."[72] At seven-thirty, ten mounted policemen arrived.

The band rehearsed, took a break, and then climbed onto the rising bandstand that was a feature of the Paramount: One of the most spine-chilling of experiences for swing band fans over the next decade would be to sit in the Paramount audience, begin to hear the faint first notes of a band's theme—Woody Herman's "Blue Flame," Glenn Miller's "Moonlight Serenade," or Goodman's "Let's Dance"—and then as the music grew louder, watch the band rise slowly and majestically into sight. It was an event that jerked fans from their seats with a roar, and the first to pull them to their feet was the Benny Goodman band on that March 3, 1937, at 8:30 in the morning. Almost from the first moment the theatre was in an uproar.[73] The kids began dancing in the aisles and crowding around the bandstand beseeching autographs. Later in the week, kids would actually climb onto the bandstand, where there was more room, to jitterbug. That first day ushers fled among them, trying to restore control. The theatre manager was frantic, certain that somebody was going to be hurt. It went on like that all day for five shows, leaving the bandsmen exhausted. Twenty-one thousand people saw that first show, and they brought a record nine hundred dollars' worth of candy. And it went on that way for the entire engagement.[74] *Variety* referred to the event as "the now historic clamor that greeted Benny Goodman's opening show at the Paramount."[75] *Billboard* said, "Benny Goodman's Orchestra is just over two years old; yet in that period the band has become one of the top drawing cards in show business."[76] Goodman's picture was on the cover of the paper. He was now famous.

# 14
# The Swing-Band
# Phenomenon

In its issue for February 1936, *Down Beat* ran a front-page story with the headline, "Flesh and Blood Bands Break Records, Set New Money High." The story went on to say, "Casa Loma's sensational success is not a 'freak' but a definite straw in the wind. . . . So look up all you cats, and get ready to leave the old milk and cracker diet, for the good old days are coming back."[1]

When this story was written, the Goodman band had been at the Congress Hotel for a month or so; the triumphant opening at the Palomar was only five months past; and the band, although celebrated in the world of dance-band musicians and jazz fans, was by no means a national phenomenon. Its impact was not yet great enough to have caused "flesh and blood bands" to break attendance records. Goodman did not create the swing band phenomenon by himself. He was, instead, riding a wave that was rapidly rising, a wave he would come to the top of, and in so doing heave it up to greater heights.

The swing band, as I have suggested, evolved out of the big jazz-inflected dance-cum-show bands of the 1920s. Some of these bands, like Ellington, Pollack, Henderson and Goldkette, played a lot of jazz; others, like Specht, Whiteman, Ben Bernie, Guy Lombardo, played mainly soft dance music. But in all cases it was a mix. Even the most commercial of these bands could play excellent jazz when called upon to do so: Specht's 1926 version of "Static Strut" is as hot as any Pollack piece, except for the lesser ability of the soloists, and Ben Bernie's "Sweet Georgia Brown" of 1925 was certainly hot. Conversely, Duke Ellington right along was recording tepid commercial pieces like "Best Wishes" and "Any Time, Any Day, Anywhere." Henderson perforce played waltzes and tangos at the Roseland Ballroom in New York, his main base during his heyday.

This distinction between what came to be known as "hot" and "sweet" bands was carried into the swing era. In fact, many of the sweet bands from the twenties went right on undisturbed into the 1930s and beyond: Bernie, Whiteman, Vincent Lopez and others remained successful well into the swing period, and Guy Lombardo continued playing in almost the same fashion for decades.

But the hot side of the equation was changing. The only one of the big hot bands from the 1920s to have a significant career in the swing era was the Ellington Orchestra. The Goldkette band died of financial difficulties in 1927; the Pollack band ran aground over personalities; McKinney's Cotton Pickers simply got lost; Henderson's group fell apart due to his own inept leadership; the Moten band in the Southwest collapsed when the leader suddenly died. With the exception of the Casa Loma and Earl Hines, the major orchestras and hot bands of the swing era were formed after 1930, and most of them were formed after 1934 or so: Lunceford and Eddy Duchin in 1931, Ozzie Nelson in 1932, Freddy Martin and Charlie Barnet in 1933, the Dorsey Brothers, Shep Fields, Kay Kayser and Goodman in 1934, and the rest later.[2]

It was the hot bands which characterized the period. To be sure, the most popular of the hot bands played a great deal of ordinary dance music, and sentimental ballads were a staple of every program. Glenn Miller's "Serenade in Blue," Tommy Dorsey's "I'll Never Smile Again," with Frank Sinatra singing the vocal, Andy Kirk's "Until the Real Thing Comes Along," Jimmie Lunceford's "My Blue Heaven," and many others were hits.

But the uptempo swingers were what mattered. Dorsey's "Marie," Barent's "Cherokee," Lunceford's "White Heat," Miller's "In the Mood," Ellington's "Cottontail," Basie's "Jumpin' at the Woodside" were the essence, the pieces that characterized the swing period.

The bands that typified the movement were formed expressly to meet a new taste, and were playing a new music. They had evolved out of the hot bands of the 1920s, especially the Pollack, Henderson, Nichols and Goldkette bands, and for a few years several of them struggled to find their audience, among them the bands of Louis Armstrong, Hines, Casa Loma, Pollack, Barnet and the Dorseys. But it was Goodman who hit upon the formula, who found the style, and after the Palomar and the Congress Hotel the music industry came alive. There was now a new music, with a large audience. A lot of musicians around the country wanted to play it, and they began putting together swing bands of their own. The band bookers and management agencies in turn quickly began looking for groups which could follow the success of Goodman, Casa Loma and others. The Artie Shaw and Woody Herman bands were formed in 1936. In the same year Hammond and Alexander went out to Kansas City to sign Count Basie.[3] With the uproar over Goodman's 1937 Paramount engagement, the floodgates opened. It was now clear that you could not only get paid to play good music, you could get rich doing it. In the months following the Paramount stay Glenn Miller, Bunny Berigan and Larry Clinton started key bands, and in the two years that followed Gene Krupa, Alvino Rey, Les Brown, Benny Carter, Tony Pastor, Teddy Powell, Jack Teagarden, Claude Thornhill, Harry James and Will Bradley formed their own swing bands. It was an amoeba-like process, with a musician becoming famous as a sideman with one band, getting backing on the strength of his name, and in turn producing famous sidemen who would start bands of their own. By 1940 there existed in the United States at least fifty celebrated dance bands, and hundreds of others scrambling to earn national reputations, and the money and glory that went with it.

The key, as everybody said at the time, was to find a musical identity, a "style" as the term was, of your own that would make your band instantly recognizable to the swing fans who could make or break reputations. Each band had a musical theme—Miller's "Moonlight Serenade," Tommy Dorsey's "I'm Gettin' Sentimental Over You," Herman's "Blue Flame," Basie's "Jumpin' at the Woodside." Each band also had its distinctive uniform, and characteristic manner of presentation, like the waving around of instruments with drill-team precision of the Lunceford band. Thus, what had started as an interest in a certain kind of music, especially among the young, had become by the time of the Paramount opening a fad, a craze, a social phenomenon. Young people liked swing, and to many of them it was a matter of intense interest, to the point where they took up musical instruments in order to play it. But there was more to it than the music, for, especially after the noise in the press about the bedlam at the Paramount, swing became a central facet of the teen culture. Adolescents felt it necessary to know about the bands, to be able to recognize this or that style, to dance the appropriate dances, to buy the records, to listen to them on the radio.

The swing-band fans—hepcats as they came to be called—were very similar to followers of sports. The hepcats had their favorite "teams" whose activities they closely followed; they knew the names of the "players" on those teams, and could recognize from their "styles" whether a particular solo was by Harry James or Ziggy Elman, just as the baseball fan is able to recognize at a distance a given batter by his "stance" at the plate. The more avid fans read Down Beat and developed a taste for arcanae: Al Klink was the saxophonist who traded "fours" with Tex Benecke on "In the Mood"; it was not Lester Young but Herschel Evans who played the solo on Basie's "Blue and Sentimental."

Fan clubs were formed, at first spontaneously, and then with considerable and entirely cynical guidance from the offices of band managers. These fan clubs usually circulated regular newsletters, often financed by band publicity departments, and heads of major fan clubs were seen as people of importance by band managements, who arranged for them to meet their heroes fairly frequently.

A surprising number of the fan club presidents were young women—indeed, girls still in high school or college. Hot music had been preeminently a male province. For whatever complex of reasons, the bulk of the early jazz musicians had been male and so had most of the early jazz fans. A Helen Oakley was a rarity.

But the swing band phenomenon swept up a lot of females as well. Photographs of swing band audiences show substantial numbers of young women.[4] Of course that was inevitable at ballrooms, where it might be presumed that the girls were there at the behest of the boys. But that was not necessarily the case in theatres. Some of the girls were there because they liked the music; others came for social and sexual purposes. These bands, after all, were stocked with sprucely uniformed young heroes, many of them barely out of high school themselves. Art Rollini, speaking of the Paramount engagement, said:

> The girls would wave at us and many of the single boys in the band would motion to the girls to meet them at the stage door. After a show there would be many girls waiting at the stage door who would do anything to have a date with these boys. . . . Fan mail poured into each member of the band, giving telephone numbers. . . .[5]

As is usually the case with social phenomena of this kind, there were special styles of dress, a code language, requisite forms of dances, informal ceremonies. For the girls the dress was saddle shoes, short white "bobby sox," a fairly short pleated dress, usually white, which cupped upwards when the wearer twirled on the dance floor, and blouses and sweaters. In reality, these costumes were more an ideal than a fact, seen more regularly in the movies than on dance floors. But they did exist, and they were the model which youths attempted to approach, if not always achieve, as a look at photographs of the time will indicate. (As a footnote, in 1966 I had the good luck to maneuver my way into a huge dance hall in Leningrad, strictly against the wishes of Intourist, where I sat in with the Josef Weinstein Orchestra, a big band on the order of the Basie band of the day. I was astonished to see on the floor in front of me literally hundreds of young Leningrad girls wearing the full costume—the bobby sox, saddle shoes, pleated skirts—all doing the suzie-Q and the big apple. When I asked some of the musicians about this later, they pointed out that the American movies Russians were allowed to see at that time most frequently came from the period of the war, when America and the U.S.S.R. were allies, and the Russians were being presented to the American public as good fellows. These kids had seen films like *Stage Door Canteen* again and again.)

The dress for males only arrived in the latter years of the swing period, and was never as widely adopted as the female version, though it had a considerable influence on male fashion of the period. This was the famous "zoot suit," which featured trousers with a tiny cuff and very wide knee to produce "pegged" pants, and a single-breasted jacket with very wide artificial shoulders and a narrow waist set artificially low. The wearer might also sport a porkpie hat and a very long watch or key chain, which he would swing round a finger as he lounged at a corner. The zoot suit, which is presumed to have originated in Harlem, was too extreme for all but a minority of males, but its effect showed in the wide-shouldered jackets and broad-legged trousers stylish during the time.

Critical to the mix were a set of dances referred to generally as jitterbugging. Hot music in the twentieth century has always spawned dances—the cakewalk of the ragtime period, the trots of the early jazz days, the Charleston of the 1920s, the twist and the frug of early rock and roll and the various dances of the discotheques more recently. In the swing era it was the shag, trucking, pecking, the big apple, the lindy hop, the suzie-Q. Like the costume, the dances have been thought to have originated in Harlem, principally at the famous Savoy Ballroom, where there was a good deal of competitive dancing by the young blacks who populated the hall. In fact, while many of these dances did originate at the Savoy, a lot of them were created by professional show dancers.

They were all quite similar. The boy and girl were joined at arm's length by their right hands, and danced separately, coming together at moments to twirl or perform other maneuvers in which the girl might be thrown in the air, or slid between the legs of the boy. When done by couples who had practiced in their living rooms, they could be quite impressive displays of coordinated and athletic dancing. But as done by kids at record hops, in high school gyms and similar places, where most of this sort of dancing took place, it was all much rougher, more improvised and spontaneous. The movie version was a much slicker article than what was brewed at home.

The language, too, was to some extent invented by publicity agents: Cab Calloway and others published glossaries of swing terms.[6] But there was nonetheless a code language in use by swing fans and musicians: the cats were hep, the swingeroos were killer-dillers, the band was in the groove, the ickies were square. And there were the little password ceremonies: to give some one some skin was to press the palms, held vertical, together. Sometimes the palms were rotated slightly a few inches apart.

It should be borne in mind that for most teenagers hearing a live band was a relatively rare experience. Only the more affluent big city kids could afford to see the bands in theatres and ballrooms more than once a month or a few times a year. In the main, most teenagers got their swing from records, from local bands, many of them composed of their fellow high-school students playing stock arrangements, from regular evening broadcasts of the swing bands on location and from the new phenomenon of the disk jockey show, like those of Al Jarvis on the West Coast and Martin Block in New York.

Youngsters who took swing seriously listened to it every day, no doubt to the detriment of their studies, but even those who followed swing mainly for social reasons heard a great deal of it. Small groups of kids might gather several times a week in a home where the parents would be absent, to listen to records, dance, drink soft drinks and sometimes beer. Not every young American was interested in swing by any means, and those who followed it closely enough to know the names of the soloists were a minority. But of some forty million people who were teenagers during the swing era, certainly a majority owned at least a few swing records and danced to the music regularly.

To some extent, the music was seen by these young people as an aspect of rebellion. The social revolt of the generation of the swing era was not nearly as marked or severe as the ones of the 1920s and the 1960s. Those were times of prosperity, when youth could afford to disavow the culture which was supporting it. The kids of the swing era were children of the Depression, scrambling to find after-school jobs for twenty-five cents an hour to earn the money for their cherished records. (You worked for as much as two hours to buy one 78, three minutes a side.) The crucial thing for the working-class youngster was a job, any job, when they were very hard to find; for a middle-class child it was to get that high-school diploma which would lead to a white-collar job. Those who could not get regular jobs could not marry, could not set up households, could not lead ordinary lives. There was neither time nor energy for a serious social revolution.

Nonetheless, these young people saw swing as *their* music, something that was anti-establishment. For one thing, at a time when sex before marriage was not generally acceptable for women—although of course it was practiced far more extensively than it was supposed to be—swing music was seen to have erotic overtones. Many songs were mildly suggestive: "All or Nothing at All," "That Old Black Magic," "Let's Get Lost." The athletic jitterbugging done by bare-legged girls in short skirts inevitably revealed a lot of thigh and sometimes glimpses of panties, and the music itself, with its regular pulse and wailing saxophones, seemed to some likely to arouse unfortunate passions. Compared with the open sexuality of today this sounds all very decorous. But that was a day when movies were censored to eliminate any overt sex, and a magazine like *Playboy* could not have been published legally.

The swing-band movement was thus an inescapable, pervasive national phenomenon which touched, one way or another, most Americans, among them millions of parents whose homes were constantly ringing with Glenn Miller's "American Patrol," Charlie Barnet's "Pompton Turnpike," Jimmie Lunceford's "For Dancers Only," Jimmy Dorsey's "Green Eyes," Count Basie's "Sent for You Yesterday." Newspapers wrote about it regularly, and by about 1940 even the smallest papers carried reviews of the recent swing records. The most famous leaders were important national celebrities, whose marriages and divorces were given press attention. Jazz—or at least a jazz-based music—was now at center stage in American culture.

This statement needs some qualification. In 1937 listeners to New York's WNEW radio station rated the top bands in this order: Goodman, Guy Lombardo, Shep Fields, Casa Loma, Hal Kemp, Tommy Dorsey, and Chick Webb.[7] Goodman and Webb were essentially hot bands; Casa Loma and Dorsey played a mix of hot and sweet music; and Lombardo, Fields and Kemp were sweet bands. I think that this ratio of hot to sweet in public taste is about correct, insofar as it is possible to make any such judgment. It clearly indicates that there was a very large audience in the United States during the period, running to tens of millions of people, for good hot music. We must bear in mind that Basie's "Jumpin' at the Woodside," with solos by Lester Young, Dicky Wells and Buck Clayton, Barnet's "Cherokee," Ellington's "Take the 'A' Train," Woody Herman's "Woodchopper's Ball," Tommy Dorsey's coupling of "Marie" and "Song of India" with Berigan's brilliant solos, Glenn Miller's "String of Pearls" with the famous Bobby Hackett cornet solo, and many other classics of the time, were hits. And so were all of those small-band recordings by Benny Goodman. The public was, of course, lapping up a great deal of milk toast; but it was also buying in large quantities some of the finest jazz records made in that day. And, as we shall see, as the swing period went on, the public taste became increasingly sophisticated, until in the 1940s it was ready for the more advanced harmonies of Herman, Stan Kenton, and others. It is startling to note that in 1940 Duke Ellington felt able to play his exceedingly thorny and dissonant "Ko-Ko" not just for a sophisticated audience in New York or Los Angeles but at a dance in Fargo, North Dakota. American taste in popular music was much more mature at the end of the swing era than it was at the beginning. And Benny Goodman played a major role in developing it.

# 15
# The Victor Classics

Goodman specialists generally divide his Victor period into three parts: the first records of April 4, 1935, to the end of 1936, when Helen Ward left; the records from the beginning of 1937 when Harry James joined the band until March 1938, when Gene Krupa left; and the remaining Victor dates from March 9, 1938, to May 4, 1939.[1] Some specialists further subdivide these periods in various ways, but this basic structure makes sense, marking off as it does the band with Ward which gave Goodman his first fame, from the one with James which many, including Goodman himself, thought was the greatest of any of his bands.

This first 1935–36 band was, actually a relatively anonymous band in comparison with some of the later ones with big-name stars like James, Cootie Williams and others. Bunny Berigan, the one true improviser of stature, left at the beginning. The trumpet soloists Kazebier, Bose, Erwin, Griffin and others who passed through were all competent jazz players, but none of them went on to become major figures in the music. Only Ziggy Elman, who joined in September 1936, would develop a name for himself, and Elman, while a player of power, was not a master improviser. Virtually all of the saxophone solos were taken by Art Rollini, competent, but not brilliant. (For the interest of Goodman specialists, the saxophone on "Small Hotel" does not sound to me like Rollini, and it cannot be Goodman, who plays a clarinet solo just before. I surmise that it is the only recorded solo made by Dick Clark with the band.) Only trombonist Joe Harris, who was in the band for a little over six months, really stands out. His replacement, Murray McEachern, was an excellent player, but Goodman rarely gave him space on the recordings. Stacy, Krupa, and Reuss were also, of course, first-rate jazz musicians, but again, at this period Goodman did not feature them much: Stacy solos twice on the fifty-two records made by this band, Reuss once and Krupa not at all, discounting the occasional brief drum break.

The soloist with the band was Goodman. He plays at least one brief solo on all but two of these fifty-two records. On average he plays about twenty-four solo bars, and considerably more on the sides without vocal choruses, which would take a third to half of a cut. In sum, Goodman plays over eleven hundred solo measures on these records; all the other soloists combined are given two-thirds of this amount, in addition to about seven hundred bars of vocal choruses, mostly by Helen Ward.

The importance of Helen Ward to the band's success is underscored by the fact she sings a full vocal chorus on about half of these records. The majority of her songs were the forgettable and forgotten pop songs of the day that were being turned out by the bushel by Tin Pan Alley songwriters, such as "Here's Love in Your Eyes," "You're Giving Me a Song and a Dance" and "Gee! But You're Swell." However, with the Trio she did get to sing some fine standards like "These Foolish Things," "There's a Small Hotel" and "All My Life."

But despite the prominence of Helen Ward, this was essentially a swing band, with all that implies. Two-thirds of the numbers were medium or uptempo numbers, including many with vocals on them, like "You Can't Pull the Wool Over My Eyes," taken at 168 beats a minute, which might be termed "medium fast."

At dances the band may have played a higher percentage of slow numbers. Surprisingly, Benny Goodman was considered to be an excellent dancer,[2] at a time when dancing well was an important social grace, and he was always conscious of the fact that he was running first and foremost a dance band. He said, "When people are dancing, you couldn't play one piece for ten minutes. I don't know whether they would have left the floor, but you had to give them a variety of tempos and tunes. Usually you'd play five or six numbers in a set; each one would be about three minutes."[3] Benny had a real feel for setting tempos. Once again this is a subjective matter; but to musicians songs "feel right" at certain tempos, in part having to do with whether they are built around a lot of eighth, quarter or half notes. Listening to Goodman records again and again, one can feel that Benny seems to have found the right "groove" for the arrangement.

He developed, James T. Maher suggests, a "marvelous instinct for programming,"[4] that is to say, finding the right mix of tempos, keys and types of tune, so that each number as it came along seemed fresh. To do this he had to include more romantic pieces than he put on records. But there can be no doubt that the essence of the band was its swing. This rhythmic feel was what mattered, more than anything else. Goodman seems to have understood that, and the bulk of what he recorded had that quality, coming both from Goodman's clarinet and from the band itself.

Of the records cut during this critical period, it was the so-called killer-dillers that have remained the best known and most frequently reissued—numbers like "Bugle Call Rag," "Stompin' at the Savoy" and "Down South Camp Meeting." But it is my perception that the popularity of the band was built as much on the simple, catchy pop tune played at a bright tempo with a certain amount of jazz soloing surrounding the light-hearted, natural Ward vocal. Among the best examples of these are "You Can't Pull the Wool Over My Eyes" and "The Glory of Love," which were recorded one after another in April 1936, and issued as a coupling.

"You Can't Pull the Wool Over My Eyes" was arranged by Jimmy Mundy and taken at that brisk tempo. The tune is not quite in the standard AABA form with the B bridge portion musically distinct from the A portions and sometimes in a different key. The tune is thirty-two bars long, but there is no bridge. Instead it is divided into two sixteen-measure segments in an ABAC form, with all three themes fairly closely related. The record consists of only three choruses plus a four-measure introduction, a six-measure modulation and a short coda, or tag. The opening chorus is a very happy example of that interplay of saxophones and brass that was a central characteristic of swing music. The brass has the first two notes of the melody, which is then snatched away by the saxophones, who play it, with brass answers, through the first eight measures. Goodman takes the second eight as a solo over simple saxophone chords, staying fairly close to the tune, which was necessary, as this was the first statement of the B theme. The first eight measures are repeated, and the final eight C theme is played by the saxophones, until they are interrupted by the brass again at the end.

Goodman then carries a six-measure modulation from C to F into Ward's vocal. Helen Ward did not have the ability of a Billie Holiday to twist a melody way out of time and metre—indeed few singers did—but she could do it to a degree, as she does here whenever she sings the word "you." This was one of the early examples of big band female singing, and it influenced a whole host of girl singers who came after. The vocal is helped by a great deal of musical activity going on underneath it. The saxophones play chords almost continuously, the brass in straight mutes play fills between the phrases, and Jess Stacy adds light, leaping, highly rhythmic figures. Everything is worked out to propel the music forward.

The third and last chorus is similar in feeling to the first, except that this time the melody is carried through the first eight bars by the brass, with the saxophones supplying fills. Goodman takes the next sixteen measures, again playing the melody relatively straight, except for a swirling upward figure at the end of the first eight measures to land on a high climatic note which leads him into the second eight. The brass again takes up the melody, with saxophone punctuation, and it winds up with a quick tag.

Taken altogether it is a very nice piece of light music, neatly put together with the elements well balanced, continually varied and played cleanly with the infectious swing so typical of this band.

Virtually everything said about "You Can't Pull the Wool Over My Eyes" can also be said about "The Glory of Love," except that the song is in the standard AABA form. Here again the melody is tossed around between reeds, brasses and Goodman's clarinet; again the vocal with support from reeds, brasses and Stacy's piano; again the relatively straight Goodman solo sandwiched between episodes of brass and saxophones; and again the swing. Even the tempo is almost the same. It is unquestionably a formula, one that would begin to sound stale in time, but it is a happy formula, and it certainly works when in good hands, as it is here.

But the hot, fast swingers were what got the audience dancing in the aisles, and have commanded the most attention since. One of the most famous pieces Goodman ever did was "Stompin' at the Savoy," which the band first played at Rose's Music Hall. Hymie Schertzer has described how elated the musicians were made by the piece.[5] The tune and the arrangement were written by Edgar Sampson, a black saxophonist who was doing a lot of arranging for the Harlem bands of the period, particularly for the Chick Webb Orchestra. Pee Wee Erwin said that in 1933 he was playing in a band at the Empire Ballroom opposite a band led by Rex Stewart, which played a lot of Sampson's arrangements.[6] Erwin was impressed by them, and later spoke to Goodman about Sampson. It is, however, also possible that Goodman had heard of Sampson through John Hammond, who usually knew what was going on musically in Harlem. The piece is hard to describe as a "song," although words were eventually put to it. Like many of the instrumental swing numbers of the time, it is difficult to tease the tune apart from the arrangement. The ostensible main theme consists of two notes, repeated three times—about as minimal a melody line as is possible. However, in the primary version each little phrase is followed by a more elaborate answering melody. Neither the call nor the answer can stand alone: the whole depends upon the conjunction of the paired phrases. The bridge, too, is idiosyncratic, ostensibly built on the basic circle of fifths chord sequence, but including several brief movements of a half-step up and back. These half-step movements make the bridge difficult for an improviser to "get loose on," unless he simply rides over these changes, as many improvisers have done, and this has prevented the song from becoming the jam session favorite it might have been.

"Stompin' at the Savoy," then, is cast in a somewhat different mold from what might be called the basic Goodman piece of this period. It does not have the contrapuntalism of the Henderson-Mundy-Murphy arrangements, but is almost all call-and-response. It is simple, and gets simpler as it goes along. There is, furthermore, an unprepared modulation up a half step from D-flat to D at the truncated last chorus, a device that was unusual in dance-band arrangements of that time, although it did occur. "Stompin' at the Savoy," therefore, was a departure from the usual Goodman piece, and this freshness was undoubtedly partly responsible for its success.

The record also includes what is probably the best-known jazz solo by trombonist Joe Harris. He has most of the third chorus to himself, with Art Rollini playing the bridge. (Goodman only plays eight solo bars on the record.) Harris certainly deserves a larger place in jazz history than he has been given. He was born in Sedalia, Missouri,[7] a small commercial center with a notorious vice district that serviced the local farmers and railroad men passing through. Around the turn of the century it was an important locus for ragtime—Scott Joplin's "Maple Leaf Rag" was named for a Sedalia saloon—and Harris must have grown up with the sound of ragtime in his ears. He was influenced first by Miff Mole, as were many young trombonists of the period, but met Jack Teagarden while gigging around the Oklahoma oil fields. He fell under Teagarden's spell before Teagarden was well known. He thereafter played with the slightly hoarse burr that Teagarden used—a whiskey voice, so to speak—and he adopted many of Teagarden's devices, including the lip trill that Teagarden made famous, which he uses to conclude this solo on "Stompin' at the Savoy." The figure he plays at the beginning of the second eight measures is pure Teagarden, but perhaps the most interesting part of the chorus is in the last eight measures, where Harris displays a five-note figure in four different guises, concluding with a tiny lip trill.

Harris's debt to Teagarden is clear, but there is no confusing the playing of the two men. Harris uses a more decisive attack, plays longer notes and fewer of them. Because of his fondness for the Teagarden style, Goodman gave Harris more solo space than anyone else in the band at the time, except himself. Harris, we remember, came into the band as a vocalist, and only began playing trombone after Lacey left. Goodman very quickly had Henderson make an arrangement of Teagarden's classic "Basin Street Blues" for Harris. Harris sings the number, and plays a long trombone solo thoroughly in the Teagarden manner. He also sings it with the Teagarden touch, but his voice has less of the hoarse bluesy quality that hung in Teagarden's voice, and little more of the sound of the crooner. Unhappily Joe Harris was the victim of a lot of bad luck. He suffered a serious injury in a car accident in 1937 and was out of music for almost two years. He died in another car accident in 1952, in his mid-forties.

Another tune cut at this time which went on to be an enduring part of the Goodman band was "Bugle Call Rag." A cut was made for Victor in August 1936, which was not issued at the time. It was remade in Novem-

ber, after Ziggy Elman had come into the band, and this is the one we are
familiar with. The tune itself could hardly be simpler, one of the common
eight-measure blues forms, in this case opening on the sub-dominant, repeated to make up choruses of sixteen bars. The bugle call is a variation of
the famous "Assembly," loathed by generations of soldiers. In this arrangement four-bar breaks are inserted between the first several choruses for saxophone, trombone and clarinet. (Actually the form is a little more complicated. As originally conceived, "Bugle Call Rag" was based on the blues,
with the player taking the first four measures as a break, and then finishing
out his solo on the remaining eight bars of the standard twelve-bar blues,
over rhythm or other accompaniment. And this, effectively, is what happens in the opening choruses which begin with breaks. However, for the
rest of the piece, both the choruses played by the band and those taken by
soloists, use the truncated eight-bar form, which is like a blues with the
first four measures lopped off. The piece is really neither quite one or the
other.)

Following the break choruses, the band plays a riff chorus with a boogie-
woogie feel, and then come solos by Elman, McEachern and Goodman.
The band comes in to play the bugle call ensemble, and then riffs to a conclusion. That is all there is to it. Indeed, it is even simpler than this makes
it seem, for the opening ensemble riffs consist of two notes by the brass
answered by three from the saxophones, and the various riffs mixed into
the closing ensemble choruses are two to five notes in length. This is very
basic big-band jazz playing, with the music mainly rhythmic, rather than
melodic, in function. Jazz like this can work only when there is a driving
intensity in the playing, and this is precisely what we have here—that
sense of playing on top of the beat, of racing heedlessly downhill, of being on the edge of falling, as Jimmy Maxwell put it. This band could not
possibly have been confused with the Basie band of the period, just then
making its first records. None of the solos is especially memorable, but
they are burning hot, and it was this sort of thing that lifted young audiences out of their seats in theatres all over the United States.

Goodman's own playing was undergoing alterations. With the band
Benny is playing, in many instances, somewhat less hot than he did in jazz
contexts, especially with other leaders. Especially on ballads like "There's
a Small Hotel," "Star Dust" and his feature, "Good-bye," he has a tendency to stay with the melody by and large. Commercial considerations undoubtedly entered in. Goodman was always conscious of his audience, always trying to make sure that they were pleased by the band, and he
recognized that many people who were dancing wanted to hear the melody of tunes they liked. Even in the small groups, which were expected to
be pure jazz, Goodman usually made a point of stating the melody at least

at the beginning of each piece. However rebellious Benny could be at times, this was his band, his recordings, his future that was at stake and he was determined that audiences should have what they wanted.

This attitude on Goodman's part was at least partly responsible for a reduction in the amount of hot intonation he was using. There are fewer of the rasps and growls with which he inflected his work before he had his own band. But the old style is by no means entirely gone; it is in evidence in such numbers as "Get Happy" and "I've Found a New Baby." An earlier version of "Get Happy," taken from the April 13, 1935, *Let's Dance* broadcast makes a nice comparison with later versions. Goodman's solo on the broadcast version is typically hot, filled with long-held notes interrupted by sudden showers of faster ones. His second solo on the version recorded in March 1936 is longer and quite different. He plays the first sixteen measures in the low register, after the manner the New Orleans Creoles enjoyed using. Goodman was, both by his early training in the dixieland school, and his inclination to fling notes skyward, mainly an upper-register player at first. But his main solo on the recorded version of "Get Happy" is built around the chalumeau; only in the bridge does he suddenly rise into the upper register, to provide a sudden contrast to the hot, smoking low chalumeau passages on either side of it. With Goodman's enormous facility and warm rich sound, the low register was a natural home for him, and he would visit there increasingly in his work hereafter. He plays these long, fast passages superbly. Note especially his breath control—he breathes only once in the first twelve measures of the tune. The sudden leap upward in the bridge provides just the right moment of contrast before he plunges back into the smoky low register. There are few examples in jazz of this kind of playing any better than this.

This second version of "Get Happy" is played markedly faster than the broadcast one. It has been said that on the *Let's Dance* show the band played with a relaxed ease that was not always evident later on. But when "Get Happy" was broadcast, the band had not played it very often. By the time of the formal recording a year later, it had played it dozens of times. Not only did it play the tune faster, but cleaner and with considerably greater intensity. Jazz musicians have a tendency to rate their music by the way they felt when they were playing it. But frequently music performed when they are tenser, a little more on edge, is actually more effective than that made when the musicians are easing along enjoying themselves. And I think we have a case of this here.

A more typical solo is the one Goodman plays on the old jam session favorite "I've Found a New Baby." The tempo is very fast, about 270, as fast as any swing band would play—you could hardly dance to anything at that tempo even with the jitterbug steps coming into fashion. Goodman takes one chorus and part of another flying through them with enormous ease, racing up and down the clarinet at high speed. There are, however, none of the growly, swirling phrases so frequent in his early work: the solo depends for its effect mostly on velocity, dash, daring.

During the years of these first Victor recordings Goodman continued to do a small amount of recording in other contexts, usually as a favor to John Hammond, who was not averse to twisting people's arms to get what he wanted. Goodman was not entirely pleased to make these outside sessions. He was now a leader, rapidly becoming successful, and it annoyed him to have to work as a sideman for somebody else. However, by mid-1935 Goodman was using Teddy Wilson, who was under contract to Brunswick, and he had to record with Wilson for Brunswick in exchange.

Wilson's leadership was nominal. These Brunswick records were produced by John Hammond, and Hammond was firmly in control of who would play on them and what sort of music would be played, although it is also apparent that record company executives had a considerable say in picking the tunes. Following his own musical philosophy, which was not necessarily that of the musicians, Hammond insisted that the groups be racially mixed and that the music be what can be termed "small-band swing"—improvised with just enough by way of head arrangement to give the pieces a little formal structure and take them out of the jam-session category which record company executives felt the public would not like, probably correctly. The bulk of these records contained vocals by Billie Holiday, which constitute the heart of her best work. The musicians included most of the finest young jazz players of the period, among them Lester Young, Bunny Berigan, Artie Shaw, Irving Fazola, Roy Eldridge, Ben Webster, Benny Morton, Johnny Hodges, Buck Clayton and many others, as well as Goodman and Wilson. These records, especially the ones with Holiday, constitute one of the finest small bodies of work in jazz history. However much the musicians may have resented Hammond's meddling and his ruthlessness in getting people fired from jobs they desperately needed, he was without question one of the best record producers in the history of jazz.

There were five of these Wilson sessions with Goodman, at which seventeen sides were cut. (Actually the last took place after the Paramount stand, but I am including it here for convenience.) Billie Holiday sings on ten, Boots Castle on three, and Helen Ward, as Vera Lane, on two; two are instrumentals. Goodman does a considerable amount of playing on these records. He generally plays the backing for Holiday, something, as we have seen, he was a master of, and he has long solos on the majority of these records, often the opening chorus, during which he states the melody for eight or so bars and then branches out—a very hot solo on the fast "What a Little Moonlight Can Do" (sixty-four bars in long metre); a nice relaxed sixteen measures on "Coquette," with a group drawn from his own band; and a full, fairly straight thirty-bar chorus on "Miss Brown to You." Particularly interesting is a sixteen-bar solo on "Pennies from Heaven," which atypically he conceives of mainly in long, held notes and empty spaces. Bar three is almost entirely untouched, and another bar consists of one dipping note. This is exceedingly spare playing for Goodman, and it shows how varied a player he could be.

Goodman made two other outside record sessions during this period, both under the ostensible leadership of Gene Krupa, and both produced by Hammond. The first of these Krupa sessions was built around men drawn from the Goodman band—Kazebier, Harris, Clark, Stacy, Reuss, Goodman, with black bassist Israel Crosby brought in from the outside, partly because Hammond wanted a mixed group, partly because he did not like Harry Goodman's playing. The session was ill-conceived. The choice of a boogie-woogie version of "The Last Round Up," as one of the tunes was, to say the least, strange. The group plays it in long metre—that is, with relatively slow melody held to its usual speed—but the underlying rhythm is doubled up. The effect here is to make some of the chord changes go on for as long as six measures at a stretch. Trumpeter Kazebier is clearly uneasy and finds himself dangling helplessly over the chords, waiting for them to change.

The other tunes are a little more successful, but not much. "Jazz Me Blues" is a dixieland tune, and the ensemble becomes a patch of mud, as dixieland ensembles almost invariably do when played by more than three horns. Goodman plays a typical, but not particularly inspired solo, and Harris a competent one in his Teagarden-derived style. "Three Little Words" is taken too fast. It contains an extremely rare item, a Dick Clark solo, as well as a good, very typical solo by Stacy. Goodman chooses to play his solo with only bass and drums for accompaniment, a mistake on this tune which is awkwardly constructed for improvising on—it has been recorded surprisingly infrequently by jazz musicians. Benny gets lost, despite some pounding by Krupa to bring him back. Finally, there is "Blues for Israel," which opens and closes with unaccompanied bass and contains pleasant solos by the others.

The second of these sessions under Krupa's name used the same rhythm section, but two of the best musicians from the Fletcher Henderson band of the moment, trumpeter Roy Eldridge and tenor saxophonist Leon "Chu" Berry, as well as Goodman. Made in February 1936, this was essentially a jam session with just enough riffing inserted into the tunes to

give them a semblance of arrangements. Three of the songs are pop tunes—
two of them sung by Helen Ward—and one, called "Swing Is Here," is a
ride on the jam session favorite "I Got Rhythm."

The sides have all the strengths and weaknesses of jam session numbers—
a lot of strong, fresh, impassioned playing, along with a good deal of confusion, especially in the ensemble passages, where the horns, rather than
looking for ways to complement each other, are simply blowing simultane-
ous solos, and forever bumping into each other and stepping on each other's feet.

The riffs, patched together hastily in the studio, are uninspired, lacking
the musical quality to be found in similar riffs worked out by good arrangers, like the Henderson-Mundy-Murphy group Goodman was using to such
good advantage. But the solos are often first-rate jazz, for example those by
Eldridge and Berry on "I Hope Gabriel Likes My Music." There is also a
pretty duet by the same two on the bridge to the riff chorus which follows
Eldridge's solo, where for once they keep their lines separate. Goodman
was in good spirits that day and plays strong solos in his hottest manner on
several tunes. His solo on "I'm Gonna Clap My Hands" is played in his
hottest, smeary style, built around long notes inflected with twists, bends
and growls and filled with broken figures. There are, for example, no eighth
notes at all in the first three measures, unusual for somebody with Goodman's facility, especially at a tempo which is only moderately fast. In the
sixth bar he begins to play a snatch of the melody, then abruptly jerks
away from it to fling out long, inflected notes, and at the beginning of the
second eight measures he plays a note which lasts approximately a measure.
This sort of playing is entirely different from the flying, low register playing he does on, for example, "Get Happy," which is like high-speed ice
ballet. The "Clap My Hands" solo is instead made up of splintery sticks and
boards of incommensurate length, flung in all directions, like a barn blown
to smithereens by a tornado. It seems clear to me that although Goodman
loved this perfervid kind of playing, he tried to stay away from it on his
own records, fearful that his audience would find it too tough.

These sessions with Krupa and Wilson put an end to Goodman's career
as a sideman. During the 1930s and 1940s he would play occasionally with
assorted all-star bands made up of winners of jazz polls, in jam sessions, and
on two or three occasions, as a favor to somebody, he would play under a
pseudonym. But essentially from this point on he always worked as leader
of his own band. There was no reason why he should do otherwise. Why
not set his own musical circumstances, instead of taking direction from
others, something Goodman was never very good at anyway?

# 16
# The Star

The Goodman band originally booked into the Paramount for two weeks, was held over for a third, and would have been held over further, but it was booked elsewhere. It was grossing something approaching $50,000 a week.[1] Further publicity was generated by a battle of the bands that Goodman played at the Savoy Ballroom in Harlem against Chick Webb, the hunchbacked drummer who led the house band there. Helen Oakley Dance was responsible for the occasion. She had been working for Webb, almost as a favor, to generate some publicity for his band.[2] She had been very helpful to Goodman in the Congress Hotel days and she was able to prevail upon him to play the event. An enormous mob turned out. "The Savoy management was forced to call out the riot squad, fire department, reserves and mounted police in an attempt to hold in check the wildly enthusiastic crowds seeking admittance with the box office closed. Traffic was held up for hours in that vicinity."[3] Some 4,000 people got into the ballroom, another 5,000 were turned away. Goodman, with the integrated Quartet, not Webb, was the draw.

The mob scene of course created a lot of interest in the press, who found that the new swing phenomenon made good copy. Musically the event was less successful. According to Hammond, the public address system was bad, and the band as a whole was "flustered."[4] Down Beat reported that Webb won the battle by a slight margin because ". . . in his very own field he is absolutely unbeatable."[5]

In the spring the band played a tour of New England, and then once more traveled to Hollywood, where it spent part of July and August making a musical called Hollywood Hotel and doubling at the Palomar again.

In September the band went to Dallas to play the Dallas Exposition. This was the first time that Goodman had taken the Quartet into the Deep South. "Teddy [Wilson] went to Dallas with considerable misgivings,"[6] Down Beat reported. For the first show Goodman did not present the Quartet, ostensibly because there had not been time to set up the vibes, a fairly weak excuse, as he could have brought in the Trio. The audience protested: it wanted the small groups. The Quartet played the second show and, said Down Beat, "There was not the slightest hint of protest during the entire eleven day stay from anyone in the audience."[7] This was not precisely correct: it was at this engagement that the incident involving Wilson and the bottle of champagne occurred. But in view of how nervous everyone had been, they were all relieved that it had only come to that.

In October the band came back to the Madhattan Room of the Hotel Pennsylvania for an extended stay. The excitement over the band, and swing in general, continued to grow. Goodman won the Martin Block WNEW poll;[8] the Columbia University Seniors' dance-band poll;[9] was the subject of a four-page story in Life,[10] rapidly becoming one of the country's leading popular magazines, a profile in the New Yorker;[11] and he was featured in dozens of newspaper stories. A few months later, the Saturday Evening Post, the nation's leading popular magazine, ran a story on Goodman in which it said, "No other band of this quality has ever had such public acceptance. In the past year and a half it has sold more records, played longer runs, and scored higher radio ratings than any band of its kind in the history of American popular music."[12] This was not just standard magazine hyperbole. The writer, Frank Norris, was a jazz fan who knew what he was talking about.

"Goodman still continues to wander around in a daze, as a result of his success at the Paramount," Hammond reported in Down Beat.[13] As well he might: three years before he had been struggling to earn a hundred dollars a week, and sharing a small apartment with Charlie Teagarden. He was now earning, according to the New Yorker story, $100,000 a year, and living in a three-room suite in the Hotel Pennsylvania.[14] His musicians were among the highest paid in the business. Krupa, who had been making two hundred and seventy-five dollars a week in April, signed a new contract for three hundred.[15] At the time, this was the sort of money important executives expected to make.

There were, as ever, personnel changes. Sometime in the spring George Koenig replaced altoist Bill DePew; the change was not consequential. In the fall Vernon Brown replaced Murray McEachern, who went to the Casa Loma Orchestra. McEachern, who played alto saxophone as well as trombone, went on to have a major career in the swing bands and the studios, but Brown, an excellent improviser, was given more solo space than McEachern got, and it is the sound of his trombone we remember when we think of the band from this period. The most significant change was the departure of Vido Musso. I have not been able to find out what happened—whether he had an argument with Goodman, or left over some slight, as others did. Art Rollini said simply that while they were playing the Pennsylvania Hotel, in December 1937:

> One night I looked over to Vido's chair and he was gone. Babe Russin, a great tenor man, had replaced him. I do not know to this day what happened. Vido said no good-byes, but just vanished. Babe was no match for Vido's strong tone but made up for it with his keen ear and great drive.[16]

I do not, however, think that Goodman fired Musso. My guess is that Musso took offense at something that Goodman said or did, and simply left. Musso had, by this time, become a fairly capable reader, and was able to handle the section work. He had that drive that Goodman liked, and it is symptomatic that Russin felt a little out of place at first. He told Rollini that the band "lagged," which meant that he was having trouble getting used to the Goodman beat, and he had his saxophone mouthpiece refaced in order to get a bigger tone.[17]

Musso drops from the record for several months, then resurfaced in the spring playing with the new-formed Gene Krupa band, and went on to play with many of the famous swing bands, among them Goodman again.

The Vido Musso case now forces us to confront the whole story of Goodman's relationship to his sidemen, which has long been one of the most chewed over subjects in the jazz world. It was sufficiently important that in February 1937, *Down Beat* made it the subject of an editorial headed "Is Benny Goodman's Head Swollen?"[18] The editorial said in part, "We were frankly amazed at the universal expressions of dislike for Benny among musicians, bookers, publishers and other band leaders in New York. Even Benny's own musicians couldn't help betraying a certain discomfiture and lack of ease with him." It went on to advise Goodman to "take a good inventory of your personal traits—is it carelessness, or fear hiding behind an inferiority complex, or just confusion?"

It was not a new story. Goodman, as we have seen, had a stubborn and at times rebellious nature. He was also a rather straightforward and blunt man. Whatever might be said about Goodman, he was not devious, or rather no more devious than anyone working in a show business infested with sharks had to be. He would, for example, haggle about money, sometimes in a most petty way, but once an agreement had been made, he would not try to depart from it. But in his nature was also an inability to understand how people were reacting to him. Almost from the moment he started his first real band he began to evidence a callous and at times brutal behavior toward his sidemen. The complaints of band bookers, theatre managers and music publishers need not be taken seriously. These peo-

ple were the parasites who always gather around a capable performer in order to manipulate him for their own ends.

But his sidemen were his allies in a project that could succeed only with
not merely their cooperation but their enthusiasm and faith that what they
were doing was important. A jazz band is like a football team: it needs
emotion, conviction, as well as skill, if it is to be at its best. A bandleader
therefore must be like a coach, cajoling, exhorting, criticizing and forgiv-
ing by turns, in order to get the best out of his men. Benny Goodman
failed almost utterly to understand this. He rarely praised anybody; his way
of dealing with the men was simply to carp—to criticize, frequently in the
bluntest terms.

As early as 1934, when the band was at the Music Hall, it was heard by
an English musician named Benny Winestone who was working on the
transatlantic passenger ships and was in New York a good deal. He later
remembered a time at the Music Hall when Babe Russin, whom Goodman
liked and respected, substituted for Art Rollini, who was ill. Russin was
sight-reading the arrangements and inevitably made some mistakes. Goodman glared—the first recorded example of the famous Goodman ray. Winestone said, "He has that queer disposition on the stand, but is quite different immediately he steps off the platform: that is what people find so
difficult to understand about him."[19]

Bud Freeman, who knew Goodman in youth and later worked with his
band, said, "Benny Goodman and Tommy Dorsey didn't give a damn what
anybody thought of them. They had this strong ego plus talent and they
were hard men."[20] Helen Oakley Dance, who knew Goodman well and was
close to the band for a period, said, "Benny lacked awareness of what an
ordinary guy feels and thinks, an ordinary musician I should say."[21] Teddy
Wilson said, "Goodman, of course, got to be kind of a bad fellow, because
he didn't spare anybody's feelings, you know. He switched the first parts,
switched solos in a minute, right in front of everybody."[22] Down Beat
writer John McDonough summed it up in a piece written late in Goodman's life: "Every time Benny has formed a new group over the years, the
inevitable result has been a fresh treasury of Goodman anecdotes, born of
anger, frustration, impatience, conflict, and bitterness."[23]

Stories about Benny Goodman have indeed circulated among musicians
for decades; musicians have been known to spend hours swapping Goodman stories, hardly any of them favorable. Their attitude is one of incomprehension: it does not seem possible to them that another human being
could do some of the things they have seen him do. There are enough of
these stories to fill a book, and it is hardly worth giving more than a sampling of them. Perhaps the most widely circulated is the "sweater" story,
which a number of musicians claimed to have witnessed. According to this

tale, Goodman brought two or three musicians to his house in Connecticut
to rehearse a trio. It was a cold day, and apparently the heat in Goodman's
private recording studio adjoining the house was turned down. Eventually
one of the musicians said to Benny, "Gee, Benny, don't you think it's kind
of cold in here?" Goodman looked a little surprised, as if he hadn't noticed it, then agreed, and walked over to the house. In a few moments he
returned wearing a sweater. The story is too bizarre to have been made up.

Another story, told by Sid Weiss,[24] Goodman's bassist off and on for
many years, involved tenor saxophonist Jerry Jerome, who was with the
Goodman band during World War II. It was, because of wartime short-
ages, very difficult to get reeds, but Jerome had a friend in an army band who
had access to them. At one point he sent Jerry a whole box of Van Doren
clarinet reeds, a top brand. This was a precious gift. Jerome brought them
to the job and left the box lying on top of his stand. During the course of
the evening Benny spotted the box. "Benny had a habit of—if a reed
didn't satisfy him, he'd put it between his first and second finger and
push his thumb up till it broke. Then he'd throw it away so he'd never have
to use it again," Weiss explained.

> "Oh, Van Dorens," Benny said. He picked up one of Jerry's reeds,
> put it on the mouthpiece, tightened the ligature which holds the reed
> in place and he played. . . . Then he took the ligature loose, took the
> reed out, and broke it. That way he went through the whole box. Every
> one of them Jerry Jerome could have used. He broke every reed in that
> box. That shows you how unconscious he was of what he was doing.
> Jerry was frozen, his mouth open, he was staring at what Benny was
> doing, just frozen.

Pianist John Bunch told a story about the Russian tour of 1962:

> I remember being in Leningrad. There were 12,000 people out there
> cheering away. It was during the intermission. I was talking to Teddy
> Wilson. We were right across the way from Benny's dressing room
> door, which was about half open. He was in there by himself. All of a
> sudden here comes four, six, big dignitaries walking back, with flowers,
> they all had suits on, with medals on their suits. The manager comes
> out, sees them, and they tell him they want to pay their respects to Mr.
> Goodman. So the manager goes in, says there are some people out here,
> they look important, they want to say hello to you. And Benny's try-
> ing out reeds. And without saying a word he just takes his foot and
> closes the door.[25]

One of the things that bothered musicians most about Goodman was
the famous "ray," which Down Beat[26] once gave a banner front-page head-

line. The ray was a long, flat stare which Goodman would direct at musicians when they made mistakes, as well as at other times for reasons they could not understand. Harry James said, "He used it only on some guys. And then there were some guys who thought he was giving them the ray when he really wasn't. Instead, he'd be looking in their direction, but at the same time he'd be completely occupied about something else, usually something about music, and he'd actually be looking off in space."[27] Ziggy Elman told Lionel Hampton that he had once been slow in putting a mute in: "The old man gave me the ray and it stayed with me four days. I couldn't sleep."[28]

There are a couple of things to be said about this. For one, in that more authoritarian day, it was taken for granted that bandleaders had a considerable amount of power over the musicians. Helen Oakley Dance said, "Bandleaders in those days were fairly big shots. They thought they were little gods, you know. They made the big money, they hired and fired. They blamed Benny for many things, that attitude. That attitude preceded Benny."[29] Jimmy Maxwell said that when he went to his first Goodman rehearsal he was dressed in casual clothes, as was customary in California where he had come from. Goodman sent him home to put on a suit, and Maxwell took it for granted that Goodman had a right to do this.[30] Goodman, for example, did not let his musicians chew gum, smoke or cross their legs on the stand. "He once even told Miff [Mole] that he couldn't chew gum on the bandstand,"[31] and in Russia he told Teddy Wilson to put out a cigarette.[32] The point is that Goodman was not alone keeping these strictures. Many bandleaders felt that it was incumbent upon them to maintain a certain decorum on the stand, especially in the elegant hotels or at the formal weddings and parties they often played.

A second thing to be said was that Benny Goodman could be a quite different person from the cruel taskmaster he sometimes appeared to be at work. John Bunch told a story of playing a date in Indianapolis, not far from Bunch's home town. "I knew a lot of musicians there. A clarinet player that I know, excellent musician who teaches out there . . . somehow got backstage and he says to me, 'You've got to introduce me to Benny Goodman. I've idolized him all my life, and you're the first guy I knew well enough to ask him to introduce me to Benny.' "

Bunch replied that he was willing to make the introduction, but he added, "I got to tell you, he's a very strange man, and he may not even put his hand out to you. So don't think it's anything personal. If he acts like that he's just thoughtless, he's just a weird guy."

It was then time to go on, and Bunch's friend went back out front. At intermission Bunch was looking around for him, when he noticed that the man had come up to the bandstand and introduced himself to Benny.

I said, "Oh, now he really blew it." At least I could have introduced him, but he just went over there on his own. And I saw them go downstairs together, and when it's time to go back on stage for the second half, George comes over to me and says, "I don't know what the hell you're talking about, he was great. He gave me a box of reeds. He was very friendly and we were talking about how they make reeds. I felt like I was holding him up from going out on stage."[33]

Goodman was notoriously close with money, as even people who liked him would admit. Helen Oakley Dance said, "Benny just didn't want to spend money. That was it, that was born in him. And you'd always come up against that."[34] This unwillingness to spend money stayed with him until the end of his life, when he was a millionaire, according to Carol Phillips, his companion in his last years, who said she tried to coax him into being a little more relaxed about spending.[35] The attitude was perfectly comprehensible in a man who had spent his youth in a family which constantly was scraping pennies together to buy food for dinner. But Goodman could be surprisingly generous at times. Once Jimmy Maxwell asked Goodman for a loan of five hundred dollars to pay for an operation his father had to have. Goodman refused. But a few weeks later Maxwell had three hundred dollars stolen from his jacket pocket. Goodman simply gave him the money. "Here he refused me a loan of five hundred dollars, but a few weeks later he's trying to give me three hundred." Maxwell also said that when he first came to New York Goodman lent him a thousand dollars to live on while he was waiting out his union card.[36]

Again, Mel Powell, who joined the Goodman band when he was a teenager, found Benny to be rather fatherly toward him, always trying to make sure that he was taking care of his money and not throwing it around, and giving him advice on his investments. He said, "I really don't think that he lacked civility, not at all. But I think that his powers of concentration and the locus of his concentration was such as to eliminate the ordinary civility. He just wasn't paying attention."[37]

And there were, of course, at least a few musicians who had nothing bad to say about Goodman. Doc Cheatham, a trumpeter who worked with Goodman in the later stages of Goodman's career, said, "I didn't ever have one bit of trouble with Benny. I rehearsed with him a lot, but I never heard him fire anyone, or tell musicians he couldn't use them. They just didn't come back. Whatever he did, he did it very quietly. I thought he was very nice, a fine man."[38]

But this was not the majority opinion. The sense that he was alone in the world was, I think, also responsible for a streak of coarseness in Goodman's demeanor. Despite his objections to smoking and gum-chewing on the bandstand, Goodman was notorious for public nose-picking, butt-scratching

and digging around in an ear with his finger. He frequently forgot to button his fly. Given his rough and tumble upbringing, it is not surprising that
he did not have the social graces when he came to adulthood. But he was
eager to acquire them, and eventually learned to dress impeccably and speak
with a Park Avenue accent. Yet in public the plug would sometimes be
out, and he would scratch, apparently unconscious of what he was doing.

Yet when all is said, it has to be admitted that there is something odd
about a man who is this unconscious of the effect he is having on other
people. Goodman simply had no idea of how much he hurt and angered
people. When interviewers would tactfully try to allude to his reputation
for coldness he would reply that it was due to his intolerance of sloppiness.
He said, "We worked every day. . . . It's the nature of the beast, and
what are you doing to do about it? If the boss works hard everybody else
has to work hard."[39] He told writer George Simon, "I guess I just expect
too much from my musicians and when they do things wrong I get brought
down."[40]

But of course that was not the trouble. Other bandleaders set high standards and worked their musicians hard without being so disliked. Goodman's problems with the musicians was, fundamentally, a tactlessness that
transcended ordinary rudeness. The excuse given time and time again by
those who wished to put the best light on Goodman's behavior was that he
became so lost in the music, so deeply concentrated on what he was hearing or thinking about it, that he was simply unaware of what he was doing
or saying. Powell said, "Of course he'd go so fuzzy he'd make eye contact,
and that could be very annoying. . . . It's not the ordinary behavior, but
he was not an ordinary guy. . . . If he didn't like someone, there was no
guessing. He'd fire them. He didn't have to stare you down."[41]

But that, really, was not it either: many people who have the ability to
concentrate intensely are not nearly so cut off from others as Goodman
was. I find it significant that Goodman had a great deal of trouble with
other people's names. All of us forget names from time to time, but with
Goodman it was carried to an extreme. Pianist Johnny Guarnieri said that
Benny called him Fletcher for a couple of months after he replaced Henderson in the band.[42] He also tended to call people "Pops," which was a
way around the problem, to the point where he even at times forgot his
step-daughters' names and called them Pops, too. He was especially weak
on the names of competing entertainers. Charlie Barnet said, "He could
never remember the names of the other acts on the bill, even though he
might have been working with them for weeks. He introduced the Condos
Brothers as the Brothers, and on one occasion the Mills Brothers became
the Ink Brothers."[43]

The using of names is of major psychological significance. It is not necessary to accept what Sigmund Freud had to say on the subject to see that whether we choose to use nicknames, formal names, first names, last names or none of these indicates something about our relationship to the person being named. The fact that Goodman so frequently failed to name people at all suggests that for Benny they did not really exist. They were mechanical contrivances—and this, of course, would especially be true of the musicians who were, in Goodman's mind, simply there to produce his music. Jimmy Maxwell has a telling story. At one point he suggested to Goodman that they play some Ellington arrangements. Goodman replied, "You think that's a good band?" Maxwell said, "Sure, it's the best band." Goodman next asked, "Who's your favorite clarinetist?" Maxwell, joshing Goodman, said, "Why Barney Bigard, of course."

"It was a stupid thing to say," Maxwell admitted. "But you don't compliment a guy to his face, you don't say you're my favorite musician." The upshot was that Goodman gave Maxwell eight weeks' notice. But the months went by and nothing happened. Eventually the band landed in California, and after hours Maxwell would go out to a club in Catalina, where there was a clarinetist fronting a rhythm section, to jam. Goodman heard about the place, and came in one night. The next day the manager approached Maxwell and told him that Goodman had finally found somebody to replace him. Maxwell, naturally, asked who it was. "It's the trumpet player at that place where Benny was last night." Maxwell blinked. "There isn't any trumpet player there, I'm the only trumpet player that was there." The manager replied, "Yeah, but Goodman doesn't know that."[44]

Maxwell admitted that Goodman's glasses were always dirty. Ziggy Elman used to pick them off his nose and clean them for him[45]—he could be as oblivious to his own dirty glasses as he was to the ketchup-bottle top on his eggs. But dirty glasses are no explanation. To Goodman, at times, the people around him became cardboard figures, the jacks and queens in a deck of cards. I find it fascinating that Goodman once said, "The fact that a musician will let his instrument be tossed around by a band boy is a tip off on how much he cares about what he's doing."[46] He never expressed that much concern about a musician. What mattered to Benny was music.

# 17

# The Famous
# Carnegie Hall Concert

In January 1938, the *New York Times* wrote, "It is hardly an exaggeration to say that swing is today the most widespread artistic medium of popular emotional expression."[1] Goodman was not only the King of Swing, he was also the Pied Piper of Swing, the man who was leading the children on a new dance. The stage was now set for what would become one of the historic moments in jazz: the Benny Goodman Orchestra's concert at Carnegie Hall.

The concert was—and still is—widely thought of as the first real "jazz concert." This was hardly the case. If by concert we mean a gathering of people for the specific purpose of listening to music, rather than, say, dancing to it, there were plenty of others first. James Reese Europe's Clef Club Orchestra played several concerts of syncopated music before World War I;[2] Paul Whiteman's famous Aeolian Hall concert came in 1924;[3] in 1928 W. C. Handy presented a mammoth concert of black music at Carnegie Hall;[4] the evenings at the Lincoln Gardens in Chicago where the Chicago musicians came to listen to the Oliver band in 1922 were certainly concerts;[5] Duke Ellington gave two concerts at a theatre in England in 1933;[6] the Chicago Rhythm Club's various shows at the Congress Hotel were effectively concerts; and Joe Helbock, of the Onyx Club, put on a swing music concert at the Imperial Theatre in May 1936, which included Chick Webb, Louis Armstrong, Artie Shaw, Bunny Berigan, Red Norvo, Teddy Wilson, Mildred Bailey and others.[7]

Which event can claim to be the first jazz concert depends a good deal on how you define both jazz and concert, but it would be very difficult to write a definition of either which would put Goodman's 1938 Carnegie Hall appearance first. Nonetheless, the concert captured the public imagination in a way that few of the others did, and it continues to do so. For jazz fans there are certain events they would like to have been present for: the Buddy Bolden engagements at Lincoln Park in New Orleans around the turn of the century; the Original Dixieland Jass Band's opening at Reisenweber's in 1917; the February 1926 Chicago Coliseum concert and dance with Louis Armstrong's Hot Five and the orchestras of King Oliver, Clarence Williams, and Bennie Moten; Goodman's Palomar opening; the Town Hall concert at which Armstrong introduced the All-Stars in 1947; the Massey Hall concert in Toronto in 1953 which presented the cream of the boppers, Charlie Parker, Dizzy Gillespie, Bud Powell, Charlie Mingus and Max Roach; Thelonious Monk's appearance at the Five Spot with John Coltrane in 1957; the Ornette Coleman-Don Cherry engagement at the same club in 1959; and others since which history has not yet chosen. Benny Goodman's Carnegie Hall concert was such an event.

It is generally agreed that the idea came from publicist Wynn Nathanson, of the Tom Fizdale Agency, which was promoting the *Camel Caravan*.[8] It was originally conceived of mainly as a publicity stunt. Nathanson called the Sol Hurok office, and asked them to promote the event. Hurok was "the legendary prototype of the impresario"[9] who at one time or another managed Chaliapin, Isadora Duncan, Pavlova, Artur Rubinstein and similar figures. His primary interest was not jazz but ballet and classical music. However, he was wide-ranging, and was responsible for promoting the career of Marian Anderson, one of the black singers of the era to break color bars in classical music. Promoting a concert of swing at Carnegie Hall, virtually his home base, called for the kind of imaginative stretch that Hurok was known for. He could hardly have been unaware of the furor the Goodman band was making, and he was perhaps the one person who could put on such an event.

Goodman was at first incredulous. He told Nathanson, "Are you out of your mind? What the hell would we do there?"[10] It should be remembered that even as late as 1938 a good many people continued to see jazz as slightly disreputable, not so much for the sexual associations it once had but because it was a low form of music, somewhat raffish. Carnegie Hall was dedicated to the presentation of higher things, and there was thus a tension between jazz and this sacrosanct hall. Even the musicians felt this. Just before the curtain went up on that famous evening Harry James said *sotto voce*, "I feel like a whore in church."[11] But it was precisely this tension which caught the public imagination.

Goodman was understandably nervous about the whole thing. What if they don't like us? What if nobody comes? He toyed with the idea of asking Bea Lillie, a famous comedienne of the day, to act as master of ceremonies, the idea being that her name would help to fill the hall. Nobody but Goodman especially liked this idea, not even Miss Lillie, who sensed that she would appear a very small noise amongst the thunder of the Goodman Orchestra, and she turned down the offer.[12] The decision was made that the concert would consist primarily of Goodman's regular repertory, the music which had made him the sensation of the day. However, Irving Kolodin suggested that the concert include a sort of musical history of jazz, with examples of early dixieland, recreations of famous solos by Armstrong and Beiderbecke, an Ellington piece and similar material.

Kolodin later said, "I apologize for it, because it probably caused more trouble in listening to old records and copying off arrangements than it was worth."[13] The feeling was that only Ellington's men could play Ellington's music, and it was arranged to have Johnny Hodges, Cootie Williams and Harry Carney added for the number.[14] Ellington himself, unwilling to play second fiddle to Goodman, turned down the opportunity to appear. In addition John Hammond, who had nothing else to do with the event, managed to wangle places on the programs for Count Basie and some of his musicians, whom he was fervently promoting.[15] It was also undoubtedly part of his general effort to bring blacks forward in the music business.

Goodman's followers and jazz fans in general shared the view that the concert would be an historic event. The house sold out almost immediately; Hurok then sold seats on the stage around the band and, on the night of the concert, standing room tickets. In a long preview piece in the New York Times Magazine, the day of the concert, the writer Gama Gilbert said, "The occasion is a landmark in the growth and recognition of a species of music that was reborn after the halcyon days of symphonic jazz some ten years ago," and added that "the event will be decisive in the history of swing. . . . Many fans are holding their breaths and fearing the worst. They foresee the same fate for swing as was suffered by symphonic jazz: the temporary success, the excommunication from its indigenous locale, the insidious stagnation of the vital force and the inevitable codification of what will be called 'swing technique.' "[16]

On the night of the concert Goodman and the musicians were unnerved. Down Beat reporter Annemarie Ewing was backstage and reported that "The boys were nervous," and that when it actually became 8:45, time to go on stage, nobody wanted to go out first. "Benny, pale as a ghost, was instructing everybody to go on together, and the boys pushing each other around in the wing space—about four feet square, filled with photographers, musicians, ticket holders with seats on the stage, a curly headed usher, trying to be dignified, and the press."[17]

In the hall, "There was quivering excitement in the air, an almost electrical effect,"[18] according to the New York Times reviewer Olin Downes, who had covered the Whiteman Aeolian Hall concert fourteen years earlier.

Goodman had decided to open with a new arrangement of a piece by Edgar Sampson, which had been written for the Chick Webb Orchestra. The piece was "Don't Be That Way." The applause at the end was uproarious, and from that moment it was clear that the concert would be a success. "Don't Be That Way" of course went on to be one of Goodman's staples. And when the concert was concluded the audience did indeed feel that they had witnessed an historic event, as anticipated.

The next day the *New York Herald Tribune* said that the concert was "warmly and vociferously acclaimed by a capacity audience. The foremost contributor to this was Mr. Gene Krupa, the group's super-expert percussionist whose gestures and facial expressions proved unusually engrossing."[19] The *New York World Telegram* said, "Swing as is swing was purveyed to the frenetic-faced throng by a frenetic-faced crew of rhythmaniacs, one of whom [Krupa] did everything but skate on the ceiling . . . the huge audience swayed and rocked and tapped its feet in tempo."[20] Irving Kolodin, who had been involved in the event and was perhaps not unbaised, wrote in the *New York Sun*, "Whether the local seismographs recorded it or not, an earthquake of violent intensity racked a small corner of Manhattan last night as swing took Carnegie Hall in its stride."[21]

The music critics, however, were not so sure. Not all of the New York papers covered the event, but those that did sent their classical music reviewers. (Newspapers at that time did not usually carry full-time pop music critics. Coverage of dance bands was haphazard and was often left to gossip columnists. Sporadic record reviews were often done by free-lancers.) They did not find the music of much interest. Francis D. Perkins of the *Herald Tribune* concluded his review by saying, "As for the value of the music itself—but that, after all, was not the point."[22] Even the redoubtable Olin Downes, who was not terribly knowledgeable about jazz but tended to be sympathetic, said that he had gone to the concert to hear this new music with "much curiosity and anticipation," but concluded, finally, that " 'swing' is a bore." He did not hear "a single player in the course of a solid hour of music invent one original or interesting musical phrase."[23] Kolodin, inevitably, found much to praise, and presciently singled out an "especially fine piano solo by Jess Stacy,"[24] which many still consider the high point of the concert. (Kolodin later remembered Downes "looking in pained incomprehension at his teen-age daughter, who was bouncing up and down in her seat with pleasure.")[25]

But it did not really matter what the classical music critics thought. The word was out that the event had been a smashing success. *Time* said that Goodman was "a far more serious artist than Mr. Whiteman," and that "in the best sense the joint was rocking."[26] *Down Beat* gave the concert its lead story:

The Benny Goodman concert has been written into the annals of swingology, for in Carnegie Hall on Sunday evening, January 16, 1938, the maestro came, played, and laid a golden egg. To some the occasion was comparable to the discovery of radium, the feats of the les freres Wright and Einstein's introduction of his mathematical theories. Others linked it to the pestiferous hot foot, annoying double-talk and Bank Night with two features plus a set of dishes. The audience was undoubtedly the strangest assortment ever gathered within the sturdy walls of Carnegie, from adolescent schoolboys attired like misprints in Esquire, who applauded everything, including clinkers, to baggy-eyed sophisticates who applauded nothing—including several enjoyable spots.[27]

As for the music, Down Beat's opinion was mixed. The show, its reviewer felt, was typical of any Goodman performance, with highs and lows. The jam session included too many players and went on far too long. Stacy's piano solo on "Sing, Sing, Sing" was "terrific." The Ellingtonians' spot was "stellar." Martha Tilton's vocals were not; and so forth.[28]

Fortunately, we can make our own judgment about the music, for almost as an afterthought, the concert was recorded. There was, then, no tape recording, and making records in concert halls and nightclubs was far more difficult than it is today. (Most of the location records we have today were not made in the clubs, but taken from radio broadcasts by avid fans at home.) According to the generally accepted story, Albert Marx, who had recently married Helen Ward, decided "on his own initiative"[29] to have the concert piped from a single overhead microphone to a nearby studio, where acetate recordings were cut. (Symphony orchestras, at the time, frequently were recorded with a single microphone, the theory being that a Toscanini or a Bruno Walter knew more about balancing an orchestra than any engineer would.) One set of acetates was presented to the Library of Congress, and Goodman was given another set. It lay in a closet of his New York apartment for twelve years, and was only discovered when his sister-in-law Rachel Speiden took over his apartment and found them. By then tape was available.[30] Goodman had the concert transferred, and in November 1950, Columbia Records issued it with the jam session reduced by half and two tunes, "Sometimes I'm Happy" and "If Dreams Come True," omitted because they were badly recorded. These concert recordings have sold well over a million copies in the United States alone and many more elsewhere, and after forty years they are still in print—one of the best-selling jazz record albums ever made.

What of the music—was the concert really as glorious as legend has made it? It seems to me that, allowing for the unevenness that is inevitable in a performance of this kind, the band was in very good form, playing with both accuracy and enthusiasm. James and Stacy in particular stand out, but there were good solos by others. As critics said at the time, the brief "history of jazz" was a mistake, the only portion of musical value being Bobby Hackett's delicate recreation of Beiderbecke's famous "I'm Coming, Virginia." The Original Dixieland Jass Band and Ted Lewis portions turned into parodies, and James's remake of Armstrong's "Shine" is too frantic. The jam session was also rather chaotic, despite a fine solo by Lester Young, because it included too many players. And, as everyone has said, Jess Stacy's solo on "Sing, Sing, Sing" was unusual, and certainly one of the best moments of the evening. But fundamentally what the crowd got was an evening of the Goodman band much like what they would have gotten in a theatre. The whole point was that it took place in Carnegie Hall.

The publicity value was incalculable. So far as most people knew, this was the first concert of swing—the first jazz concert—and it was Benny Goodman who had put it on, thereby proving that jazz was an art. It did not matter that there had been jazz concerts before, and that jazz had been written about as an art early in the 1920s. The press showered the credit on Goodman.

The publicity, as is often the case, multiplied. The Strand Theatre had booked a Goodman film, *Hollywood Hotel*, to run at the time of the concert, and on January 26, Goodman opened at the Paramount. His name was all over New York—in newspapers, on theatre marquees, on radio, in record stores. Less than four years after he had put together his first band to play Billy Rose's Music Hall, Benny Goodman was at the top of the American popular music industry—the central figure of the booming new swing music, and on his way to earning his first million dollars.

There was a second concert, this one at Symphony Hall in Boston in April. Unfortunately, an unruly crowd helped to make it less than a success. *Down Beat* said that the audience "behaved so bastardly that some magnificent jazz was drowned out,"[31] and Goodman was reported to have shouted at the audience, "For heaven's sake, shut up,"[32] although it is unlikely that "For heaven's sake" was the exact phrase.

Later on Goodman said, "Well, I think the band I had at the Carnegie Hall Concert, about that time, was the best band I ever had. It was a really close-knit organization and they had just a wonderful ensemble and great soloists, and I think I got more satisfaction out of that band than any other."[33] Unhappily, it was about to fall apart.

The first man to depart was Gene Krupa, amidst an uproar in the press which today seems somewhat ludicrous but which at the time was terribly important. The main problem was a conflict of egos. Gene Krupa had a flamboyant and aggressive stage personality, and he attracted a great deal of attention from the swing fans, who loved to see him hunched over his drums, hair flying, arms pumping, apparently in a frenzy as he roared

through "Sing, Sing, Sing" and the other pieces. Krupa was more important
to the band's success than any of the other musicians, aside from Goodman
himself, and as a member of the popular small groups he got additional
exposure. By 1938 Krupa was the highest paid sideman in jazz,[34] and generally got featured billing wherever the band went.

Goodman's musicians have always complained that Benny was an "ego-
tist" who resented having to share the spotlight with his sidemen. Paul
Quinichette, who was with Goodman briefly in the 1950s, said that after
an engagement in Montreal, "I got a big write-up all on the front page.
Coming back on the plane he started to scream at me. 'Everybody thought
it was your band,' he said. 'Well, thank you, Fletcher Henderson,' I answered." Goodman never used Quinichette again.[35] Other stories of this
kind have been told, and at the time a great many people believed that the
trouble had grown out of Goodman's resentment of Krupa's popularity.

This may well have been true in part, but as was usually the case with
Goodman, things were not that simple. For one thing, Goodman was never
afraid of hiring the best jazz musicians available, people who he knew
could challenge him. Some of these men, like Sid Catlett and Lionel
Hampton, were also aggressive crowd-pleasers who courted audiences. However egotistical Goodman may have been, he was usually willing to give
good players room. The rupture with Krupa then was not due solely to
egotism on Goodman's part.

An important element was Goodman's growing disenchantment with
his audiences. Some show business figures devour furor and love nothing
better than to stir an audience to a frenzy. Benny Goodman was not that
sort of a man. There was an element of reserve in his character, and he was
coming more and more to dislike the kind of uproar that went on at the
Boston Symphony Hall concert. There was now more of this everywhere.
An appearance by the Goodman band was coming to be seen by some high-
school kids as an event, with the music of only secondary importance.

But for Goodman the music was the heart of it, the one thing that mattered, and it was always his goal, no matter how rich and famous he became, to play it right. It made him angry to see audiences full of rowdies
whose interest in his music was limited, preventing people who cared for
it from listening. And he saw that it was Krupa, more than anything, who
was stirring up the crowds.[36]

Thus, while the ego question may have played a role in his antipathy to
Krupa, what really mattered, I think, was that Krupa seemed to be throwing red meat to wild animals. There might have been some way to handle
the situation tactfully, but Goodman barely knew what the word "tact"
meant. He made some remarks; Krupa made some remarks back. They
began to quarrel on stage, and early in March, at the end of a week's en-

gagement at the Earle Theatre in Philadelphia, Krupa quit.[37] His contract with Goodman still had months to run, but Goodman did not press the issue. So Krupa was gone—at least for the moment—and gossip swept the band world.

Both Goodman and Krupa made an effort to paper over the rupture, at least for public relations purposes. Krupa issued a statement which said in part, "John Hammond and the other critics have made too much of our differences. It's not dramatic at all, but simply a case of ragged nerves, the strain of 40 shows a week, riding trains, etc.—which can happen to any musician."[38] Krupa quickly formed his own orchestra, and in the middle of that May both the Goodman and Krupa orchestras were in Philadelphia. Goodman made a point of going around to hear the Krupa band. He was introduced, and made a short speech in which he said that Krupa's band "really sounds fine." They put their arms around each other, had a drink together, and the fracas was thus smoothed over.[39]

There was yet one more element which may have entered into the dispute with Krupa, and subsequent other problems with personnel. According to John Hammond, writing in Down Beat in April, "Benny's health has been none too good in the last few months. His nervous system is slightly shattered. . . ."[40] Precisely what Hammond meant is hard to know, but it is clear that Goodman was under a good deal of tension. Managing a band of jazz musicians, many of them independent-minded people who do not like being told what to do, is not an easy task; and since the Paramount opening about a year earlier, Goodman had been dealing with the pressures that come from sudden success. "Benny Goodman" was now a big business with millions of dollars involved. There was not only the ordinary routine of seeing that the band was booked to best advantage, but music publishing and recording contracts to be negotiated, promotional schemes to be decided upon and a great many other purely business decisions to be made.

Additionally, Goodman continued to take care of his family. In the spring of 1938 he sponsored a band for Freddy, which had its debut at Ocean Pier in April; the band was not a success.[41] Far more profitable was Regent Music, which Benny helped to establish for Harry and Gene.[42] The business eventually made a lot of money, which allowed Harry to retire to the south of France, where he began collecting vintage wines.

And then of course there was the frenzy of the fans. Goodman had set out to put together a successful band, but what he had in mind was a success on the order of, say, Red Nichols or Ben Pollack. He had certainly not expected to become the central figure in an upheaval in popular culture, and I think that the uproar going on around him added substantially to the tension he was suffering from.

Benny Goodman lived inside a shell, cut off from other people to one extent or another a good deal of the time. Such a personality is likely to have its weak points. Later on Goodman would see a psychologist who actually traveled with the band for a period. And it is my suspicion that the very considerable pressures he was under were causing him emotional problems. These, I think, made it difficult for him to more easily manage the problems with Krupa and other bandsmen. In any case, in the weeks after Krupa left, Reuss, Koenig, Schertzer and Russin quit or were fired; and before the year was out Koenig's replacement, Dave Matthews, and Russin's replacement, Bud Freeman, had also left. In March 1939, Teddy Wilson left to form his own band. Still other men were in the band briefly, while others left and returned.

The greatest blow was the loss of Harry James, who left early in the year. James's own explanation, which he gave to George Simon, is this:

> I don't think I ever told anybody this, but I was going through a real mental thing and it was all built around "Sing, Sing, Sing." I'd been sick; they gave me some experimental pills—sulpher pills [probably sulfanilamide]—only they weren't very refined yet. Well, they wigged me out, and it happened the first time I was supposed to get up and play my chorus on "Sing, Sing, Sing." I just couldn't make it. I fell back in my chair. Ziggy said to me, "Get up!" but I couldn't; so when he saw what was happening, he got up and played my solo. I was completely out of my mind. It happened again another time, too, and so every time the band played "Sing, Sing, Sing," I'd get bugged and scared it would start all over again. You know, that Stravinsky-type thing that the trombones and then the trumpets play just before the chorus? Well, that would really set me off. I tried to explain it to Benny, and I'd even ask him to play "Sing, Sing, Sing" early in the evening, so I could relax the rest of the night. But of course, that was his big number and I couldn't blame him for wanting to hold off. So finally I just left the band. I couldn't trust myself any more. At least with my own band I could play the tunes that I wanted to play.[43]

Undoubtedly there was a good deal more to it than that. It was obvious to a lot of people that James had a real chance to make a considerable success of himself as a big band leader, as proved to be the case. And it cannot have been simply pills that threw him into a panic at the thought of playing "Sing, Sing, Sing"—some other kind of emotional pressure was also at work. It suggests how much strain there was on star performers with these big bands to produce a stirring performance for mobs of excited fans night after night.

One of the strangest of personnel problems occurred when Goodman brought in a group of men from the Basie band for a recording session.

According to Art Rollini, one day just before the *Camel Caravan* radio show Goodman's manager Leonard Vannerson came up to him and said he had something to tell him. The band was about to go on the air, and Rollini asked Vannerson to wait until after the show. But when the show was over Vannerson was gone. Rollini thought nothing of it, but:

> We had a recording session scheduled for the next morning. When I went down to the Victor recording studio for that session I saw Lester Young sitting in my chair. I stayed in the small lobby outside. Benny came rushing out. Tears welled in my eyes. Benny said, "Don't worry, Schneeze [Rollini's nickname], I am just trying something."[44]

What precisely Goodman was doing has not been made clear, but it is possible that John Hammond was involved. It has always been difficult to know exactly how much influence Hammond had on Goodman. Benny owed Hammond a lot, and furthermore, as a boy from the ghetto, he tended to be impressed by Hammond's social status. On the other hand, Goodman was a prickly and independent-minded man who did not take easily to being told what to do. According to Helen Ward, at one session an unhappy Peggy Lee had to do something like fourteen takes on a song. Finally Hammond turned to Goodman and said, "Oh, Benny, she can't sing."[45] Benny threw a chair at him. Hammond's meddling was frequently resented by the members of the band, said Ward, in part because they felt they knew more about how the music should be played than Hammond did, and partly because they knew his tastes were fickle, and he might at any moment start urging Benny to fire any one of them in favor of somebody he had recently heard.

However, Hammond cannot have wanted Benny to hire Lester Young or Freddie Green away from the Basie band. Hammond was at the moment very aggressively promoting the band and was rebuilding it; and he would hardly have wanted to lose key men like Young and Green. No explanation for the whole thing was given, but certainly the loyal Art Rollini, who had been an important member of the band from the start, deserved better treatment than this.

Among the most important of the new arrivals were Bud Freeman and Dave Tough. Freeman has been for decades a celebrated figure in jazz, author of two books on his life and times, an intelligent man who has always been a favorite of the older jazz buffs. Freeman's mother was a pianist, and in his childhood there were in his home both classical and dance records.[46] At the age of about fifteen he met Jimmy and Dick McPartland, who drew him into the Austin High group, where he met Dave Tough, the group's house intellectual. Freeman and Tough formed a friendship which lasted until Tough's early death.

Freeman, eager to get in on the new jazz music, coaxed his parents into buying him a C-melody saxophone. He never studied the instrument formally, and was by his own admission a very poor player for some time. But Tough shoe-horned him into a job he had, and gradually he began to improve. At nineteen he switched to tenor saxophone. Like others in the gang he was influenced at first by the New Orleans Rhythm Kings, but he began hearing the black bands at Lincoln Gardens and later at the South Side black-and-tans. He got some formal study and moved to New York at the end of the 1920s when the heart of the jazz scene shifted there from Chicago. He worked with Pollack briefly, gigged around New York, finally landing with the Tommy Dorsey band, with whom he made a well-known and characteristic solo on the hit recording of "Marie."

Freeman, although well liked by jazz fans for his vigorous, bouncy style, has never had the critical reputation of men such as Lester Young or Coleman Hawkins. Hawkins spoke of having been influenced by Freeman, but the influence is at least mutual. Clarinetist Bud Jacobson, another of the young white Chicagoans, said, "Bud played very ordinary sax until he heard Hawkins. And from then on Bud's rise was perpendicular. He'd play those Hawkins things and then let that develop out of himself until he played about the best sax in the business."[47]

Freeman tends to have a rough, somewhat guttural sound which he at times smooths out. He depends to a considerable extent on a set of stock figures, and his solos are in part worked out in advance. He lacks the rhythmic fluidity generally associated with the saxophone, but his style is markedly individual and easy to identify. Although he spent some years in the big bands during the swing heyday, he is more generally known for his work in small bands, especially the dixieland groups around Eddie Condon.

Freeman's pal Dave Tough has always had a larger critical reputation. He worked with the important Goodman small groups, and also with the modern Woody Herman groups of the post-war period. Tough lived one of those tragic lives that jazz is shot full of. His father was, according to Freeman,[48] "learned," "a highly educated, sensitive man." But "I think [Dave] saw his mother die in a certain drunken fit." Whatever the case, Tough grew up to be a small, wiry, sensitive and troubled youth. He went to Oak Park High, where Ernest Hemingway had gone, read *The Sun Also Rises* when it appeared in 1926, and by the age of sixteen was going to the Chicago Art Institute to see the Cézannes, an advanced taste for a boy at that time. He was also playing with the Austin High group, and eventually made a way for himself in the music business. But he continued to have intellectual interests and in the late 1920s moved to Paris with a new wife. She had an affair with a member of the band he was working with, and, according to Freeman, Tough returned to New York, broken-hearted. He was by now an alcoholic, and was virtually out of music from 1932 until 1935, when he began to play with the emerging swing bands. In the following years he was in and out of many bands, among them those of both Dorsey brothers, Berigan, Red Norvo and Goodman.

During one of his stints with Tommy Dorsey the band was playing in a black theatre which had a show with black dancers. Freeman and Tough asked the black pit bandleader if there would be any problem about dating the girls in the show. They were assured there would not be. Tough fell in love with one of them, who was named Casey Majors, and married her. Freeman said, "She was a darling little girl. And she was so marvelous for him. He quit drinking for three years because of her." But the moment did not last: Tough began drinking again, suffered a series of illnesses, and finally, in 1948, while at a veterans' hospital in New Jersey, died from head injuries incurred in a fall. The implication was that he committed suicide, but it may well have been accidental.

Freeman said, "Oh, Dave Tough was one of the most delightful [men] you would ever want to meet; he had a brilliant sense of humor." According to Freeman, Tough was once having an affair with a nymphomaniacal woman whose husband led a very commercial band. When the husband once walked in on them Tough's response was, "Thank God it's you."

In 1945, after eighteen months with the brilliant Herman band, Tough won first place in the *Down Beat, Esquire* and *Metronome* polls. Sid Weiss said,

> Buddy Rich is supposed to have that fast foot. But Davey could play faster than Buddy, and also play faster than Louie Bellson with two drums. Davey was unbelievable. Take charge. As small as he was, he knew just how to do it. When I played a note his bass drum would go through the note and amplify it. He had a way of playing the bass drum so it would not cover—the tonality was right or whatever. The way the pedal struck the drum, it was just absolutely perfect. Most drummers didn't really understand about the bass drum, they weren't really listening to the bass.[49]

(String bass players frequently complain that a hollow, booming bass drum, of the kind that Krupa played, would swallow up the bass notes through a considerable range of pitches.)

But what was really important about Tough was his ability to swing a band. A number of years ago I was listening rather haphazardly through the Goodman small band sides, in order to pick out a few for further analysis. I was astonished to discover that all of the ones I had chosen as particularly worthy had Tough on drums. This was something musicians felt. Tough could swing. And I think that there is substantial opinion that among drummers of the period only Sid Catlett was Tough's peer.

With the departure of Krupa, Lionel Hampton filled in for three weeks, and then Goodman brought in Tough from the Berigan band. Freeman was eager to join his old friend—they had previously spent twenty months together in the Dorsey Orchestra—and it was arranged for him to come with Goodman.[50] But Tough was drinking. He began missing dates, and eventually, in October 1938, Goodman had to fire him.[51] According to Art Rollini, Tough "was a fine drummer, but heavy on the cymbals. Benny eyed him cautiously. . . . The pressure began to take a toll on little slender Davey. He was losing weight. Benny was very critical with drummers."[52] Mel Powell said, "His cymbal playing was wonderful, but I don't think he was the best ideal drummer for Benny. . . . Davey was subtle. Subtlety was not for Benny's band. Davey would work better even with Tommy Dorsey's band. Even with the small group. Benny's kind of drummer was Krupa. Driving. For all the show biz and maniacal stuff, Gene was a driving, ferocious drummer."[53]

Between Goodman's tenseness and the arrival and departure of so many musicians, the band began to lose some of its crispness and sparkle. Rollini said, "The [saxophone] section was falling apart. . . ."[54] Whether the fans felt this, or simply were looking for new faces, as is often the case, they named Artie Shaw's band number one. A core of the Carnegie Hall band still remained, including Elman, Stacy, Brown and Goodman himself. If the band had slipped a little, and was not the automatic first choice of swing fans, it still had an enormous following, and was greeted by throngs wherever it went. But it had more competition. As the swing wave mounted, more and more bands were pulled together to cash in on the demand. In the two years after the Carnegie Hall concert bands were formed by Benny Carter, Tony Pastor, Jack Teagarden, Claude Thornhill, Will Bradley, and two Goodman alumni, Gene Krupa and Harry James. Goodman no longer had the field to himself.

The personnel shifts continued through 1939. James's replacement, Cy Baker, was in turn replaced by Irving Goodman, only to be replaced by Corky Cornelius. Hymie Schertzer came back; Art Bernstein came in on bass, George Rose on guitar. Finally, the last of the key men, Jess Stacy, left. This was entirely Goodman's fault. With the departure of Teddy Wilson, Stacy had begun to play with the small groups, something he had wanted to do for a long time, after having sat in Wilson's shadow for years. Not long after, Flecher Henderson gave up on his most recent band and rejoined Goodman as a staff arranger. Very soon Goodman put Henderson into the Trio in place of Stacy. Jess was hurt and bewildered, but for the moment he hung on.

The jazz writers were equally bewildered. *Down Beat* said, "After four years with Benny Goodman's band, during which time he rose to be acclaimed one of the greatest jazz pianists in the world, Jess Stacy gave way to Fletcher Henderson last month."[55] All Goodman would say by way of explanation was, "Maybe Fletcher isn't the best pianist going but at least he knows what we want."[56] Jerry Jerome remembers that Goodman began " 'conducting' Jess, who started drinking and became upset. . . . Benny had the ray working, but would not fire Jess. By late July, Jess could not take it any longer."[57] According to *Metronome*, "It is understood that Jess quit the band in very much of a huff. There had been some friction, friends say, but it wasn't until Benny put Fletcher Henderson into the Trio and Quartet in place of Stacy, then asked him to take Jess' chorus of 'Stealin' Apples' [Henderson's arrangement] with the full band that the quiet Chicagoan flared up."[58]

Henderson, however fine an arranger, has never been considered an important jazz pianist, whereas Stacy was one of the best of the day. Even Henderson's biographer, Walter C. Allen, was puzzled. He said, "It seems strange now that [Goodman] would have in effect driven as great a pianist as Jess Stacy out of the band in favor of one who—let's face it! didn't have a tenth of Jess' soloistic ability."[59] Stacy was very angry, but he said only, "I never want to play with Benny Goodman's band again. . . . There were no hard feelings between Benny and me. He's a fine guy. But it was too much of a strain. You never knew where you were with Benny, and I feel terribly relieved that it's over."[60] He said later that although nobody could surpass Teddy Wilson in the Trio, "for the band, he didn't have the oomph." His own style, Stacy said, was "more dense, two-handed. Teddy played lots of little runs. Did you ever notice that Teddy would never attack a note? It's pretty piano. I played more barrel house style." And he continued, "If I tried to play like Teddy Wilson I'd make an ass out of myself. So I can only do what I do. If people like it, fine."[61] Stacy toyed with the idea of forming his own band, but in the end accepted an offer to go with the Bob Crosby band. And in time, when the Crosby band folded during the war, he came back to Goodman.

It is hard to understand what Goodman's motives were. It is true that Goodman had been hard on Stacy for some time. Otis Ferguson, writing in 1937, spoke of Benny "raising his eyebrows in the signal for what-the-hell-goes-on-here, or coming over to buzz a couple of high clarinet tones right in Jess's ear. . . . Jess proves to be just the butt for that sort of thing, because his face begins to get red and flustered. . . ."[62] Ferguson was hearing the band frequently during this period, admired it greatly, and his story can be trusted.

I think, fundamentally, that in the small groups Benny had gotten used to hearing a certain kind of piano that Teddy Wilson provided. He was no longer hearing it, and Stacy was obviously the villain. I also have a feeling that Goodman tended to probe where he felt weakness; Jess was not weak, but he was a gentle man, and Goodman may have felt he could bully him with impunity. In any case, Jess proved that while he could be pushed, he could only be pushed so far, and he was gone.

There was one more change that needs to be commented upon. That was the addition of a third trombonist, played by Bruce Squires. One of the main aspects of the history of the modern dance band, from the first Hickman groups until the end of the swing era, was the steady increase in the number of wind instruments. Hickman had two saxes, one trumpet, and one trombone. By the early 1920s bands were using two or three saxes and at least two trumpets and a trombone to make up a three-piece brass choir, the point being that a chord requires three notes, and a three-piece section can therefore be harmonically much more sophisticated than a two-piece one. By the late twenties some bands were using three trumpets, two trombones and four saxophones; and by the early thirties some, like the Henderson and Ellington bands, had added a third trombone to make a true trombone choir possible.

This trend would continue into the forties, when the swing band typically carried four trumpets, five saxes and three trombones. Finally some were using five trumpets, four trombones and five or even six saxophones; and groups like the Kenton band might have as many as ten brass.

There were a number of reasons for bulking the sections up this way. For one thing, it was a time when leaders and fans liked a lot of power. For another, there was the show business aspect of it: the serried ranks of horns looked very impressive on band stands. Finally, the modern chords being used in the mid- to late forties often called for five notes.

Yet there was always the feeling of some people that what was gained in power and harmonic richness was lost in the ability to swing. One of the most critical aspects of playing jazz with a big band is the close coordination of tiny details by members of a section. Just hitting a note together with a timing that most symphonic players would find difficult can be critical to swing, where fractions of a second are involved. It is obvious that three people can do this more successfully than five or six. At least Goodman thought so: "I don't know why arrangers want to use eight brass," he said. "It's got to make an orchestra sound tubby. They can't get eight brass to play as well as you can get five or six."[63] But the fashion was now for larger sections, and Goodman would, over the next few years, follow the trend, though reluctantly.

But all of these changes were just a prelude, for in the middle of 1939 Goodman changed record companies, brought in a new and very different arranger, and revamped the whole band. It would all be different. The so-called Victor band that Goodman had built to a peak at the time of the Carnegie Hall concert in January 1938 was now, after eighteen months of slow bleeding, finished. The switch to the new record company was fitting, for the old ways, and most of the old musicians, were gone. It would be a new beginning.

# 18
# The Carnegie Hall Band

Benny Goodman's favorite of his bands was the one that played the Carnegie Hall concert, sometimes referred to as the 1938 band by Goodman fans.[1] Many critics and ordinary fans agree; that band seemed to have a greater verve than some of Goodman's other groups and, according to Goodman's admirers, most other swing bands of the day. I am not sure that I entirely agree; but it certainly is true that this 1938 band was the one that comes to mind when we think of Benny Goodman's music.

Actually, the "1938" band can really be dated from the beginning of 1937, when Helen Ward left and Harry James arrived. The band was not really complete until Martha Tilton came in the summer of 1937, but the arrival of James roughly coincides with the explosion at the Paramount that March, and it is reasonable for the purposes of analysis to group the records made by the band during James's tenure through the beginning of 1939. All but three of the fourteen men who played James's first recording date were still with the band for the Carnegie Hall concert the following January. Thereafter Krupa and Reuss left, and various saxophonists came and went. But eight of the fourteen were still with the band for James's last record date with it.

Of the roughly ninety-five records made during this time, fifty included vocals, mainly pop songs that lived very brief lives. Some were longer lasting, like Tilton's classic "Loch Lomond" and a few standards like "'S Wonderful" and "I Can't Give You Anything But Love, Baby," but some 90 percent of the vocals are on tunes like "Let That Be a Lesson to You," "You Took the Words Right Out of My Heart," many of them tunes from movies the band appeared in, which were recorded to exploit the film.

Martha Tilton was as important to this band as Helen Ward was to the earlier one. Goodman's liking for her singing is indicated by the fact that in the months before her arrival, when Goodman was trying one singer after another, only a third of the records the band made included vocals;

once Tilton was in place, the ratio jumped to a half. At one point, during the summer of 1938, when the band was at a peak of popularity, it cut eleven consecutive vocals.

In fact, during this two-year span Tilton had more solo space than even Goodman. Benny, as usual, was the dominant instrumental soloist, taking about half the solo time for himself. This was particularly true of the vocal numbers, where solos were limited by the full chorus given to Tilton. On these Goodman usually played patches of the tune here and there, sometimes staying quite close to the melody and usually at least suggesting, or paraphrasing it. One or two other soloists might get an occasional eight bars for variety. There was a certain justice to this. Goodman was the best soloist in the band, and furthermore the sound of his clarinet was basic to the musical identity of the band; the fans expected to hear it regularly.

But on the more jazz-like swingers, Goodman substantially reduced his solo time. His was still the dominant voice, but on these records he takes only a little over a third of the solo measures. Goodman was aware of the fact that he could not keep players of the caliber of James, Stacy and the others if he did not give them room in which to blow; but, perhaps more important, Goodman liked to hear these people play. Stacy in particular, despite the dissatisfaction that Goodman would eventually feel about him, was getting much more solo time than he had previously.

The case of Dave Matthews is instructive. Until his arrival, alto solos on Goodman records are virtually nonexistent. In Goodman's view people like Hymie Schertzer, Toots Mondello and Bill DePew were excellent section men but not exciting jazz improvisers. Dave Matthews, neglected by jazz historians, was one of the finest alto saxophonists of his day. He had a warm, full tone approaching in richness that of Duke Ellington's Johnny Hodges, the preeminent altoist of the period; he swung hard, and he was fluent in ideas. Matthews spent most of his working life in big bands, successively Pollack, Jimmy Dorsey, Goodman, James, Hal McIntyre, Woody Herman, Stan Kenton and Charlie Barnet, which is some indication of the respect he was held in. Jazz reputations, with the exception of a few, like those of Bunny Berigan and Ellington's stars, are made with small band recordings, where the musicians can play extended solos. Matthews made far fewer of these than his peers, and his reputation has suffered for it.

A second important soloist with the band during this period was Goodman's old friend from Chicago, Bud Freeman, who came in when Russin left. However, of all the soloists who played with this Goodman group, the most important beside Krupa was unquestionably Harry James. James has been given short shrift—or no shrift at all—by many jazz writers, who have tended to see him as a slick commercial trumpeter, addicted to showy effects, who eventually made a lot of money playing over-ripe ballads like

"Sleepy Lagoon" and "I Cried for You," both of which were big hits for him when he had his own band. All of this is certainly true. James never denied that he intended to give the public what it wanted, which included a lot of fulsome ballads. James, we remember, was in show business when he was a little boy, and had been trained from childhood to think in terms of audience appeal. As a circus musician he came from the trumpet tradition of the famous Herbert L. Clarke, which demanded flashy effects, a strong high register, and a lot of showy grace notes, turns and cadenzas. This brass tradition is evident in his playing from the beginning.

But it is also true that Harry James could be, when he wanted to, a very fine jazz musician. He was all of his life a great admirer of Louis Armstrong, and he thought of himself primarily as a jazz man. Most of his recordings were with big bands, mainly his own and Goodman's, but he did record with small bands, which often show him to good advantage. For example, in the middle of 1937, a few months after he joined Goodman, he made sixteen cuts in the famous Teddy Wilson series masterminded by John Hammond. In these he shows none of the flashy stunts and excessive half-valving that marred his ballad playing later on. He plays clean, nicely constructed solos on "Coquette" and "Honeysuckle Rose," but particularly fine from this set is the doubled-sided blues, issued as "Just a Mood." The record includes a wonderful, delicate xylophone solo by Red Norvo, but James has five choruses which are thoughtfully worked out to build to a climax in the manner suggested by what Louis Armstrong was doing on the Hot Five records a decade earlier. James's solos on these records show him to be a thoughtful player with an immaculate technique. He virtually never fluffs, a rare thing in an improvising trumpet player. He can stand comparison with most of the today more highly regarded jazz musicians who played on these Wilson sides.

However well James handled himself in the small-band context, he was really the quintessential big-band musician, with the power to drive his solos over a whole band. His roaring solo in his own "Two O'Clock Jump" —a version of the old "One O'Clock Jump," with the modulation into D-flat in the middle—is a classic hard-driving big-band solo which was copied by young trumpet players all over the United States. With Goodman he plays a ferocious, purely hot solo on a radio broadcast version of "Ridin' High," later issued as part of what was called Goodman's *Jazz Concert #2* to capitalize on the surprise success of the Carnegie Hall album. On the formal recordings with Goodman, James plays many fine solos, often quite brief, as on "Bumblebee Stomp," "Margie," "When It's Sleepytime Down South" and a dozen others. Two excellent examples of his work with Goodman are on "Peckin'" and "Roll 'Em." The first is an arrangement James had made when he was with the Ben Pollack Orchestra to feature the trumpets. The main theme is built around the trumpet section half-valving the opening notes to create the impression of "pecking"—that is to say of the sudden brief peck which the dance of the same name featured. It is a small tour de force, requiring some very nice coordination on the part of the trumpets. James's own solo is typical—the sudden sky-rocket bursts into the upper register followed by quick patches of eighth notes, the occasional grace notes which are a trade mark and, most characteristic of all, the endless fluid, powerful forward motion.

To my mind the finest of James's solos with Goodman is on "Roll 'Em." He runs up to it with a novel figure which he keeps on unwinding through the next two bars until he creates another version of it in bar four. This run carries up to the natural phrase break at the fifth bar, and then keeps on unwinding through the seventh measure, to make one long, steadily rolling phrase, played with great restraint, to give us a sense of something impending. Particularly striking are the three parallel figures in the first three measures, each three beats in length, which make a displacement in meter.

The last four bars of the chorus give us the climax which we have been awaiting. However, instead of holding at the peak, James winds down briefly, a sound tactic which allows him to create a second climax at the opening of the next chorus. Again he falls off, then rises and falls and rises, to make the chorus a series of climaxes. James had a very good sense for this sort of thing. Very frequently improvising musicians reach a peak too early, and then, feeling that they must not lose ground, keep struggling to find yet higher ground, which remains out of reach. Here James, by winding down from each peak, gives himself a chance to rise again.

On the Concert #2 album version of "Roll 'Em," possibly broadcast from Pittsburgh, James plays four blazing hot choruses which so stirred the audience that it began yelling from excitement, an effect the band often had. This, too, is a memorable solo; but the one made in the studio, with its restraint, is ultimately more satisfying, and I have no hesitation in calling it one of the finest trumpet solos made during the swing era, the equal of the best work of Bunny Berigan, and approaching that of James's own idol, Louis Armstrong. It is worth noticing that some of James's best moments in jazz come on the blues: "Just a Mood," "Two O'Clock Jump," and "Roll 'Em." He was raised in Texas, a blues hotbed during his youth.

Nor should it be thought that once James left Goodman he turned into a commercial hack. He continued to play a lot of jazz, some of it excellent. In 1947 he formed a band to play the new bebop music that was sweeping jazz. The group was never as deeply committed to bebop as, say, the Dizzy Gillespie big bands to come a little later; but it was capable of playing very hot music. James himself even changed his style to absorb some ele-

ments of bebop, and he plays boppish solos on some of the recording with
this group, as for example "Tuxedo Junction" made with a small group
drawn from the big band.

Unfortunately, James was an uneven performer. At his best he was as
good as any of his peers and better than most. But he was not always
at his best. Far too often his solos are thrown off with a casual glibness, or
marred by showy effects, and because his best moments come infrequently,
he has never been ranked with other featured trumpet players of the big
band years, like Buck Clayton, Cootie Williams, Berigan and others. But
he was not nearly so far behind them as critics have believed, and he was
enormously influential in his day. From the moment he came into the
Goodman band he was the model for thousands of aspiring jazz trumpet
players all over the United States, black as well as white. It has always been
said that Dizzy Gillespie's first model was Roy Eldridge, and it is certainly
true that by 1939 or so Dizzy was schooling with Eldridge. But Gillespie's
earliest records with the Teddy Hill band show him to be a big-band trumpet player directly in the James mold. It is hardly surprising that James was
so influential: he was a hot, swinging trumpet player regularly featured
with the country's leading swing band and possessed of a flawless technique
that was the envy of trumpet players everywhere.

But equally important to the band was the ensemble work. First-class
arrangements played with crispness and swing continued to be the essence
of big band music. During this period the bulk of the arranging was being
done by Fletcher Henderson and Jimmy Mundy. However, it was also the
period when Edgar Sampson made his major contribution. (Actually
Mundy did most of the writing in 1937, Henderson and Sampson in 1938.)
Two of the band's most famous arrangements from this period were Sampson originals, "If Dreams Come True" and "Don't Be That Way." Both are
built around Sampson's trademark, a rather evenhanded call-and-response.
As we have seen, in the usual system the call is the main statement, the
answer simply punctuation, or a murmured reply. In Sampson's hands the
answer was given as much weight as the call, and the effect is sufficiently
different that these Sampson pieces are immediately identifiable as his.

"If Dreams Come True" consists of three thirty-two-bar choruses. Each
chorus is divided into two virtually similar sixteen-bar segments. These are
further subdivided into related eight-bar sections, which are further subdivided into similar—in some instances identical—four-bar passages. Structurally it could hardly be simpler or more four-square. The harmonies, built
around a basic two-five-one pattern, are equally simple.

The opening line, or call, which is the putative melody to the song,
consists for the most part of two notes played over two bars, which are
then answered by a somewhat more complicated figure. In the first chorus

these are played respectively by trumpets in cup mutes and unison clarinets. Then follow sixteen bars of Goodman's clarinet over the saxophones, and another sixteen bars by trombonist Vernon Brown, who had come into the band only a week or two before. Brown's solo, as befits the general tenor of the piece, is made up mainly of relatively long half, whole and less definable notes. Goodman's trombone soloists during the 1930s—Jack Lacey, Joe Harris and Brown—all tended to play this way. It is certainly true that on fast numbers trombonists may fall back on quarter notes, rather than the quicker eighths and sixteenths, but at the tempos that the Goodman band usually played, none of these men would have had any trouble playing faster passages. Indeed, Teagarden, who influenced all of these men, was noted for his loquacity at high speeds. Benny Morton, one of the most admired trombonists of the time, also built his line around quarter and half notes, although he was a fine technician who could easily negotiate faster passages. This kind of trombone playing was really a stylistic preference, a way of implying, rather than stating, the rhythm. Instead of subdividing the beat with notes of various lengths, in this system the player holds the note and lets the beat subdivide it, so that, as in the best poetry, what is not said echoes in the mind with a force it might not have were it made explicit. In this case it is the rhythm that is implied. It is a very effective method and Brown used it frequently.

Brown's sixteen measures are followed by another variation on the call-and-response device. For the first eight measures the band and Goodman alternate two-measure phrases. For the second eight the order is reversed, with the band answering back exactly what Goodman had first played. Although it is possible for a band of well-schooled musicians to do this sort of thing spontaneously, this was undoubtedly written into the arrangement and rehearsed. The effect is startling—a case of the man answering the parrot.

There is, finally, eight bars of tenor solo by Vido Musso, and then a last eight by the whole band playing a wrap-up which suggests the main melody. That is all there is to it. The imaginative use of call-and-response, a couple of nice solos and not much else. It all depends on the lightness of the arrangement, and the crisp, easy way it is played, so that the whole piece seems to float over the rhythm, like a swimmer in the air.

"Don't Be That Way" is almost simpler. It is cast in the standard pop song AABA thirty-two-bar form, again cut into subdivisions of eight, four and two measures. This time the call-and-response program gives major weight to the call, and uses the answer exactly as punctuation. After a four-measure introduction the saxophones play the famous melody line in unison—just as Sampson used unison clarinets for the answering figure in the opening chorus of "If Dreams Come True." The answers are trumpets

in straight mutes, playing a very simple syncopated two-note figure that
was used again and again by swing bands. For variety, at the "turn around"
at the end of the first eight measures the trumpets play the connecting
passage and the saxophones open out into harmony. The first eight is
repeated and then at the bridge roles are reversed, and the melody—if so
simple a phrase can be called that—is reduced to an absolute minimum,
just two notes by the trumpets, two by the saxophones in each two-measure
segment. The first eight measures are then repeated to round out the
chorus. There follows a four-bar interlude to modulate from D-flat to F,
after which Goodman and James split a chorus, with James playing a great
many of the grace notes he favored. The final chorus is divided first into
eight bars of call-and-response between orchestra and drums, and then an
eight-bar solo for trombone, which is introduced by a very trombonistic figure on single bass notes by the piano so that remembered later it seems to
be part of the trombone solo. Goodman solos on the bridge, and then the
piece jumps abruptly into D, and repeats the opening. Again, we remember
that in "Stomping at the Savoy" Sampson went from D-flat to D, although
in this case there are several intervening key changes. But this is not the
end; for the eight-bar conclusion repeats three times, fading away a little
each time until a sudden drum break brings the band back at full steam
with the brass this time playing a somewhat more elaborate figure forte
against the main line in the unison saxes.

Once again it is amazing how little there is to it—and how little actual
writing was involved. Seven of the sixteen eight-bar segments are virtually
identical, one other is quite close, and six others are solos, all supported by
brief, repeated figures, reharmonized where necessary. But Goodman
thought so much of this piece that he used it to open the Carnegie Hall
concert. And it became one of the most popular pieces Goodman ever
played.

There is a lesson in this. Jazz has always been a music of a very limited
formal structure. This was partly because ballrooms and records limited
performances to three minutes. But it was also because the musicians
themselves have always been primarily concerned with matters other than
form—invention, rhythmic impulse, a particular sound and the like, and
do not want to have to worry about following an elaborate formal structure
while they are improvising. A limited form cannot bear too much traffic,
or too elaborate a superstructure. It requires an economy of line, shape,
event. Only a very few of the great jazz musicians have been able to get
away with the level of complexity Ellington brought to pieces like "Ko-Ko,"
and even the masterful Ellington at times fell when he tried to do too
much. The temptation to over-write is always present. Goodman under-

stood this, and habitually pruned arrangements to make sure that first the piece would swing. It is no accident that some of the best-liked pieces from the swing era are very simple, indeed basic, as Glenn Miller's "In the Mood," Ellington's "Take the 'A' Train," Basie's "Jumpin' at the Woodside" and Goodman's "Don't Be That Way," all of which open with unison reed riffs.

Mary Lou Williams's "Roll 'Em," which contains the wonderful solo by James, is also classically simple. Williams grew up musically in Kansas City where the big band had evolved somewhat differently. According to Eddie Durham, who arranged for a number of bands from the Kansas City region, among them the important Bennie Moten band, the riffs favored by the Kansas City musicians were melodic, not just punctuation, as they frequently were with the Eastern bands. "You could always write a song to it," Durham said.[2]

This is very much the case with Williams's "Roll 'Em." It is a boogiewoogie piece formed, like most boogie-woogie, on the blues. It utilizes four-bar breaks by soloists, and the full band at times, on the first four bars of the blues chorus, a device popularized by Pine Top Smith's well-known "Pine Top's Boogie Woogie." In Sampson pieces very frequently the call, answer, or both, are made up of just two or three notes, as for example the main "themes" of "If Dreams Come True" and "Stompin' at the Savoy." In "Roll 'Em" the trumpet answers over the boogie-woogie bass in the saxes are relatively long, constituting real, if abbreviated, bits of melody. In the second chorus the first response by the trumpets is punctuation; but very quickly the brass sweeps up the whole band, which plays a long, eight-measure melody that unfolds without repeated phrases. In the third chorus, after a four-bar break by the band, both saxes and trumpets play continually, rather than the one answering the other. You could indeed "write a song" to a lot of the material in "Roll 'Em." Only in the last chorus does the brass punctuate the saxes in the riff system that was by this time standard for big-band writing.

What made the piece go as far as the audience was concerned was the boogie-woogie bass. Boogie-woogie became a national fad after John Hammond's first spirituals-to-swing concert at Carnegie Hall in December 1938, which featured boogie pianists Pete Johnson, Albert Ammons and Meade Lux Lewis, whom Hammond was promoting. In the middle of 1937, when "Roll 'Em" was recorded, the boogie-woogie craze had not started, and it struck audiences as something fresh. It is also clear that Goodman himself loved the piece. At this time he was playing a more contained, rather melodic style; but here, pressed forward by the pile-driving boogie beat, he reverts to the growl that had been so much a part of his style in his first days.

Particularly neat are the variations he makes on a brief phrase through the last nine bars of the first chorus. "Roll 'Em" stayed in Goodman's repertory for years, and he continued to whack away at it ferociously.

"Roll 'Em" was something of a departure for Goodman, and so was another piece that became a hit for him, "Loch Lomond," one of Martha Tilton's best-known vocals. By the middle of 1937, as the swing era was heating up, bandleaders, beset by the need for constantly finding something fresh to do, were somewhat desperately reaching out in various directions for novelties. One device was to produce swing versions of pieces from classical literature. Early in 1937 Tommy Dorsey produced arrangements of Mendelssohn's "Spring Song," and "The Blue Danube." There was also a fad for swing versions of old standards: Louis Armstrong sang "My Darling Nellie Grey" and "Carry Me Back to Old Virginny" in April 1937; Connie Boswell and the Crosby band recorded "Home on the Range" that fall; the Casa Loma Orchestra recorded "My Bonnie Lies Over the Ocean" the following February; Tommy Dorsey did "Annie Laurie," "Old Black Joe" and "Comin' Through the Rye" in 1938; that spring Jimmy Dorsey recorded "The Arkansas Traveller"; and in the summer Casa Loma cut "Swing Low, Sweet Chariot."

In August 1937 Maxine Sullivan, one of the best vocalists of the period, made "Loch Lomond" with a small group using an arrangement by Claude Thornhill, who played piano on the recording. It was a hit, and Goodman commissioned Thornhill to make a big-band arrangement for Tilton.[3] It consists almost entirely of the vocal (which includes a brief bit of recitative by Goodman), and a short eight-measure solo by James. This is one of the few records the Goodman Orchestra ever made in which Goodman does not play at least a brief solo, but he can be heard behind Tilton in the second chorus. Musically the surprise is the open fifths in the introduction and elsewhere meant to imitate the drones of the bagpipes. What made the piece a hit, however, was the idea of swinging a tune which most Americans had learned to sing in their elementary-school music classes—the old familiar in a new guise, like Cinderella dressed up for the ball.

Yet one more novelty from this period that remains well known is "Bach Goes to Town." "Going to town" was a slang phrase of the period that meant making a thorough job of something—in the case of swing musicians, a perfervid performance. The piece was composed by Alec Templeton, a blind pianist who became something of a celebrity in the 1930s and 1940s, especially as a radio personality. He was a serious composer but was best known for a series of parodies written in the manner of masters like Mozart and Haydn.[4] This piece was arranged—or let us say orchestrated—for Goodman by Henry Brant, a serious experimental composer who at periods earned his living writing for radio, films and other commercial mar-

kets.[5] "Bach Goes to Town" is a genuine fugue. It is played first by clarinets (including bass clarinet), after which the full band is employed. It is
subtitled "A Fugue in Swing Tempo" but in fact it swings very little—
although the band tries—primarily because the orchestration is almost
entirely lacking the syncopated notes that are essential to jazz rhythm.
Nonetheless, it is an amusing tour de force.

Yet one more fairly strange set of records was cut in March 1938—the
sides which included Lester Young in place of Art Rollini. Krupa had just
left, and Hampton moved over to play drums with the orchestra. For this
session Goodman brought in Basie's bassist Walter Page and guitarist
Freddie Green from what has often been considered the finest of all big-
band rhythm sections, and, much to Rollini's dismay, Lester Young came
in on tenor.

What Goodman was attempting is not known, but it is clear that he
had, by this time, become a great admirer of Young. According to John
Hammond, the story was this.[6] Hammond had, sometime in the middle of
1936, discovered a guitarist working in the Black Cat, an obscure Greenwich Village club a few blocks from his apartment. Hammond felt that he
had the finest beat of any rhythm guitarist he had ever heard. This of
course was Freddie Green. Hammond was in the process of revamping the
Basie band, and he wanted Basie to fire his guitarist, Claude Williams, and
bring in Green. Sometime in late November or early December 1936, he
brought Basie and some of his musicians, including Young, down to the
Black Cat. He also asked Goodman, who was finished for the night at one
o'clock, to join the party.

Both Goodman and Young sat in. Hammond said:

It was quite a night. Benny had brought his clarinet so he sat in. Basie
took over at the piano and Jo [Jones] on drums, but Frank Clarke remained on bass and, of course, Freddie Green continued to play guitar.
Goodman played so beautifully that everyone in the room was overwhelmed. Lester had brought along a metal clarinet, an instrument
much less expensive and not so tonally rich as the wooden clarinet
most players use. Lester did not have much clarinet technique, but he
did have the same intimate sound and sense of phrasing he had on the
saxophone. After Lester played a while Benny handed Lester his clarinet. "Here," he said, "take mine"—meaning, keep it. Goodman could
get as many clarinets as he wanted; still, it was an extraordinary gesture,
a tribute to Lester's playing, an indication that if Benny cared he could
be very generous.[7]

John Hammond is never an entirely trustworthy source, but it is clear
enough that Goodman was enormously impressed by Young. And this
finally led to his inviting Lester to the March 1938 recording session which

so distressed Art Rollini and apparently caused Allen Reuss to give his notice.

Benny Goodman played alto saxophone regularly as a member of saxophone sections with Pollack and during his free-lance period, and occasionally soloed on the instrument. He also soloed, but rarely, on baritone sax and bass clarinet. He could, of course, play tenor, and he apparently did so with the Music Hall orchestra when the arrangement called for a fourth saxophone. However, he recorded so little on tenor it is difficult to make a judgment about his style.[8] But Bud Freeman said he and Benny once swapped instruments, just for fun, and Freeman said, "I was amazed when I heard Benny play tenor."[9] And the English saxophonist Benny Winestone said that he once heard Goodman late at night in a half-empty Music Hall play on "California Here I Come": "about twenty choruses on tenor that were as fine as anything I ever heard from any tenor man."[10]

On the basis of the relatively few alto solos on record, it is clear that Goodman was certainly a competent soloist with a light, clean sound, undoubtedly modeled on that of Frankie Trumbauer. Furthermore, Goodman kept, as his principal saxophonist for years, Art Rollini, who also played with a clean, flowing sound. Although he eventually began using tenor saxophonists like Vido Musso and Georgie Auld, who played with the rough, hard-driving style developed by Coleman Hawkins, he also used players like Wardell Gray and Stan Getz, who played with the light, airy sound that was the antithesis of Hawkins's manner. There is, therefore, good reason to believe Hammond's story, and it is not surprising that Goodman was interested in trying Young in his band.

Goodman's own playing on the date is quite odd. For one thing, he does not play at all on "Make Believe" nor on "oooOO-OH BOOM!" on which he sings—undoubtedly the only recording session Goodman ever made in which he does not play on two cuts. And when he does play, his solos are atypical. In "Please Be Kind," the first record made on the date, he plays brief phrases just before the vocal, and in the tag, that are deliberately staccato at moments and almost devoid of jazz feeling, as if they were being played by a symphonic musician. He opens his solo with a wholly atypical figure consisting of a repeated note played increasingly faster, and does the same thing again two measures later. His tone, furthermore, is less full, a little lighter and clearer than was usual for him. On "Ti-Pi-Tin," a novelty number popular at the time, he opens his chorus with three measures of repeated eighth-note B-flats. For the second eight he plays a series of sharply attacked, abrupt B-flats an octave higher. The last eight measures comprise a sequence of staccato quarter notes. Sequences of repeated notes, played for some rhythmic purpose, are very typical of jazz playing, especially at beginnings of solos to help the player get under way. But they are rare in the work of Goodman, whose astonishing facility allowed him to start off immediately with a complex figure.

On "Always and Always," a typical pop song with a vocal by Martha Tilton, Goodman's opening solo has a tentativeness, almost diffidence, and the legitimate sound heard on "Please Be Kind." There is also a strange moment after the vocal where Young doubles Goodman's line two octaves lower for a brief four bars. On "The Blue Room," Goodman plays with a very fast, emphatic vibrato, and his tone thins out and becomes shrill on the bridge. There follow some extremely high notes, much higher than he was accustomed to play.

What was going on? Page and Green are under-recorded, and do not appear to be any improvement over Goodman's own men. What was the point of having them on the date? For another, why bring in Lester Young and then give him one brief solo in six sides? As Rollini pointed out later, Young does not blend well with the section, although given more time he might have. The episode alienated Rollini and possibly others as well. Allan Reuss left soon after, although he may have already decided to go, and was replaced by Ben Heller, who would stay with the band for some time.

We cannot, of course, know what was going on in Goodman's mind. My guess, however, is that he heard something in Young's playing that he wanted to capture. This is something that often happens to jazz musicians. It is not so much a question of imitating another player's style—that is to say, attempting to replicate his particular sound, and play figures similar to his—but of adopting a more general approach to improvising that the other player seems to be working from. It is my feeling that Goodman recognized in Young's work the existence of clear statements which were rarer in his own playing, or indeed in the playing of all but a handful of improvisers. I think Goodman in these records, and in some later ones, was trying to pare down his usually very busy playing to the kind of cogency he was hearing in Young. And I would further guess that he brought in Page and Green because he suspected that the Basie rhythm section may have had something to do with Young's effectiveness: What would happen to his own playing with such a rhythm section?

I would also suspect that when he played the records back he did not find what he was looking for, and for the most part his playing during this period was in the old, familiar manner; but here and there the Young mode, if we may call it that, breaks out.

In any case, the records from this session are among the least important Goodman made with the James band. Far more significant were the classic "One O'Clock Jump," "Big John Special," "Wrappin' It Up" and of course "Sing, Sing, Sing," possibly the most famous single record of the whole swing band era.

At various times "One O'Clock Jump" has been credited to Count Basie and Buster Smith, a Kansas City alto saxophonist who was an important figure there. Undoubtedly it was developed over time out of riffs cooked up in the famous Kansas City jam sessions of the 1930s. Basie recorded it in 1937, and it would become a big record for him. It was really just a vehicle for blowing, with just enough riffing to provide a framework. Basie recorded it more than once, and the routine and choice of riffs vary.

It is of course a blues, which utilizes several different riffs in various combinations, mostly in the call-and-response system. In the Goodman version, there are solos by Harry James, Harry Goodman and Jess Stacy. Benny's solo is really a statement of a riff. The effectiveness of the piece lies mainly in the soloing and in the three-tiered riff choruses at the end which pit trombones, trumpets and saxophones against each other. There are two such choruses, using somewhat different riffs, taken higher, and it was really this riffing which got audiences in theatres to screaming.

There is an aircheck of "One O'Clock Jump" made two months earlier which is quite similar to the formal recording but with somewhat more space given over to solos. The main difference is that in the recorded version Goodman signals the band to repeat the final riff chorus three times, allowing the momentum to build and build. We must remember that these hot swingers varied somewhat from performance to performance. Goodman was always conscious of how his audience was reacting, and which of his soloists was particularly strong on a given night, and would adjust the arrangement accordingly. He would sometimes limit his own solo space to give some to others. On this aircheck he plays three choruses himself, but gives two each to Babe Russin, Vernon Brown, and James. Stacy, who was in particularly fine form that night, has four choruses. Goodman liked to hear good jazz men play, and when he had strong soloists, as he had in this band, he gave them room. The result, in any case, is that the formal recording of these tunes is only one variation among many, although as listeners came to know these hit numbers from repeated playing, they grew to expect the live versions to be identical to the record.

Fletcher Henderson, who was touring a lot with his own orchestra, was less active as an arranger for Goodman in 1937 than he had been, but he contributed increasingly to the band's book in 1938. The best known of his arrangements to be recorded at this time was "Wrappin' It Up." The tune was an old one: Henderson had recorded it with his own band in 1934, and Goodman had cut it for the Thesaurus Rhythm Maker's series in 1935. However, he did not record it for regular distribution until 1938. The Goodman band plays it almost exactly as the Henderson band did, even down to the routine of the soloists. It is typically spare Henderson arrangement, with not more than forty bars of original writing, aside from the simple backing for the soloists. Furthermore, there is far less of the interaction of brass and reeds than one expects in a Henderson arrangement. Over the first sixteen measures of the main theme the "answers" consist of single notes by the brass every two bars; for the next sixteen measures there is no answering at all. Only when the band reappears after the trumpet solo do we have any real answering. It is provided by a clarinet trio, a device which had long been a favorite of Henderson, or more correctly, Henderson and the man who had done most of his arranging in the beginning, Don Redman. Redman was asked by James T. Maher where he had gotten the idea for the high, skirling clarinet trios which appear so frequently in his arrangements; he laughed and said, "Oh those: we stole them from the polka bands,"[11] which were a commonplace in the United States at the time. Wherever it came from, it was a useful way of varying the diet of saxes and brasses the swing bands subsisted on, and although its popularity ebbed as the swing period went on, it continued to be employed by Goodman through Henderson arrangements Goodman played to the end of his life.

"Wrappin' It Up," then, is really a minimal piece, basically a vehicle for the soloists. There is a full chorus by Dave Matthews, and shorter solos by Goodman, Freeman and a trumpeter who I think is Ziggy Elman. But simple as it is, it swings, and Goodman would go on playing it for a long time.

One of the problems of determining the value of Fletcher Henderson to the Goodman band is that at least some of the arrangements usually credited to him were written by his brother Horace. Like Fletcher, Horace had a college education, and had studied music. He led bands of his own and at times worked as a sideman in other bands, including his brother's. He also wrote a number of arrangements for his own and Fletcher's band, and when Hammond asked Fletcher to sell Goodman some arrangements at the time of the *Let's Dance* show, some of Horace's were included. It is agreed by both Goodman and Henderson specialists that Horace wrote "Always," "Dear Old Southland" and "Big John Special," as well as the version of "Chicago" available on airchecks. The archivists at Yale, where twelve hundred Goodman arrangements are lodged, credit Horace with eight other arrangements, and James T. Maher would add "Walk, Jennie, Walk" and "I've Found a New Baby."[12] Russell Connor agrees with the Maher attributions, but does not agree with the Yale attributions in every case,[13] although much of the Yale work is based on Connor's research.

However, based on the generally agreed-upon arrangements, it seems to me that Horace Henderson was at least as good an arranger as his brother. In particular, it seems to me that his counter melodies, answering figures and the like, are fresher and more imaginative than those of most other arrangers. They are not there simply for contrast or rhythmic punctuation, but very frequently have real melodic content, as for example the figures played by the saxophones behind the muted trumpets on "Always," the various paraphrases of the melody of "Dear Old Southland," the melodies in the main theme of "Down South Camp Meeting." Horace's writing, judging from this small sample, are less relentlessly in the call-and-response form. He tends to use the sections more contrapuntally, with one running along behind the other, so that when the call-and-response passages appear, they seem fresh.

However we judge Horace, it is certainly true that a high percentage of the arrangements ascribed to him turned out to be important for Goodman. One of these was "Big John Special." Goodman did not get around to recording it until May 1938, but he obviously thought well of it, for he used it as the encore at the Carnegie Hall concert. Once again it is almost identical to the Henderson band's version, with a couple of alterations in the solo routine.

The piece opens with the famous riff played by the saxes, with brass punctuation. Thereafter it is built around a judicious mix of solos and various sections of the band. Except for a twenty-four-measure solo by Stacy, in no instance do things stay the same for more than sixteen bars, and in most cases there is a shift every eight bars. This continuous movement of the music around the band was basic to the system developed by the Grofé-Hickman-Whiteman combine. Don Redman seized on the device when he began writing for Henderson in the early 1920s, sometimes moving the music around every four bars, so that everything was always on the boil. This was overdoing it: Redman's early arrangements are often frantic and distracting. By the end of the decade, however, arrangers were using the device more judiciously, and "Big John Special" demonstrates this good judgment at work. There is just enough motion to keep us interested, but not so much that we are annoyed by interruptions.

However important pieces like "Big John Special" and "Don't Be That Way" were to Goodman's success, without question his biggest number was "Sing, Sing, Sing." It is a fairly chaotic piece of music. It was ostensibly written by Jimmy Mundy, but most of it was a head arrangement put together by accretion over several months. From time to time, usually in live performance, somebody would add something, which might become a permanent part of the piece. It also incorporates a pop tune of the time, "Christopher Columbus." According to Pee Wee Erwin, he and Chris Griffin got some of the material from an arrangement Rex Stewart had been using with a little band he led a few years earlier at the Empire Ballroom in New York. There is also a snatch of "Yankee Doodle," and a "waterfall" inspired by Stravinsky.

The young Benny Goodman, probably about twenty. (From the Benny Goodman Papers in the Music Library of Yale University.)

*Top left:* The Midway Gardens where Goodman would get early dance-band experience. These casino gardens were typical of the time and attracted a varied crowd. *Bottom left:* Goodman with several people who were important to him: Helen Oakley, Fletcher Henderson, his mother, and his favorite sister, Ethel. *Top right:* Some of the brothers: Louis, Irving, Eugene, Freddie, and Jerome in front. (*All from The Benny Goodman Papers in the Music Library of Yale University.*)

*Top left:* The Ben Pollack Band in California in 1927. Goodman is second from left, followed by Gil Rodin and presumably Harry Goodman with tuba. Glenn Miller is at far right, Pollack kneeling with the snare drum. (*Ken Whitten Collection.*) *Top right:* The band at the Congress Hotel in Chicago, 1935. Saxophones are Dick Clark, Bill DePew, Hymie Schertzer, and Art Rollini; trombones are probably Red Ballard and Joe Harris; the rhythm section is Stacy, Reuss, Harry Goodman, and Krupa; the vocalist, of course, is Helen Ward. *Bottom right:* Benny, Helen, and Mr. and Mrs. Red Ballard, in a snapshot taken by Ralph Muzzillo during the 1935 cross-country trip. (*Last two from Goodman Papers at Yale University.*)

*Top left:* The classic Benny Goodman Quartet in 1937. *Bottom left:* The famous trumpet section of Chris Griffin, Ziggy Elman, and Harry James. *Top right:* They really did dance in the aisles at the Paramount. (*All from Ken Whitten Collection.*)

*Top left:* The principal figures in the famous Sextet: Charlie Christian, Cootie Williams, Georgie Auld, and Goodman. *Bottom left:* The brief-lived 1948 small group with Wardell Gray and Stan Hasselgard. (*Both from Ken Whitten Collection.*) *Top right:* The Goodman boppers with Buddy Greco, Wardell Gray, Francis Beecher, Benny, Doug Mettome, Clyde Lombardi, and Sonny Igoe. (*Goodman Papers at Yale University.*)

*Left:* The family, with the new baby, Benjie, in 1946. *Right:* The proud father. Rachel performed classical concerts with Benny on a number of occasions. Benjie studied the cello but was less serious about her music than her sister. (*Goodman Papers at Yale University.*)

*Left:* A youthful looking John Hammond with Benny at the Newport Jazz Festival in 1958. *Top right:* The famous photograph of Goodman and Soviet leader Nikita Khrushchev, during the 1962 Russian tour. (*Both from Goodman Papers at Yale University.*) *Bottom right:* A rare photograph of Goodman's altoist for the tour, Phil Woods, with the legendary Russian jazz musician Gennadi Golstein. In the rear are Soviet drummer Valery Myssovksy, who did some translating for the band, and his wife, Alla. (*Photo courtesy of Valery Myssovsky.*)

*Top left:* Goodman with the Budapest String Quartet, probably in 1938. *Bottom left:* With the great choreographer George Balanchine and Goodman's close friend, composer Morton Gould, during a rehearsal for the ballet *Derivations. Top center:* Goodman with Leonard Bernstein during the recording session for *Prelude, Fugue, and Riffs* in 1963. *Top right:* With Charles Munch, conductor of the Boston Symphony, at Tanglewood, 1956. (*All from Goodman Papers at Yale University.*)

Four famous middle-aged men, a long way from the kids dancing in the aisles at the Paramount, at a 1972 reunion of the Quartet for a television special. From left to right are Benny Goodman, Teddy Wilson, Lionel Hampton, and Gene Krupa.

By the time the band was finished adding to Mundy's kernel, it had sprawled out so much that it took two sides of a twelve-inch record to accommodate it. The basic principle was the alternation of Krupa's tom-toms with various band figures. There is little soloing throughout the first half of the piece, but the second half is devoted to solos in duet with the tom-toms, again alternating with stretches by the whole band, often roaring along all at once.

The piece, then, was a paste-up, in which elements were tossed together without much regard to how they related. The only structure it has is provided by the tom-tom episodes; but it raised audiences, at times, to a frenzy. It was simple stuff, with a lot of pounding of the drums, and Krupa's gum-chewing, hair-flying show was no detriment to its popularity.

Goodman was forced to play "Sing, Sing, Sing" to conclude nearly every performance, and, as we have seen, it eventually helped to drive Harry James from the band. Gene Krupa had made a success of his band, after leaving Goodman, and other bands were sprouting up everywhere. Goodman could hardly have been pleased to lose James, but he recognized that it was inevitable, and he even helped James with some financing.[14] Irving Goodman came in temporarily to play third trumpet, with Ziggy Elman again becoming the principal trumpet soloist. Irving was soon replaced by Corky Cornelius, and thereafter began the parade of new men coming and going that in time led to the dissolution of this Goodman band.

The key, however, was the loss of James. He was an enthusiastic young man, respected for his brilliant musicianship, and liked for his cheerful manner. It seems to me that the band began to play with more fire and verve the moment he arrived. Through the last months of 1936 the band sounds a little tired, and was, in any case, recording a great deal of inferior material, mostly undistinguished pops. The musicians had worked very hard for two solid years building the band, playing endless one-nighters, and often doubling between theatres and hotel restaurants. They had a right to be tired. James seems to have galvanized them, and it was probably this new spirit, rather than any change in the music, that caused Goodman to remember this as his favorite band.

By the same token, when James left some of that spirit left with him. In any case, the band's Victor period was almost over. There were only fifteen more records before Goodman moved on to Columbia. Most of these are routine renderings of forgotten pop tunes, but among them are an excellent band version of "Pick-a-Rib," an arrangement celebrating the publication of the Goodman autobiography, The Kingdom of Swing, and one of Goodman's most lasting hits, "And the Angels Sing." The latter is a fraelich, out of Jewish klezmer, a sometimes wild and shrill music featuring horns and drums that was a folk music of the East European Jews. Goodman, growing up in a neighborhood populated by East European Jews, was familiar with klezmer, but it was Ziggy Elman who worked out the idea of basing a tune on a fraelich. Turned into a pop song, it has an attractive melody and was fitted out with a better-than-average lyric by Johnny Mercer, who was at the time appearing regularly on the *Camel Caravan* radio program. However, the song attracted attention primarily because of the sudden introduction of the original fraelich in 2/4 played by Elman supported only by drums and almost inaudible chording by the band. It was essentially a novelty piece, but its popularity gave Elman a reputation with the dance-band public, and eventually led to his forming his own band.

Finally, Goodman appeared on two sides as a member of an all-star band made up of winners of a *Metronome* magazine poll. The band included two of Goodman's favorite musicians, Jack Teagarden and Bunny Berigan, both of whom play excellent solos. The tunes were "Blue Lou" and a head on the blues. Goodman plays sixteen bars on "Blue Lou" and a chorus on the blues. This last is particularly interesting for the two long notes Goodman plays in the first four measures, on which he toys with the pitch, letting it sag and rise, a device he had learned from the blues singers and the New Orleans players he had heard as an adolescent in the black-and-tans of Chicago's South Side. However sophisticated a musician Goodman had become, he never lost sight of where jazz came from, and what it was supposed to be all about.

Withal, by the spring of 1939 a period in Goodman's recording career was over. There would be by the middle of the year a number of new musicians, an important new arranger and a new record company. But to many of Goodman's fans these Victor records, made between April 1935 and May 1939, constitute the heart of the Goodman canon. It is really "Stompin' at the Savoy," "Don't Be That Way," "Sing, Sing, Sing," "Bugle Call Rag," "Down South Camp Meeting" and the others that leap to mind when we first think of Benny Goodman. These were the records that made him famous, the records he cut when his orchestra was at the top of the American popular music heap, and to many they will continue to best exemplify what the swing era was all about.

# 19

# The First Small-Group Recordings

The records made by the Benny Goodman small groups stand as one of the finest bodies of work in jazz. There is really nothing else like them. To be sure, in Chicago Goodman had frequently heard Jimmie Noone working with clarinet, alto saxophone and rhythm section. And a number of musicians, among them Jelly Roll Morton and Johnny Dodds, had recorded in duets and trios with clarinet leading one or two rhythm instruments: Morton's "Shreveport" and others were made with the same instrumentation as the Goodman Trios—clarinet, piano and drums. Goodman himself made the Trio recordings of "That's A Plenty" and "Clarinetitis" in 1928. Thus, there was precedent for the small jazz group using one or two horns in front of a small rhythm section.

However, few horn players willingly risk carrying a three-minute jazz performance by themselves. Louis Armstrong made two duets with pianists, "Weatherbird" and "Dear Old Southland"; Dicky Wells made "Lady Be Good" and "Dicky Wells' Blues" with trombone and rhythm section; Coleman Hawkins made "Picasso" as a solo; and more recently some modern players have recorded in duets or even alone, as for example Ornette Coleman's duets with bassist Charlie Haden, "Soapsuds, Soapsuds." But these ventures are relatively rare, simply because few musicians are capable of improvising for long stretches without repeating themselves or falling back on clichés. It is not surprising that a substantial proportion of such efforts have been arranged for clarinet, an instrument which allows the player to execute fast, showy passages which will hold the listener's attention.

Confident of his ability to spin endless tales around a theme, Goodman was entirely unfazed by the challenge. He was aided in making his Trio records by having as his partner Teddy Wilson, an imaginative, sensitive and facile pianist who could be counted on not only to carry his weight but to interact with Goodman to create the interplay essential to the success of small groups of this kind. But there is no question that Goodman's small groups, despite the excellence of the other musicians in them, were built around Goodman's clarinet. And it is worth noting that when other band-leaders began putting together small groups on the model of Goodman's, they almost always included two horns, because there were few other horn players who could carry a whole number alone.

Between July 1935 and April 1939 Goodman cut for Victor almost fifty Trio and Quartet sides. It is clear that he was, at first, a little apprehensive about how the public would receive these purely jazz records. Goodman always wanted to play as much jazz as he could, but he was conscious that he must make a financial success of the orchestra. In 1935, when he cut the first four Trio sides, he was still a relatively obscure bandleader a long way from being established with the public. The last thing he wanted to do was make a set of records that would not be to the general taste.

The consequence was that at the beginning he played it safe. Virtually all of the early Trio and Quartet records use popular standards, tunes which would to an extent sell the records. The first four were "After You've Gone," "Body and Soul," "Who?" and "Someday Sweetheart," songs that are still regularly heard. About 40 percent of the tunes for these early small groups had been popular in the years from 1922 to 1925. It has been said more than once that the music we are closest to throughout our lives is that which we fell in love with during adolescence. These were the years when Goodman was between thirteen and sixteen. He was just be-ginning his professional career and was playing the tunes popular at the moment. He liked them and was comfortable with them, and it is not surprising that he turned to them frequently for his small groups.

Generally, although not always, the Trio and Quartet records paired a slow ballad with an uptempo number, as for example the first, which cou-pled "After You've Gone" with "Body and Soul," the idea being to spread the widest possible net. Furthermore, on both fast and slow tunes Good-man was careful to open the record with a full chorus of the melody played very much as written. Even after it was clear that the small-group records would sell, Goodman persisted in playing standards with a good deal of straightforward melody. For example, early in 1937, when he was well es-tablished, he cut "Ida, Sweet as Apple Cider," "Tea for Two" and "Runnin' Wild," three very popular songs. The main exceptions to this rule occurred when Helen Ward was brought in to sing a current pop song.

However, as time passed and Goodman grew more confident of the ap-peal of the small groups, he began recording an increasing amount of spe-cial material and even novelty numbers, many of them based on the blues.

The first of these was "Vibraphone Blues," cut in August 1936 and featuring Lionel Hampton shortly after he began to record with the group. By the end of the period about half the small-group recordings were specials, like "Opus 1/2," "Pick-a-Rib" and the novelty "Dizzy Spells."

The addition of Hampton was a felicitous choice, demonstrating Goodman's musical sense. The small groups required musicians who could play at high speed with facility, which Hampton could do on the vibes. Furthermore, the sound of the instrument was of a similar character to the piano and clarinet—bright, quick and fresh. It is almost impossible to play legato on the vibraphone: the notes are sharply attacked, and this, generally, was true of both Wilson's and Goodman's playing, although of course Goodman could, and did, frequently employ slurs and more legato passages. All three tended to play long racing strings of notes, like shattering glass. Yet the vibraphone had a sufficiently distinct sound to demark it from the other instruments.

The vibraphone clearly fascinated Goodman. It was, at the time, a novelty instrument, almost unknown in jazz, used mainly as a specialty in vaudeville. On Hampton's first recording with the group, "Moonglow," Goodman gives him a full chorus, which at a slow tempo, takes up a substantial portion of the record. Hampton also has two full choruses on "Dinah," which was issued with "Moonglow." Hampton inspires the group to a hotter performance than usual. The cut opens with a strong, fast introduction by Hampton, and Goodman follows with the usual statement of the theme. Hampton next plays two driving choruses, with Krupa for once departing from the steady beat, throwing in accents all the way along. Goodman charges in for the ride-out choruses, apparently meaning to play some sort of paraphrase of the melody. Instead, he is caught up in the excitement, and the Quartet rolls into the final chorus as if it were jamming at the Paradise Club—so much so that Goodman is taken by surprise at the arrival of the ending, which he only barely manages to negotiate, an ending quite different from the neat way he usually ties these packages up. Once again we see the naturally cautious Goodman abandoning constraints in his music he could not cut loose from in life.

Even after Hampton joined the group Goodman occasionally recorded without him in the old Trio format, as for example "Sweet Lorraine" cut in 1938, or "Exactly Like You," on which Hampton sings but does not play. Hampton also played drums occasionally with the small groups after the departure of Krupa. His drumming style was very similar to Krupa's, built more on the snare than on the cymbals, as was the case with Tough.

The Benny Goodman small-group recordings from this period are of such a high order that it is difficult to single out a few for discussion. Not one of them is boring or tossed off haphazardly. All of them are played with intensity and polish, difficult enough to do occasionally much less every time. This consistently high level of performance is a tribute both to the musicianship of the players and to Goodman's characteristic insistence on holding himself and his musicians to the highest standards. It was not in Benny Goodman's nature to go slack, to take an easy route. He always strove to give the best performance he could and he demanded the same of his sidemen, and whatever they may have felt about Goodman personally, they did not like to fall short in his eyes: musicians just did not want to appear lacking in front of Benny Goodman. The results are apparent in these records.

These early Trio records are far simpler in construction than later Goodman small-band arrangements would be, but the men do not simply go into the studio and jam. Goodman was particularly aware of the potential monotony in three instruments playing the same song over and over, as was necessarily the case with a relatively brief tune taken at a fast tempo. On "Who?" for example, recorded at the first Trio session, Goodman has carefully worked out a routine to avoid sameness. The piece opens with a brief introduction for clarinet and piano which was planned in advance. Wilson then plays a chorus, which was unusual, for Goodman almost always takes the first chorus in these pieces in order to give listeners a full chorus of melody. Goodman then follows with an improvised chorus. He sounds a little uneasy to me, which may once again be due to the fact that the chords sometimes go on for several bars at a stretch because of the long meter. Krupa then has a solo, followed by Goodman playing a solo in his low register for contrast. Wilson has another chorus and Goodman a final hot chorus. Of the seven choruses, only two resemble the one that has gone before it, and this constant shift in the character of the music keeps it fresh.

For "Oh, Lady Be Good!" Goodman utilizes a standard device, used by classical composers for variety long before there was any such thing as a swing-band arrangement, changes of key. After a brief introduction Goodman and Wilson take turns playing solo choruses: Goodman in G, the standard key for the tune, Wilson in A-flat, Goodman in B-flat; and then for further variety, Goodman plays half a chorus in C-minor, opening out to C-major to end the tune. Additionally, Goodman plays the minor portion of the arrangement in low register, with a smoky tone, over Krupa's tom-toms, to produce a spooky effect that is entirely different in character from the joyous quality of the record as a whole. All of this was rather basic stuff, of course, but in the very small format in which most jazz is played, basics are often more effective than more imaginative and complex ideas. Goodman utilizes these simple devices very well to give this record more variety than a jammed version would have had.

The use of the tom-tom was relatively rare on these records. For perhaps 95 percent of the time in these sides Krupa plays steadily on the snare, for the most part with brushes, although occasionally with sticks. Cymbals, tom-toms and the cowbell he used frequently with the big band in his solos are heard very rarely. Goodman had also attended the New Orleans snare-drum school which Krupa had been trained in, and was used to this kind of playing. But it is also my guess that Goodman had instructed Krupa to keep it simple and use the brushes.

As a rule, Goodman was playing more conservatively on these records than he had in the past. He avoids bent notes, growls and the twists and turns that were so evident in his earlier work, and he plays a lot of very straight melody, in both the big band and the small groups. Occasionally there would come perfervid performances, like "Dinah," but overall Goodman's playing was sparer on these records than was typical. We find this spareness in one of the prettiest of this series, "Sweet Sue—Just You," a tune that Goodman was playing in adolescence. It is taken at a moderate tempo, with a light, easy swing. Goodman plays the first chorus almost as written. Wilson plays the next chorus, and then Goodman comes back to improvise a very easy, light-hearted chorus that is nonetheless both thoughtful and felt. He uses long held notes, leaves open spaces and produces a very clean line with few extraneous notes. Over roughly the first six bars, counting the pick-up, he plays only eighteen notes, where in a busier mode he might well have played forty or fifty. The great trumpet player Roy Eldridge, who like Goodman could play very fast, said in speaking of his apprentice days, "I was a young cat, and I was very fast, but I wasn't telling no kind of story."[1] Goodman's primary weakness, especially as a young man, was precisely this, allowing his facility to run away with him so that he was not producing a coherent musical line. But in this "Sweet Sue" chorus he seems to be deliberately trying to tell some kind of a story, and it is to my mind one of his best solos from the period.

He is similarly spare on another tune from his adolescence, "Tea for Two," which is taken at a slow, somewhat bouncy tempo. Here Goodman uses many long notes, leaves gaps and plays few of the long eighth-note passages we expect of him. There are, for example, only six notes, counting the pick-up, over the opening three measures of the second chorus, a similar spareness at the beginning of the second eight measures, and a sequence of very lazy eighth notes in measures twelve through fourteen. The group achieves a nice rocking swing throughout, especially in the Goodman solo. On this chorus Krupa picks up his sticks and plays press rolls, a device he learned from the New Orleans drummers, broken by off-beat rim shots. Wilson, recognizing that there is a lot going on, simply comps, playing a very common quick figure used again and again by brass sections to punctuate a saxophone line. It is worth noting that although both "Sweet Sue—Just You" and "Tea for Two" are taken at slow, quite danceable tempos, they achieve a tremendous swing—more, if such a thing can be measured, than the group often manages at faster, more "jazzy" tempos.

Goodman was not playing in this spare style all the time, however. "Tiger Rag" includes a good many fast passages, especially during the low register chorus which Goodman plays on the number's final strain and in the hot ride-out ending. But even on a tune like this, which is meant to be a rip-snorter, he plays a good deal of straightforward melody, and there are spare patches, as in the opening measures of his chorus after the drum solo, where he plays a string of quarter notes.

Goodman, of course, was by no means the whole show on these small group recordings. Wilson and Hampton usually, although not invariably, had extended solos, and Krupa soloed on some of them. Hampton was a very busy player, leaving few open spaces and frequently using long strings of eighth notes which cascade down the instrument. He uses many repeated phrases and imitations, often at the beginning of an eight-measure segment of a song, which then break up into a shower of eighth notes. His solo on "Dinah" shows all these characteristics. There are repeated figures at the opening of the second chorus, on the second half of the bridge that follows, and on the opening of the last eight measures of this chorus; and imitations in bars nine through twelve of the opening chorus and again at bar nine of the second chorus.

Hampton also deliberately turns the beat around at times to produce conflicting meters. In his introduction to "Dinah" he accents away from the meter so much that it is difficult to find the downbeat until Goodman comes in with the melody. This solo, like much of Hampton's work, is swirling with activity.

Teddy Wilson, too, was a very active player and, like Hampton, a brilliant uptempo improviser, able to fly through fast passages without strain. But I prefer him on slower tempos, as for example his solo on the medium tempo "Sweet Sue—Just You." Two traits stand out: the use of dynamics to accent throughout the line, and a tendency to delay notes just fractionally, which he is better able to do at slower tempos. These characteristics are present throughout this solo. Delayed notes are pratically evident in bars three and twenty-eight, and accents in the opening measures of the solo.

The solo also exhibits Wilson's strong preference for strings of single notes, rather than the heavier chordal right hand of stride players like Fats Waller. He does not play a single true chord with his right hand through the entire thirty-two bars of the chorus, an extraordinary thing for a pianist to do. The solo also shows how spare Wilson could be with his left hand—much of the time he is playing single quarter notes, or even half notes, with the left hand. We do not think of Wilson as a particularly economic player, but in fact he plays fewer notes in this solo than most pianists would have.

As Goodman's confidence in the popularity of the group grew, he became a little more musically daring. One of the most popular of the small group records was "Bei Mir Bist du Schön," a pop tune adapted from a Yiddish theatre song, which Goodman made as a two-sided record. (The title is a Yiddish phrase meaning roughly "by me, you're beautiful.") It is sung by Martha Tilton and well played by the Quartet. However, the interest in it for audiences of the time lay in the appearance of Ziggy Elman on the second side to play the original Jewish melody, anticipating his great success with "And the Angels Sing," about a year later.

Another novelty was "Dizzy Spells," a tour de force apparently cooked up by Wilson, Hampton, Goodman, or all three. It consists of two themes, organized to make up a forty-bar piece. The trick to it is the "cycling" or metric shift which makes up the first theme. The playing off of two or more meters against one another has an ancient history, and is at the core of much West African drum music, where several meters are played simultaneously, worked out so that occasionally they come together. That is to say, the drums are playing not only different tempos but different patterns so that, for example, a three-beat pattern locks and unlocks with a four-beat one. The principle has been widely used in so-called minimalist music of today.

The idea came into jazz quite early, in its simpelst form, in which a three-note phrase is cycled over a 4/4 meter at the same tempo. This device was used to create the principle themes of a number of songs, among them "Twelfth Street Rag" and "Fidgety Feet." So widespread was the practice in early jazz that Winthrop Sargeant, the first musicologist to write a book on jazz, took it to be one of the main principles of the music.[2]

"Dizzy Spells" is based on a metric shift of this kind, and taken at a very swift tempo it does seem dizzying. There are solos, and it is some indication of Goodman's musical good sense that he does not simply blow on the changes, but produces a number of cascading figures in keeping with the general tenor of the piece. It is, in any case, a demonstration of Goodman's extraordinary technical prowess.

One set of recordings of particular interest in respect to Goodman's musical development was that of March 1938, about three weeks after Krupa walked out of the band. This session came about two weeks after the "Ti-Pi-Tin" session with Lester Young. The tunes were "Sugar," "Sweet Lorraine," and a double-sided blues which was issued as "The Blues in My Flat" and "The Blues in Your Flat," as well as the idiosyncratic "Dizzy Spells."

Goodman opens "Sweet Lorraine" with a full solo chorus played virtually as written, except for short improvised figures at the end of the first sixteen and the closing of the chorus. His tone is thin and clear, with a distinct terminal vibrato. The sound is remarkably like the somewhat plaintive tone that Lester Young had on clarinet, which can be heard on his famous Kansas City Six sessions. Furthermore, the two brief improvised figures Goodman plays are typically Young.

"Sugar" is to my mind the best effort made by anyone to capture the Young clarinet style. (I am referring to the second take.) It opens with Hampton and Goodman in duet, with apparently neither of them quite sure who is supposed to be playing lead, a species of diffidence hardly typical of either man. Goodman then takes a solo, playing in the light, plaintive tone, and employing the short, stubby figures, the empty spaces, the abruptly shortened notes that are characteristic of Young's work. Goodman stops the fifth note of the solo suddenly, to leave an empty space, much as Lester frequently did; and in bars four and five, seven and eight, and at the opening of the bridge he uses figures which, if not drawn directly from Young, are certainly typical of his manner. It is all extremely sparse, a far remove from the busy, fluid Goodman style with its long figures running without cease across two, four or eight measures. Nor is there any of Goodman's usual muscular exuberance here: it is withdrawn, introspective playing.

The two blues sides, really one long piece, are even more interesting. (I am referring to take one.) Goodman's opening chorus is very simple, in the middle register, spare and wistful, and he employs more complete figures than he normally does. During the piano solo that follows he irregularly reiterates the tonic alone, and again in Hampton's solo plays very quiet, tentative figures made of two or three notes. For his final solo he plays a paraphrase of the sequence of descending figures that Louis Armstrong used on the last chorus of his immortal "West End Blues." The second half of the piece opens with Goodman almost alone playing a few very spare figures in the low register built around the tonic and minor third. During Hampton's three vocal choruses he pokes brief, unobtrusive notes into the empty spots; and for the final chorus he again plays a somewhat different paraphrase of the "West End Blues" material.

This new attitude continued to inform Goodman's playing. "Sweet Georgia Brown," made in October 1938, is taken at an easy pace instead of the horse-race tempo it is frequently played at. Goodman opens his solo with a long, four-measure figure, which he follows with a similar one, and then another which, although different, still manages to reflect what has gone before—three long related figures over twelve measures. The rest of the solo is cut less regularly, but consists of long phrases and is, for Goodman, thoughtful playing.

His work on the Gershwin classic " 'S Wonderful" (take one) is much the same. The tune again is taken at a slower tempo than is customary with jazz versions of a song—a quite danceable tempo. His opening chorus is played straight, and with a good deal of tenderness, not a quality that appears frequently in Goodman's work. To back Hampton's solo he repeats piano figures, a graceful little ploy obviously worked out in advance. Goodman's own solo opens with long, looping phrases which he drapes across the first eight measures. At the final bars, instead of heated high-register notes he might have used, he plays a variation on the melody in the middle register.

By this time Dave Tough was with the band. With the small groups, he usually played with brushes as Krupa did but worked on the cymbals a good deal, especially the hi-hat. Playing with a light, swinging drummer, rather than the hard-pressing Krupa, may have been in part responsible for Goodman's less heated approach during this period. But even after Tough was fired, Goodman continued to play in this low-keyed style a good deal of the time—on "Pick-a-Rib," for example, which was cut with a "Quartet" which included bassist John Kirby as well as the usual instruments. Goodman plays most of his lengthy solo on this two-sided performance in the middle and low register. There are many passages of simple riffing, with Goodman playing one figure over and over. The piece is a medium-tempo blues with an unusual ten-bar interlude inserted at points, and is mainly solos, with a lot of boogie-woogie on the second side. In the past a vehicle like this would have driven Goodman to the perfervid manner, with a lot of high-register playing and the growls and snarls he liked. Instead the playing is easy, casual, almost tossed off.

It is not safe to say that this less driven, somewhat more thoughtful manner can be entirely ascribed to the influence of Lester Young. As is usually the case in such instances, motivation was undoubtedly complicated. It is probable that the example of Young suggested to Goodman that he search deeper in the music for meaning. Nor was the old way abandoned: Goodman would certainly continue to play in the old hot manner, as the later "Roll 'Em" compilation with Sid Catlett makes abundantly clear. But he had expanded his emotional range to include a more thoughtful vein.

Goodman would go on to make many more small-group recordings throughout the rest of his career. Certainly the Sextet records of the early Columbia period, featuring Charlie Christian, have been as highly valued by jazz critics as these earlier Victors. But these first small groups were the model, not merely for the other Goodman groups to come but for a great deal of jazz that followed, for they showed that there was a large audience in America for small-band jazz, and that the big dance orchestra had not driven the improvising jazz group underground. The success of the Goodman Trio and Quartet led directly to the recording of a whole great body of classic jazz—the Kansas City Six and other groups featuring Lester Young, the host of Blue Note and Commodore records and dozens of others on the small labels which followed, and eventually the first records of the beboppers. It cannot be said that without Goodman none of this material would have been recorded. But it was these early Goodman groups that gave small-band jazz an impetus that it had lacked. And they were, besides, among the finest jazz records of their kind ever made.

It must be borne in mind that, despite the contribution of the others, these were Benny Goodman's records. Teddy Wilson eventually came to dislike Goodman, but even so, he later said, "All those intricate trio, quartet and sextet arrangements were put together by the whole group, but it was Goodman who would put everybody's ideas together to form the final product, and only then would we record. It was Goodman who decided whose idea would be used for the introduction, whose idea would go into the interlude and whose idea to change the key at a certain point would be used, and where, and of course he contributed ideas himself."[3]

# 20

# The Columbia Band

The American recording industry, moribund in the early 1930s from the effects of the Depression, radio and sound films, had made an astonishing recovery by the late thirties. In 1932 total record sales for the country were roughly ten million; in 1939 they were fifty million.[1] The main factor in this new prosperity was swing music which comprised 85 percent of all record sales.[2] The majority of the most-played records on juke boxes were the hotter swing records, although there remained strong interest in the sweet variety.[3]

Interest in the new music was general. In 1938 Goodman was broadcasting to two million fans three times a week.[4] In 1937 the New York Board of Education announced plans to have weekly jazz lectures by Goodman, Ellington, Tommy Dorsey, Red Nichols and others.[5] At the beginning of 1938 Down Beat announced, "Sugar music makers such as Lombardo, Olsen and Hal Kemp . . . still out-number the ace swing units, such as Benny Goodman, Tommy Dorsey and Bob Crosby. Outstanding development of the year, however, was the increasing popularity of swing, and its influence on all bands."[6] And by the end of 1939 Down Beat's circulation had reached 80,000, and it had gone from a monthly to a bi-weekly period.

For the recording companies, the game was swing. Columbia had not climbed out of the slough of the Depression as successfully as Victor had. Victor's Red Seal label dominated the classical music market, and the company had scooped up a number of important swing bands at an early date, among them those of Glenn Miller, Tommy Dorsey and of course Goodman. An upstart concern, Decca, formed in 1934 as a low-price label, had also signed a number of popular performers, among them Louis Armstrong, Casa Loma, Guy Lombardo, Jimmy Dorsey and Bing Crosby. Columbia had fallen behind.

In 1938 the C.B.S. radio chain bought the Columbia record company. It put the invalid company into the hands of Ted Wallerstein,[7] who would become one of the most highly respected men in the history of the American recording business. Wallerstein had been the man who had ordered that Goodman be signed to Victor,[8] and he immediately hired John Hammond as associate director of popular music, with the admitted hope that Hammond would be able to persuade Goodman to sign with Columbia.

Precisely what Hammond said to Goodman is not known, but sometime early in 1939 Goodman decided to make the change, and when his contract with Victor ran out, probably in June, he signed with Columbia. Not long afterwards his Camel cigarette radio show was switched to N.B.C., with Bob Crosby taking over the C.B.S. spot.

Goodman was by this time facing a number of strong competitors. Clarinetist Artie Shaw, who as Art Shaw was one of the free-lancers around New York Goodman had competed against, had established his own band on the heels of Goodman's success. Very quickly he had an enormous hit with his arrangement of "Begin the Beguine," which went on to become one of the most popular records of the entire swing era. In the 1938 *Down Beat* poll, the Shaw Orchestra beat Goodman's by a slim margin. Goodman's Trio and Quartet won first place in the small-band category, and Goodman himself was named the top soloist, with Shaw second. Eighteen months earlier it had been Goodman first, everybody else way back down the track. Now Goodman was being jostled by a crowd of competitors which included, besides Shaw, Bob Crosby, Duke Ellington, Tommy Dorsey, Count Basie, Jimmy Dorsey, Jimmie Lunceford, and two of his former sidemen, Harry James and Gene Krupa.

Goodman was feeling restless, itchy. He said later, "My band was in a slump. I was more worried than I'd admit."[9] What exactly the problem was he did not say. However, in looking at Goodman's behavior over a long period it is obvious that he was frequently dissatisfied about things, often without any very clear sense of what exactly was bothering him. He tended to brood at times; and then he would suddenly decide that thus and such a player was the cause of the trouble and would start picking on him. Sid Weiss, who was in and out of the band several times, said that once he came into the band when Krupa was playing with it. He saw that Gene was not always taking Benny's beat, but setting one of his own. Benny realized that there was something wrong with the rhythm; and according to Weiss, when he looked around he saw only one new man in the rhythm section, Weiss, who thereupon became the target of a great deal of criticism from Goodman, to the point where Weiss threatened to quit.[10]

The point is that the dissatisfaction that Goodman felt so frequently at times had nothing to do with music, but was a more general malaise that was an expression of his underlying psychology. But to Benny, music was everything: if he felt dissatisfied, the cause must lie with the band, and the solution would be there, too. Goodman, thus, was temperamentally prone to make changes, and that by itself is enough to explain the move to Columbia and the other changes that followed.

But Benny was also becoming aware that something had gone with the dissolution of the 1938 band. The loss of James, Reuss, Krupa and Musso had taken the heart of the band, and he was ready to believe that sweeping changes were necessary. The change of record company seemed to offer a good moment for it. The entire rhythm section was replaced: Arnold Covarrubias came in on guitar, Hammond's old friend Artie Bernstein on bass, Nick Fatool on drums, and Fletcher Henderson took over the piano in place of Stacy. Toots Mondello came in again, causing Schertzer to leave as before; Art Rollini, who was tired of the road, quit, although he had a feeling he was about to be fired.[11] Trumpeters Jimmy Maxwell and Johnny Best, and trombonist Ted Vesely came in. Thus, between May and September 1939, all but four members of the band had been replaced.

The personnel of the group that began to record for Columbia was now quite different from the one that made the last records for Victor. One of the most interesting of the new arrivals was trumpeter Jimmy Maxwell, who would play with Goodman off and on for years and was at moments his principal trumpet soloist.[12] He was born in Stockton, California, in a country district where there was still no electricity. Various members of his family played instruments, and when Maxwell was four his grandfather gave him a cornet he had played in the Spanish-American War. Maxwell grew to be six feet tall by the time he was in the eighth grade, and eventually was six feet four. He was an inveterate reader—he liked to read encyclopedias, and Goodman once gave him one—and his first ambition was to study for the priesthood. However, as an adolescent he heard Louis Armstrong and committed himself to jazz. "I never liked Bix Beiderbecke. I never understood what the hollering was all about. And the funny thing, the first person that made me see any value at all, was Lloyd Reese, a black trumpet player. . . . He said, 'There's a lot to learn from [Bix].' "[13]

The area in which Maxwell grew up was racially mixed. He played with black and Japanese children as a boy, and remained sympathetic to ethnic minorities. He picked up some Japanese, eventually studied Zen, Japanese language and culture, and went on to learn Spanish, French and some Russian. His education was eclectic and hand-hewn, but he became a much broader person than most of the musicians around him, who had, like Goodman himself, devoted themselves almost entirely to music from an early age. He impressed the others.

The arranger Eddie Sauter, who was relatively well educated himself, said, "When he came with Benny, he was very taken with Eastern cultures. He used to sleep on a straw mat, lived on bananas, and studied Japanese. He used to talk Japanese. This was in 1940, before the war. He was always a unique human being and turned out to be a very good trumpet player."[14]

Maxwell was one of those purists who did not like to compromise with commerce, and wanted to do nothing but play hot jazz. He said,

> When I was young, I . . . was going to sit there and wait for my solo and to hell with the parts. And I was talking to Bunny Berigan when I was about eighteen or nineteen, at the time when I wanted to be a great soloist and everything, and he gave me a long lecture about it. He said, you know, you're no kind of a musician in the band if you can't sit there and play your part. In those days jazz players had to play leads. So he said, it's one thing to play jazz but you have to sit there and listen to the lead trumpet player and learn to guess what he's going to do and play it with him perfectly. He said, then you can call yourself a trumpet player.[15]

Maxwell became, in time, a first-rate musician who could play lead and hot solos with power and drive, as for example on "After You've Gone," from July 1942. He eventually became a trumpet teacher and clinician and helped Jonah Jones and Buck Clayton through some embouchure problems.

As important as the new musicians were to the band's sound, the most significant change was the introduction of a new arranger with an entirely different approach to the swing-band arrangement from the one used by the Henderson-Mundy-Murphy team which had given the Goodman Orchestra its original sound. Eddie Sauter was a prickly and complex man, with a good deal of intellectual sophistication, and a quite different personality from, let us say, Fletcher Henderson. He would inevitably write in quite a different way.

Sauter was born in Brooklyn in 1914 to a relatively affluent family.[16] His father was a florist. Eddie fell in love with music listening to a ship's orchestra on a trip to Germany when he was ten. His father bought him a trumpet—actually a flugelhorn in F—in Bremen, and on his return Sauter began listening to the name bands whose music was pouring out of the radio. There was an organ in his home, and a lot of Caruso records which he listened to. He learned to play drums and began to take mail-order arranging lessons from bandleader Archie Bleyer. He joined a high school dance band, which worked summers on the French Line. He arranged for this band, and then for the Blue Lions, a student band at Columbia University. Eventually he went to work for Bleyer.

He had become a relatively accomplished arranger, and, barely out of his teens, he began writing and playing trumpet for the struggling Charlie

Barnet band. From there he went to the Red Norvo–Mildred Bailey combination.[17] But he was ambitious, and he continued year after year to study music, with Louis Gruenberg at the Chicago Music College (he was then with Norvo at the Blackhawk), at Columbia Teacher's College, and then privately with Bernard Wagner of Juilliard, and eventually with Stephen Volpe, who taught him philosophy as well as music. Although he was making his living as a dance-band arranger, and was entranced by the Ellington Orchestra in particular, his "guiding lights" were Stravinsky and Bartók.[18] Eddie Sauter was, thus, at a far remove from the mainly self-taught arrangers upon whom Goodman had been dependent.

In 1939 Norvo and Bailey were suffering from both marital and musical disputes, and their band broke up. "Red was scuffling and split with Mildred," Sauter said. "He had gone off on his own and I guess Benny needed somebody at that point, so they offered and I made a decision and went. I always felt I was leaving home."[19] He added, "I think my real reason for going with Benny was to get enough money so I could pay these teachers. I was putting out about thirty, thirty-five dollars a week for lessons in those days. . . . I suppose I [had] a touch of ambition at that point. I didn't know what I wanted but I wanted something more, and that's what drove me to take those lessons and I realized later that one of the reasons was to keep my mind working in an area that it wasn't given in a normal daily routine."[20]

"Benny had built his band around Fletcher's arrangements," Sauter said, "and I was supposed to imitate that, I think, but I never really could. Maybe Fletcher respected me because I didn't. . . . I was wary about joining Goodman from the start."[21] He added, "Those black and white interpretations that characterize his band made me realize that I'd be pretty limited."[22]

With all of his training in music, Sauter was well ahead of most of the others who were writing big band arrangements. Ferde Grofé, who had started the whole thing, had had some formal training, and so had Don Redman. But many of the most respected arrangers of the time, like Mary Lou Williams, Eddie Durham and even Duke Ellington, were mainly self-taught, working out ideas for themselves on the piano, or in Durham's case, the guitar. Sauter's formal training gave him a substantial advantage over the others, for he had a vast fund of musical ideas and devices to draw on, and furthermore he knew the solutions to problems others struggled to find. But all of this training was also a curse. His arrangements were inevitably more complex than was acceptable in a dance band. "I was put down early for being too wild. . . . I got a reputation at that point for being uncommercial, which is the kiss of death."[23] Jimmy Maxwell said that Goodman always thought that Sauter's music was too busy, and would edit it a lot in rehearsal. Sauter would argue with him, but Maxwell believed that Goodman was right, because he would make the arrangements swing more.[24]

For a second matter, the musicians often found Sauter's arrangements difficult to play. Jerry Jerome said, "The guys almost stepped on their joints trying to play it, it was so tough."[25] Sauter himself admitted that the musicians "didn't quite cotton to it. They wanted something else."[26] Goodman, with his cautious nature, tended to stay away from the more complicated Sauter pieces except in special circumstances. "Benny didn't play this stuff for a long time, because he used to complain they were too classical. He made records of them, but after that, no."[27]

Yet, despite the problems that Sauter's work sometimes caused, he and Benny had a surprisingly good relationship. Goodman had a tendency to respect people whose musicianship was more advanced than his own, as Sauter's certainly was. Sauter said, "I always liked Benny. I always got along with Benny. He did strange things, he always did. . . . I think this was all a result of growing up in a ghetto. I think that anyone who has to go through that sort of thing will have some residue. All his brothers have it too in different ways, they're not the same. It leaves its mark. I guess all living leaves its mark, but to grow up in an urban ghetto, it has to do certain things to you."[28] Goodman in his turn treated Sauter cordially, even if he did not always play the more complicated pieces Sauter wrote. When Sauter became ill with tuberculosis in 1942, then a much more serious, often fatal, disease than it is now, he kept Sauter on the payroll. And of course, Sauter's arrangements were not always troublesome. He was required to turn out arrangements of two or three pop songs each week, many of which were quite ordinary. And some of the most memorable things that Goodman did at this time, like "Superman," "Clarinet a la King" and "Moonlight on the Ganges," were written by Eddie Sauter.

But as far as musicians and the dance-band public were concerned, the most important of the new additions was Charlie Christian, who would go on to have an enormous impact not only on jazz but on all of popular music through his exploitation of the electric guitar, and who would die young, a jazz legend.

Details of Christian's life are exceedingly sparse. The best source is a memoir of Christian written by Ralph Ellison.[29] Christian was born in Dallas. The generally accepted date is 1919, but there is a picture of him in first grade dated 1923, which makes an earlier date likely. His father was a blind guitarist and singer, and Christian got an early apprenticeship in music guiding his father around Oklahoma City, where he grew up. It has generally been said that Christian started as a rough country player, modeling himself on the local blues musicians. However, Ellison, whose younger brother was a classmate of Christian's from the first grade on, said that in fact Christian got a relatively sophisticated musical education in the local high school. At the time, it was generally believed by both blacks and whites that blacks had a special talent, or perhaps affinity, for music, as the great black social thinker W. E. B. Du Bois said explicitly in *The Souls of Black Folks*.[30] Blacks, as a consequence, took considerable pride in their musical skills, and in black public schools music was not seen as adjunctive, but as a central part of the curriculum. At the Douglass School, where Christian studied, "There was an extensive compulsory music-appreciation program."[31] Harmony was taught in grades nine through twelve. Charlie's brother Edward sang in high-school operettas, and had a band which included some of the legendary Kansas City jazz people, among them Hot Lips Page, Walter Page and Sammy Price.

But the breadth of Christian's musical education was not reflected in his general environment. "Although he was from a respectable family, the wooden tenement in which he grew up was full of poverty, crime and sickness," Ellison wrote. "It was also alive and exciting, and I enjoyed visiting there, for the people both lived and sang the blues."[32] Ellison believes it is probable that Christian got the tuberculosis which eventually killed him in this tenement.

Christian started his musical career with his brothers Clarence and Edward, strolling through white middle-class areas of the city playing light classics among other things. His first important jazz influence was Lester Young, who arrived in Oklahoma City in the early 1930s and "upset the entire Negro section of town."[33] Young later said that he and Christian, who was perhaps fifteen, "used to go out in the alley and jam."[34] Young's influence was lasting; Jimmy Maxwell said that Christian always wanted to play tenor saxophone like Young, sang Young's solos on the band bus and learned to play them all on his guitar.[35]

By adolescence Christian was working professionally around Oklahoma City, and in about 1937 he took up a novel instrument, the amplified or electric guitar. Precisely who invented the electric guitar is a matter of dispute. It was not Christian, certainly. Credit has frequently been given to Floyd Smith, who made a record in March 1939 called "Floyd's Guitar Blues" with Andy Kirk, featuring the amplified instrument. However, Eddie Durham, guitarist, trombonist and arranger for many important swing bands (he wrote the swing classic "Topsy"), claims to have invented the instrument when he was with Lunceford in 1935.[36] He said that at first he simply tilted a microphone down over the F hole, but then began using an amplifier, presumably from a simple public address system, and shoving the microphone into the F hole. He then rigged up a movable bridge attached to a coat hanger, and by hooking his finger in the coat hanger could produce the effect of a resonator. Durham also claimed to have showed Floyd Smith his invention, and to have taught Christian how to downstroke.[37] Eddie Durham was an intelligent and sensitive man, and there is no reason to disbelieve his story. In fact, there did already exist in 1935 the so-called steel guitar, which was electrified, but Durham appears to have come up with the idea of amplifying a standard guitar on his own.

It is surprising that the electric guitar was not more quickly taken up. Only a few guitarists were using the instrument before Christian rose to prominence, among them George Barnes, Allan Reuss, Art Ryerson with Paul Whiteman, and Bus Etri with Charlie Barnet. The point of course was that an electric guitar could solo over a big band, while an acoustic one could not. The idea seems obvious; but it was only when Christian got wide exposure with the Goodman Sextet that the electric guitar became popular. The consequences for music thereafter were enormous.

The story of how Charlie Christian became part of the Benny Goodman Sextet and entered into jazz history has been told many ways. John Hammond's version[38] is that Mary Lou Williams, a Kansas Citian, had told him about Christian, who was then working in that city. Hammond made a point of hearing Christian, and was so taken with him that he arranged to fly him to Los Angeles, where the Goodman Orchestra was about to open at a restaurant called Victor Hugo's. Goodman gave Christian a perfunctory audition beforehand and dismissed him. Hammond then arranged for Christian to meet him in the Victor Hugo kitchen that evening, and while Goodman was eating supper after the opening set, he and bassist Artie Bernstein carted Christian's equipment onto the bandstand, where Goodman would open the next set with the Quintet. When Goodman came out to find Christian, wearing a purple shirt and yellow shoes, installed on the bandstand, he was furious. However, he did not want to make a fuss before the opening-night crowd. He called for "Rose Room," which—according to Hammond—he believed Christian would not know. But Christian played it so brilliantly that the tune went on for forty-five minutes, and the Quintet was enlarged to make room for him.

However, there are other versions of the story. Walter C. Allen said, "Benny was still looking for new talent. On the basis of a newly released record by Andy Kirk, 'Floyd's Guitar Blues,' . . . Benny tried to get Floyd for his own band." He reportedly offered Kirk $5,000 for Floyd's contract, but Joe Glaser, Kirk's agent, interfered.[39] Mary Lou Williams said that Christian wanted to stay in Kansas City, and was in no rush to join Goodman. She also said that Christian's family wanted him to stay home, possibly because they knew how sick he was. But finally he went.[40]

Although Christian eventually played with the big band for a brief period before his death, for the most part he played only in the Sextet, and it was with the small group that he made an enduring mark on jazz. Aside from bringing the electric guitar to national attention, he is best known for having contributed ideas to the bop movement which would begin to coalesce around 1942. For one thing, Christian was using some of the upper notes of the chord—ninths and elevenths—more frequently than other jazz players. He was also prone to substitute a diminished chord for the dominant seventh in places. The boppers would eventually develop these practices to the point where chromatic alterations and the upper-chord notes would be a major characteristic of the music.

For a second thing, Christian liked to use long lines of unaccented eighth notes. This was in part due to the nature of his instrument. It cannot be made to accent notes with anything like the subtlety of a wind instrument. But it was also a matter of taste—Charlie Christian liked to run long lines. There is a surprising lack of syncopation in his work. This use of long lines of relatively uninflected notes also became characteristic of bebop.

Finally, Christian habitually phrased against the grain of the tune. Jazz musicians have always played asymmetrical phrases, but there is nonetheless a tendency to design a solo to match the two-, four- and eight-bar segments most tunes are constructed of. Christian persistently played phrases of odd lengths—one of three-and-a-half bars, followed by another of five, and then one of two—interjected at irregular points in the chorus. This use of disjunctive phrasing also was typical of bebop.

Finally, Christian frequently ended phrases on the second half of the last beat of a measure. This is the weakest point in a measure, and in most standard music, ranging from the operas of Mozart to the worst material from Tin Pan Alley, phrases are ended at stronger points, often at the first beat of a measure. But this inclination to plunk down at a weak point also became characteristic of bebop.

Charlie Christian was by no means the most important of the bebop fathers, nor was he essentially a bopper himself, although he undoubtedly would have been had he lived. But he spent a lot of time jamming after hours at the legendary Minton's, a Harlem club that was a cradle of bop, and he was influential on the young boppers who were about his age.[41]

By the second half of 1939 Goodman had a new band with different soloists, a different type of small group, a different principle arranger. However, the cautious Goodman did not totally abandon the old for the new. He continued to include in his programs a good sampling of the music which had got him where he was: "One O'Clock Jump," "Don't Be That Way," the inevitable "Sing, Sing, Sing," and the rest. He also played with a trio, as well as the new Sextet, and in general departed from the model of the Carnegie Hall band only to an extent, as indeed he would do for the rest of his life. The band's popularity remained high. The 1939 Down Beat poll had Goodman back in first place, followed by Glenn Miller, Bob Crosby and Shaw. The Sextet was the top small group; Goodman remained the readers' favorite soloist; Christian was named best guitarist; and "And the Angels Sing" was voted best record. *Down Beat* readers were more knowledgeable and intense in their concern for swing music than the mass of big band fans, who would probably have chosen Glenn Miller and Tommy Dorsey over Goodman. But the poll indicates clearly that the changes had not hurt the band's popularity.

Nor was there any shortage of work. In October 1939, there was a second Carnegie Hall concert which has been almost forgotten, because it was not well recorded and has only been issued on a bootleg version. This concert was in celebration of ASCAP's twenty-fifth anniversary and included four swing bands.[42] In November the Goodman Sextet opened on Broadway as a special feature in a swing version of *A Midsummer Night's Dream*, which also included Louis Armstrong and Maxine Sullivan. The show closed after thirteen performances. In December Artie Shaw gave up his band, and Goodman picked up from him his vocalist Helen Forrest. He also brought in pianist Johnny Guarnieri to replace Henderson. Goodman may finally have tired of hearing criticism of Henderson—*Swing* magazine called him a "sore spot"[43]—but Walter C. Allen has suggested that Henderson himself was happy to be relieved of the burden of arranging and playing with both the band and the small groups.

Just at this point, when Benny seemed finally to have pulled together a second band that was both musically interesting and widely popular, he began to have problems with his health, some of which would dog him for the rest of his life. Sometime in the early part of 1940 he began to suffer from what was reported to be sciatica, which was affecting his lower spine. His left leg ached constantly. He carried on until the beginning of March when "sharp pain, apparently caused by a nerve ailment in his spine, was constantly doubling him over. . . ." He broke up the band temporarily and "rushed to Hot Springs to spend three weeks."[44] By March 19 he was somewhat better, and flew to the West Coast for an opening at the Coconut Grove.

But the improvement to his health was only temporary. On July 10 he was forced to quit again. He flew to the famous Mayo Clinic in Rochester, Minnesota, for spinal surgery on July 12.[45] The band finished out its current engagement without Benny, and then Goodman simply broke it up. It was the first time in over six years that he was without a band for an extended period.

His motives for dropping the band were not entirely a matter of health. For one thing, he had had very little vacation over the years—a brief visit to London in the summer of 1938, an occasional week off here and there.

We must keep in mind how hard these swing bands worked, especially very popular ones like the Goodman group, which could be booked three hundred and sixty-five days a year. The people who were leading bands in these earlier years of the swing era had been through the bad years of the 1930s; they knew how hard the music business could be, and few of them had much faith that the sudden gold that had come upon them would keep coming indefinitely. They were determined to capitalize on the popularity of swing while it lasted, and this meant taking every reasonable job that came along. As a consequence they doubled at theatres, playing at least five shows a day, while working at hotels and ballrooms, which meant playing from perhaps ten in the morning to one or two in the morning. Although at times they were able to "sit down" for a long run at a hotel, it was critical for them to play long tours of one-nighters. The hotels, which could accommodate only a few hundred people, were only modestly profitable for the bands; the real money was made in the big ballrooms scattered all across the country, which could hold several thousand people. These one-nighters were exhausting, often requiring the men to climb into the bus immediately after a job, and drive several hundred miles, in a day before superhighways, to the next town, where they might have time for a little sleep before they started over again. Between all of this there were weekly rehearsals to prepare new material, radio broadcasts and record dates, which came along perhaps once or twice a month. It was a very hard pace, even for young men and women as these mainly were, and it is no wonder that a lot of them had recourse to liquor and drugs—marijuana mainly at that period—to keep them going.

Goodman not only had to do everything that his sidemen did, but he bore the additional burdens of being the musical director, main soloist and chief operating officer of what was now a million-dollar-a-year business. He was undoubtedly tired, and perhaps "burnt out"—that is to say, unable to work up much enthusiasm for music. But it seems to me that he was once again suffering from that generalized dissatisfaction that afflicted him. It is apparent that he intended to make changes, and this time it would be a clean sweep.

For the moment he kept on salary Charlie Christian, Lionel Hampton, his vocalist Helen Forrest, Artie Bernstein, Eddie Sauter and two key trumpeters, Jimmy Maxwell and Ziggy Elman.[46] The rest of the men departed, a number of them joining a new band that Artie Shaw was putting together. Then, in the late summer Elman, unsure of his future with Goodman,[47] joined Tommy Dorsey. And in October Lionel Hampton decided it was time to follow the path of Krupa and James and form his own band. Goodman was sympathetic, and gave Hampton some financial help, as he had done for James earlier.[48] Hampton went on to become an inter-

national star with a band which lasted for decades. The old guard was now
gone for good. Nobody who had been at Carnegie Hall was still with the
band, although a few of them would be back from time to time over the
years.

The operation at the Mayo Clinic was apparently successful, and for the
moment relieved the pain. But Goodman would suffer from considerable
back pain intermittently for the rest of his life, to the point where, in his
last decades, it would be so painful for him to stand for long periods that
at times he had to simply walk off the bandstand and lie down. He was,
however, stoic about it and said little about it publicly.

Goodman rested through the summer and in the fall began to put together a band which, he hoped, would be fresh and exciting. Through the
early part of the fall he added and subtracted musicians, and played casual
gigs to try the group out. One of the musicians who made a brief appearance with the band was Henry "Red" Allen, a New Orleans pioneer, extravagantly admired by many jazz fans.

The key recruit, however, was Cootie Williams, considered by many to
be one of the finest trumpeters in jazz history. Williams was from Mobile,
Alabama, only 150 miles from New Orleans.[49] There was a good deal of
travel back and forth between the two cities and consequently as a boy
Williams, who was born in 1910, heard many of the early New Orleans
players. He thus soaked up at the source the new jazz that was sweeping
out of New Orleans across the rest of the country.

Williams's mother died when he was young, but his father, a tough and
intelligent man, who was at one time or another a strikebreaker in the
Texas oil fields, a professional gambler and a minister, kept the family together. Williams studied the trumpet with a teacher who disliked jazz and
made him work his way through the famous Arban exercise book, which
young brass players have cursed for generations. He thus had the best possible training for a jazz man—early acquaintance with the music at its
source and good legitimate training. He began hearing Louis Armstrong's
records and radio broadcasts as a teenager, and was instantly smitten, as
were thousands of trumpet players around the country. For the rest of his
life Williams was an Armstrong disciple, frequently quoting his solos in his
work.

In 1928 Williams came to New York. His abilities were quickly recognized, and he got jobs with the Chick Webb band, and then the Fletcher
Henderson Orchestra at the peak of its fame. Henderson, however, had a
competitor in the Duke Ellington Orchestra, which was rising into prominence as a result of his nationwide broadcasts from the Cotton Club,
America's best-known cabaret. In 1929 Ellington was growing impatient
with the bad habits of his star trumpet player, Bubber Miley, who had es-

tablished the band's basic "jungle" sound with his growling into the plunger mute. Bubber was critically important to the Ellington band, but he was a heavy drinker and very unreliable. Early in 1929 Duke reluctantly fired Bubber. He then reached out for Williams, who decided to join the band. At first he continued to play open horn, as he had always done, in the Armstrong manner. He was, in fact, amused by the growling of the other brass men. "Night after night, I had sat up there and nobody said a word. When trombonist Tricky Sam [Nanton] played, I laughed, because I thought it was funny. . . . But it dawned on me, finally, I thought, 'This man hired me to take Bubber's place.' "

Williams thereupon set about developing a growling style. He had never heard Miley in person, and says that he took nothing from him. Instead, he modeled his style on that of Ellington's great trombone growl specialist, Joe "Tricky Sam" Nanton. Very quickly he developed into the finest player in this manner in jazz, as convincing as Miley and perhaps even more expressive. Because he could also play open horn with power, he had a variety that Miley lacked, and he went on to become, through the 1930s, a central figure in the Ellington band, recognized as one of the major figures in jazz.

In 1940 Benny Goodman decided he wanted Williams in his band. It was a typical Goodman choice: Williams was a strong and fiery player along the lines of so many of the other soloists Benny picked out. It was, however, a rather curious choice. Cootie Williams was seen as so much a part of the Ellington band that it was difficult to imagine him playing elsewhere. It was a move that was sure to enrage Ellington's fans, although this would not have mattered to Goodman, if it even occurred to him. So in the fall of 1940 Benny asked his brother Irving to sound Williams out.[50] Williams was torn: on the one hand he felt a great deal of loyalty to Ellington; on the other, Goodman was offering him a sum that Ellington could not, or would not, pay him. Perhaps more important, exposure with the immensely popular Goodman band could give him a far greater national reputation than he could achieve with Ellington, although in fact the Ellington band would eventually become as popular as Goodman's.

There was, however, something else. Cootie Williams was a disciplined man who was very serious about his music. The Ellington band had always been filled with naughty boys whose mischievousness frequently led them to come late for engagements, be drunk on the stand and pay less attention to the music than Williams thought proper. Indeed, he at times undertook to provide the discipline that Duke was reluctant to impose, turning around in his seat to glare at evil-doers. He was particularly annoyed by Ellington's drummer, Sonny Greer. Greer was never considered a hard-swinging drummer, and an addiction to alcohol had made him increasingly unreliable. The Goodman band, however, was highly disciplined, musical and always had hard-swinging rhythm sections—"Terrific rhythm," Williams said. "That was the main thing. The band had a terrific beat." Temperamentally he would fit in with the Goodman band better than he did with Ellington's.

Williams went to Ellington. He said later that if Ellington had urged him not to go, he would have stayed. But Ellington, a princely man, was not one to ask people for favors. He not only urged Williams to take the offer, but said he would negotiate the salary for him. And early in November Williams left.

He was hired primarily to play with the Sextet, but he did have some solos with the big band. At times he also played with the trumpet section, filling in for a man temporarily missing. He may also have supplied a fourth trumpet in arrangements that called for one, but I have difficulty hearing four trumpets on the records with Williams I have listened to carefully: after Williams left, Goodman kept to three trumpets, which he could not have done if any substantial proportion of the book called for four.

Cootie Williams came into the Goodman band with the intention of returning to Ellington after a year. He did, in fact, leave when the year was up, but the stint with the Goodman Sextet had given him the larger public image that was forecast, and Ellington now urged him to form his own orchestra. He did so, but the band was not successful. Williams fell on hard times, and eventually returned to Ellington, where he finished out his career. He said later of his stint with Goodman, "That was the most relaxed thing that I ever had in my life in music. . . . And that Sextet used to romp. . . . I enjoyed that so much."[51]

A second key addition was tenor saxophonist Georgie Auld, a Canadian born in 1919. He came with his family to New York when he was a boy, and had some formal study on saxophone. He was just at the right age to capitalize on the swing boom and, starting at age eighteen, worked his way through bands led by Bunny Berigan, Artie Shaw and Jan Savitt, establishing a reputation as a man who could read well and swing. He became for a period the Goodman band's principal saxophone soloist, but gained more fame as a member of the Goodman Sextet with Williams and Christian. Auld came out of the Coleman Hawkins–Ben Webster school of saxophonists, always hard-driving and busy. His tone was not as thick and furry as Webster's, but somewhat more dulcet. He tended to play repeated riff-like figures and series of off-beat notes which are rhythmic, rather than melodic, in intent.

An even more important musician than Auld, who quickly became famous with the Goodman band, was a very young pianist named Mel Powell, born in 1923, and hardly more than a boy when Goodman first climbed to fame. Powell's[52] background was substantially different from that of the typical jazz man, who got his training in school marching bands, high-school dance bands, and jam sessions at local clubs. Powell was born Melvin Epstein in the Bronx of parents who had, like Goodman's, immigrated from Russia. His father was, at times, a quite successful business-man, and Powell was given piano lessons at four or five. It quickly became clear that he was, if not perhaps a child prodigy, at least enormously talented, to the extent that he attracted the attention of Walter Damrosch, a composer, educator and conductor who was a power in American music.

Powell had an older brother Lloyd, who followed the new swing music. "One day he came wide-eyed and said to Mom, 'Benny Goodman's band is coming to the Paramount. I want to go downtown,'" Powell related.

He talked her out of a quarter for both him and for me, and he took me down to the Paramount Theatre. That was my first exposure to jazz. That band, I can still remember it coming up. It was marvelous, that was the band with Krupa, Teddy Wilson. [This of course was the famous 1937 Paramount stand.] That was the introduction, I became fascinated with it, quite knowledgeable. I think the following summer I went to work in the Catskills. I went to work in a little band, and there were real smart jazz buffs there. They showed me a great deal. One of the fellows from the Catskills took me around by the nose. . . . He took me to Nick's. He introduced me to Sidney Bechet and Zutty Singleton. The piano player was very good, he was Nat King Cole. Hell of a piano player. And Bobby Hackett was playing, and George Brunies and Brad Gowans, and Eddie Condon. . . . So that was my crowd. They let me sit in. . . .[53]

Powell had graduated from high school at fourteen, and was attending City College, where he was studying not music, but French literature. He was also working with bands of various kinds to help pay for his education, sitting in at Nick's, and eventually working there regularly. He was taken in hand by Willie "The Lion" Smith, one of the masters of the stride piano style, whom Duke Ellington had taken as a mentor some fifteen years before. Smith later said of Powell,

He had musical ambitions and played in a dixieland band up in Nyack, New York. He was short on money, but long on talent and I could see he really wanted to be a professional pianist. Instead of cash he used to bring me strudel cakes, a half-dozen cigars, or a bottle of absinthe with a lump of sugar in it. It took me six months of constant training to get him to develop some speed and to use his left hand. In later years, when he got with Benny Goodman's band, his head got as big as a house, and he said Teddy Wilson taught him all that he knew.[54]

However, when Powell was with Goodman he told a *Down Beat* reporter, "The Lion was wonderful to me, and I'll always be grateful for his help and advice."[55]

Powell spent two years working at Nick's with Zutty Singleton and others. He was with Muggsy Spanier's dixieland band briefly, and by the time he was sixteen or seventeen he had developed a reputation in New York jazz circles. In particular, jazz writer George Simon touted him to Goodman, who was dissatisfied with Johnny Guarnieri. Guarnieri was a fine jazz pianist but was hamstrung by a reputation which said that he could play in any style but his own. According to Jess Stacy, Guarnieri "always hated Goodman," because Benny, in his tactless way, said to him something like, "Johnny, why don't you get a style of your own."[56] In time Guarnieri left and went back to Artie Shaw, where he made his first fame as a member of Shaw's small group, the Gramercy Five.

Undoubtedly Goodman would have liked to have had Wilson back in the band, but by this time Wilson intensely disliked Goodman, and was in any case a star who could work as a soloist or with small groups. Finally Goodman auditioned Powell. According to a frequently told story, Goodman's secretary was present at the audition. After hearing Powell, Goodman turned to her and asked her, "Is he any good?" She replied, "I think so, and besides, he's cute,"[57] or words to that effect. (Powell was tall, gangling, blonde and not yet twenty at the time.)

Goodman hired him. Powell was elated to be going to work with the same band he had been thrilled by only four years earlier at the Paramount, although the men he had been playing with at Nick's and elsewhere believed that Goodman was a commercial huckster who had abandoned the true faith and told Powell that he was selling out. But the chance to play with a celebrated band was something few teenagers would have turned down for the sake of purity; and, besides, at the time the Powell family needed the money.

Powell managed to establish a much better relationship with Goodman than most of the sidemen did. For one thing, they were both sons of Russian Jews who had seen hard times; both were ambitious, determined to rise in the world. Powell, like Goodman, went on to develop an upper-class drawl, became a professor of music at Yale University and later at the California Institute of the Arts, and in time a recognized composer of modern music. Later, when Powell was teaching at Yale, he lived not far from the Goodman home in Connecticut, and the two families saw a good deal of each other.

Musically, Powell drew on a number of sources. Like most of the young pianists of the day he was influenced by Teddy Wilson and had the deftness, speed and ability to interact with Goodman which characterized

Wilson's work with the Trio and Quartet. But he appears also to have developed a more "barrel-house" style very reminiscent of Stacy, especially in the heavy dynamic accentuation from note to note that was typical of Stacy, which can be clearly recognized in Powell's solos on the "Roll 'Em" compilation.

Powell thinks that he was able to get along well with Goodman because

> . . . in some respects I was a stronger musician than he was, and he probably respected that. I knew a lot of things he didn't understand. I'm certainly not speaking in terms of jazz playing, but my theoretical background, my knowledge. I suspect that had something to do with it. Even at that time I was very, very, well trained. I'd had a terrific musical education. He got a big kick out of the fact that I had a certain sense of historicity of jazz. For example, we could wink at one another and do a Joe Sullivan—Pee Wee Russell. He'd start growling, you know, the way Pee Wee did, that struggle, that angst that Pee Wee Russell would play on the clarinet—not being able to play it very well. It was all playing from the viscera and so on. So I'd immediately do Joe Sullivan, or Earl Hines, or stuff that would go to the period where Benny had grown up.[58]

Powell's contribution to the band was significant. He played both with the band and the Sextet, and wrote arrangements as well. He quickly became respected as one of the finest jazz pianists in the swing style.

One more important musician who played with the Goodman band during this period was drummer Sid Catlett. The stories about Catlett mainly regard his unceremonious departure from the band about four months after he came in, and the considerable regret felt today over his leaving. Sid Catlett was born in Evansville, Indiana, in 1910.[59] He played a little piano, but quickly found his métier when he shifted to drums. At some point in his youth he moved to Chicago, where he drummed at Tilden High School on the South Side. He was thus in the heart of the jazz ferment when the great New Orleans pioneers were beginning to make their national names. He heard all the major black drummers in Chicago at the time—Baby Dodds, Zutty Singleton, Jimmy Bertrand and others. Louis Armstrong said, "I remember when I was playing with Carroll Dickerson at the Savoy, Big Sid frequently showed up in his knickers and pestered Zutty to let him take over those tubs."[60] Catlett developed into a broad-shouldered man over six feet tall and a fine drummer. He came to New York where he worked with Elmer Snowden at Small's in Harlem with a band that included a number of coming stars, among them Roy Eldridge and Chu Berry. He eventually worked for Fletcher Henderson, and by the mid-1930s was considered one of the finest drummers in jazz.

He was, moreover, a showman. He would toss a stick in the air, then light a cigarette while waiting for it to come down or dance around the drums while playing a solo. He said, "Think of all the fine musicians you've met who are playing for cakes because they haven't got showmanship."[61] These displays did not always please his fellow musicians, nor the more purist jazz fans, but they forgave him almost anything, because of his enormous talents as a jazz drummer. Connie Kay said, "Catlett was the only drummer I liked to hear take a solo. He seemed to play musically."[62] Max Roach called him "my main source of inspiration."[63] Mel Powell said: "Big Sid, an absolute magician. I think he's one of the greatest drummers who ever lived. If I had to have my druthers, I think it would be Big Sid. Taste. He never did anything wrong. The enormous power, under constraint, which always fascinates me. . . . He made pitches out of everything. . . . Like a cushion. Utterly conscientious and reliable. You could count on him."[64] There is widespread agreement that Catlett was, perhaps, the finest drummer of the swing age.

But Catlett was not always an easy man. He could be friendly and jovial, but was temperamental and could appear "tense, sullen and agitated."[65] This was not the sort of man who would get on well with Benny Goodman. What happened, precisely, nobody is sure. Catlett joined the band in New York in June. By July they were in Chicago, and here Catlett was able to persuade Goodman to bring in his friend, bassist John Simmons. According to Hammond, Benny was trying to tell both Catlett and Simmons how to play. Whatever the case, Simmons stayed in Chicago when the band left at the end of August. By this time relations between Goodman and Catlett were going rapidly downhill. Then, at a September 25 recording session in New York, a drummer who is present on some takes in the early part of the date is missing thereafter, and "The Earl," cut at this session, is without drums. The record caused a good deal of gossip in swing-band circles, and a rumor was passed around that Jo Jones had been hired for the date but was pulled out at the last minute because his union card was not in order. Goodman's memories of the date varied over the time. Russ Connor, who has heard the out-takes, says that it is clearly Jones, and Connor certainly would know the difference between two drummers, which was especially marked in any case.[66]

Catlett was back with the band the next night, but basically it was over, and within a month he was gone. I agree with many others that it is a matter for regret. Catlett was noisy, showy and difficult. But he was also a brilliant drummer who not only swung himself, but drove the band, as the "Roll 'Em" compilation makes clear. Unfortunately, most of the records he made with Goodman were of straightforward pops, which do not show him to best advantage. But he is on "Pound Ridge," "Roll 'Em" and "Clarinet a la King," as well as on the airchecks. Unhappily, Big Sid Catlett died of a heart attack in 1951 at just over forty.

Yet again, Goodman acquired two vocalists who would be identified with the band. The first was Helen Forrest, who joined the band at the end of 1939 and stayed through the middle of 1941. A pretty brunette, she had made a national reputation with Artie Shaw, and when her predecessor with Goodman, Louise Tobin, quit to have a baby, she came to the band.

Helen Forrest had a pleasant, warm, but fairly light voice, with a touch of terminal vibrato which was not as pronounced as Helen Ward's, and good intonation. Between her stints with Shaw, Goodman and James—at times when each of these leaders had one of the two or three most popular bands in the country—she came to be seen as the quintessential female swing-band vocalist.

Helen Forrest was yet another who found working for Goodman a strain. She quit suddenly "to avoid having a nervous breakdown. Then just on a hunch, I decided to contact Harry [James]."[67] And it was with James, despite the attention she had gotten with Shaw and Goodman, that she became one of the most famous of the girl singers of the big-band era.

Her replacement was one who became even more famous, Peggy Lee. She was born Norma Egstrom in 1922 and grew up in Fargo, North Dakota. She began singing on a local radio station at fourteen and eventually landed with the band of Will Osborne, which tended toward novelties.[68] Goodman heard her singing in a cocktail lounge at Chicago's Ambassador Hotel shortly before Helen Forrest quit, and hired her. In time she went on to become almost as important to the Goodman band as Helen Ward had been. She became involved in a romance with Goodman's guitarist, Dave Barbour. Barbour left the band in February 1943, and a month later Lee left as well. According to George Simon, "Peggy may have looked sophisticated and sensuous, but in reality she was rather insecure, extremely sensitive, and terribly sentimental."[69] The twenty-month stint with Goodman made her one of the most famous female vocalists of the time, and she went on to have a long career as a singer. In addition, she wrote a lot of songs, mostly in collaboration with various people, some of which were minor hits, like "What More Can a Woman Do?" and "Mañana." She also did a little television acting, and had a role in the film Pete Kelly's Blues.[70] She sang in a somewhat more legato manner than many of the female vocalists of the time, with a less pronounced vibrato—a style that was not quite so bouncy as some of the others. She used a great many slurs and pitch sags which gave her singing a bluesy quality, although she was not really a blues singer in the old tradition. Her weakness was occasional uncertainty of intonation. Peggy Lee has always been considered a somewhat more jazz-oriented singer than many of her competitors.

As was the case with the instrumentalists, there were between times a good many vocalists coming and going. Mildred Bailey sang with the band on the *Camel Caravan* for a short period, and others, like Frances Hunt and June Robbins, were with the band for longer or shorter stays. Goodman also began at this time using a male vocalist regularly with the band, which he had not done before. He was Art London, or Art Lund as he eventually became known, who was in and out of the band for a number of years.

Yet despite the success, both critical and popular, of this band, Goodman continued to exhibit that restless need to tinker. Personnel came and went at a faster pace than ever. From the formation of the new band in November 1940 until the beginning of the recording ban in August 1942, a period of twenty months, Goodman used some sixty-five musicians who can be identified on recordings, and undoubtedly more who came and went so fast that they have eluded discographers. Eleven trumpeters passed through the band, an equal number of drummers and no less than twenty-three saxophonists. Going through the revolving door were some old familiar names, among them Hymie Schertzer, Vido Musso, Irving Goodman, Dave Tough and, for a brief guest appearance, Gene Krupa.

Not all of this turn-over was Goodman's fault. The Selective Service draft began in 1940, and as the musicians were exactly the young men who the army was looking for, the draft very quickly began to disrupt the swing bands generally, creating an increasingly competitive scramble for the best men, and not incidentally driving salaries up to levels that would have astonished the players who had staffed the swing bands only a few years earlier. James T. Maher, during this period, once heard Tommy Dorsey complain, "I'm paying this kid trumpet player $500 a week, and he can't even blow his nose, for Christ's sake."[71] Furthermore, as Maher also points out, the swing band sidemen tended to be nomads, leaving bands for more money, over a real or fancied injury, for women who wanted them at home, because they were tired of the road or just on a whim.

But it is also true that Goodman was getting less and less patient with the men. There were instances when he would fly in a new hope at considerable expense, and then fire him at the end of the first night, hardly a fair hearing for a musician who was unfamiliar with the book, undoubtedly nervous and possibly very tired as well. It seems clear that when Goodman brought a new man in, it was not after a considered judgment that he was the right man for the job, but on a trial basis, as an experiment. Goodman frequently chose men not because he was familiar with their work but because they had been recommended to him, and under this procedure he was bound to find some of them not to his taste after he had heard them play for a few days. But beyond all of this was that ceaseless dissatisfaction that gnawed at Goodman so much of the time. Somehow, things were never quite right, and the answer would be to make changes.

The effect was to keep the men, especially the younger ones and the newcomers, very tense. Jimmy Maxwell, speaking of this period, said that the old hands like Schertzer and Mondello, who had known Goodman since the free-lance days, were not so easily upset by what Goodman did, nor was Ziggy Elman, who, Maxwell said, "wasn't afraid of anybody. But the younger guys were in awe of him."[72]

Working for Benny Goodman was not always fun.

# 21

# The First Columbia
# Recordings

As we have seen, the Benny Goodman band which began to record for Columbia in August 1939 was entirely different from the Victor band in almost every respect. Although Fletcher Henderson and Jimmy Mundy continued to arrange for Goodman, and the band still played many of the pieces from the old book, the significant arrangers for the period were Mel Powell and Eddie Sauter. Both of these men were thoroughly schooled musicians, with a far more sophisticated grasp of music theory than most of the earlier arrangers—or indeed most people in jazz—had. They were able to handle more complex ideas and thicker harmonies: Goodman, out of both personal taste and a sense of what his audiences could take, frequently simplified the more complex arrangements Sauter and others brought in. As we shall see when we come to examine Goodman's ventures into the world of classical music, he had little early exposure to the chromaticism of the late nineteenth-century composers such as Mahler. The dance-band harmonies he had grown up with were triads and sevenths: Eddie Durham said that he learned to write in four and five voices, and when he was arranging for Bennie Moten in the early 1930s, the men in the band were both startled and annoyed by the sixths and ninths he was using.[1] By the 1940s sixths and ninths were clichés which Goodman had become accustomed to, but he was not going to let his arrangers go much further into dissonance. Nonetheless, Sauter persisted in writing these advanced arrangements.

For another thing, the voices from the Victor band, some of them as familiar as old shoes to Goodman fans, were gone. Cootie Williams, in his growl mode, was one of the most individual voices in jazz, entirely different from James or Elman; Lou McGarity was a rough-voiced punchy player quite different from the much easier Brown or Ballard; Mel Powell had some of Wilson's deftness, and some of Stacy's abundant swing, but he was nonetheless a different kind of player.

Taken as a whole, this band had a very superior collection of soloists. Powell was in a class with Stacy and Wilson; Cootie Williams was one of the finest trumpeters in jazz, and Jimmy Maxwell was an excellent improviser; Auld was not of the rank of Coleman Hawkins or Lester Young, but he was better than most of the tenor saxophonists in the swing bands of the time; and McGarity was one of the best trombonists of the day. Finally, Charlie Christian, who occasionally soloed with the band, was the most influential guitarist of the period, and a pivot in jazz history.

This cadre of soloists gave Goodman a considerable advantage in putting together his small groups. These would now, like everything else, be substantially different in instrumentation, texture and structure. I will discuss the small groups in more detail shortly. For now I would only point out that they were usually made up of six or seven pieces, instead of three or four; they would contain as many as three horns, instead of clarinet alone; and they would be more frequently built on carefully worked out riffs and other devices, instead of being largely improvised.

The band was now recording an increasingly higher percentage of popular tunes, as opposed to hot swing numbers—about 75 percent. However, the pops were usually clothed in swing arrangements, many of them by Eddie Sauter in his relatively complex style. On "Bewitched," a tune from the hit show *Pal Joey*, which was recorded in January 1941 and taken at a very danceable 112, Sauter uses the full band for the introduction, including a unison trombone drone effect which sounds like an auto horn. Goodman takes the opening four measures over brief saxophone figures, after which the whole band picks up the melody. The arrangement is repeated for the second eight measures. The bridge is given to a solo saxophone backed by both trumpet and saxophone sections. Behind the vocal chorus that follows, Sauter uses saxophones and brass both jointly and separately. On the next bridge he uses trumpet, saxophone and trombone choirs behind Goodman's solo clarinet. These choirs are not playing punctuation or simple repeated riffs, but in many cases quite complicated figures. This is a far different way of writing from the manner of Sampson and Henderson of the Victor period, with their open spaces, punctuation of one section by another, and general airiness. Sauter was putting down on score paper at least twice as many notes as Henderson or Sampson typically would, and often far more than that. Among other things, Sauter would write out lines for the bass, rather than simply letting the bass player work out his own lines on the chord changes, in order to make sure that the bass was functioning harmonically as he wanted it to. He often frequently wrote out piano parts, for the same reason, frequently with the bass line on the piano doubling that of the string bass.[2]

Again, on "I Found a Million Dollar Baby," in the twenty-eight measures which precede the vocal Sauter passes the melody along every four bars and in some cases every two. The section is filled with sharp contrasts: a bit of very gentle piano suddenly interrupted by flaming brass, a rolling saxophone figure shot from ambush by the trumpets. Behind the vocal which comprises the rest of the record Sauter has something going on, and sometimes two things, at virtually every point—here the saxes, now the trumpets, there a bit of solo saxophone. This is in marked contrast to, say, Spud Murphy's "The Glory of Love," in which he backs the vocal mainly with some simple saxophone figures and bits of sparkling piano by Stacy.

Sauter is not always so busy; his arrangement of "When the Sun Comes Out" is comparatively simple. The simpler arrangements came about, I think, because Sauter had to turn out two or three scores for pop songs each week, which he viewed as a chore. "Some of them were awful," he said. "There were certain things that Benny wouldn't accept. He didn't say don't do it, but he simply wouldn't play it. So why knock yourself out on something that he's not going to use?"[3] For these pieces, which would have a very short life, Sauter did not bother to extend himself, but in general his method was to enrich rather than pare away, as the earlier arrangers tended to do.

The pieces that Sauter is best known for, like "Superman," "Clarinet a la King" and "Moonlight on the Ganges," are all very complex for what was, after all, supposed to be dance music. In fact, these pieces have to be seen as jazz compositions, rather than arrangements of songs. "Superman," one of Sauter's best-known pieces for Goodman, runs four and a half minutes and was issued on one side of a twelve-inch record. It was written as a feature for Cootie Williams, who had just come to Goodman from the Ellington Orchestra. Sauter thus had in front of him the famous "concertos" that Ellington had written for Williams and other of his star soloists. In particular, "Concerto for Cootie," which would be transformed into the hit song "Do Nothin' Till You Hear From Me," had been issued not long before. Sauter was not especially under Ellington's influence, as is apparent from his work: "I'm sure I was overwhelmed by Ellington's band . . . but I couldn't do that because I wasn't there,"[4] he said. Nonetheless, the idea of writing concertos for instrumentalists was an innovation Ellington had brought to jazz.

"Superman" consists of about seven different sections, depending on which ones are seen as individual episodes or variations on other ones. The episodes are made up mainly of four- or eight-measure units, as in the ordinary pop tune, but there are six-, ten-, twelve- and twenty-measure units as well. Furthermore, some of these units are unevenly subdivided; for example the opening ten-measure unit has Cootie solo over the band for three measures, and then exchanges phrases with the trombones for the remainder of the unit. Again, the putative eight-measure unit which comes just before the twelve-measure interlude leading into the saxophone solo— I can think of no easy way of pinpointing this—is truncated in favor of the interlude. After the saxophone solo the trumpets have a passage with a metric shift, in which a repeated figure keeps turning up a beat earlier than we expect. Yet again, in a passage towards the end, in which Cootie growls into the mute, the saxophone accompaniment is cut into unusual lengths which entirely disrupts the meter. It is no wonder that the musicians "stepped on their joints" trying to play it. Jazz musicians, even when they are reading music, work as much by feel as from what is on the paper. Trained as improvisers, they are always conscious of where the down beat is, and they can feel, without thinking about it, four, eight, and other groups of measures. There is nothing terribly difficult about this; it is a matter of training, and more recently musicians, even students, have trained themselves to feel groups of measures of three, five and even seven and a half beats. But in 1940 these musicians were thinking in fours and eights, and they were thrown off by the metric shifts and units of unusual lengths. The trumpets, for example, stumble while playing the aforementioned passage with the phrases a beat short; and Georgie Auld, in his long solo near the middle of the piece, is never quite able to shake himself loose from the obstreperous behavior going on around him.

The development of this piece is not entirely satisfactory. It is not always clear how successive episodes are supposed to relate. But on the whole the composition works, in considerable measure due to the splendid playing of Williams in both open horn and a variety of mutes. His part is largely written, and Sauter has used him well, taking him through the whole range of timbres that he had developed with Ellington.

A second Sauter piece that became well known was "Clarinet a la King," a feature for Goodman, as the title suggests. Structurally it is somewhat simpler, with the units mostly eight measures in length, usually divided into four-measure subsets. There are six sections, in addition to an eight-measure introduction. The first and last are built on the same theme, which bears more than a little resemblance to "My Little Cousin," a pop song Goodman recorded a few months later, but this may have been coincidental, in that both are based on the fraelich genre which Goodman had used so successfully in "And the Angels Sing." As the introduction is also used to announce a long coda, the ending is a mirror image, with variation, of the opening, giving the piece a certain structure. However, the main idea of the piece is a constant dialogue between Goodman's clarinet and the orchestra, beginning with the introduction, where the orchestra and clarinet exchange two-beat phrases. In the main theme following, Goodman plays four measures accompanied by the rhythm section, and is then answered by the band, which sometimes actually recapitulates a portion of the clarinet line. In the bridge, roles are reversed with Goodman answering various sections of the band—now the trumpets, then the saxophones, and so on. Thus it goes throughout the piece: Goodman plays a simple figure, which is repeated by the piano, then by the whole band. Goodman has a brief conversation with the drums, and so forth. At only two points is this scheme abandoned: in the middle Goodman is given a fairly lengthy space in which to improvise in his usual fashion, and at the conclusion of this section there is an atempo passage, very much in a symphonic manner, in which Goodman, the saxophones and the brass all play more or less continuously. This is a nice little piece of music, entirely unjazz-like, rather pastoral in feel, and fairly dissonant in spots, at least for the time.

Once again this is not a dance-band arrangement, but a relatively complex composition that draws on many sources outside of jazz. Goodman did not play pieces like this one very often. He recorded them and would bring them out for special occasions, but he was wary of offering them to his regular fans. They could not be danced to, in any case.

The same can be said of "Benny Rides Again," one of the best-known pieces Sauter did for Goodman. As the title suggests, it is another concerto for Goodman, with long solos, atempo passages, breaks and the like. It features a good deal of hard-driving brass, but is notable mainly for a long thirty-two-measure passage (with a four-measure transition at the end) for the saxophone section, prefiguring later advanced pieces like Woody Herman's famous "Four Brothers." Typically, it is a very busy section, especially after the first sixteen measures, when Sauter brings in trumpets and trombones to pile up layers of sound as he so often did.

Most of the ballads Sauter wrote for Goodman were tossed off quickly, but when challenged by a good song he could produce some wonderful moments. His arrangement of the Gershwin tune, "Love Walked In," a beautiful melody, is particularly fine. The opening has Goodman improvising over fairly dissonant harmonies. Goodman then plays the theme, with a counter-melody by solo trombone for the first eight measures. In the second eight the counter-melody is provided by tenor saxophone; and for the three following quite similar phrases of the melody, the clarinet is harmonized successively with muted trombone, muted trumpet and saxophones. The last sixteen measures of the melody are played by one trombone, with another providing the counter-melody. It is a very imaginative, not to say fanciful arrangement, somewhat regal, and is played majestically by the orchestra. Trombonist Trummy Young was in the band at this time.

He became best known as the mainstay of Louis Armstrong's All-Stars in the 1950s and 1960s, playing leather-lunged and at times ham-fisted solos built to suit the antic atmosphere Armstrong often created; but he had been a sensitive player with an impeccable tone, and he shows it here. Trumpeter Al Cuozzo plays a very straight but powerful solo as well. As a whole it is a brilliant demonstration of the kind of music a good dance band could make given the right materials. "Love Walked In" is a long way from "The Dixieland Band." This is truly "symphonic" jazz.

Goodman's other principal arranger for the period, Mel Powell, did not do nearly as much work as Sauter did—he was, after all, the pianist with the band—and his material was not nearly as complex. Powell was only eighteen when he wrote his first arrangement for Goodman, and although he was clearly talented beyond his years, and extremely well schooled, he had not, at that point, had as much training in composition as Sauter had. Even as a youth Powell had a good deal of confidence in himself, but given his inexperience, he was bound to tread a little more cautiously than Sauter, who had been writing for dance bands for many years. One of the best-known Powell arrangements is "Mission to Moscow," named for no particular reason after a popular book and movie of that title.

The piece, fundamentally, is a march: although it is played in 4/4, there is a 2/4 feel to it due to the fact that the main theme is built entirely out of quarter and half notes. Furthermore, Powell again and again uses the trombones as Sousa did, marching them up and down scales to link the phrases of the melody, as in the third measure after the introduction. The march-like quality is further enhanced by the use of a lot of triadic harmony; and the piece closes with a trumpet figure that has been used to conclude a substantial proportion of all the marches ever written. Finally, the brass heavily dominates, where of course in a swing-band piece the saxes are at least as important.

Structurally, the piece is quite simple. It consists of two themes, each sixteen measures long, which are for the most part alternated. The main, or A, theme is based on a common set of chord changes; the second uses a less common set, and includes a device which Duke Ellington used frequently, beginning as early as "Black and Tan Fantasy" (first recorded in 1927)—movement of the chord on the lowered six to the tonic.

But it is not all march music. Goodman plays a very hot, intense solo in his bristly staccato style, which includes bent notes. There is also a clever chase passage in which the piano imitates the clarinet. And there is a very fast passage for saxophones, all rolling eighth notes, which the saxes do not articulate as well as they might have.

Another well-known Powell work is "The Earl," dedicated to Earl Hines, who founded the school of jazz piano Powell descended from. (Powell also wrote a piece called "The Count," for Count Basie.) "The Earl" bears a considerable resemblance to "Mission to Moscow." There is an emphasis on the brass, a chromatic movement in the harmonies to the second strain (actually the bridge to what is essentially a thirty-two-bar pop song form), and a chase chorus between piano and clarinet. It is a feature for Powell more than anything; what is surprising about it, given the title, is that the main theme, especially as played by Powell in the introduction, is not Hines-like but derives from the older stride style and could have been dedicated to Fats Waller.

Powell's writing in these and other pieces is much more direct and less complicated than the work of Eddie Sauter—quite sunny and filled with youthful exuberance, in contrast to the somewhat convoluted approach of the older man with philosophic inclinations. Unlike Sauter, Powell was not under contract to produce a lot of pop songs, and could write more or less what he wanted, but he did do some more standard swing numbers. One of these was "String of Pearls." Glenn Miller's version, containing a famous cornet solo by Bobby Hackett, was a big hit, but the Goodman version was also very popular.

The tune—if it deserves to be called one—could hardly be simpler, based as it is on repeated dotted quarters on the same pitch. There are eight measures of this, eight similar measures a fourth higher, and then the first eight are repeated. As there is only a minimum of chord changes, after one playing of this theme in C, the band modulates into a blues in A-flat on which Auld and McGarity have solos. Goodman takes his solo on the original theme in C, adds a chorus of the A-flat blues, and the band plays a chorus of blues and returns to the original theme to end it all. The piece gets its lift from the unremitting syncopation of the successive dotted quarters, the sprightly piano figures Powell lays under it, the simple countermelodies and the solos. Particularly fine are the two choruses of blues played by Lou McGarity, all tough, gutty staccato trombone with the burry front edge to the notes that was characteristic of his playing. McGarity has been unduly neglected by jazz writers; although he used Teagarden's style as a point of departure, he is a far more forceful player with an instantly recognizable manner that is always hot—the kind of powerful musician Goodman liked and hired so often. This is one of his finest solos on record. Finally, "String of Pearls" contains a device that was becoming a Powell trade mark—a little instrumental chase, this time moving from saxophones to trumpets to clarinet.

One of Goodman's biggest records from this period was a coupling of "Six Flats Unfurnished" and "Why Don't You Do Right?" which were cut in the next-to-last recording session before the 1942 record ban. "Six Flats Unfurnished" was an original by Richard Maltby, the only piece he

ever wrote for Goodman. The number is similar to the work that Sauter
and Powell were doing in that it is based on counter-melodies running
along in parallel, rather than the call-and-response system that was at the
heart of the music of the Victor band. Like Powell's pieces, it is cut into
eight- and sixteen-bar units, with shorter interludes at points. After an introduction, the trombones play a very basic and widely used figure for eight
measures, and then, while the trombones continue, two melodies, one of
them related to the trombone melody, are played by saxophones and trumpets. The three melodies recur throughout the piece in different guises and
variations. The number's attraction lies in the fresh melodies that Maltby
has provided, and the contrapuntal effects. This is also one of the rare records by the band on which Goodman does not solo. The only solo is by
tenor saxophonist Jon Walton, an early disciple of Lester Young who died
young. "Had he lived, he'd have been great," Benny told Russ Connor. It
should be noted that by this time Goodman was carrying five saxophones—
two altos, two tenors and a baritone. This had become standard in dance
bands, because the five voices allowed arrangers to write thicker, more advanced harmonies than they had been. But as we have seen, Goodman preferred a trimmer band, and he is still carrying only five brass, whereas by
this time most bands were carrying seven.

"Why Don't You Do Right?" was primarily a feature for Peggy Lee,
which became important to her success. It is basically a blues in D-minor,
but the lyric is structured somewhat differently from the standard blues
system. The song was written by blues guitarist Joe McCoy, a featured
singer with the Harlem Hamfats, the first rhythm and blues group. Lil
Green had had a hit record with the song several months before, and Lee's
version owes a good deal to the Green recording. The song has a typical
Depression lyric about failed men and put-upon women, and even though
the country was rolling out of the Depression by 1942, it had a certain rel-
evance. The arrangement is fitted out with portentous stings, and Goodman plays very tense, staccato passages here and there. But the main point
are the four choruses and a tag which Lee sings in her bluesy manner, with
a somewhat sardonic edge to her voice, and it put her on the road to fame.
There is also some very nice plunger accompaniment by Jimmy Maxwell
behind Lee's last chorus. He roomed with Cootie Williams[5] when the
band was on the road for a period, and it is apparent here, and in the
throat tones of his "After You've Gone" solo, that he was influenced as
much by Williams as by Armstrong.

Actually, although "Why Don't You Do Right?" was an important record for Peggy Lee, it was not typical. On it she sings in a tough, clipped
manner supposed to suggest the complaint of the hard, put-upon woman
of the lyric. Her usual style, as on ballads like "My Old Flame" and "Let's

Do It," is more dulcet, in the standard manner of the romantic big band girl singer.

Among the writers for the band was Goodman himself, who is credited with a piece called "Pound Ridge," named for a village in Westchester County where Goodman lived for a period. However much Goodman contributed, the piece is in part a head, with ideas coming from various members of the band. In particular, the background line for the saxophones was taken from an Ellington piece called "Frolic Sam," and was probably brought in by Cootie Williams, although no doubt others were familiar with the line, which is very basic in any case. The piece is very simple—an AABA thirty-two-bar pop form with almost primitive chord changes. "Pound Ridge" is not far removed from a jam session. Goodman and Williams have full thirty-two-bar solos, Powell and tenor saxophonist George Berg each have sixteen. This was one of the few sides that the band cut while Big Sid Catlett was with it, and his presence shows, for the number develops a hard-driving swing from the outset. Catlett always listened carefully to what was going on around him. He was not simply laying out a beat, but finding appropriate things to do as the music flowed around him. Behind Goodman he plays a ride beat on the cymbals; he pushes the trumpet with off-beat pistol shots on the snare, something of a trademark of his. (These are actually so-called rim shots, in which the stick hits both the skin and the metal rim of the drum at once, to produce a ringing sound.) For the piano he again provides a light, deft backing on the cymbals; with the band he accents in carefully chosen spots; and on his own solo he produces a rolling beat on the snare with tom-tom accents that does not make a showy interlude of the solo, but remains an integral part of the piece, propelling the band forward at the end of it. Sid Catlett was hardly the only drummer who constantly adjusted his playing to the band, of course; but he was a master at it, almost always finding just the right thing to do. It is interesting that Goodman's solo is rather more thoughtful and less busy than is usual with him. A soloist who is backed by a superlative beat usually finds it necessary to do very little to make his line swing, and he is likely to play less rather than more. I think something of the kind was happening here.

It is also to the point that Goodman, to the extent that "Pound Ridge" was his work, kept to basics. Goodman never forgot what was at the heart of the music. Before anything he wanted his bands to swing, to be exciting, to drive. Even though he was buying fairly complex arrangements from Sauter and others, he constantly returned to simple vehicles, playing "Roll 'Em," "One O'Clock Jump" and similar pieces night after night so that he, and the other soloists, could relax and blow. "Pound Ridge," not "Superman," was Goodman's taste.

Nonetheless, it was the more complex pieces which interested the critics and the more knowledgeable jazz fans, and even the more casual dance-band listeners. "Six Flats Unfurnished," which five years earlier would have been considered almost impermissibly avant-garde, was popular. In fact, the more adventurous dance bands had been educating the American public. The leader in so doing was of course Duke Ellington, who had been giving the public a lot of advanced compositions from as far back as "East St. Louis Toodle-Oo" and "Black and Tan Fantasy" in 1927, and had continued to produce strange and different works regularly through the 1930s, among them "Creole Love Call" with its wordless vocal, the tour de force "Daybreak Express," the sequence of concertos for his star soloists and dozens of others. By 1940 he was turning out some very sophisticated pieces, like the thorny "Ko-Ko," "Harlem Airshaft," "Warm Valley," "Main-stem" and many more. Ellington had not invented the idea of the complex or symphonic arrangement for the dance band; that had been done by Grofé and Whiteman when Ellington was still a novice. But he was the first, and greatest, master of the form.

The Ellington band did not exactly fit the basic mold of the swing band—its music was too various and at times too complex to be fitted into what was really a very simple form—and few dance bands imitated the Ellington style directly, the Barnet band being one that sometimes did. But Ellington had shown how expressive a medium the dance-band arrangement could be, and it was undoubtedly his example that inspired other arrangers to more fully exploit the possibilities in the form. By 1939 Charlie Barnet was occasionally producing more venturesome pieces, like, not surprisingly, "The Duke's Idea"; but most leaders continued to stay with the formulas that had made them successful. Goodman, in playing a fair number of works like "Superman" and "Clarinet a la King," was once again in the vanguard. He was by nature a cautious man and this more advanced music was not exactly to his taste, and as a consequence he would not continue in the direction he was going. But his example helped to inspire leaders like Stan Kenton, Woody Herman, Boyd Raeburn and Claude Thornhill to create the "progressive jazz" of the mid- to late 1940s. This music—Herman's "Early Autumn" and "Four Brothers," Kenton's "Artistry in Rhythm," Raeburn's "Boyd Meets Stravinsky," and others—brought the level of big-band music to a peak, and the fact that it was widely popular in the United States is an indication of how far popular taste had developed. The Goodman of the early Columbia period provided a stepping stone along the way.

# 22

# The Sextet

The Benny Goodman Sextet of the Charlie Christian era, which had seven musicians including Goodman, was one of the most important and influential jazz bands in the history of the music. The earlier Trios and Quartets with Wilson and Hampton were also very significant, in part because of the racial mixing, in part because of the wonderful music they produced and in part for proving that the purest kind of jazz still had a real audience in America. But the Sextet was innovative in a way that the early small groups were not. Those had brought to a peak a form which had long existed in jazz; the music of the Sextet was new and different from anything that had gone before. And, as a bonus, it contained some of the most important musicians in the history of jazz.

The group cut its first record, "Flying Home," which Hampton would go on to make a career of, in October 1939, not long after Goodman moved to Columbia. This six-piece group was a precursor to the famous Sextet. The personnel were Goodman, Hampton, Christian, bassist Artie Bernstein, drummer Nick Fatool and Fletcher Henderson on piano. In December Guarnieri replaced Henderson; but in fact Goodman at times brought in Count Basie to play on the records, although Guarnieri or the pianists that followed him played in live performances.

Then, in November 1940 Cootie Williams joined the group, and Benny put together the memorable seven-piece Sextet that cut about two dozen masterpieces. It consisted of Goodman, Christian, Williams, Auld and other rhythm players who shifted according to Goodman's moods but at various times included pianists Guarnieri, Basie and Ken Kersey; drummers Tough, Harry Jaeger and Jo Jones; and Bernstein on bass. In Goodman, Christian and Williams the group had three of the finest players of the time. It is difficult to think of many other permanently constituted small groups which contained so stunning an array of talent: perhaps only the Charlie Parker groups with at various times Miles Davis, Dizzy Gillespie and Max Roach, or the classic John Coltrane group with Jimmy Garrison, Elvin Jones and McCoy Tyner could match it.

In the Victor groups the key figure had always been Goodman, despite the brilliance of Teddy Wilson. In the Columbia Sextets the key was Charlie Christian. Young musicians today are sometimes puzzled by the high place Christian holds in jazz history; they hear more recent guitarists playing faster and using more complex ideas than Christian did. The point is that Christian cut the trail down which the new players so easily run. Christian was the one who brought the electric guitar to prominence and showed what could be done with it. Had he not played with the brilliance he did, the lesson might not have taken. The others who had used the in- strument before, and even recorded with it, collected no chain of imitators. Before Christian the instrument was seen as an eccentric novelty; after his brief flight into the sun the guitar, hitherto a subordinate member of the rhythm section, moved into a central place in jazz, and ultimately came to dominate popular music in the latter half of the twentieth century. Chris- tian's bell-like tone, the confident strength of his line, his more venture- some chords and his angular phrasing all seemed fresh and exciting to his contemporaries, and they began to track after him.

But Christian did more for the Sextet than just play his solos. In Good- man's first groups the main vehicles had been standard songs, and only as he became confident of public acceptance did he start to work out originals for the group. With the Sextet, however, almost two-thirds of the cuts were originals. It is generally conceded that Christian created many, if not most, of the melody lines for these pieces. He is given partial credit for a number of them, among them "Shivers," "AC-DC Current" and "Seven Come Eleven." According to Mary Lou Williams, she and Christian used to jam in the basement of the Dewey Square Hotel, with rats running over their feet, and a lot of the ideas produced at these sessions later appeared in Sextet pieces.[1]

The originals were almost always based on the simplest structures—the blues ("Gone With What Wind," "Boy Meets Goy," "Wholly Cats"); "Honeysuckle Rose" ("Gilly"); or variations on "I Got Rhythm." In most cases the melody lines are made up of two-measure figures, repeated the requisite number of times. Because the chord changes used for these tunes are so basic, the riffs do not require much, if any, adjustment to suit the progressions, and are frequently identical throughout. This is very simple music, unlike the more complex polyphony of the New Orleans bands, or bebop, with its advanced harmonies. Nonetheless, the lines themselves seemed novel, because of the timbre of the electric guitar playing in unison with clarinet, muted trumpet or other instruments; because of a lot of dis- placed accents; and because of more scalar movement than was customary in riffs, which usually tended to move up and down the chords. Inevitably, given the limited instrumentation, the constraints of the three-minute recording, and Goodman's penchant for working from basic material, there is a certain sameness to these records. Goodman, however, was aware of the problem and often coupled one of the uptempo riff tunes with a standard: "Flying Home" with "Rose Room"; "Boy Meets Goy" with "I Surrender Dear"; and "Six Appeal" with "These Foolish Things."

Like the Trio and Quartet sides, these Goodman Sextet records are of so consistently a high order that it is difficult to single out any for discussion. There is not a poor one in the lot—Goodman would not have let any failures be issued in any case—and many of them are brilliant. One which has always been a particular favorite of mine is "Gilly," which was also issued as "Gone With What Draft." (Several of the pieces acquired two or even three names.) The number is based on "Honeysuckle Rose," and it is made up of several riffs, with only Goodman taking a full-dress solo. The opening riff features Williams in the plunger playing a figure that consists of three tones over four measures; the accompanying figure is one note repeated. The whole thing could hardly be simpler, but it is extremely effective because of the contrast of timbres—the rather wry plunger against the hollow sound of the repeated notes. This playing with sound was important to the effect of the Sextet. The sounds of the clarinet, electric guitar, tenor saxophone and trumpet contrasted markedly, and the variousness was expanded by the fact that Williams, and to a lesser extent Goodman, was capable of producing a variety of sounds.

Following the opening riff Goodman takes a chorus, backed by a riff by guitar and saxophone; there is an interlude built on the tune's bridge, followed by a second riff, a series of tumbling figures played by Goodman, Christian and Auld, which are abbreviated to create a metric shift as they go, and which are answered by a growling Williams. The horns split "twos" on the bridge, we are given the tumbling figures again, and then a final simple riff which consists of Goodman and Christian together answering themselves in replicated two-bar figures. There is very little to any of this, but it is all very cleverly worked out with call-and-response, rapid changes of timbre, and the regular introduction of new material, so that it seems to shift like a kaleidoscope—colorful, gay and played with a swinging verve. This was precisely what Williams meant when he said the group "romped." Goodman's solo is particularly fine, made up of a series of relatively long figures, some of them four measures in length. It is a very hot solo, but at the bridge Goodman suddenly changes to a lighter mood with a series of shorter, more delicate figures, growing in intensity as he swings back into the final eight measures.

By this time Benny Goodman had been playing twenty or thirty jazz solos a night, almost every night for six years. He had played everything there was to play on the clarinet in his idiom, and a good many things that many clarinetists would have said could not be played on the instrument. He had an ease and fluidity that was the envy not only of clarinetists but of all other musicians, who were regularly faced with the frustration of conceiving ideas that they could not execute. Goodman at least seemed to have got beyond this problem, and the rest could only marvel.

One of the best of the slow standard tunes is "As Long as I Live." The tune is usually played at a jump tempo, but the Sextet played it like a ballad, slowly and with great tenderness throughout. It opens with Basie playing a sketch of the melody in his "one-finger" style. The chords for the main theme of the piece are worked out so that the third of the scale can be played throughout. Goodman takes advantage of this by playing a rapid low-register trill on the third through Basie's solo. He takes the bridge himself, playing it more or less as written. Williams has the next chorus with Christian playing the bridge, and Auld the following one with Goodman taking the bridge. It closes as it opened with eight measures of the theme played by Basie with the Goodman tremolo over him.

Williams plays his chorus in the plunger mute, as he does most of the time with the Sextet. (The plunger specialists in the Ellington band placed a small mute inside the bell when using the plunger, the purpose being in part to help steady the intonation, which will change as the plunger is opened and closed. The effect is somewhat of a plunger being used in tandem with a straight mute, which is the sound Williams gets here.)[2] It is a very thoughtful solo, particularly in the last eight, where Williams plays a figure, a variation on it to suit the new chord, and then a kind of extension of the idea for the remainder of the eight measures. We think of Williams as a rip-snorting growl specialist, or a bravura open-horn player in the Armstrong mode; but he was also capable of this sort of introspection which came close to the manner of his competitor in the Basie band, Buck Clayton.

Auld's chorus is similarly tender. Auld, too, is usually thought of as a hard-driving player with something of the sound of Ben Webster. Never considered one of the great masters of the tenor saxophone, he was nonetheless a fine improviser who developed enough of a name for himself with the public to lead his own bands, mostly small groups, for a long time after the swing era was over. His style was built around glissandos, frequently upwards and often combined with a swell, as of a balloon suddenly puffed out. His solo on "As Long as I Live" is characterized by these "balloon" effects, and carries through the tender mood established by the others. The piece as a whole is once again very simple, and gets its effect from the pensive mood that is maintained right through, and the constant passing of the melody through the band, so that no voice speaks for too long.

Charlie Christian was, of course, a dominant voice in these Sextet re-cordings and played one brilliant solo after another. Perhaps his best-known solo came on a riff tune based on the blues called "Breakfast Feud." The cut has been reissued with Christian's solos spliced in from several takes, which, however confusing to discographers, gives us a fine sample of Chris-tian at his best. We note particularly the long lines of relatively uninflected eighth notes, fairly evenly played, as for example on the first chorus on the Columbia CL30779 version, in which he plays a run of uninterrupted eighth notes from bar three into bar eight. Strings of eighth notes this long would be rare even in a piano solo.

Charlie Christian played mainly with the Sextet. He could not read mu-sic,[3] and although he certainly could have picked up the chord changes by ear, the band had a guitar book which was supposed to be followed. There is also the fact that the electric guitar would not have blended with piano and bass as well as the acoustic guitar did. Despite the fact that big-band rhythm sections usually use electronic instruments today, they never do achieve the blend that the acoustic instruments did in the hands of good players. Arnold Covey (Covarrubias) and then Mike Bryan played with the big band.

But Christian did cover for brief periods between other guitar players, and he generally took such guitar solos as there were with the band, as on a version of "Honeysuckle Rose" made in November 1939. His best-known big band piece, however, is his famous "Solo Flight," which was based on his own ideas but arranged for the band by Jimmy Mundy. It is basically a concerto for guitar, along the lines of the ones Ellington created for his star soloists and Sauter pieces such as "Superman" and "Clarinet a la King." It was originally called "Chonk, Charlie, Chonk," a name which was fortunately dropped when the piece was recorded. It is built on two simple themes, one in C, the other in F, and, aside from a relatively brief Goodman solo, features the guitar and the band.

I have never thought that "Solo Flight" was Christian's best perfor-mance. For one thing, Mundy's arrangement is very heavy-handed, con-sisting for the most part of the brass, and at times the whole band, chasing forward like a locomotive. The guitar would have been better served by a more easy-going approach. Certainly more contrast was needed. Nor do I think that Christian's playing was up to the standard of his work with the Sextet, as it hardly could be with so much slamming and banging going on around him. But a concerto for the electric guitar, as hard as it may be to believe today, was something of a novelty in 1941, and "Solo Flight" be-came one of the best known of the Goodman sides from the period.

There is one more session by the Sextet which needs to be mentioned. In October 1940, just days before Cootie Williams joined the band, Goodman brought into the studio a seven-piece Sextet consisting of men drawn from both his own band and the Basie band—Lester Young, Buck Clayton, Walter Page, Jo Jones, Basie, Christian and himself. What Goodman had in mind we do not know. He apparently saw the session as some sort of experiment, and it is my guess that he wanted to see how trumpet and tenor saxophone would work in the Sextet format in order to know how best to use Williams. Goodman never showed any interest in issuing the cuts, nor even in preserving them. According to Russ Connor they turned up years later along with a heap of other Columbia material in a second-hand store in Manhattan.[4]

It was a serendipitous find. Young, as he usually seemed to be when he was playing with white musicians, was challenged. He was in any case at a peak in his playing career, and he played as well as he ever did on that day. In my view his solo on "I Never Knew" is simply superb, one of his very finest statements. He completely eschews the little devices he would often fall back on—the alternate fingerings, the honks. It is all one seamless, direct unfaltering statement, made up of long rising and falling lines in the middle register. The phrase leading up to the bridge is almost ten measures long, an almost unheard of length for an improvised jazz phrase at a moderate tempo. Note the little figure in the ninth and tenth bars which effects a shift of meter and therefore accent and is then brushed over again immediately after. Goodman's entrance following this solo is in the Young clarinet style, and is extremely tentative, hardly a Goodman trait, and we can understand why: Young had left nobody anything else to say.

Unhappily, by the spring of 1941 the Christian Sextet was coming to an end. Christian was fatally sick and had to leave the band. He would not return. He spent his last days in Seaview Sanitarium on Staten Island, with Goodman covering his medical bills. It has been said he might have recovered but friends kept smuggling women, drugs and liquor to him, and the touches of the high life weakened him. Christian was an extremely unsophisticated young man, and it does seem possible that he would not have had the sense to see the risks in too much socializing. Whatever the case, he died in March 1942.

Cootie Williams departed at the end of October, and this famous Sextet was finished. A few days before Williams left, Goodman recorded with a new sextet, this one actually containing six men, built around his clarinet, Lou McGarity's trombone and Mel Powell's piano. The combination of clarinet and trombone is unusual: the only other well-known group I can think of which used this instrumentation was the Louisiana Five, a popular New Orleans dixieland group which recorded in 1918 at the beginning of the jazz boom with Charlie Panelli on trombone and Alcide "Yellow"

Nunez on clarinet. (This was probably a mixed band. Panelli was white, and although Nunez was officially termed a "Spaniard" he was probably of mixed blood.) It was, however, a felicitous combination because the use of quite different voices makes the lines distinct, as we can hear in the ensembles passages of, for example, "Wang, Wang Blues." However, Goodman's reason for choosing this combination was undoubtedly much simpler: he liked playing with McGarity, whose strong, driving style suited his own. This group made only a few records before the recording ban.

However short-lived, the Christian version of the Goodman Sextet made a large mark on jazz. Aside from its importance in giving Christian and Williams wide exposure, it produced a body of records, small though it was, which remains one of the little treasures of jazz.

# 23
# Marriage and Family

In 1942 Benny Goodman was thirty-two years old and had never been married. This was unusual. At the time, allowing for the temporary dislocations occasioned by the war, American men married at about the age of twenty-four, women at about twenty-one.[1] Many millions of Americans married in their teens. It was not uncommon for young people to announce engagements at the time of their high-school graduations. In staying unmarried for so long Goodman was far from the norm.

To be sure, it was not easy for a musician, who was forced to travel so much, to maintain a relationship with a woman which might lead to marriage, and to keep the marriage going once it was celebrated. Sometimes married musicians managed to bring their wives on tours, but that was not always possible, and certainly not practicable when there were children. These were young, active males, and inevitably, after a few weeks on the road, they tended to fall into casual liaisons, which sometimes became more serious, further straining longer-established relationships back home. Nonetheless, a lot of the musicians traveling with Goodman married. Art Rollini, Red Ballard, Sid Weiss, Lionel Hampton, Jimmy Maxwell, Vido Musso, Chris Griffin and others managed to keep marriages going despite the travel and other problems. In fact, it was somewhat easier for a leader to take a wife along, because he could usually afford to make relatively pleasant travel arrangements for her, whereas the wives of the sidemen would usually travel with three or four people in cars. Most of Goodman's major competitors of the swing era were married, among them the Dorseys and Glenn Miller; two others, Charlie Barnet and Artie Shaw, were notorious for marrying and divorcing repeatedly.

Goodman was, however, not celibate. He had come out of a social circumstance where sex was often taken casually and was easily available, even to fairly young boys.[2] The Chicago of Goodman's youth was being run as a wide-open town by the mobsters who bossed, among other things, an extensive prostitution trade. Furthermore, the black-and-tans that Goodman and the other youthful musicians were visiting offered a fairly erotic brand of entertainment, with a lot of semi-nudity, blue jokes, songs with sexual content, shake dances and the like. There were in or about these places women prepared to slake the thirst the shows aroused. Unlike many middle-class boys of the day, to whom sex was a dirty secret, these children of the slums and ghettos were fairly well acquainted with sex by their mid-teens. Goodman, said Carol Phillips, "was a rather sensuous guy. He was very comfortable with the flesh."[3] Goodman did not report on his sexual adventures in his memoirs, as a number of musicians of the time have. It has been said that in 1933 he was seeing a dancer named Thelma,[4] and a year or so later he was involved with Hannah Williams,[5] part of a well-known vocal duet called the Williams Sisters, which recorded with Pollack. Then, when the band went into the Music Hall in 1934, he is reported to have been involved with the beautiful Ann Graham, who occasionally sang with the band.[6]

But the big romance of the period was the one Benny had with Helen Ward—a "heavy romance," according to Benny Winestone, who was around at the time.[7] Helen was apparently in love with Benny. What Goodman's feelings were have never gone on record, but there is some information that Goodman genuinely cared for her and at least considered marrying her. But, according to Ward, now Mrs. William Savory, Benny was at this time totally focussed on his music and his career and felt that marriage would interfere with his work.[8] Eventually she left the band to marry another man, and it is possible that she was impelled to do so when she came to realize that Goodman was not ready to marry. But she and Benny remained good friends until his death, meeting from time to time, the last time just a month before he died. And she is one of the few people who worked for Benny whose fondness for him remains undiminished. Others of his compatriots from the old days today play down their ancient grievances, but their ambivalent feelings about Benny seep through; this is not the case with Helen Ward. Women, in fact, seemed to like Benny, to feel affection for him in a way that men did not, and there never was any shortage of them in his life, although there is no evidence that he was a compulsive womanizer. Aside from the fact that he married late, there appears to have been nothing out of the ordinary in Goodman's relations with women.

However, the primary influence on Goodman was his father. David Goodman was, if he was anything, a good father and fervent family man, and we can take it for granted that Goodman wanted to emulate his father in this respect and marry and have children of his own. But the choice he finally made was a strange one which surprised, and in some cases dismayed, his friends and family.

John Hammond had four older sisters, but his favorite was Alice, the third oldest. He said:

> My third sister Alice was the family rebel. She had a sharp wit and a fanciful way of embroidering a narrative. She would tell the family one quarter of the truth about her escapades, a fraction so horrifying that they could not imagine anything worse. Alice, of course, fascinated me and became my favorite sister.[9]

Alice, in turn, was attracted to the Bohemian life her younger brother had chosen and "was always fascinated by my friends in music and the theatre."[10] The Hammond family, we must remember, was dominated by the mother, Cornelius Vanderbilt's great-granddaughter. She succeeded in imposing her rigid morality on all the others, including her husband. John and Alice's father was "by no means master of his own house, exercising his authority only occasionally, and otherwise accepting the house rules laid down by my mother."[11] The net effect was that the children of the household were eager to get away from these constraints as soon as they could. This was a time when a new, open spirit was in the air—a time of freer sexuality, open drinking, dancing, going to cabarets to hear jazz, and the rest of it. It was precisely the moment when young people would be exceedingly restless under the firm hand of a Victorian teetotaler. John, as we have seen, moved out of the mansion into Greenwich Village the moment he became twenty-one and had money of his own, and the girls married as quickly as they could. Alice became engaged to a man who later married one of her sisters when she was eighteen or nineteen, and then in 1927 she married a man who would not only take her out of the house but out of the United States. He was George Arthur Duckworth, a Tory member of the British Parliament.[12] She took up residence in England, and had three girls, who would eventually become Benny's step-children. But the marriage failed, and in the late 1930s she was back in the United States with the children—in part, undoubtedly, to safeguard them against the impending war.

Alice had met Benny Goodman briefly on a visit to New York in 1934. John Hammond had brought her around to the Music Hall, and had introduced them casually, but Benny, typically, quickly forgot the meeting.[13] Then in 1939 or 1940 Goodman went out to Westchester County to visit Hammond at the gentleman's farm which Hammond's father maintained in Mount Kisco. Alice was there, and that was the beginning.[14]

It was, from any viewpoint, a very strange match. Benny Goodman was a rough-edged son of immigrants, a Jew, a jazz musician with little formal education. Alice was from one of the great American families, raised to a style and manner which few Americans would recognize, much less emulate. Among other things, people of this class in that day by reflex avoided Jews, and many were openly anti-Semitic. Further, the folkways of people of old wealth are several removes from those of the middle class. Embedded in them are customs and rituals the meaning of which may escape even fairly attentive observers, but which exist primarily to mark off the outsider from those born to the select group. They are lost on most people who come into contact with these old moneyed families, who do not even realize that they are being snubbed. Goodman and Alice Hammond had come from opposite ends of the social scale, and although Goodman was by 1939 rich and famous, a big name in America, this by itself was not enough to bridge the large cultural gap between the two of them. Alice had, furthermore, spent the previous ten or twelve years living in England, which widened the gap even more. They did not, really, have much in common.

Yet interestingly enough, somebody like Benny Goodman would actually be more acceptable to people like the Hammonds than a person from the middle class. Goodman could be seen by them not as somebody a few rungs down the ladder aggressively trying to push his way up, but as an exotic, an Arab prince, or a Chinese philosopher might be viewed—somebody whose folkways were so removed from theirs that he became a curiosity.

Once it was clear that Benny and Alice were serious about each other, a lot of people became concerned. One of these was John Hammond. The relationship between Goodman and Hammond was always stormy and grew worse in later years, when Hammond was prepared to say quite bitter things about Goodman.[15] Hammond of course admired Goodman's playing and he had been important in getting Goodman his start toward wealth and fame. They were, in a sense, allies rather than friends, and as in most alliances, there were frictions. Among other things, Hammond always felt free to leap into print with criticism of his brother-in-law. He wrote, for example, that Benny "no longer defies convention by breaking down racial barriers, and thinks primarily of the commercial appeal of his music."[16] This sort of thing could hardly have endeared Hammond to Goodman, although no doubt he came to expect it.

In his autobiography Hammond gives the whole story of the marriage only a passing brush over, saying only that "Alice had divorced Arthur Duckworth, and in 1942 she and Benny were married." He added that his parents liked Benny and "gave the marriage their blessing."[17] He does not go on to say that he blessed the marriage as well, and it is clear enough from this and other sources that he was not entirely pleased.

Why Alice Hammond Duckworth was attracted to Goodman is hard to know. He had that streak of peasant coarseness that would not be well taken by her social group; he was a penny-pincher; and of course there

were the considerable cultural differences. But in all the furor over Goodman's treatment of his musicians, and his general fear of being taken, we
must keep it in mind that he could, when he wanted to, be a very person-
able man. He was overgenerous with his children; he did give money to
people in trouble, as the cases of Jimmy Maxwell and Bunny Berigan suggest; he had private philanthropies that few people knew about; and he
could be pleasant and charming in the right circumstances. The three
women in his life about whom we know the most—Helen Ward, Alice
Hammond and Carol Phillips—were all handsome women with a good
deal of style and attainments of their own, and both Hammond and Phillips belonged to the upper echelons of American society. Women of this
kind do not need to put up with brutes and boors, no matter how rich and
celebrated. They clearly knew a pleasanter and more charming Benny
Goodman than the sidemen saw.

For her part, Alice was, like her brother John, a rebel, and she may have
found the idea of marrying somebody so socially inappropriate satisfying a
need to shock. Mel Powell said, "John and probably Alice were of a very
special kind of Vanderbilt, and that is there was a bit of rebel in both of
them. So part of Alice's rebellion would be the marriage to a Jewish
clarinet player."[18]

For another thing, Goodman was part of the world of show business,
which had always had a certain fascination for Alice.[19] It needs to be
pointed out that in the years when Alice was growing up, musicians, actors
and vaudevillians were considered outcasts, a disreputable rabble not much
above prostitutes and drug addicts. Working people might well aspire to
become dance-band musicians or vaudeville dancers, but for a middle-class
youth to do so was to drop down the social ladder. For someone of Alice's
class, it was unthinkable. By 1942 this attitude had changed to an extent;
show business had gained a measure of respectability. But the old disdain
for show people lingered, and Alice clearly found entry into this slightly
disreputable, but somewhat freer world, attractive.

For a third thing, Benny Goodman was both famous and rich. Outside
her own circle, where her antecedents were known, it was much better to
be introduced as Mrs. Benny Goodman than as Alice Duckworth. The fact
that Goodman had his own money mattered, too. The rich cannot help
suspecting that people of ordinary means are seeking their friendship
mainly for money. Goodman, then, might not have suited every woman
in Alice's social class; but he suited her.

If John Hammond was somewhat perturbed by the affair, the Goodman
family was dismayed. Benny, after all, had been the principal breadwinner
of the family for perhaps fifteen years. He had put some of his brothers
into a business which was earning them a good deal of money, and he had

supported others, as well as their mother; and with his growing wealth and celebrity could do a great deal more for them. They felt in their bones that if Benny were to move into the Hammond social circle they would lose him; or rather, they would be shucked off like out-worn clothes. But there was little anybody could do about it, and on March 21, 1942, Alice and Benny were married in Reno, Nevada.

As might have been predicted, the marriage of such opposing types was not without problems. Alice was raised always to exhibit civility, and many of the musicians, who did not understand her world very well, liked her. Sid Weiss said, "I knew Alice. She was a charming person," and his wife Mae said,

> She was unpretentious. People were in awe of her, knowing she was a Lady. [This was not the case: Duckworth was not a peer.] She was always knitting. She used to make his socks, argyle socks. She never dressed in a way, you know, high couture. One day we were at rehearsal and we went to the ladies room. I admired the coat she had on, she had a beautiful coat that was very British-looking, lovely tailoring, and I said to her, "Such an attractive coat you have." She said, "Oh, do you really like it? My sister sent it to me. When she gets tired of her coats she just mails them to me." . . . She put everyone at ease by being, not self-effacing, but natural. . . . Many people thought she might be stand-offish, but she wasn't.[20]

And Mel Powell said, "I adored Alice. Alice was everything that you ascribe to the word charming. Light, vivacious, all those good words. She would radiate all those attributes. She, on the other hand, was all civility, highly sophisticated. She was like an old shoe—marvelous combination."[21]

This civility, this ease with people who were not from her own social stratum was not, however, so much a matter of unpretentiousness but what her social group would have called breeding. She had been taught never to be discourteous to servants and the lower orders in general. In particular, it was a rule in her group never to make a show, especially in regard to material possessions. Such people do not dress like movie stars or high fashion models. It is all low-key and in quiet good taste, and they do indeed think it only sensible to accept hand-me-downs which still have a lot of wear in them.

What the musicians were seeing, then, was breeding: it was Alice's social duty to be pleasant, and she would no more have put on airs with the musicians than she would have belched in public. But behind that breeding was a good deal of iron. Alice Goodman was a far more formidable woman than the picture drawn by the musicians suggests. For one thing, she apparently took it as a matter of right that she would dominate the household. She came from a line of women who were used to running things. Her mother had told her father where and when he could drink and smoke, and her grandmother had been a daring and imperious woman, who made her own Fifth Avenue mansion a "haven"[22] for her Hammond grandchildren when they needed to escape the restrictions their mother enforced in their own house. At Alice's grandmother's, her boy friends could get a drink. Alice was from birth used to seeing women rule.

For a second thing, she was well aware that Benny needed a lot of making over before he would really be suited to the family he married into. Among other things, she would have to draw Benny away from his family. It was one thing to make over a husband, an entirely different matter to take on a large and unruly brood, including a mother who was illiterate. Given the somewhat asperious relationship between Benny and his brothers, it was not difficult to pull Benny away from the family. Relations between the brothers became less than cordial. Harry sniped at Benny for his penny-pinching, and Benny complained about Harry's bass-playing. "All I can hear is piano bass," he told Jess Stacy.[23] Eventually Mamma moved back to Chicago.

The truth is, however, that Benny was willing to be made over. James T. Maher spoke of Benny's "sense of style and class," which was part of his makeup from quite early in life. Goodman had seen his father coming home exhausted and stinking from having spent the day shoveling raw fat at the stockyards, and he had determined early to get away from that. Now he was a member of a family at the very pinnacle of the social system, and he began trying to learn their ways.[24] It was bringing up Papa," Powell said, referring to the famous Maggie and Jiggs cartoon. "Alice taught Benny a great deal about a lot of things."[25]

The first and most obvious manifestation was a change in his manner of speaking. Art Rollini, speaking of the early 1930s when he first got to know Benny, said, "In those days Benny had a Chicago accent. Years later he developed an affected Park Avenue 'society' accent."[26] This was the somewhat nasal drawl used by the old families of the American Northeast. Goodman began to adopt it, probably before he met Alice, for use in appropriate circumstances. It is not evident on the *Camel Caravan* broadcasts from the late thirties, although he may already have been using it in other places, but it can be heard on recorded interviews from later periods. It has been reported that he took elocution lessons, and it is certainly true that, when he could afford it, he began sometimes buying the most expensive sort of British tailoring. Maher says, "Now, he did develop a very, very suave presence and manner, and had all kinds of mannerisms, speech mannerisms, that could be very warm and jolly and intimate, and then the next time, all of a sudden it sounds like you're talking to a don of Christ Col-

lege." Maher also said that Goodman had been observed by his old sidemen
to switch from the old mode of speech and presentation—"address," as it
has been termed—to the new one when somebody of Alice's social circle
came in.[27]

It is, of course, a very old tale, the kid from the bottom who is determined not only to rise to the top but, by aping the manners he finds
around him there, to show that he is worthy. He would become one of
them, and to an extent he did.

Nonetheless, given the disparity of their formative experiences, the marriage of Benny and Alice must necessarily have contained strains. Benny
was apparently a little afraid of Alice. At least some of the musicians disliked having her come on the road with them because her presence made
Benny tense, and the band would feel the effects. She would sit at a table
and knit, as a consequence of which the composer Alec Wilder began to
call her Madame Defarge, a name which caught on. Benny at times chafed
under Alice's authority.

But the marriage lasted until Alice's death in 1978, and from the outside
it appears to have been a reasonably good one. Mel Powell said, "She
adored, idolized, she thought there was no one more important in the
world than Benny."[28] Mae Weiss said, "They were very warm together.
He really deferred to her. He deferred to her, as absent-minded as he was,
he was always very conscious of her being there. He deferred to her, although she didn't make a big thing out of it, either."[29]

James T. Maher told an illuminating story about their relationship:

> We [Maher and Goodman] were having lunch one day at a lovely
> French restaurant. It was rather narrow, and there were banquets against
> the wall going back. So Benny and I were having lunch and all of a
> sudden he looked up and said, "My God, there's Alice." Alice was
> having lunch with somebody, and they were on the far end of the room
> on the opposite wall. So Benny said, "Have you got a pencil?" and he
> sat down and wrote her a mash note, and sent it to her. And she sent
> a sexy little note to him right back.[30]

Benny Goodman appears to have been a good father. He took on responsibility for his three Duckworth step-daughters and treated them as his
own. "He adored, loved" his own children, Rachel and Benjie, "dearly,"
Mel Powell said. Rachel especially has been concerned about her father's
ultimate reputation. "She just worships her father, she's doing everything
she can to preserve his memory,"[31] Powell said. My own brief exchanges
with Rachel would bear this out.

Benny Goodman was not a perfect husband and father. He could be moody and withdrawn at times—"difficult." But he had nonetheless before him the image of his own father. His family was important to him, and he was determined to do right by them. On the whole, then, we can say that Goodman was as good a family man as most, and better than a good many, without question.

# 24

# An Era Ends

One of the major upheavals in the world of the swing bands in the 1940s was not the arrival of a new style or the emergence of new bands, but something extra-musical. It had begun to occur to the president of the national musician's union, James C. Petrillo, a musician from Chicago who had risen in union politics, that mechanical entertainment would eventually cut drastically into the employment of musicians. In the 1920s, as we have seen, the demand for dance bands of any kind was so strong that salaries were driven to extraordinary heights, with top players earning as much as the president of the United States. But beginning in about 1930, radio and sound films threw the music business into total disarray. Tens of thousands of musicians were out of work, and the record industry nearly foundered. In about 1934 the juke box suddenly caught hold and all across the country was replacing more thousands of musicians in taverns and small restaurants that had previously employed pianists, trios and other entertainment. By 1937 there were 150,000 juke boxes operating in the United States.[1]

The swing-band boom at least temporarily masked the inroads that mechanical entertainment was making into the music profession. Swing bands, employing twelve to fifteen musicians in 1940, were providing a great deal of work, and once the draft began snatching men off band stands, it was the glory days all over again with salaries skyrocketing. But it did not take a great deal of prescience to see that once the war was over there would be far too many musicians around for the amount of work available.

In particular, the phenomenon of the disk jockey was growing at an alarming rate. The successes of the early disk jockeys like Al Jarvis and Martin Block had quickly been imitated by others. Records, donated free by the record companies, were an obvious source of very cheap program-ming; why hire an orchestra of local players when you could have Benny

Goodman, Glenn Miller, Duke Ellington on disc for nothing? Petrillo saw the dangers, and of course he was absolutely right. By the 1960s the proliferation of devices for the mechanical reproduction of entertainment had produced a condition where the bulk of musicians were part-timers, dependent upon what musicians still call "day jobs"; and by the 1980s conditions had reached the point where the union had given up even trying to enforce pay scales in all but a handful of major venues.

In 1940 Petrillo saw that the main problem lay with recordings, which were, effectively, being supplied to the public free through the mediums of radio and juke boxes. (The public paid a nickel a time to play a record on a juke box, but none of that money reached the musicians.) Petrillo wanted some compensation from the record industry, and he decided to pull records out of the juke boxes and off the air unless his demands were met. However, he quickly saw that this was going to be difficult. There was no law preventing people from doing whatever they wanted with a record once they had purchased it, including playing it on the air. Petrillo then concluded that the only effective way to force concessions out of the music industry was to shut down the record companies. After several months of huffing and puffing on both sides, on August 1, 1942, Petrillo ordered the musicians to stay out of the recording studios, which his mandate from the union board allowed him to do.[2] V-discs cut for the armed forces were an exception.

Not all of the musicians agreed with Petrillo's reasoning; in fact, probably a majority opposed the ban. But Petrillo had the power to enforce it, and in any case there were many musicians who did agree with him.

The record companies were much more unhappy than the musicians, the bulk of whose work consisted of live performances. The Big Three—Columbia, Decca and Victor, who constituted almost the entire recording industry—had a fair amount of stock in their files, and, as the deadline rolled toward them, they raced the orchestras under contract into the studios to cut whatever they could. Goodman cut three sides on July 27, including his hit coupling of "Six Flats Unfurnished" and "Why Don't You Do Right?" and four more on July 30, among them "Mission to Moscow." The record companies were determined to hold firm, and as stockpiles dwindled in 1943, they began to record singers who were not in the musicians' union with choral backgrounds; Bing Crosby, Frank Sinatra, and Dick Haymes were among those who were recorded in this way.

As it happened, the ban worked to the advantage of jazz fans, for in order to develop product, the Big Three began reissuing long out-of-print masterpieces from the 1920s and 1930s, including sets of Armstrong's Hot Five, various Beiderbecke groups, early Ellingtons, Morton's classic Red Hot Peppers, some Red Nichols combinations, and, not least, the Bennie

Goodman and His Boys sides with Glenn Miller, featuring what were now two of the biggest names of the swing era. These records did not sell in massive quantities but they did well enough to prove that there was an audience for the older music, and eventually led to regular reissue programs that gave a new generation, attuned to the swing bands, an awareness of the virtues of the earlier jazz.

Decca, founded in 1934, had a much smaller backlist than Columbia and Victor, who had, among other things, extensive stocks of classical music which did not date as pop music did. In the fall of 1943, after about fifteen months, Decca made a deal with the union.[3] Victor and Columbia were still determined to fight on, and not until 1944 did they finally settle with the union. For Goodman, the consequence was that he made no formal recordings, aside from V-discs from mid-1942 until November 1944.

However much the record ban disrupted the music industry, the war did much worse. There was a certain feeling in the government that dance bands were needed for morale, to keep both servicemen and civilians cheered up, but draft boards did not necessarily follow this line. Goodman was deferred because of his back problems, but many of his men were taken, among them Mel Powell and trombonist Cutty Cutshall.[4] Finally, in the fall of 1943, the government issued its "work or fight" edict, which required men to go into industry or risk being drafted. One who felt the force of this edict was Vido Musso, who was told by his draft board to take a war job or face immediate induction.[5]

Furthermore, in October 1942, the government put limits on travel, and the next month introduced gas rationing.[6] Space on trains jammed with servicemen being moved around the country was at a premium, and over the next months tires and other replacement parts for buses and cars became harder and harder to get. When it came to a choice, the government had to see that workers driving to war plants had what was needed to keep their cars moving—no new cars were made after 1941—rather than keep a swing band on the road. The one-nighter almost disappeared. Bandleaders much preferred location jobs, where they could sit down for weeks at a time, even at lower fees, than struggle with the problems of transportation.

Yet despite everything, for those leaders who could keep going, and for the musicians who managed to stay out of the armed forces, the war years were a time of prosperity. Bookers were desperate for any kind of entertainment and willing to pay what they had to. There was a lot of money around. People working in war plants, especially those with critical skills, like welders and machinists, could command huge salaries, and in any case millions of workers were putting in a lot of overtime at salaries which seemed fantastic to working people who only a few years before were struggling to hang onto jobs at rock-bottom wages. There was nothing to spend this money on—no new cars, no new houses, none of the huge assortment of durables that would become available after the war. Furthermore, there was a *carpe diem* spirit in the air. Who knew when you, or your boy friend, would be drafted and shipped off to fight and perhaps die? The swing bands—and show business in general—benefitted.

But Benny Goodman was no longer really the King of Swing. He was now just one among many—one of the most popular, certainly, but not inevitably at the head of the pack. Duke Ellington was now winning the majority of the *Down Beat* polls, both Dorsey orchestras were crowding him, Harry James was "rated as the hottest B.O. attraction,"[7] and the Glenn Miller Orchestra, until Miller disbanded it to join the service, was probably the most widely popular of them all. By early in 1943 the music press was saying that Goodman had entered "a period of decline which had him changing personnel almost nightly and had critics wondering whether Goodman was at the beginning of the end. . . ."[8]

The end had not yet come, however. In December 1942, Bob Crosby broke up his band in Boston, and Jess Stacy, despite what had happened, rejoined Goodman the next night. By summer Benny had a number of old hands back, among them Hymie Schertzer, Ralph Muzzillo, Allan Reuss, along with some of the veterans of the early days, like Miff Mole and drummer George Wettling. The *Down Beat* reviewer said of an opening at the Astor Hotel, "Looking like the proverbial million dollars and really working at his music, Benny brought the crowd in just as always, and the swarms of youthful and enthusiastic fans around the bandstand reminded more than one old-timer in the music game of the days in the 1930s."[9]

Another of the old hands made a dramatic return to the band, if only for a brief stay. That was Gene Krupa, who in the spring of 1943 was arrested on a drug charge that got heavy coverage in the national press. Precisely what happened is difficult to know with any certainty: Krupa's story differs somewhat from what was reported in the press. It should be remembered that marijuana was at the time a substance that the vast majority of Americans had never seen, much less smoked, and was generally viewed as a dangerous drug that could bring on a frenzy. It was, however, much better known to jazz musicians, and show business people in general, than it was to the public. The lyrics to jazz songs and the blues were rife with references to it, and most jazz musicians had at least experimented with it. It was well known that Louis Armstrong smoked it on a daily basis, and was once convicted for possession.[10]

Police of course were aware that musicians were likely to use marijuana, and from time to time they investigated. According to Russ Connor,[11] Krupa was tipped off that a police search of his band was imminent. He

told his bandboy to check everybody out and flush whatever of the drug
he found down the toilet. The bandboy collected the marijuana but, instead of disposing of it, kept it. He was caught and arrested. However, he
skipped town, and when he failed to turn up for sentencing, it came out
that he was an alien, technically a minor and a draft dodger. Because he
was a minor Krupa was held responsible for his behavior, and he was
charged with possession of the drug and impairing the morals of a minor.
The first charge was dismissed, but the second one was sustained, and
Krupa eventually was sentenced to ninety days in San Quentin. However,
the charge was reversed on appeal, and Krupa ended up spending only
eighty-six days in jail.

The newspaper stories are a little different,[12] for they say that the bandboy claimed he had been given six hundred and fifty dollars "to get out of
town," presumably so he could not testify against Krupa. These stories also
said that Krupa had sent the bandboy back to the hotel to bring the drug
to him. This, in any case, was how the jazz press, which was fundamentally
sympathetic to Krupa, reported the story. Whatever the truth, the jazz
world felt that Krupa had been unfairly picked out for prosecution because
he was a celebrated musician, because he was not in the service and because his drumming style suggested that perhaps he was in a drug-induced
frenzy when he played his famous solos. The episode was disastrous for
him, for it destroyed his band, exhausted his finances and, he believed,
might have irreparably damaged his reputation with the dance-band public.

Goodman, like other people in the jazz world, was quick to support
Krupa. He immediately said, "You know, he's a wonderful guy, and a wonderful drummer. Anytime, any place, anywhere he wants his old job back,
it's his."[13] Krupa, unsure how the public would react if he put together
another band, took Goodman up on his offer. He joined the Goodman
band in the fall for a U.S.O. tour of army and navy bases. According to Sid
Weiss, who was with the band at the time:

> Some big mucky-muck at one of the bases, a naval base I think, said
> that no way could Gene Krupa get on that stage. So Benny said, "No
> Gene Krupa, no band." There would have been a riot, really. He played
> toward the end of the tour—it was a big U.S.O. tour we did, we did
> other things, too, we did a guest shot with Al Jolson, but towards the
> end of the tour we played at Annapolis in a big concrete amphitheater,
> and we played "Sing, Sing, Sing" during the course of the evening—
> packed of course. And when we came to the part where he started play-
> ing that drum solo, he went on for ten or fifteen minutes. And I mean
> it was really great, it was out of this world. And [Goodman] gave the
> signal for the band to come in, and you couldn't hear, the applause was
> so tremendous that I couldn't even hear Gene, and I was standing right

next to him. So Benny had to wave the band out and Gene played for another ten minutes.[14]

Weiss also felt that as a rhythm player Krupa was never better than during this period because the traumatic experience had humbled him.

> Gene had all that humility. And he played under the band. It was just unbelievable what he did, oh Jesus. Again that was one of those times when I couldn't wait to get to work at night. His control, his sensitivity, his ears—during that period I'm talking about, when he had all that humility. Of course Benny hired him for scale. It's no denigration of Benny. He's a businessman, too.[15]

However, Krupa and Goodman, although there was a sense of old comradeship between them, remained a little wary of each other, and when the Goodman band closed at the New Yorker Hotel on December 11, Krupa went to Dorsey at the Paramount. "Gene's joining Tommy was not advertised, for Gene was apprehensive of the reception he might get from a more general audience than he'd faced in the New Yorker. So once more the pit lift rose in the Paramount, and as the audience caught sight of Gene, they rose to give him a 20-minute standing ovation. Gene wept with joy."[16] Krupa eventually re-established his band, and went on to a long success in music.

The year 1943 had begun well, but once again the moment would not last. In its August 15, 1943, issue *Down Beat* ran a famous front-page story which it headlined, " 'Ray' Upsets Goodman Band." Mole, Harris, Wettling, bass saxophonist Joe Rushton and bassist Jimmy Stutz left. Four vocalists followed one another swiftly. *Down Beat*'s Amy Lee wrote:

> Miff Mole has handed in his notice. Miff was showing all the rest how to play jazz trombone and make it beautiful before anybody heard of Benny Goodman. Taking Miff's choruses away from him and turning them into clarinet choruses didn't look right to Miff. . . . Joe Harris has handed in his notice. Trying to play solos while the King argued with another band member didn't help Joe's morale. Joe used to do a pretty nice job of singing with the old Goodman band. Benny has taken over many solos that would normally be Harris's. Joe Rushton has handed in his notice. He got rather tired of hearing about being tired of the bass sax in the band.[17]

It was this kind of behavior which puzzled—and still puzzles—jazz writers and Goodman fans. He had in his band some of the best of the swing-band musicians, men with long experience who could read anything and play hot solos. He was playing the kind of music he wanted to play. Dance-band fans had been educated up to a new level, as critics recognized even then. *Metronome*, in an article under Lionel Hampton's byline, pointed out that a lot of music the critics in 1942 were calling commercial would have been considered good stuff a few years earlier. "Maybe the public is still 'square' at heart, but it's accepting good jazz more today than ever before. . . . Today even bands like Kay Kyser are playing the brand of music that Benny started to popularize."[18]

Goodman had everything going his way. He was celebrated, rich, possessed of a first-rate musical organization and free, within limits of course, to make the kind of music he liked. Instead of enjoying the band, he groused about the men, picked at them for small mistakes, gave them that glare, and in general failed to understand that they had human feelings. So the musicians came and went.

Next Goodman began to quarrel with M.C.A., who had been handling the band since 1935. Willard Alexander's early faith in the band had been critical to its success, and whatever else might be said about M.C.A., it had provided Goodman with excellent management. Through the last months of 1943 Goodman wrangled with the agency, trying to get out of his contract in order to go to William Morris. Finally, on March 9, 1944, he put the entire band on notice, and announced that he was willing to wait out the remaining two years of his contract. He said, "I'm tired of working hard, doing six shows a day in theatres and stuff like that. I'd like to take it easy for a while. You know, be a family man."[19] It is true that his first child Rachel had been born ten months earlier, and that undoubtedly played a role in his decision. M.C.A., for its part, said, "Benny was dissatisfied with many things for the past year or so, but so are most people these days. If Benny wants to take a long vacation, that's his business. But if he works, he works for us."[20]

For several months Goodman did very little but rest, enjoy his family, play a few dates. He made some V-discs with pick-up groups, cut the music for the Walt Disney movie *Make Mine Music*, and made occasional radio broadcasts, especially for the Armed Forces Radio Service and with pick-up groups. In the fall he put together a quintet with Red Norvo, Teddy Wilson, Sid Weiss, drummer Morey Feld, and vocalist Peggy Mann, for a kind of variety show produced by his old boss, Billy Rose, called the *Seven Lively Arts*. He stayed with the show into March 1945, playing occasional broadcasts along the way. One of these featured winners of the second *Esquire* poll and included Louis Armstrong playing from New Orleans, Duke Ellington from Los Angeles and Goodman from New York. Armstrong and Goodman both played along with Ellington's "Things Ain't What They Used to Be"; Goodman, listening to the others through earphones, at one point heard his own clarinet in the loudspeakers in the Los

Angeles hall, and thinking he was hearing Armstrong, played answers to himself.[21]

What sort of music were these wartime Goodman bands playing? There were of course no formal recordings, but there are available a number of airchecks from various locations and in particular a lot of material from Goodman's Armed Forces Radio Service shows.

The bands that Benny Goodman had during the record-ban period of the war years were exceedingly good. They played the arrangements accurately and with verve, and they contained some very fine jazz soloists—at one time or another Billy Butterfield, Jimmy Maxwell, Chris Griffin, Al Klink, Miff Mole, Zoot Sims, Bill Harris, Jess Stacy, Ernie Caceres, and others. The band of the fall of the 1943, for example, had Klink and Harris, and a wonderful rhythm section of Stacy, Krupa, Allan Reuss and Sid Weiss. As time went on, Goodman more and more returned to the older men, even though they were likely to be higher paid, in part because they were less likely to be drafted than the younger ones and in part because they were more experienced musicians. By this time a lot of musicians who at the beginning of the swing era had been a little shaky in their ability to read and not thoroughly proficient on their instruments had picked up thousands of hours of playing time on increasingly more difficult arrangements. There now existed in the United States a large cadre of highly skilled dance-band musicians who could read almost anything at sight, play a full dynamic range, handle a variety of mutes, blend with a section almost by instinct and play hot solos when called upon to do so. These players had developed saxophone technique, building on the advances of the pioneers Rudy Wiedoeft, Art Ralton, Clyde Doerr, and a few others, which was making the saxophone into one of the dominant instruments of the twentieth century.

They had also brought about an astonishing development of brass technique. Before the rise of the modern dance band, brass instruments were almost invariably played in "fanfare," quasi-military manner, generally loud and forceful. The dance-band brass played plenty of loud, forceful passages, but they also had to be able to play dulcet ballad melodies and backgrounds for vocalists, and they developed a dynamic range, and a skill at legato playing that had hitherto been considered beyond the capacity of the brasses. When the swing band era ended, the brasses were being played quite differently from the way they had been played in the first modern dance bands. The technical skills of these dance-band musicians were amazing, and Goodman was turning to the seasoned players. We find, for example, in a mid-1944 band Hymie Schertzer, Art Rollini, Vernon Brown, Billy Butterfield, Charlie Shavers, Teddy Wilson, Cozy Cole, Weiss and

Reuss, all experienced men, nearly half of whom had been with Goodman before the war.

But despite the quality of the people in the band, Goodman was increasingly featuring himself to the exclusion of the others, at times taking more than one chorus for himself and allotting only eight to sixteen bars to everybody else. Only Jess Stacy was getting any reasonable solo space. Goodman had also come to think of himself as a singer. He had sense enough to realize that he did not have the warm, supple voice required for ballads and used other vocalists for the sentimental pop songs he was required to play—Art Lund, Ray Dorey, and others. But he generally sang the uptempo novelty numbers himself, tunes like "Paducah" and "Minnie's in the Money," which came from the movies he was appearing in. He had a pleasant, husky voice, but it was totally untrained and did not project well. There is a certain amateurish quality to his singing which does not fit with the high professionalism of the rest of his music.

His dominance of the band continued into the Quintet, which had become for the most part simply a four-piece rhythm section backing Goodman, although in some versions it had Red Norvo instead of a guitarist. The pianist, usually Stacy or Wilson, did of course solo, and bass or drums might have brief breaks, but essentially they had become showcases for Goodman's clarinet.

Furthermore, the arrangements, at least the ones Goodman tended to play, were less interesting than many that had come before. This was in part because Goodman knew, or believed, that a lot of the younger players he was forced to use would have trouble playing the more difficult ones. A contributing factor was that by 1942 Eddie Sauter was suffering from a very serious case of tuberculosis which threatened to kill him. According to Sauter, during Charlie Christian's final days Charlie would during recording sessions come into the engineering room to rest on the sofa, coughing steadily, and this is how he picked up the disease.[22] Goodman kept him on salary for some time, but Sauter's work for the band was curtailed. He turned out what arrangements he could through 1943, but in 1944 he left, although he continued to arrange for Goodman from time to time. His reasons for leaving were not only medical. He said, "After awhile though, it got so that I couldn't hear one note going to another, it was too repetitive, too much of the same thing. I just had to stop it."[23]

It is probably true that this sort of emotional fatigue was afflicting others as well. The carefully thought-out interplay of sections which had been the hallmark of the band's music before was less in evidence. Yet the band was actually playing the music very well, and Goodman himself was in excellent form. The influence of Lester Young, whatever it had come to, was going. Goodman was playing with fire and drive, frequently using his upper register, which had developed in strength. And his facility had increased. There now seemed to be nothing he could not play at any possible tempo. Yet taken altogether, the music from this period is not up to that of the early Victors or the Columbias before the record ban. There were really too many problems to be overcome.

As we have seen, Goodman was without a permanent band through 1944. But by the beginning of 1945 it was clear that the war in Europe was about over, and that the Japanese, although still dug in and fighting, were defeated. The record ban, too, ended late in 1944. Goodman would not be free of his M.C.A. contract until September 1945, but he decided to organize a band anyway; he would pay M.C.A. the required percentage but would otherwise let them have nothing to do with the band.[24]

The new orchestra was built around a group of younger musicians, many of whom never established themselves as important jazz players. But it did include guitarist Mike Bryan, who would be with Goodman off and on for some time; drummer Morey Feld from the previous group; trumpeter Sonny Berman, who would be a star with Woody Herman and who would die very young from drug abuse; and Trummy Young, who had been a star with Jimmie Lunceford for some time.

The band opened at the Paramount Theatre in March 1945, eight years after the great triumph there of 1937. Goodman made his own deal with the Paramount's Bob Weitman.[25] The engagement was a popular success, and early reviews were hopeful. Metronome said that it was "obviously a promising band, we'll have to hear a lot more of it. . . ."[26] But as the weeks wore on reviews of the band's recordings in the music-business press were lukewarm, and stories of fuss and feathers within the band increased. Throughout the first five months of the band's life there were constant changes of personnel. Among others, Schertzer, Griffin and Freeman all came back for brief stays. Finally in November Goodman brought in nine new men to open at the Terrace Room in Newark, New Jersey, among them Stan Getz and Kai Winding, who would go on to become celebrated jazz musicians, and trumpeters Johnny Best and Conrad Gozzo, both of whom became highly respected professionals. In December there were five more newcomers, including trumpeter Bernie Privin, reedman Peanuts Hucko, and old hands Billy Butterfield and Mel Powell. In January there were eight new men, among them Lou McGarity and, of all people, Mannie Klein, and in February there were more changes, with Nate Kazebier being another surprise.

There was a lot of turnover in the Sextet as well. In February 1945 it consisted of Goodman, Norvo, Wilson, Bryan, Feld and bassist Slam Stewart. By May Norvo and Stewart were gone; by August Wilson was out; in September Norvo and Stewart were back; by January they were gone again, and so was Mike Bryan, so that of the original group only Goodman remained.

Some of these personnel shifts were caused by the fact that certain musicians would not, or could not, travel and were used by Goodman mainly for recording. Other musicians, especially the blacks, disliked playing in the South, and would avoid making tours there as much as possible. Nonetheless, the restless changing of personnel had become unreasonable. In the year since this new band had been founded, a roster of some of the best musicians of the period had passed through it: trumpeters Berman, Griffin, and Butterfield, saxophonists Freeman and Getz, trombonists Young, Winding and McGarity. Whether these men quit or were fired does not really matter. The fault was Goodman's, and there was no possibility that he could develop a first-rate band with this much turmoil inside it.

It is possible that Goodman was affected by the complaints of the critics, who were coming down hard on the band's recordings. *Metronome* liked Powell's "Clarinade,"[27] and *Down Beat* said, "It's pretty in spots, listenable throughout and seldom if ever jazz."[28] *Metronome* disliked "Gotta Be This or That."[29] *Down Beat* was lukewarm on a coupling of "Omph Fah Fah" and "Slipped Disc" by the Sextet.[30] The critics tended to be more enthusiastic about the small-group records, but there was a feeling that Goodman was grinding some very old cornmeal. In May 1946, Barry Ulanov, writing in *Metronome*, said, "The Benny Goodman show which ran for seven weeks at the New York Paramount would have been a sensation in 1935. As late as 1941 it would have been interesting. But by 1946 it was a good deal less than neither [sic] of these qualities."[31] Three months later the paper headed a long, unfavorable report on the band with the line, "The King of Swing Abdicates."[32] George Simon, also writing for *Metronome*, differed: "Benny's band, now playing more modern, interesting arrangements, many by Mel Powell, would turn out to be Goodman's finest in years."[33] But this was a minority report.

The band still was playing with accuracy and sometimes enthusiasm, and Goodman's own work was as brilliant as ever. The problem was the material they were working with. Through 1945 and 1946 about 60 percent of the numbers Goodman was playing were current pops, some of them fairly good tunes, but many of them execrable. Some 35 percent were only slightly updated versions of the things he had been playing since 1935. The small groups, similarly, were using a lot of old tunes. Only a small fraction of the material, perhaps 5 percent or so, consisted of important new pieces, like Mel Powell's "Clarinade" and two-sided "Oh Baby!" and Sauter's lovely "Love Walked In." Why on earth was Goodman remaking "You Turned the Tables on Me" and "Blue Skies"? Why were the small groups still doing "Tiger Rag," "Body and Soul," "Oh, Lady Be Good!"?

Making matters worse, Goodman was not bringing to the small-group sessions anything like the imagination he had brought to the earlier pieces—the modulations in "Oh, Lady Be Good!," the dazzling riff work in the Christian-era Sextet, the interplay with Wilson in the first Trios. Most of the small-group pieces are just jam sessions, with little attempt to give them freshness by working out background figures, changes of instrumentation and the like. For example, the new version of "Oh, Lady Be Good!" is played in G throughout, where the original version passed through several keys, including a patch in minor.

But there were a few interesting pieces. Probably the best known of them was Mel Powell's extended composition on an old pop tune, "Oh, Baby," which was issued on two sides of a twelve-inch record. A few months earlier Goodman had recorded a piece called "All the Cats Join In," originally written for the Disney movie *Make Mine Music*. "All the Cats Join In" included both the Sextet and the full orchestra, probably more for filmistic reasons than musical ones. "Oh, Baby" opens with the Sextet playing in its standard manner. Then clarinet and vibes play a little figure, which is parroted by the whole band. This parroting of brief Sextet figures of the whole band goes on for a considerable period; it is meant to be humorous, as much as anything, and succeeds in being cute. Finally the Sextet drops away, and the full band finishes off the piece. There is not much to be said about the writing, the little exchange between the band and Sextet aside, but there are first-rate solos by Johnny Best, Lou McGarity, and probably tenor saxophonist Gish Gilbertson, as well as Goodman.

A more successful piece is Powell's "Clarinade," a feature for Benny which he preferred to Sauter's more complicated "Clarinet a la King." The piece is structured in standard four-, eight- and sixteen-bar segments. There are two primary themes—a twenty-four-bar ABA form for the clarinet, with a rather Baroque-like melody line and the B segment in minor; and a hard-swinging thirty-two-bar AABA section for the band over which Goodman cavorts in spots. The B segment also goes into the minor. The themes alternate, with some variation. There is also a lovely pastoral interlude for Goodman with subdued band accompaniment, which Benny plays in his classical manner. Goodman improvises very little, if any, of his part. The only improvisation in the piece is a brief solo by Powell. It is really quite simple and hangs together well. Reviewers at the time suggested that it was not jazz, and in part it is not. But I think it is one of the most successful marriages of jazz and classical elements to come out of this period.

But on the whole, the music is rather pedestrian, and it seems to me clear that Goodman had lost interest. He had broken up the band in 1944, revamped it entirely in 1945, and I think he was dissatisfied, tired and going through the motions, in so far as Goodman, with his temperament, could do that. Why did he keep going? Probably partly as a matter of pride, partly because he had devoted his life to music. And what else was he going to do with himself if he got out of the band business? But the music he was playing was not fresh, was not what the best bands of the time, like the Herman, Kenton and Raeburn bands, with their advanced compositions, were playing, and it does not grip us today as the earlier music did.

In fact, as is now apparent, the whole swing-band movement was running down. In the fall of 1945, when the war was over, *Down Beat* ran an optimistic story about a number of new dance bands being formed, and others in the planning stages, one of them to be led by Mel Powell.[34] But the optimism was not supported by the facts. New bands were indeed being started, but they were not catching on very well. The *Down Beat* poll for 1945 was indicative. The winners were all the same old names: Ellington, Dorsey, Goodman, Mel Powell, Ziggy Elman and the like.[35] Artie Shaw, who may have seen the handwriting on the wall, and was fed up with the band business anyway, announced in October that he was going to retire.[36] *Down Beat* struggled to remain optimistic. It announced early in 1946 that it would eventually become a weekly, and that "the outlook for dance music, and we use the term in a broad sense to include all music in a popular vein, is much brighter than at any period since the days of the first one-nighters."[37]

But by summer a certain uneasiness was taking hold. One of the problems was a tax on nightclubs, which had been instituted in 1944 as a wartime measure. The rule was that clubs which permitted dancing had to add 30 percent to the customers' bills. It had begun to hurt almost immediately. *Down Beat* said, "The 30 percent tax is cutting into night club business here,"[38] and in another story it reported that "operators in most areas have felt a sharp decline in patronage," and that a number of cabarets were eliminating music.[39] The tax continued even after the war ended and the cabarets and hotel restaurants which had been vital to the swing bands began making changes.

The effect was to make the ballrooms critically important to the bands; but they, too, were suffering. Willard Alexander told *Down Beat* editor Mike Levin, "Musicians are getting over twice the money in salaries they did before the war, and transportation and arranging costs are way up. But the hotels and spots which must be the home base for any new outfit have only gone up about 40 percent in their band bids—they literally can't afford anymore."

Alexander estimated that a new band must expect to lose five hundred dollars a week and go $10,000 into the red before there was any hope of turning a profit. (This was a time when newspapers cost three cents and you could still find a nickel beer.) With personal managers taking only 5 percent, "a man can't gamble at all in the music field—because he can't get a return for his dice throwing."[40]

From this point on the slide came with astonishing speed. In August Charlie Barnet, who for several years had had one of the most popular and most swinging of the dance bands, announced that he was giving up:

> I wish I could keep up the present payrolls, but it just won't work. The band business is in a slump and getting worse. Take Pennsylvania. The other day I spoke to an executive of a big booking office. He told me how the last six Pennsylvania tours by a half dozen of the really top bands left promoters in such a flattened state that they're going back to booking only small, territory combos. . . . Bands can't keep asking such big prices that promoters on one-nighters have to charge dancers $2.50 instead of $1.10 in hopes of making a profit. The orchestra leaders, in turn, will have to cut expenses to be able to accept smaller guarantees. That means either smaller bands or smaller salaries or both. . . . I know now that we must forget about the few screaming fans who line up against a bandstand and applaud the flag-wavers. We'll have to look over their heads and watch the bulk of the audience to see whether or not they're walking back to their chairs in disgust because they can't dance to the music.[41]

Barnet cited Goodman's current engagement in Pennsylvania: the band had a guarantee of $2500 but drew only 750 customers. Barnet concluded, "As far as the band business is concerned, the party is over."[42] In the same month a group of West Coast ballroom operators convened a meeting to discuss ways of cutting costs. Most, or all, had been "operating at a loss in recent months," Down Beat said.[43]

In the face of this it seems incredible that the unions would choose this moment to demand raises; but in September New York and Chicago locals raised their scale by 20 to 33 percent. This would not have much effect on the top-name bands, who were paying their men considerably above scale in any case. But it would hurt, in some instances badly, the smaller dance halls where local bands were working for scale. The operators reacted predictably. In Chicago a lot of places cut the size of the bands, or fired the "relief" bands who played the intermissions. In New York, "Nearly all the 41 members of the powerful hotel association of New York City . . . gave two weeks' notices to those bands making less than the proposed scales, and that included all but a few of the very top names."[44]

The attitude of the musicians' union was that, yes, pay for musicians had gone up, but the increases were not commensurate with salaries in industry.

Even though raising scales at a time when the band business was sinking seems in retrospect like poor policy, it is easy to sympathize with musicians. The entertainment industry—and the arts in a more general way—has always been dependent upon the ability of the entrepreneurs to exploit "talent." The musicians had done very well for a brief period of the 1920s, when there was a great demand for dance music and mechanical entertainment was in its infancy. But otherwise they were traditionally badly paid. The men who staffed the name bands during the years before the war found it difficult to save anything at all while they were on the road even if they were single, and impossible if they were married, and it was the willingness of hundreds of musicians to work for very low salaries that allowed the swing bands to exist. During the war they had gotten used to being able to buy decent clothes, good cars when they could find them, and to support families. But they were still running behind. Sidemen who were paying $9 a night for hotel rooms insisted that they couldn't live on the road for less than $125 a week, a reasonable claim. But bandleaders replied that with salaries in that range they would have to demand $1750 to $2500 in guarantees, and Harry James was actually getting $4,000. At that level, the operators had to charge two dollars to two dollars and a half admission; and the public's response was that that was too much.[45]

There really was no solution. In November the Down Beat headline was "Music Biz Just Ain't Nowhere," and the story which followed was long and dolorous. The Meadowbrook, one of the premier spots for dance bands, was going to start using "only lesser name bands." Hotels "are recording cover figures almost 40 percent lower" than in 1945. Fifty-second Street "is financially flat," and the Harlem clubs were "so hard hit by the business slump and the new night club scales enforced by Local 802 that three of them will probably be out of business by the time this hits print."[46] Both record and sheet-music sales were down. In November Les Brown announced that he was giving up, and Gene Krupa told his sidemen that he would be paying a hundred dollars a week to everybody but the section leaders.[47] The next month Down Beat counted up the scorecard. In addition to Brown, Teagarden, Tommy Dorsey, Harry James and Woody Herman were giving up their orchestras. And so was the man who had started it all, Benny Goodman.[48] Jimmy Dorsey would attempt to continue, although his recording company, Decca, had released him from his contract;[49] he succumbed anyway, and the rest of the swing bands disappeared rapidly.

It was, finally, over. It had been a ten-year balloon ride, with everybody apparently endlessly ascending. Some people got rich and famous; a lot more had a moment in the sun, and made enough money to retire at an early age; hundreds of others built solid careers for themselves as professional musicians. It had not all been glory. For the sidemen it had been ten years of pounding their way for the thousandth time through a worn arrangement; of long, exhausting bus rides; of meals skipped and sleep missed; ten years of too much liquor, too many drugs.

But for these mostly young men and women it had been a heady time, a time when saying that you worked with such-and-such-a-name band was as important as saying you were on a major league baseball team; a time when the women—mostly the girl singers—were adored by tens of thousands of men, and the men found women eager to take them to bed in even the smallest towns. For most of them the end came as a shock, and when the tide went out it left a lot of them drying on the beach, twenty-five or thirty-five years old and trained to do nothing but play dance music. Many of them found jobs in high schools and junior-high-school music departments. Others took "day jobs" and played with small combos at Elks Club dances and at small lounges on weekends. Art Rollini ended his working life as a concrete inspector;[50] Jess Stacy was working for Max Factor after 1963;[51] Nate Kazebier was a golf instructor in Reno, Nevada.[52] Only a few of them made places for themselves in radio, movies and eventually the television studios.

What really happened? The changing economics of the business was of course important in killing the big bands. But probably the most important factor was one of those changes in public taste that from time to time bring forward a new style of music, with a new set of heroes. When the dance band was coalescing in the late 1920s, singers were seen as strictly adjunctive. In a time before one-nighters, when bands might play in the same location for months, or even years, at a stretch—as the Pollack band did at the Park Central and the Ellington band did at the Cotton Club— the band was there primarily to play for dancing, as a backdrop to dinner and to accompany the show, if there was one. The singer or singers would be part of the show, usually providing their own music for the band to play. Duke Ellington, for example, did not carry a singer with the band until he left the Cotton Club in 1931, and he did not have a boy singer until long after the band was famous.[53]

But by the late 1930s, bandleaders were beginning to find that it added to their appeal to carry attractive boy and girl singers. Jimmy Dorsey's team of Helen O'Connell and Bob Eberly was very important to his band's success. Soon leaders began adding singing groups like Tommy Dorsey's Pied Pipers and Glenn Miller's Modernaires. They might also have a male singer who specialized in novelty numbers, like Glenn Miller's tenor saxophonist Tex Benecke, who came forward to sing hits like "Chattanooga Choo-Choo," a role Goodman played with his own band.

The singers, inevitably, began building followings of their own, and very quickly the tail began wagging the dog. Bing Crosby had long since gone on his own after earning his popularity with Paul Whiteman. But it was the really enormous success of Frank Sinatra with Harry James and then Tommy Dorsey that suggested what the future might be like. Sinatra became the center of a cult of teenaged girls—"swooners," as they were called, who were analogous to the teenagers who clamored after the Beatles a generation later. In 1943 Sinatra left Dorsey to set up in business of his own, and his astonishing success encouraged others to follow his lead. Thus, even before the war was over, popular fancy was shifting from the bands to the vocalists. The effect was masked by wartime prosperity, when ballroom operators were begging booking offices to send them bands and everybody was making a lot of money. But when the war ended, the mask fell. The stars were now the singers, and from the late 1940s until well into the next decade, when the rock-and-roll surge brought another change, the biggest names in popular music would be Eddie Fisher, Patti Page, Jo Stafford, Vic Damone, Perry Como and many others, singing rather easygoing romantic tunes of love and marriage. Among the most popular shows on television, the new medium of entertainment bursting into American culture, were those of Perry Como and Bing Crosby.

Still other factors were at work in the social system to bring about the end of the swing era. The main support for the big bands had been provided by a generation who were teenagers between the early 1930s and early 1940s. They had seen their lives disrupted, and marriages delayed, by the Depression and then the war. They were now in their twenties, and some of them in their thirties, and they were intent, in the midst of postwar prosperity, on building families and careers and buying the new tract houses that suddenly made it possible for even struggling young families to own homes. They no longer had the time or energy to go out dancing, collect records, learn the words to new songs.

The new generation of teenagers coming along, which might have taken up swing, did not. Why is always a question, but it may have had something to do with the spirit of the times. The big dance band had been spawned as part of a new feeling in the American air, an electric spirit of a new openness, a new freedom. The Depression had brought with it an aggressive mood which demanded change. But the post-war period was a time of consolidation, of prosperity, and the romantic love-and-marriage tenor of the music of the singers suited it.

Another change, less sweeping but in its way even more dramatic, was under way. In the early 1940s a group of young black musicians was creating a new music in Harlem clubs, among them Minton's, where Charlie Christian frequently sat in. This was of course bebop, or bop as it is now generally known.[54] Its heroes were Charlie Parker, Dizzy Gillespie and a few others. It was a new, fresh sound, once again being made by young men, and it drew to it not only a lot of young jazz musicians but also a substantial proportion of the younger jazz fans. These young people, who a few years earlier would have become admirers of Goodman, Berigan, Shaw and the rest, were following Parker and Gillespie. Swing was seen by these people, both the musicians and the fans, as an old-fashioned, commercial music. Blacks also saw it as a white man's music, and the blacks in it, like Cab Calloway, Louis Armstrong and Fats Waller, with their mugging and comic jiving, as Uncle Toms.

Thus, while the vogue for singers was drawing off the mass audience, bop was taking away the hard-core jazz fans who had followed the music closely, bought a lot of records, kept up with *Down Beat* and *Metronome*, and stood in front of bandstands applauding solos by their favorite sidemen. *Metronome* went with them, pulled particularly by Leonard Feather, who saw himself as a spokesman for the new music. Swing was not only losing its congregation but its acolytes as well.

The big bands did not disappear entirely. During the post-war years the bands of Stan Kenton and Woody Herman, playing an advanced version of swing colored both by bop and by devices drawn from modern classical music, particularly the work of Ravel and Stravinsky, surged to the top and for a brief period created some excitement like that which had been occasioned by the rise of the Goodman band ten years earlier. The Duke Ellington band never stopped for a moment until the leader's death in 1974. Lionel Hampton kept his band going for a long time. Count Basie, with one brief hiatus when he led a sextet, kept the band going until his death in 1984. Buddy Rich and Woody Herman fielded bands from time to time. Goodman himself put together big bands occasionally for special events. So-called "ghost" bands continued the music of Glenn Miller, the Dorseys, Basie and Ellington after their deaths. And new bands came into being, mainly because there were musicians around who wanted to play the music and struggled to varying degrees of success—the Thad Jones–Mel Lewis band, the Toshiko Akiyoshi–Lew Tabackin band, the Widespread Band and others. And along the way other leaders have come and gone—Doc Severinson, Maynard Ferguson, Sauter-Finegan, and more.

Most of these bands did not work full-time, and some of them died early deaths. But there were always swing bands: the swing era was dead, but the swing band would continue to have a real, if smaller, audience.

# 25
# The Bop Band

The bebop movement was more than just a shift in music; it had important sociological overtones.[1] Black musicians—and black entertainers generally—of Benny Goodman's generation had taken it for granted that they must work within the stereotype of the comical darky with the razor, bandana and stolen chicken that was widely accepted by whites. The best known of these musicians, people like Louis Armstrong, Fats Waller, Cab Calloway and others, almost invariably offered their audiences a good deal of jivey patter and comic songs, like Calloway's famous hit, "Minnie the Moocher," Waller's "Your Feet's Too Big" and Armstrong's "I'll Be Glad When You're Dead, You Rascal You."

To be sure, Duke Ellington refused to stoop to such antics, and by the 1920s at least a few blacks, like the great bass Paul Robeson, were accepted as serious stage artists. But even Ellington made his first fame at the Cotton Club playing "jungle" music for shows that included a lot of "African" shake dances and the like.

By the 1940s, however, a new generation of blacks had begun to think differently. They had grown up in less difficult times for blacks, many of them in the North, in contrast to Armstrong and some of the others, who had been children in the South at a time when a militant black could expect to be lynched or, if he was lucky, severely beaten. These younger blacks were willing to speak out, frequently in quite harsh terms, against the injustices visited upon their people. They were bitter, and they were prepared to turn their backs on the Calloways, Armstrongs and Wallers; indeed, they were prepared to turn their backs on American society as a whole.

In the very early 1940s there began to coalesce in New York a small group of young black jazz musicians who shared this attitude. Their leaders were Dizzy Gillespie, an obstreperous trumpet player with enormous skills whose wise-guy attitude had got him fired from at least one band;

Thelonious Monk, an eccentric who was developing a strange, angular piano style; the naive Charlie Christian; a strong-minded drummer, Kenny Clarke; and an erratic genius named Charlie Parker who would be the main musical inspiration for the group.

These people, and others around them, were men of marked individuality, who were determined to follow their own course, and could not be easily bent. They were, thus, both philosophically and by dint of their personalities, rebellious, not politically but musically. Many young musicians of this generation, having grown up on swing music, had by the early 1940s become bored with the simple harmonies and relentless thirty-two-bar popular song form they were forced to work from most of the time. As we have seen, Goodman himself was looking for something different in 1940. Some of these young men were turning to the twentieth-century masters, especially Stravinsky, for inspiration, a move that would result, a few years later, in the advanced dance music of the Herman, Kenton, Raeburn and Thornhill bands and the so-called "cool" jazz of Dave Brubeck, Gerry Mulligan, the Modern Jazz Quartet and others.

But Gillespie, Parker and their followers, whose familiarity with the classical composers of the day was not large, turned inward, to produce a music which they created by standing swing music on its head. They were seeking something different, something new, something that would be their own. Whatever had been wrong was now right; whatever had been essential was now discarded. In the bop which burst out of the underground in 1945, all of the old rules were reversed. Where swing favored the first, third and fifth notes of the scale, the beboppers began to emphasize the second, fourth, flatted fifth and ninth. Where the swing musicians tailored their lines roughly to the two-, four- and eight-measure segments of the popular song form, the boppers began casting their phrases in odd lengths, which began anywhere and ended anywhere. Where the swing musicians in various degrees divided beats into markedly unequal parts, the boppers tended to divide them more equally. Where the swing players valued richness or purity of tone, the boppers often used coarse or astringent sounds. Where the swing musicians phrased to the first and third beats of each measure, the boppers favored the second and fourth. It was all new and different.

Musicians first became aware of bebop through informal jam sessions held after hours at Harlem clubs. Some of these players moved into a band led by Earl Hines, and then a spin-off group led by Hines's former vocalist, Billy Eckstine. These bands, which included Parker and Gillespie, were turned into schools for the new music. By 1944 some of these men were occasionally appearing on New York's Fifty-second Street, and in 1945 Parker, Gillespie and a few others were beginning to get occasional gigs at major clubs and were making the first of a highly influential series of records.

Benny Goodman was aware of bebop from the beginning. As early as 1940 Charlie Christian was sitting in at Minton's. Goodman was curious and went up from time to time himself. He was one of the most celebrated jazz musicians in the world, a man who had broken the color barrier in the music business, and a brilliant instrumentalist, and was quite welcome at Minton's. The regulars there tended to temper their playing to stay within the swing school Goodman was comfortable with.[2] Nonetheless, he heard a great deal of bebop one way or another.

By the second half of the 1940s, bop had sprung into full bloom and had become, for a musician at least, unavoidable, an exciting new direction for some, a thorn in the side to others. Dizzie Gillespie especially was beginning to get a certain amount of attention from the national press, as the apostle of a new and antic form of music. The goatees, the horn-rimmed glasses, the conservative suits, the rumors of drugs and hints of decadence behind the natty tailoring all made good copy. Indeed, bop was as much a cast of mind as it was a music. Its partisans adopted a reserved, "cool" bearing of the all-knowing insider, used an arcane language which was meant to confound the outsider at the same time that it implied possession of a special knowledge. It had all the trappings of a cult, with special handshakes, passwords, high signs, dress and manners. Much of it was a sham, and in the case of some of the musicians, a "put-on," meant to mock both the unknowing outsider and the cult itself. Bebop was infused with irony, although built on a sharply limited intellectual base.

But the music was real enough to threaten the older generation who had risen to fame on the swing movement. The first reaction of many of them was to attack it. Louis Armstrong said, "These young cats now, they want to make money first because they're full of malice, and all they want to do is show you up and any old way will do as long as it's different from the way you played it before."[3] Many others felt the same, among them Goodman, who said, "I guess I'm just an old-fashioned cornball. Maybe I'm behind the times. I can't figure out what those so-called critics mean by progressive music. If playing bad notes all night is progressive music just call me the golden Bantam and leave me alone."[4]

A lot of fans, particularly the ones who had come of age with swing, or the dixieland that had gone before, agreed. Bop seemed like a noisy menace to a great many of them. The problem was not so much the use of more advanced chords. This chromaticism had long been a part of classical music, and was familiar to many people through the works of Mahler, Brahms, the Impressionists, Stravinsky and others. People with good ears for music, especially musicians, would have quickly adjusted to the thicker harmonies, which in any case were beginning to creep into the arrangements of Herman, Kenton, Raeburn and some others. This more chromatic language was bound to have come to jazz sooner or later.

But the rhythmic innovations of the boppers were something else again. The shifting of the pulse onto two and four, the disregard of the conventional two-, four- and eight-bar units in favor of irregular phrases, the phrase endings suddenly coming at odd points in the meter, troubled the older players, most of whom simply were not able to figure out exactly what was going on.

A jazz musician can quite consciously choose to employ new or different harmonic schemes; it is not difficult, with a little practice, for an improvising musician to learn to think in terms of minor ninth chords instead of sevenths, although it may never come quite as naturally as his primary harmonic system. But playing a specific type of jazz rhythm is something that is not easily learned in the practice room. A player may understand the devices required—syncopation, metric shifts, secondary attack and the like—but it is exceedingly difficult to apply them consciously. They must be felt, instinctive as it were, simply welling up from inside. What most jazz musicians do when improvising is to think in terms of a sequence of pitches; the rhythmic pattern they apply them to must be automatic, must spring out unconsciously. That is to say, a player can direct himself to play, for example, C, B-flat, G, F. He cannot consciously think that he will begin the C on the second half of the beat, play the B-flat fractionally late, and so forth. In a certain sense the improvising musician does not "cause" the music; it "happens to him," and part of the pleasure he takes in it is to listen to the ribbon of music he is producing as it appears. This is particularly true of the rhythmic aspect of jazz.

The swing players had internalized one rhythmic style; and virtually all of them found it impossible to root this one out and replace it with another. Some, fearful of being left behind, tried, among them Roy Eldridge, Coleman Hawkins and Wardell Gray. But none of them really made themselves into true boppers. To my mind, the only swing musician who managed to cross the line was Don Byas, except of course for the young boppers themselves, many of whom had started their careers in swing bands.

In 1946 when Armstrong was excoriating bop, it seemed possible that the new music was faddist gimmickry which would dry up and blow away when its essential emptiness was exposed. It turned out, however, that there was substance to the music and it did not dry up and blow away. Rather, swing fell further and further behind, and by the end of the 1940s the swing players had come uneasily to realize that they had better make a truce with bebop.

Benny Goodman's reluctant liaison with bebop began in 1946 when

Mary Lou Williams, an arranger he regarded highly, presented him with a boppish arrangement called "Lonely Moments." Goodman tried it out with the band and, according to Williams, said, "Oh, bebop," and refused to play it.[5] Eventually Williams persuaded Goodman to use it by telling him to play the blues on his solo. Goodman, however, as he frequently did, tinkered with the arrangement, in particular removing the flatted fifths, which jarred his ear. He told a *Metronome* reporter:

> I've been listening to some of the rebop musicians [Rebop at the time was an accepted alternate term]. You know, some of them can't even hold a tone! They're just faking and are not real musicians. From what I've heard, rebop reminds me of guys who refuse to write a major chord even if it's going to sound good. A lot of the things they do are too pretentious. They're just writing or playing for effect, and a lot of it doesn't swing.[6]

There was some justice to Goodman's comments. It was true that a number of young musicians coming into bebop at the moment, playing in public and making records, had not mastered their instruments. The early Miles Davis is a case in point. On the other hand Parker, Gillespie, drummer Kenny Clarke and some others had established themselves as first-rate swing players before bop was ever invented. Others like pianists Al Haig and George Wallington had backgrounds in classical music. No matter what the detractors said, bop would not go away.

Early in 1947 Goodman moved his family out to Westwood Station, a wealthy suburb of Los Angeles.[7] He was now approaching forty; he was wealthy and celebrated; and he had seen the movement in which he had been the major force wane and die. He had spent a major portion of his adult life on the road, sleeping on trains and eating in diners. It was time to relax, spend some time with his family, and enjoy all the things that his enormous success had brought him. Among other things, he now had two little girls, Rachel and Benjie.

But as he said repeatedly, music was his life, and he found he could not walk away from it. Almost immediately on arriving on the West Coast, he signed a contract with a brash new record company called Capitol, which had been founded in 1942 by Johnny Mercer and others. Mercer was a prickly man who could be troublesome when drinking, but he was one of the leading songwriters of the day, a brilliant lyricist who wrote the words to hits like "Come Rain or Come Shine" and "Skylark," as well as tunes like "Dream" and "I'm an Old Cowhand." He had worked with Goodman on many of the *Camel Caravan* shows as a singer and master of ceremonies, and he undoubtedly played a role in signing Goodman with Capitol. The label had prospered by developing its own artists—Nat "King" Cole was one of the first—but it would hardly turn down a chance to sign somebody like Benny Goodman.[8]

The band Goodman put together for his first Capitol recordings was built primarily around a group of the older hands, including Nate Kazebier, Red Ballard, Lou McGarity, Babe Russin, Jess Stacy and Allan Reuss, many of whom were now living on the West Coast. Over the next several months players came and went, but among them were a number of younger musicians who had at least one foot in the new music: pianist Jimmy Rowles, Stan Getz, drummer Don Lamond, all of whom would go on to make names for themselves in jazz. Stan Getz, for example, was never really a bebopper, but his light, airy approach fit with the modern "cool" mode coming into fashion. Goodman could not help being affected by what he was hearing on the stand night after night, and by bit by bit, however reluctantly, he began to accept the new music.

It was, however, always two steps forward, one step back. On the one hand he was playing Mary Lou Williams's boppish "Lonely Moments" and "Whistle Blues." On the other, he was playing small group versions of " 'S Wonderful" and "Sweet Georgia Brown." Yet the trend is clear. At the beginning of the year he was still playing a lot of the older numbers with the small groups, although not with the big band. But by April he was using Jimmy Rowles, who had been with the band in 1942 but had moved toward the modern school. He shortly added guitarist Al Hendrickson, a bopper, and then in June Don Lamond to create a modern rhythm section. In the spring, too, he began buying arrangements from Ralph Burns, a noted modernist who did important work for the Herman band, and pianist Tommy Todd. Their work was by no means pure bebop, but it was certainly more venturesome than some of the music Goodman was playing.

In June Benny recorded a quintet version of the bebop anthem, "Cherokee," with the modern rhythm section. Charlie Barnet had made his fame with his version of the tune, but in 1945 Charlie Parker had recorded a superlative version of it, retitled "Ko-Ko," and it had become a favorite vehicle for the boppers who, following Parker's example, had worked out their own system for playing the rather complicated bridge. Negotiating the tune at a fast tempo, especially the long bridge with its flying chord changes, was a test for the boppers, as Jimmie Noone's "I Know That You Know" had been for clarinetists of the 1920s. I have no doubt that Goodman chose to record the tune as a response to the challenge of bop. The artists are Rowles, Hendrickson, Red Norvo, Lamond, bassist Harry Babasin and Goodman. Benny plays a full sixty-four-measure chorus of the tune, relatively straight, to open the record, after which Rowles gets the major portion of the space to solo in the more modern style. This is not pure bop piano, but his solo is filled with modern touches, as for example the turn-around at the end of the first sixteen measures, and again in the descending chromatic approach to the tonic in bars twenty-nine and thirty, which was something of a bebop cliché by this time. (Coleman Hawkins had employed this device for some time, but the boppers made a habit of it.) Al Hendrickson's solo is more clearly in the bop idiom; and the riff behind Goodman's opening solo is adapted from the main figure to "Jumpin' with Symphony Sid," another theme popular with the beboppers of the day.

It is impossible to put percentages to anything as elusive as the amount of bebop in a given performance, but this version of "Cherokee" is certainly brushed with bop. It sounds today rather mild; but at the time it sounded disquietingly modern to Goodman's older fans.

It is interesting to notice the way the famous bridge is handled. It appears three times. The first time Goodman plays the melody much as it is written; the last time it is given a very simple riff by clarinet, guitar and vibes. Only in its second appearance does Goodman attempt to improvise on it, and he is playing very cautiously and tentatively. The chord changes are not at all unusual, being made up of related two-five-one patterns, one of the most standard of all harmonic sequences. (This was not the way Ray Noble had originally harmonized the bridge, which suggested bitonality, but the scheme the boppers worked out.) The problem for players new to the tune is first to discover what the pattern is and then to improvise against a long train of chords flying by at high speed. Goodman was entirely capable of doing the last, and I suspect that his tentativeness on the bridge stemmed from the fact that he had not quite caught on to the harmonic system. Musicians who have worked with Goodman have sometimes questioned his ability to hear chord changes. Sid Weiss said, "I tend to agree" with the idea that Goodman sometimes had trouble hearing changes, but added, "That's nit-picking."[9] John Bunch, who played piano for Goodman for as long as anybody, said,

> He didn't have near the ear that Zoot Sims, Scott Hamilton, even myself. I don't think he had as good an ear. If he made a mistake he'd want to know sometime down the line what was going on there harmonically so he wouldn't make the same mistake again. I remember one time [in the early 1960s] we were rehearsing up at his house in Connecticut, "I've Grown Accustomed to His Face." I didn't think he'd ever learn that tune. We must have done that tune for four hours. He insisted that we keep going on and on and on. I wished I'd never started it. I felt, Jesus, when will this ever end.[10]

What is interesting about this is that Goodman could easily have got hold of the sheet music for the tune, or even asked Bunch to write it out for him, which would not have taken more than a few minutes. Bunch said, "If he had the changes written out for him he could read them, but he wanted to memorize them. He didn't want to have to read them. As a bandleader I can understand that."[11] It is true that so long as a musician depends on paper for his notes, they never stick in the memory. To memorize a tune it is necessary to play it by ear without music. This was what Goodman wanted to do, for he did not wish to appear in public reading music.

Jess Stacy supports this story. He said that before a recording session Goodman would ask Stacy to come in early to go over the tunes with him. (During the swing era the bands tended to record new tunes, so that when they went on the road they would be playing the material they had just recorded. Reversing the procedure would have often left them recording songs which were already fading.) Stacy would say, "Benny, that's a D7," and Goodman would respond, "No, no, don't tell me, just play it."[12] He wanted it in his ear, not his mind.

Stacy, however, added that Goodman "had an ear like a snake" and had no trouble learning tunes. What is the truth? Mel Powell was probably correct when he said, "I think that his harmonic sense was restricted to the style that he played. My own guess would be that musicians who would say that [he did not hear chords well] might have been younger. . . . After all, Benny did not continue to grow with Dizzy Gillespie and Charlie Parker. Benny played from the 1930s. So when it comes to major, minor, diminished, augmented and 7th chords, which the language of jazz of that time was, he was impeccable."[13]

The problem, basically, was that Goodman never really liked the advanced chords, the thicker harmonic textures. Powell said, "He'd be annoyed by it. His taste was very good, but limited. Limited is an unkind word. He was a bit of a purist. He did not like fancy things. He thought that good playing was what would make a B-flat major chord sound wonderful."[14] Marian McPartland, who also worked with Goodman frequently in later years, said,

> As marvelous a musician as Benny is, I did notice, however, his seeming lack of interest in rich harmonies. His music reflects this; he always has concentrated on the beat, rhythmic excitement, the melodic line. Lush voicings and chord changes evidently leave him cold. He seems to want the blandest possible changes behind him, and his improvisations are carried out strictly within this framework. It bothers him to hear an unfamiliar voicing—as I found out. This is his style, however, and his taste; I respect it as such.[15]

This probably is the essence of it: any musician will have trouble learning to hear chord changes he does not really like. And Goodman, clearly, did not really like the more dissonant chords that were being brought into jazz by the modernists. This, perhaps, was a failing on his part. A musician who is willing to give up his hostility to the new, and spend time letting his ear soak it up, will usually find something there he likes. Goodman did not do this. But in his defense, it might be pointed out that the music of Bach, as well as Louis Armstrong, was built on the simpler harmonic system he had espoused.

Nonetheless, although he continued to play a lot of music in the old manner, he was moving gingerly into a more modern style. For one thing, he had largely, if not entirely, abandoned the repertory of the 1930s. He was not regularly playing "Sing, Sing, Sing," "King Porter Stomp," "Don't Be That Way," as he had ten years before. To be sure, he continued to use a lot of the old tunes as vehicles for the small groups: "I Know That You Know," "After You've Gone," and other war-horses turned up regularly. But the big band was playing new material.

During the first half of 1947 Goodman was appearing on The Victor Borge Show, recording and playing various other engagements. That summer he was involved in a movie eventually called A Song Is Born, which featured a lot of the biggest names from the swing era, among them Louis Armstrong, Charlie Barnet, Tommy Dorsey, Lionel Hampton and, of course, Goodman.

Then, at the beginning of 1948 there came a second recording ban. As a consequence, we have only a spotty record of Goodman's work as he was moving firmly into bebop. What bop Goodman was listening to at this point is hard to know. However, West Coast promoter Gene Norman was using Goodman on some of his "Just Jazz" shows through late 1947 and early 1948.[16] These very successful concerts included a mixed bag of musicians drawn from various schools. Among them was Wardell Gray, a young tenor saxophonist who was beginning to make a substantial splash in the jazz world. Gray was not initially a bebopper: his primary influence was Goodman's old favorite, Lester Young, whose style Gray could ape almost perfectly when he wanted to. Rhythmically he was in something of a halfway house between the old swing manner and the new system of Parker and Gillespie. He used a good many of the bop harmonies in his line, and as time went on he moved further into the bop movement. As a Lester Young disciple he was exactly the sort of modernist to appeal to Goodman, who later said, "If Wardell Gray plays bop, it's great."[17]

Also appearing at the Just Jazz concerts were pianist Dodo Marmarosa and trumpeter Howard McGee, who were bop stalwarts. One way or another, Goodman was getting some exposure to the music. But the catalyst which pushed him to really give the new mode a try was a young Swedish clarinetist known in the United States as Stan Hasselgard.

He was born Ake Hasselgard in 1922,[18] and raised in the town of Bollnas, some fifty miles north of Stockholm, where his father was a judge. He was given a solid middle-class upbringing, during the course of which he heard the new swing music coming out of the United States. Like so many other adolescents, he was taken by the sound of Goodman's clarinet, and began trying to capture the style. In 1939, by this time handsome, blond-haired and six foot, three inches tall, he matriculated at the famous university at Uppsala. He ran the college dance band which was making regular radio broadcasts and thus began to earn a small local name for himself. He spent 1943 and 1944 in the Swedish army and returned to Uppsala to earn his degree in English and art history in May 1947. His father then agreed to send him to the United States to study both English and art at Columbia University. It would have been more customary for a European to send a son to England to study English, but England was still suffering from a good deal of dislocation and privation as a consequence of the war. It is also probable that Hasselgard pushed his father to send him to the United States, the fount of the swing music he loved.

He arrived in New York on July 1, 1947, and went immediately up to the Famous Door on Fifty-second Street to hear Jack Teagarden and clarinetist Peanuts Hucko.

He began sitting in around New York and playing in jam sessions. Sometime that fall he met a young trumpet player named Johnny Windhurst, who was attempting to make his way in jazz. By this time music was pulling him away from his studies at Columbia, and when Windhurst told him that he was going to drive to the West Coast, Hasselgard decided to go along. In Los Angeles he found places to sit in and very quickly met Barney Kessel, one of the leading guitarists of the period and an important influence on guitar to come. Under Kessel's influence, Hasselgard began trying to play bop. Kessel also introduced him to the people at Capitol, who grew interested in recording him. Then, according to the generally accepted story, in February 1948 Goodman came into the Club 47 in Los Angeles where Hasselgard was jamming. He was immediately struck and asked Hasselgard to have lunch with him the next day. Over lunch he asked Stan to join a new sextet he was forming.[19] Hasselgard had never intended to become a professional musician and had never learned to read music very well. But he accepted the challenge: the chance to work with his boyhood idol was too good to turn down.

The puzzling question is why Goodman wanted to hire a second clarinet player. In the early days he had been on good terms with competing clarinetists. He had roomed with Jimmy Dorsey for a period during his freelance days and during his apprenticeship in Chicago he had known Buster Bailey, Jimmy Noone, Frank Teschemacher and others fairly well. But he had never given solo space in his band to any other clarinet player, although at times he had some good ones, like Peanuts Hucko and Ernie Caceres, in his saxophone section. Furthermore, from a musical viewpoint it made a lot more sense to bring in some other horn rather than a second clarinet, if only for the sake of variety. The only explanation that occurs to me is that, if he were going to have a modern group, he thought it might be a good idea to carry a clarinetist who could cover for him in the new idiom.

In May the new Sextet opened at Frank Palumbo's Click Restaurant in Philadelphia. The musicians were Wardell Gray, guitarist Billy Bauer from the modern school, Teddy Wilson from the swing days, bassist Arnold Fishkind, drummer Mel Zelnic and vocalist Patti Page, who would become one of the most popular singers of her time, as well as Goodman and Hasselgard.

The group broadcast regularly from the Click. Some of these broadcasts were recorded and later issued. On the broadcasts Goodman tended to dominate, and the clarinetists sound very similar, but according to a reviewer who heard the group in the restaurant,

> Hasselgard's role varied in size from night to night—Goodman being reasonably generous in allowing his protege solo space. [There was] an unusual contrast in clarinet styles, with Hasselgard's modernity very noticeable. The only sour note was struck by the fact that the Swede, comparatively untrained technically, had some difficulty reading his parts.[20]

From Philadelphia Goodman took the group north to play a series of dates at the huge Westchester County Center, north of New York City. Trumpeter Red Rodney, who had been with Charlie Parker for a period and was a pure bebopper, was added and a few other personnel changes made. The *Down Beat* reviewer said, "The King rides along on the ensembles with his cohorts, but gives the solo spotlight to his protege, Stan Hasselgard. The star of the evening from the applause standpoint was tenor star Wardell Gray. Trumpet star Red Rodney was a one-man bop section."[21] But although the job was successful musically, it did not draw well enough, to Goodman's disappointment. But he still had enough enthusiasm to start planning a band to play bop.

Whether he planned to include Hasselgard in the band is not known. After the County Center engagement, Goodman played a number of dates which did not include the Swede. Hasselgard was still living in the United States on a tourist visa, and it was necessary for him to leave the country from time to time and re-enter, in order to maintain his tourist status. In November he set off for Mexico in the car of Mrs. Billy Eckstine and her chauffeur. Outside of Decatur, Illinois, the car went off the road. Hassel-gard was thrown out and killed instantly.[22] It was a great loss to jazz. One of the peculiar characteristics of bebop was that hardly anybody learned to play it on the clarinet. The main exception was Buddy DeFranco, a bril-liant technician who has always been considered by critics, perhaps un-fairly, as a cold, mechanical player. The clarinet virtually dropped out of jazz, except as it continued to be used in the older dixieland and swing forms. This is surprising, because the clarinet was the instrument best fitted to play at the rapid tempos the boppers favored. If Hasselgard had lived, he might have found a way of playing bebop that would have given the in-strument a place in the new music. But he did not, and even today the clarinet remains a secondary instrument outside of the older schools.

Whether Goodman had planned to include Hasselgard in his bebop big band is moot, but he went ahead anyway. According to trombonist Milt Bernhart, who joined the band in rehearsal at the M.C.A. studios in New York, probably in November, the group was supposed to include alto saxo-phonist Lee Konitz, trumpeter Fats Navarro, and baritone saxophonist Gerry Mulligan, all leading modernists. Mulligan, in addition, was to supply arrangements. When Bernhart got to the first rehearsal, neither Konitz nor Navarro was present. At some point, "Suddenly Benny began to scream, got the bandboy, screamed 'Get him out of here and give him his music.' He was talking about Mulligan. And Mulligan left with his mu-sic, and we never saw him again."[23]

Bernhart thinks that Mulligan may have been asking Goodman for his money; but his point really was that Goodman was only paying lip service to modern music, and after about three weeks they were playing a lot of the old tunes.

His original idea was to build the band around Wardell Gray and Fats Navarro, who was rapidly becoming recognized as the leading bop trum-peter after Gillespie. Navarro actually cut one record with a Goodman Sex-tet, permitted under the record ban because it was for a charity. However, Navarro was not included in the band as finally formed. By this time he was suffering from a considerable drug problem, and my suspicion is that Goodman did not want to deal with any drug-induced unreliability. Fats would die in 1950 of drug-related illnesses.[24]

The band, which began to work in November 1948, included, besides Gray as the primary saxophone soloist, Doug Mettome as the trumpet so-loist and Eddie Bert as the principle trombonist. The pianist was Buddy Greco, a classically trained musician from Philadelphia who would eventu-ally become a minor star as a singer. Almost all the arrangements were by Arturo "Chico" O'Farrill, a recent immigrant from Cuba, who also had had considerable classical training. O'Farrill not only wrote a number of originals for the new book but revamped some of the old numbers, like "Don't Be That Way." Bernhart felt that Goodman stuck with O'Farrill because his work was not too far into the bebop style.[25] The band broke in with a tour of the Northeast, and then went into the Hotel Syracuse in up-state New York, an area which had a number of colleges and universities which might provide a basic audience for the band. Goodman flew in some critics to hear the band, which had with it a vocal group called the Clarinaders, and an English woman singer named Terry Swope who had worked with Buddy Rich and Woody Herman. Leonard Feather, writing for *The Melody Maker*, said, "The youngsters who crowded the room to capacity seemed more interested in standing and watching the music than in dancing with their partners."[26]

In January 1949, the band played at the ball for the inauguration of President Harry S Truman. By this time the second recording ban was over, and the group began to make formal recordings. Throughout the spring and into the summer it toured, recorded and did a lot of broadcasting. In the summer Goodman shelved it for six weeks, in order to go to England and France with a sextet. (It should be noted that by this time "sextet" had become a courtesy term applied to groups with as many as eight members.) But the British were still refusing to let American musicians play in England. Goodman offered to come by himself and use British musicians but was not permitted to do that either on the ground that he would scoop up the best musicians to the detriment of their regular leaders.[27] In the end, Goodman flew over with pianist Greco to work with a regularly constituted English group, but the whole project was aborted when Benny discovered that he could not take his money out of France.[28] He came back to the United States in August and worked with the bop band to the end of October and then, suddenly, gave it up.

Once again, as we so often do with Goodman, we ask why. During the years of his flirtation with bop, Goodman at times spoke with somewhat grudging approval of the music, as when he told nightclub columnist Earl Wilson, "Some of [his new young musicians] are nuts about bop. If I like the way they play, I don't care what the hell they call it."[29] Given that he was playing, or at least trying to play, the music, he could hardly say anything else. But in 1950 he told a Danish jazz writer, "Bop is on the way out in America. And you know, I have never liked it."[30] This, undoubtedly, was the truth. By the late 1940s bop was getting a good deal of publicity from the national press but the actual audience for it, however, was smaller than the press interest suggested. The major figures like Gillespie and Parker were by the late 1940s working regularly for good fees, and their records sold well enough to encourage some smaller labels to record them. But the majors did not believe that there was a sufficient audience even for a Charlie Parker to make recording him worthwhile. Similarly, the jazz clubs, like Billy Berg's in Los Angeles or the Three Deuces on Fifty-second Street in New York, could do well with a bop band, but the big venues, like the hotel restaurants and major theatres, were not interested. The Kenton and Herman bands, to be sure, were attracting large followings; however, these were not playing pure bop but an advanced version of swing which owed more to Eddie Sauter and Stravinsky than it did to Gillespie and Parker.

Goodman had overestimated the popularity of bebop. When it finally dawned on him that critical interest in the new music was far greater than popular interest, he quickly dropped it. He was undoubtedly encouraged to do so by the reviews he was getting. A review of "Blue Lou" said, "It opens with a Goodman-Gray duet; Wardell takes over shakily; Doug Mettome follows firmly; Benny returns the group to an antiquated groove, and Buddy Greco comes up with some facile modern piano."[31] San Francisco columnist Ralph Gleason, long a Goodman supporter, wrote, "Even the nonboppers wish Benny would make up his mind as to what kind of a band he wants."[32]

Goodman found the response to the bop band puzzling. He had been chastised by the critics for being old-hat, but now, when he had modernized his music, they were still not happy. He said, "It's just too confusing to me. I don't know why they don't like it more. I don't think it has taken hold the way swing did in the 30s."[33] And so he quit.

What, then, of the music of Goodman's bop bands? The early bop of Parker, Gillespie and their associates was a very narrow form with quite rigid conventions—as strict, in its way, as a sonnet. If the music had too high a proportion of triadic chord tones as opposed to non-triadic ones, too uneven a division of beats, too many accents on first and third beats, it was cast away. The system had to be swallowed whole, or it was not bop. Goodman was simply not willing to go whole hog, and as a consequence his bop bands were in a halfway house. Including the various small-group sessions, there were fewer than thirty cuts altogether, some of which were never issued. A number of these were pop numbers with vocals by Buddy Greco, Terry Swope, Dolly Huston and various vocal groups. The pure, or at least reasonably pure, bebop cuts were relatively small in number.

Probably the best known of the big-band sides is "Undercurrent Blues," an O'Farrill original. It has a nice bebop line, played by the saxophones in unison, as was the standard bop practice for opening lines. There is a good solo by Eddie Bert, which owed something to Bill Harris but was more thoroughly bop than Harris's work was, and an excellent solo by Doug Mettome. However, Goodman's own solo is wholly out of place in the context of bop. Heard today, the piece sounds derivative, with reflections of Parker in the main line, and references to the "Salt Peanuts" lick, even then a cliché.

Others of these bop big-band pieces, like "Egg Head" and "The Huckle-buck," are even more derivative. The latter was a pop tune cooked up out of Charlie Parker's "Now's the Time." The Goodman version is taken at a tempo which is far too slow for the tune, giving it a rather lugubrious sound inappropriate to a tune supposed to celebrate a jolly new dance. Wardell Gray's solo echoes Parker at moments, and the appalling lyrics are sung in a flatfooted fashion by one of the vocal groups audiences of the time seemed to want. "Egg Head" is pedestrian, and a lot of it is not far removed from the kind of music Goodman had been playing years earlier, as, for example, the introduction, the opening chorus and the chorus following the saxophone solo.

To my mind, the small-group pieces are far more successful. These groups were basically composed of Goodman, Gray, Mettome and a four-piece rhythm section. The best known of the pieces, however, is the strange bop version of "Stealin' Apples" made with Fats Navarro in September 1948. It is a Fats Waller tune which Goodman had made a specialty of in the 1940s. The tune has been modified to give it a bop flavor, which works because the original tune, with its repeated figures, was similar to many bop lines. Wardell Gray's solo is not pure bop, but closer to the Lester Young style; only Navarro's solo, a typically fine underplayed chorus taken in the middle range in a mute, is pure bop. As a consequence, Goodman's clarinet playing is less out of place than it seems in other of these bop numbers. Indeed, Goodman actually plays some bop figures, as for example in bars seven and eight of the first chorus, which were almost certainly written out for him.

My preference, however, is for the small-group version of "Blue Lou." The tune, written by Edgar Sampson, has a certain amount of chromatic movement in the chords, and fits into the bop mode fairly well. Wardell Gray has a very fine solo, Mettome a good one, and because of the chromatic structure of portions of the song, Goodman's own chorus has a slightly more boppish flavor than it might otherwise have had. Overall the piece is played with a drive and enthusiasm that does not seem to be present in many of these cuts.

In sum, the effectiveness of the Goodman bop band depends mainly on the soloists, especially in the small groups. Bop has always been pre-eminently a soloist's music. Even the idiom's genius, Charlie Parker, never really figured out what to do with the ensemble, and usually left it to state a line in unison to open and close a piece, with the remainder of the space devoted to solos. As a consequence bop has always been less effective when played by a big band than by a small group. This is certainly the case here.

And while it is generally agreed that Goodman's experiment with bebop was not successful, I think that these small-group sides are worth attention, especially for the soloing of Mettome and Gray. Gray, who would die in a few years apparently of a drug overdose, has always been seen as an important saxophonist of the period. Doug Mettome, however, has never had the recognition that he deserved, in part at least because he spent most of his career in big bands, some of them fairly commercial, and did not record as much as he should have, especially with the small bop groups in which the reputations of Navarro, Clifford Brown and others, were made. Mettome had the strong upper register which was critical to bebop trumpet playing, and although he had originally been influenced by the swing players, he had come to understand the bop idiom thoroughly. He has good solos on Septet pieces "Bedlam" and the aforementioned "Blue Lou" and an exceptional solo on "Undercurrent Blues" in which through the first eight bars he unfolds successively higher figures into the top of his range.

The remaining question is how much Goodman's own playing was affected by what he was hearing around him. The answer is not much. He virtually never uses any of the so-called altered chords, with their flat fifths, diminished ninths and raised thirds, which are essential to the bop mode. Nor does he reach for any of the complex shifts of meter that are characteristic of bebop. His playing remains firmly in the swing system. However, he is playing far fewer of the bent notes, growls and other devices of hot playing than he used ten years earlier. His line is somewhat more even, purer and taken as a whole, a little "cooler" in manner than it had been. This, as we have seen, was a direction Goodman's playing was already taking. But the bop revolution probably re-enforced this tendency toward a more relaxed, less impassioned style than the one he had made his reputation on.

# 26

# The Classical Goodman

Over the decades after World War II, Benny Goodman became increasingly interested in what still has to be called classical music. It never supplanted his jazz playing; in fact, his work with small groups and the occasional stints with a big band still occupied far more of his time, so far as public appearances were concerned. Nonetheless, by the late 1960s he was playing perhaps a half dozen classical concerts a year and sometimes more.

Goodman's career in classical music, however, was fairly limited. Months, or even years in some cases, would go by without any classical concerts, and his repertory was small. He generally chose to play the Mozart Quintet for Clarinet and Strings (K. 581); the Mozart Concerto for Clarinet and Orchestra in A (K. 622); the Brahms Trio in A minor for Clarinet, Cello and Piano (Op. 115); Aaron Copland's Concerto for Clarinet and String Orchestra (with Harp and Piano), which Goodman had commissioned in 1947; and various Weber pieces, especially the Grand Duo Concertante for Piano and Clarinet in E-flat Major (Op. 48). He did occasionally play other pieces—the difficult Bartók "Contrasts" for violin, clarinet and piano, which Goodman and Joseph Szigeti had commissioned in 1940; Igor Stravinsky's "Ebony Concerto," which had been commissioned by Woody Herman in 1945; Morton Gould's "Derivations for Clarinet and Band," which was written for Goodman in 1954, and includes some almost straightforward swing band writing in the fourth movement; Leonard Bernstein's "Prelude, Fugue and Riffs," also composed for Herman, in 1949; and pieces by Poulenc, Debussy and others. But the Brahms, Mozart, Copland and Weber pieces constituted the heart of his repertory, and he used them in his concert performances about two-thirds of the time, so far as can be judged from the record.

Benny Goodman began his classical career rather late. There is no evidence that he had any interest in classical music in his youth. The family did have that cheap phonograph by the time Goodman was ten or twelve, and late in his life Goodman said that he listened to Mozart, Brahms, and Haydn as a boy.[1] But it could not have been much, nor often, for he says nothing about hearing any classical music as a youth in *The Kingdom of Swing*, nor in earlier interviews he gave when he was first starting his classical career. For one thing, the family, in those early days, could not have afforded to buy very many symphonies and operas, which on seventy-eight records would come in sets costing many dollars. Nor is there any evidence that Goodman was taken to concerts, except the band concerts that were given everywhere in the United States at that time, at which the music would be marches, band arrangements of rags and popular tunes, and familiar overtures like "Poet and Peasant." The fact that Goodman was studying with the famous classical clarinet teacher Franz Schoepp was not significant. In the main he was working his way through exercise books. Had he continued his studies beyond two years he would eventually have been taken through the literature for clarinet, but he did not.

During his free-lance days in New York, when he was not working every evening, he would have had the time and the money to do more listening, either to records at home, or at any of the many concert halls that exist in New York. Once again, there is no evidence that he did much, if any, listening to classical music. His first real experience with classical music apparently came about in the spring of 1935, when Hammond approached him about it. Hammond had for years played viola in a string quartet, and he suggested to Goodman that they work up the Mozart Quintet, or something similar. Goodman admitted that he had never even heard of the piece before, but he was willing to try it.[2] Hammond got some excellent string players for support, and they rehearsed once a week for three months. Goodman found the music intriguing. He said, "Naturally, I had a tough time at first adapting myself to this sort of thing . . . but the music did appeal to me."[3]

Eventually the group played the piece at the Hammond mansion for a group of some two hundred people, among them a lot of people from the jazz world, including Mildred Bailey and Red Norvo.[4]

Apparently Goodman attempted to follow up the success of this amateur concert by recording the Mozart Quintet with the Pro Arte Quartet. According to the story, he walked into the recording studio cold, after playing a one-nighter and almost immediately realized that he was not properly prepared, and walked out again in considerable embarrassment.[5] He then began to work more seriously on the piece, and on his classical playing in general, and eventually felt confident enough to schedule a recording of the same work with the celebrated Budapest String Quartet, for April 1938.

Playing classical clarinet is quite different from playing jazz on the instrument. Classical musicians tend to use a heavy reed, with a small opening between reed and mouthpiece for better control. Jazz players use a softer reed and a wider opening, which allows them to bend notes more easily. For Goodman to learn to play classical clarinet after spending years as a jazz musician was not something that would happen overnight. The 1938 Mozart Quintet recording with the Budapest was received politely by the classical reviewers, and with considerable hoopla from the jazz press, which at the time was concerned about making the music respectable, and thought that by showing the world that a jazz musician could also play classical music it would raise jazz in the eyes of those who looked down on it. Otis Ferguson in the *New Republic* called it "a beautiful piece of recording all through."[6]

But Goodman himself was not so sure. Many years later he said, "I just plunged into it. I had a kind of jazz vibrato, but I just played. Later it struck me that I really would like to know what the hell I'm doing."[7] He then began to study with the Russian émigré Simeon Bellison, clarinet soloist with the New York Philharmonic, and with increasing knowledge of classical playing, he eased further into the field. In 1940 he and violinist Joseph Szigeti commissioned a piece from Béla Bartók, which they eventually recorded with Bartók at the piano. It was a very hard piece, and Goodman did not play it frequently thereafter. Later the same year he recorded the famous Mozart Concerto for Clarinet and Orchestra which became the piece he is most associated with. For reasons that are not clear, this first recording has never been released. On the same day he recorded Debussy's "First Rhapsody for Clarinet," which was issued; and with these pieces behind him, his classical career was truly begun. It developed slowly, however, and not until the latter years of the 1940s and the early years of the 1950s did he finally build a significant repertory, adding the Weber, Copland and Brahms pieces.

In the late forties he began to study with Reginald Kell. Kell was an Englishman who had come to the United States where he enjoyed a minor celebrity as a virtuoso clarinet player, and was widely recorded. According to Ernest Lumer, one of the few clarinetists who has worked in both symphony orchestras and as a jazz musician, and is therefore aware of the problems of crossing over, "Kell was one of the first symphonic clarinetists to use a vibrato. He had a small, light sound, and used a lot of rubato. American players get a big, dark resonant sound."[8] In fact, many of the American players were disdainful of Kell's approach, claiming that he had "vulgarized" the instrument. His admirers insisted that they were simply jealous of his popular success.

Of particular importance was the fact that Kell used the so-called double-lip embouchure. Most clarinetists curl the lower lip over their teeth and rest the clarinet on it; the upper lip remains in its normal position, so that the teeth are actually touching the mouthpiece. In the double-lip system both lips are curled over the teeth. The double-lip system is supposed to open up the throat and encourage lighter tonguing. Few jazz musicians use the method, and only a relatively small number of symphonic players. But Goodman, despite a good deal of advice against it, decided to learn the double-lip system, and once he had learned it, he continued to use it at times for the rest of his playing career. Lumer says, "He didn't have as much bite afterwards. He lost some resonance, and had a thinner sound."[9] I agree with this assessment. It seems to me that by 1950 or so Goodman's tone was purer, with less of the darker, woody sound than it had previously, especially in the middle and lower end of the range.

In the two decades that followed the studies with Kell, Goodman gave some classical performances in most years, either recordings, concerts or some of both. After 1970 the pace slowed, and by the 1980s he was giving fewer classic concerts, indeed, was playing less generally. He left, however, about twenty recorded performances of classical works, the number depending on whether you count more jazzlike pieces written by Morton Gould, Leonard Bernstein, and others, most of them cut in recording studios, but some of them taken from live performances.

The general view among critics qualified to comment on these pieces is that they do not entirely succeed. As early as 1938, with the appearance of the Mozart Quintet recordings with the Budapest, Patrick "Spike" Hughes, an English composer and early jazz critic, set the tone when he said, "As a player of Mozart he has not yet developed a personality. There is nothing in his playing individual enough to make the listener say next time he hears a Goodman recording: That is Benny, of course. . . . Taking the performance as a whole Benny Goodman's share is frankly undistinguished."[10] Rudolph Dunbar, an English clarinetist, who conducted a clarinet column for The Melody Maker, said, "I feel that he is not at ease in his 'New' music—he is feeling his way too much, a little awed by it all."[11] Goodman eventually agreed. He said of this early piece, "What's wrong with that set of records is Goodman. I was still reading notes, and that's only part of the discipline. If I were to do it over now [two years later] it would be ten times as good. And I mean ten."[12]

But the critics were not sure that ten was the right number. The New York Times said of a 1940 Carnegie Hall performance of the Mozart Clarinet Concerto, "Mr. Goodman . . . approached the Mozart rather warily, but in a most self-effacing manner. Its most difficult passages were met with utmost ease and accuracy. The phrasing was impeccable, the legato of the smoothest. As for the tone produced it was somewhat more open to question. . . . Many of the pages would have benefited by a suaver and more refined and varied tone. . . ."[13] This was the general tenor of much of the criticism of Goodman's playing. A 1947 *Times* review of another concert said that his playing "while correct and expert, was dull."[14] Henry Simon, critic for the newspaper *P.M.*, and brother of the jazz writer George Simon, said that Goodman "didn't seem entirely at home on the classical stuff."[15]

Not all the criticism was adverse. A 1946 *New York Times* review of Alex North's "Revue for Clarinet," which Goodman had commissioned, called it "a brilliant and disarming performance,"[16] and a review of the Handel "Concerto Grosso No. 12 in G" said, "Here the playing was intelligent in conception and vigorous in execution."[17] But these were the exceptions: the rule was that while Goodman's playing was invariably technically flawless, it failed to bring the music to life.

R. D. Darrell, an important critic of both jazz and twentieth-century music in general, said in 1956, "What licks him, surprisingly enough, is just that straight forwardness—for he's so intent on doing justice to the letter of Mozart that he misses out in the flexibility of phrasing, buoyancy of melodic line, and delicate variety of tone-coloring, which are the quintessence of the Mozartian spirit."[18]

Critics continued to say the same. In 1976 the English newspaper *The Guardian* reviewed a concert in London of the Mozart Clarinet Concerto and said that Goodman's reading of the Mozart work was "unexceptionable,"[19] which is fairly faint praise. Mel Powell, speaking of the Bartók "Contrasts" and a Hindemith commission, said, "I don't think he heard those things well, but that's complicated stuff, and it's always a question of who does hear it terribly well."[20]

The problem, according to many, was that Goodman really did not understand the idiom. Ernest Lumer, speaking of the Mozart pieces, said, "I don't think that Benny got the essence of the music. He played it correctly and well, but he didn't get to the heart." Lumer added that he thought the Bartók "Contrasts" was among Goodman's best: "This is closer to the music he understands."[21]

The point being made by these critics and musicians is that, like jazz, classical music gives the listener the feeling that he is being told something. This sense comes from relationships in the music between notes, phrases, small and large episodes, movements. The listener must understand these relationships—that this figure is supportive of the one before it, or is antagonistic to it, or amplifies it, or whatever. The problem seems to have been that Goodman did not entirely grasp the relationships in the music, that he was playing the notes one after another, of course paying attention to the expression marks, but not really adding the small details which would have shown the relations, made the line "speak." There is no argument about Goodman's technique: he played these classical pieces impeccably. I am by no means an authority on Mozart, Brahms or classical clarinet playing in general, but it does seem to me that Goodman's line in such as the Brahms and Mozart pieces lacks the strength and confidence brought to it by other players. Learning to play classical music well is an arduous task, which generally begins when the player is young, and requires the player to be thoroughly at home in the musical language he is supposed to be speaking—the classic style of Mozart, the romantic sense of Brahms, the harsh pessimism of the twentieth-century music of Stravinsky and the others. This really was what Goodman lacked—enough time spent with classical music to absorb into his system the forms he was attempting to play.

# 27

# The Last Bands

Although he could not have known it, when Benny Goodman broke up his bop band his career as an influential popular musician was essentially over. Over the course of the rest of his life, he would continue to put together bands of various kinds, often small groups, to play specific events—tours, concerts, radio and television broadcasts, recording sessions and various anniversary events. But never again would he have a band which worked steadily for more than two or three weeks at a stretch. From now on his groups would be formed for specific purposes, and disbanded when the task was finished.

Benny Goodman was just over forty, and, like many of the swing musicians, he found himself working in a métier for which there was only modest demand—a maker of bread slicers and candle snuffers. Goodman and the others could not predict the future. They could not remotely conjure up in their imaginations figures like Elvis Presley and the Beatles, who in 1950 would have seemed to them as strange as creatures from space. Many of them believed that fashion would cycle back to them. After all, Ellington, Basie, Kenton and others were still playing the old music, or something like it in any case. Goodman remained busy. Through the next several years he was working more often than not, usually with small groups which could be put together easily, but sometimes with big bands, which included various of his sidemen from the past. He was also playing concerts of classical music, usually as a guest artist with symphony orchestras and chamber groups. It would certainly not have seemed to Goodman that he had been put out to pasture, and this feeling was reinforced in 1950 when Columbia decided to issue the records made at the 1938 Carnegie Hall concert, by this point a legend in jazz.

Goodman had brought the records to Columbia, which was his company again, and Columbia had decided to issue them. The records were received with enormous enthusiasm, not only by old Goodman fans, as would be expected, but by jazz reviewers and a lot of younger people to whom the Carnegie Hall concert was only a tale. The set of records, which is in print today, went on to sell well over a million copies, making it the largest selling jazz set ever made.[1] To capitalize on the sudden and surprising success of the concert recordings, Columbia issued a set of airchecks from the 1937–38 period, which is called by the misleading title, *The 1937–38 Jazz Concert No. 2*. This set, too, got excellent reviews and sold briskly. *Down Beat* made it a front-page story.[2]

It was clear enough from the sales of these records that Goodman's music from the old days still had a lot of fans across the United States. It seemed that perhaps the cycle of fashion was coming back already. Goodman decided to see if he could put together the original band for a cross-country tour. Who knew what might come out of it? Perhaps there was a whole new audience of youngsters out there who would be as stirred as their parents had been at the Paramount Theatre in 1937.

According to John Hammond, who discussed the tour in detail in his autobiography,[3] Benny first asked Harry James to join the tour. James was now enormously successful himself, and asked for 50 percent of the profits. Goodman thought this was excessive, but in his cautious way he decided he did not want to risk the tour without a co-star of some kind. He then went to Joe Glaser, Louis Armstrong's manager. Armstrong had, like Goodman, been hurt by the collapse of the swing era, and had for a period right after the end of the war fallen almost into obscurity. He had, however, on Glaser's advice junked his big band and formed a small "all-star" group, ostensibly to play the dixieland music he had grown up on. In fact, the jazz content of the music dwindled over the years, as Armstrong came more and more to the front as a singer of pop songs and a show business personality, and by 1953 he was on the way to becoming one of the most famous entertainers of his day.[4] He was a sure draw and Goodman was willing to give up 50 percent to get him.

Goodman now asked Hammond to manage the tour. Hammond was not at all sure he wanted to take the job. He said:

> I had not wanted to become involved with him again, either musically or in a business way. He was now a part of my family, our relations in the past had often been strained, and my contributions and suggestions, once so welcome, now struck Benny as interference. It seemed wise to restrict our future relationship to merely a personal one. Still, the offer was a challenge. I loved the original Goodman band and I thought it would be fun to get it together again.[5]

As it turned out, this series of decisions would prove to be disastrous. But this was not immediately apparent. Hammond and Goodman were able to round up enough of the old hands to give the impression that it was the original band, among them Ziggy Elman, Gene Krupa, Teddy Wilson, Vernon Brown and Helen Ward. Georgie Auld, who had been with a later Goodman band, joined, and the group was filled out with excellent musicians, including trumpeter Charlie Shavers, alto saxophonist Willie Smith, guitarist Steve Jordan and bassist Israel Crosby, who had played on the "Blues for Israel" session some twenty years before. It was an excellent band, playing the old arrangements, and Goodman as always saw that it was well rehearsed.

The band played three break-in engagements in obscure locations in New England, away from the eyes of the New York critics. The halls were packed and the crowds "wildly enthusiastic," according to Hammond.[6] Goodman, clearly, had not needed Armstrong to ensure the success of the tour.

The band then returned to New York to rehearse with Armstrong. According to Hammond, Armstrong showed up in the middle of the rehearsal with his full entourage, and there followed twenty minutes of greetings, back-slapping and general merriment. This sort of thing was not to Goodman's temperament, especially when he was conducting a rehearsal. He let it go on as long as he could stand, and then asked Louis to tell his hangers-on to wait outside. Armstrong took offense, stalked away, and failed to turn up the next day for a scheduled rehearsal.[7]

As Hammond pointed out, somebody ought to have realized that those were two very bristly egos, and that the difficulty might have been anticipated. Armstrong was now recognized by the jazz fraternity as probably the greatest musician of them all. Moreover, he had become a major figure in show business, beloved by a large audience, and he commanded large fees. At this point he was a more important figure than Goodman was. Louis Armstrong is widely seen as a humble natural philosopher oozing good nature, and it is perfectly true that most of the time he was affable and easygoing. But he also had a jealous streak and a well-developed amour-propre which surfaced when he felt he had been pressed too hard.[8] In order to establish his position vis-à-vis Goodman he showed up three hours late at the rescheduled rehearsal, and on opening night in New Haven stayed on stage for eighty minutes instead of the allotted forty. At the close of the show, when Goodman was supposed to bring Armstrong back out to join the finale, Louis simply did not come out of his dressing room.[9]

Goodman made efforts thereafter to meet with Louis and smooth the matter over, but Armstrong was not ready to make up. They staggered through two Carnegie Hall concerts, which "produced the largest grosses of any jazz concert"[10] up to that time, and went on to Providence, Rhode Island, and then to Boston. By this time Goodman realized that he had not needed Armstrong in the first place, wanted to get rid of him and was trying to find ways around the contract.

But it was not Armstrong who would go. In Boston on April 19, Goodman collapsed from an ailment, the exact nature of which has never been clear. The rumor spread that it was a heart attack, but that was not true. *Down Beat* reported, "Benny was stricken with nervous exhaustion and a respiratory attack in Boston on April 19, requiring the services of an emergency pulmotor squad that worked nearly two hours to revive him."[11] Hammond's theory was that the illness was psychosomatic, brought on by the tensions the tour had engendered, and he suggested that Goodman was taking advantage of a minor seizure of some kind to get Armstrong off the tour through trickery. Sick or not, Goodman did not return to the tour.

Gene Krupa now fronted the band, and Armstrong took over as master of ceremonies. One side effect of the whole disaster was that the relationship between Hammond and Goodman came to an end, for the moment,[12] and Goodman virtually withdrew from the music business. *Down Beat* said, "There is also no doubt that Benny, broken-hearted about the way his return to the band business backfired, suffered a severe breakdown. For the past few weeks he has been completely incommunicado under doctor's orders."[13] He was virtually inactive for the rest of 1953, and played only sporadically through most of 1954.

What actually happened is difficult to determine. For one thing, Hammond strongly implies that Goodman was drinking heavily at least on some occasions during the tour.[14] The whole question of how much Goodman drank is problematic. Not a single one of the musicians who have touched on the matter saw Goodman as anything but a very moderate drinker. Although he was surprisingly tolerant of heavy drinkers if they were talented, like Berigan, Teagarden and Tough, he certainly did not permit drinking on the stand, and, driven as he was to produce the best music he could, he would not go on stage unfit to play. Popsie Randolph, Goodman's famous bandboy, said flatly, "One thing he didn't tolerate, and that was drinking."[15] Others, like James T. Maher, who had lunch with Goodman occasionally over a period of years, find it difficult to believe that Goodman was ever an excessive drinker.

Yet there is the testimony from Hammond and other sources who cannot be quoted, that at a time, or times, in his life, Goodman was drinking too much.[16] It is possible, although not certain, that this was such a time.

It is known, too, that both Benny and Alice Goodman were seeing a psychologist, who at least some of the time traveled with the band.[17] Some of the musicians believed that Alice had got Benny into therapy in order to "make him over" into a man more suitable to her class of people, but in view of the fact that she was also seeing the same psychologist this is not a very sound hypothesis. What the trouble was has never been made public, but it appears that Goodman suffered from sieges of depression.

Some of this depression could well have been situational. He had been a child star, an admired professional in adolescence and finally the King of Swing. Now, in his early forties, it was all slipping away, and it would not be surprising that he felt the loss of the spotlight deeply. But I do not think it was entirely a question of the fleeting glory of the world. Goodman's relationships with most people were not easy. He appears to have been closer to his daughters than others in his life, and his marriage was enduring. But his relations with his siblings were strained, and he never really made himself part of a group of males who he could turn to for emotional sustenance during a time of trouble. He quarreled frequently with his ally and brother-in-law John Hammond, and his relationship with the musicians, his comrades in arms, was exceedingly poor. This is particularly striking, for jazz musicians who work together for a period are likely to become close, in the same way that players on an athletic team frequently do. Even those who today speak well of him, like Mel Powell and Jimmy Maxwell, admit that he was not an easy man to know. Maxwell expressed his ambivalence when he said, "You know, with all the stories about Benny, I owe a great deal to him, really. He is a strange man, but I always feel guilty when I say anything against him, because I owe so much to him."[18]

It is my feeling that Goodman tended to see himself surrounded by enemies, which at times included some of the people in his bands, whom he felt were "out to get him." Bassist Bill Crow, in a long piece he published in Gene Lees's *Jazzletter* on the tour of Russia, said, ". . . he seemed to be always on his guard against us, as if we had been shanghaied and had to be watched for signs of mutiny."[19] Carol Phillips said, "He was paranoid about being taken by people, especially in regard to money."[20] Of course some of this feeling that he had to be on guard was justified, as it always is with wealthy and celebrated people who have the power to do a great deal for others. John Bunch said, "I felt frankly, that most every telephone call that I ever heard him take when I was up there in that apartment [Goodman's apartment-office in New York] was really not anybody being friendly with him, but they wanted something from him, wanted him to do a benefit, or business."[21] I think we can best explain his behavior toward his musicians if we understand that he felt any failure on their part to perform well was a deliberate attempt to sabotage him. He tended, at times, to see this one or that one as his enemy. Teddy Wilson said, "When things seemed wrong he would center his criticism on one man. Then suddenly he might decide he was wrong and switch to some-one else."²²

In any case, the tour with Armstrong seemed to have brought Goodman to an emotional crisis. He had come into it believing that the old days were—or at least might be—coming back, and the enthusiastic crowds at the tryout dates had bolstered that belief. Then it had all gone wrong. The dream was dead. The old world, Goodman must now have seen, was gone. The result, hardly unusual in such cases, was too much drinking, a physical and emotional collapse and a withdrawal from the world of music. From this point onward, Goodman would be a part-time performer, still vastly admired by thousands, but a figure out of the past. He would live on old glory henceforward.

However, the glory was sufficient to inspire a movie company in 1955 to decide that a film of Goodman's life would be profitable. Not long before, a film on the life of Glenn Miller, called *The Glenn Miller Story*, had been a considerable box office hit, and the idea was to do the same with Goodman's life. There was trouble almost from the outset. John Hammond's role in Goodman's career would have to be depicted. Accord-ing to Hammond, Alice was assigned to broach the subject with him.²³ Hammond, who was still smarting from the fiasco of the 1953 tour, in-sisted on seeing the script. He was horrified to discover that the Ham-monds were "portrayed as schnooks. . . . Alice was shown proposing to Benny. I was a rich dilettante attempting to help Benny, although he made all the decisions."²⁴ Furthermore, there was no mention of Willard Alex-ander, whose early faith in the band had been important to its success. Hammond went to his lawyer, who suggested that they ask the movie com-pany for $50,000 in compensation for what they saw as unsympathetic treatment of him. The movie company turned Hammond down, as Ham-mond expected, and then changed the Hammond character's name to "Willard Alexander," or so Hammond says. Now Alexander balked; and the upshot was that Hammond, and apparently Alexander, were paid a few thousand dollars each, and their roles in the film were substantially re-duced.

Steve Allen, then a rising television star, was hired to play Goodman. On the surface it seemed a good choice: Allen looked a little like Good-man, played a little jazz piano, and was sympathetic to the music. Unfor-tunately he was not a professional actor, and the film suffered from his rather wooden portrayal of Benny.

Other problems arose from putting together a band to play the sound track. It included some of the players from the old band, among them Griffin, Schertzer, Reuss, Krupa, Russin, McEachern and Martha Tilton;

some from later groups, like Stan Getz; and some, like Buck Clayton, who had not been with the old band at all. Some of the omissions were un-avoidable. Harry James, for example, was by now too big a star to work as a sideman, although he did appear as a soloist in "Sing, Sing, Sing" and replicated his Carnegie Hall "Shine" solo, and both Red Ballard and Dick Clark were out of music. But the omissions of Jess Stacy and Vido Musso, two of the band's primary soloists, rankled. Friends of Musso said, "Vido was the biggest tenor star Benny ever had. . . . Vido was very hurt that Benny didn't use him in the concert sequence." Stacy was even more bitter. He said:

> Benny—or rather one of his underlings—called me and asked me to do some recording as a favor. So I get out there and discover that they have given most of the things I did with the band to Teddy Wilson, who was never actually a member of the band. And I was supposed to do just some little thing on one number—for flat scale for one session. Then Benny, trying to be funny, said I was playing like I needed a blood tranfusion. I told him ———— ———— and walked out.[25]

The Benny Goodman Story was, in the end, a travesty which bore little relation to Goodman's life or to the band business in general. Goodman was portrayed sympathetically as inarticulate and so preoccupied with his music that he failed to notice that he was in love with Alice. Alice's first marriage was eliminated, and she was brought into Goodman's life at a time when she was still living in England with Duckworth. All of this, of course, was not surprising. Hollywood has never been notorious for the faithful rendering of human life. Jazz fans were inevitably annoyed, but the film did reasonably well, and continues to be shown occasionally on late night television, mainly to audiences of by now middle-aged men and women reliving the days of the big bands.

The music, in any case, was surprisingly good, in view of how Hollywood has usually treated jazz. The presence of Hymie Schertzer and Babe Russin, who had played these arrangements thousands of times, made the saxo-phone section sound as good as ever.

The trumpets do not quite have the precision and bite of the classic James-Elman-Griffin group, but they are not far off. Teddy Wilson's play-ing of the piano solos that were originally Stacy's are somewhat tentative, lacking the confident flash that emanated from the old Trio and Quartet sides. It is my feeling that he had been told, if not exactly to play like Jess, at least to emulate Stacy's more spare style, which was not natural to him. On the second half of the bridge of his solo on "It's Been So Long," he uses a very Stacy-like tremolo, and then dashes briskly away from it, as if annoyed, with a very typical Wilson run.

Yet on the whole the band sounds very good. The more modern sound of the primary saxophone and trombone soloists, Stan Getz and Urbie Green, is a little out of place against the backdrop of music by this time twenty years old, but both men were among the best of their time. Buck Clayton, who does the bulk of the trumpet soloing, was of course one of the leading trumpeters of the swing era. The rhythm section was as close to the original as it could have been. Mannie Klein does a fine job of re-creating Elman's "And the Angels Sing" solo.

Goodman's own playing—and there is a lot of it—is excellent. The movie version of "China Boy" for example is as exciting as any he ever made. It remains amazing that he could continue to bring enthusiasm to a piece like this one, which he had by this time played many thousands of times.

As had happened on the heels of the issuance of the Carnegie Hall album, the movie led to a spate of activity—radio and television appearances, interviews, magazine stories. The tone, however, was nostalgic. Interviewers wanted to hear about the Pollack days, the opening at the Paramount, the Carnegie Hall concert. Although there was still a substantial audience for his music, Goodman was now seen by younger people as a relic, a hero from the past on the order of a retired baseball player ready for the Hall of Fame.

He put together a new band which played sporadic one-nighters through the spring. It was held in abeyance over the summer, but was then re-formed in November to play a tour of the Far East under State Department auspices. The band continued to work occasionally through the spring of 1957, and then Goodman's interest ran out. From now on Goodman would increasingly go out with small groups of various kinds—trios, quartets, sextets or octets which might use abbreviated arrangements to give some of the feeling of a larger orchestra. There was a 1958 European tour, built around appearances at the Brussels World's Fair, which resulted in a number of recordings. A great deal of this activity was occasioned by radio and television appearances. But sometimes weeks, or even months, would go by with little or nothing musical happening.

In putting together these groups Goodman usually reached out for the best musicians he could find. At one time or another through the 1950s and 1960s he employed Zoot Sims, Urbie Green, Milt Hinton, George Duvivier, Bob Wilber, Jerry Dodgion, Red Norvo, Bill Harris, Flip Phillips, Clark Terry, Jimmy Knepper, Phil Woods and others of the best jazz musicians of the time. He also occasionally reached back for the veterans— Murray McEachern, Hymie Schertzer, even, on special occasions, Gene Krupa. But he was depending more and more on less well-known people, many of them highly competent young players who were flattered to be asked to play for Goodman and were more tractable than established stars might be.

He continued to add to the repertory, putting in the book occasional recent hits like "People," "Ode to Billy Joe," or older tunes he just happened to like. But the heart of the book remained the same—big band versions of "Don't Be That Way," "One O'Clock Jump," "I'll Never Say Never Again, Again," small group renditions of "Avalon," "After You've Gone," "Memories of You." Even the famous Sextet pieces from the 1940s began to slip away. Goodman continued to play "Slipped Disc" and "Air Mail Special," but others, like "Wholly Cats" and "Gone With What Wind," virtually disappeared. Nor was he playing many of the Sauter and Powell arrangements from the 1940s. He would play "Clarinade" and "Mission to Moscow" from time to time, but most of the Sauter pieces were trotted out very rarely. Goodman, it is clear, had his heart fixed on the 1930s. It was this music—the things that he played on *Let's Dance*, at the Palomar, the Congress, the Paramount and Carnegie Hall—that he was focused on. In part, of course, this was the music his older fans wanted to hear. A lot of them had never really got used to the later pieces, and although the 1940 band had been very popular, the older repertory had always been seen by his first fans, the ones who shouted and danced at the paramount, as what the Benny Goodman band was all about. "King Porter Stomp" and "Bugle Call Rag" were as much a part of their youths as their young loves and early rebellions. This was the music they wanted to hear, not "Superman" or "Clarinet a la King."

But it is equally true that this was the music that Goodman himself liked best. It is an interesting fact that once a jazz musician absorbs into his head a certain way of playing, usually in adolescence, he or she has great difficulty going beyond it. Only the greatest players have been able to adopt a new way of playing, and none has ever done it twice. Louis Armstrong, for example, made the change from the old New Orleans style to the new swing music he played such a large role in developing, but he was not able to cope with, or even understand, the modern styles that came in the 1940s. Duke Ellington's music constantly advanced, but it did so primarily within the confines of a basic style which was more or less in place by the early 1930s. Goodman, like Armstrong, began as a dixielander imitating the New Orleans pioneers Shields, Roppolo and Berendsohn; and like Armstrong he moved into the new swing style which he also had a considerable hand in developing. But there he stuck. Even when he was leading what was ostensibly a bebop band his attempts to play the music were few and futile. He did not want to play another kind of music, and the consequence was that for the remainder of his life he was simply repeating what he had done a thousand times already. He was not alone in so doing, of course.

None of his contemporaries from the swing period, even masters such as Coleman Hawkins and Roy Eldridge, really became boppers. Nor is this to say that the music was bad: although as time went on he sometimes seemed to be only going through the motions, he could, when properly inspired, still play as well as he ever had. But the music was the same as it always had been.

Furthermore, he was no longer influencing the younger players. Where in the 1930s he had spread over jazz like an enormous cloud, his influence so strong that it was almost impossible for anyone to follow him, after 1950 only rarely would there come along a young player whose basic allegiance was to Goodman. The young musicians were choosing other models.

One of the results of this concentration on the older music was that the young musicians he increasingly had to hire quickly became discontented. To begin with, they had grown up learning the thicker harmonic textures of the postwar period, the altered chords with their chromatic intervals, and they found the endless triads and seventh chords on which much of Goodman's music was based insipid. For a second thing, they quickly discovered that, even when Goodman had more advanced music in the book, he tended to play the tried and true pieces again and again. The sidemen would become bored, restless, scornful, and this in turn would lead to too much drinking and a too casual attitude toward the work. This, for example, happened in the course of a series of European tours Goodman made in 1970 and 1971 with a band of English musicians. In 1969, Goodman had used English musicians perforce when he was asked to record in London while there on vacation. He liked what he heard, and the fact that English musicians would come cheaper and would not have to be transported from the United States made it inevitable that he would try them again. At first the experiment was a great success. Goodman was challenged by playing with new musicians, and the English players were excited by the chance to play with a legend. But soon, after reading down "King Porter Stomp" and "Don't Be That Way" yet one more time, the sideman began to grow restless. Discipline broke down, and in the end Goodman called a halt.[26]

The same problem caused a good deal of difficulty on the 1962 excursion to the U.S.S.R., which has since become notorious in the small world of jazz. In the spring of 1961 the State Department, perhaps unaware that Goodman was no longer one of the leading figures in jazz, announced that he would take an orchestra to the Soviet Union the next year, the first American group to tour there since the 1920s. There were, inevitably, complaints that Goodman's music was old fashioned and that a more modern band ought to have been selected. In particular, many critics felt that the Ellington band, playing a more complicated and perhaps more worthy kind of music, ought to have been given the honor. But whatever the State Department's thinking, Goodman's audience appeal was extremely broad, making him a safe choice.

In fact, by 1962 Russian jazz musicians and the underground jazz fans were far more sophisticated about the music than Americans were aware.[27] By means of smuggled records and especially the Voice of America broadcasts of Willis Conover, they had heard a great deal of jazz, and many of the best of them, like the famous Gennadi Golstein and the legendary Roman Kunsman, now in Israel, were beginning to go beyond bop into various kinds of experimental music. The jazz community would find Goodman's music out-dated, although they were nonetheless eager to hear the band. But the boppers constituted only a very small group in the Soviet population, and the State Department was probably right, although the Ellington band, which could have satisfied both the jazz community and the general public, might have been the optimum choice.

The projected tour generated a lot of publicity. Russia had been, for most Americans, closed tight in the years of the cold war. It seemed a mysterious and forbidding place, that had only recently been opened up a little by Nikita Khrushchev with the so-called "thaw," especially in the area of the arts. The idea that an American jazz band would visit there was intriguing.

Goodman was excited by the scheme: among other things, his parents were both Russian émigrés. He set about recruiting what would be an all-star band, including Jimmy Maxwell, Phil Woods, Zoot Sims, Jimmy Knepper, Joe Wilder, Ellington's former singer Joya Sherrill, and an exemplary rhythm section of John Bunch, Bill Crow, Mel Lewis, and Turk Van Lake. Teddy Wilson was brought along to work with the small group, with Vic Feldman on vibes.

In fact, Goodman had a certain amount of difficulty getting the men he wanted. The rumor was circulating that Russia was not exactly Disneyland. Furthermore, many of the men had worked for Goodman before and knew how difficult he could be. Jimmy Maxwell kept refusing, even though Goodman pushed his salary up to a thousand dollars a week, a very high salary for the time, and only consented to come when Benny offered to include Maxwell's son David, who was eager to see Russia, as bandboy.[28] John Bunch similarly resisted. He said:

> A friend of mine had just been to Russia and he told me, don't go. It's awful, it's the most depressing place. I didn't want to go. So I asked more money than he was willing to pay me, and we must have talked for half an hour on the phone, long distance, which was sort of a big deal then. I probably asked four hundred dollars, and he was only willing to pay three hundred dollars, or something like that. But I got

it out of him, because I really didn't want to go. It was so hard to get
him not to be thinking of money in terms of 1938.[29]

Despite everything, initially the morale of the band was high. Goodman
had commissioned a considerable number of new, more advanced, arrangements, which the men enjoyed playing. They knew they would have to
play a lot of the old book, but they were assuming that Goodman wanted
something more contemporary for the tour. It was a considerable mistake.

In 1986 and 1987, several months after Goodman's death, Gene Lees
published in his *Jazzletter*[30]—a rather personal and prickly newsletter devoted to music and other matters Lees has on his mind—a series of pieces
on the Russian tour by Bill Crow, along with a storm of letters the series
engendered. The pieces constituted a fairly complete catalogue of all the
criticisms which have been leveled at Goodman by musicians—his insensitivity, his tendency to shove himself into the spotlight, his public butt-
scratching, his niggling over money and his general attitude that he was
King and the musicians were lackeys expected to accept with a smile whatever abuse he heaped on them. It was an important story in the sometimes
ingrown world of jazz, because it was one of the few times that anybody
had said in public the things that people in the music business had been
saying about Goodman privately for years. (The jazz press has always considered it close to criminal to write honestly about musicians, especially
revered figures like Goodman.) Predictably a number of people were angry
at Crow and Lees, especially as the pieces had run so soon after Benny's
death. Lees, in his defense, pointed out that the pieces had been written
and scheduled to run while Goodman was still alive, and, so far as anyone
knew, was likely to remain alive long enough to sue. The pieces undoubtedly exaggerate Goodman's defects. Although the majority of the letters in
response supported Crow's view of Goodman, a number of correspondents
described generosities and decencies Goodman had shown to them or
others. It must be borne in mind that Goodman treated his musicians far
worse than he treated most other people in his life, especially important
jazz writers, some of whom wrote to Lees in Goodman's defense. We must
keep it in mind that musicians were seeing a somewhat different Benny
Goodman from the one many others saw.

But it cannot be denied that he treated musicians badly, and the Russian
tour ended with virtually all of the musicians enraged at Goodman, although some of them would continue to work for him afterwards. A major
source of annoyance was that Goodman stuck almost entirely to the old
book, ignoring the new arrangements which had been carefully rehearsed.
It was "King Porter Stomp" and "One O'Clock Jump" all over again. (For
the LP package issued in conjunction with the tour, producer George

Avakian was unwilling to issue yet another album of Goodman standards and so concentrated on the new material as much as possible. The album does not reflect what the band played on the tour.)[31]

As it worked out, the general Russian public liked the older pieces, and the tour was a popular success, but predictably the jazz people were disappointed. Alexey Batashev, then president of the Jazz Section of the Musical Youth Club and today considered one of the Soviet Union's leading authorities on jazz, said, "He is a bit old-fashioned," but, he added politely, "very interesting."[32] Valery Myssovsky, a jazz drummer who did some translating for the band when it was in Leningrad, said:

> At the Winter Stadium, which was full to the brim, the band played wonderfully, but unfortunately, after 3-4 numbers our young dixielanders began shouting for "Bei Mir Bist du Schön," which B. G. understood at once as "a must" for us, illiterate Russians—and that was the end of the big-band concert. He started playing only with the rhythm section and vibes . . . and only dixie numbers. Which was not very interesting and disappointing, for we wanted to listen to those great arrangements, played by such men as Joe Newman, Phil Woods, Zoot Sims, et al. But of course the public went wild.[33]

Myssovsky, who had met the band at the airport, added one more story to the Goodman archive. Benny almost immediately asked Myssovsky to see that he stay at a different hotel from his musicians. Myssovsky quickly explained that he had not the authority to make such arrangements, saying that he was not from Intourist but was "only a musician." Suddenly Goodman was shaking Myssovsky's hand enthusiastically, saying how delighted he was to meet the eminent composer. Myssovsky had to explain that he was not the eminent composer Nicolai Myaskovsky, upon which Goodman broke off the conversation.[34]

Whatever the musicians thought about the tour, to everybody else it was a great success. Russian leader Khrushchev attended the first concert, and once the official audience was gotten out of the way, ordinary fans piled in and responded with great enthusiasm to the music. The State Department was pleased, and so was Goodman, who was invited to the White House to be personally thanked by President John F. Kennedy on his return. Life, at the time the most prestigious of the popular magazines, ran a story on the tour, there were major television and radio interviews, and the governor of Connecticut, Goodman's home state, proclaimed "Benny Goodman Day."[35] On the strength of this publicity Goodman put together a new band, which included Cootie Williams, and went off on a two-month tour.

Over the next few years Goodman continued to play regularly, but it was again with groups put together for special engagements—a concert, a television appearance, a brief tour, or a two- or three-week stand at a room like New York's famous Rainbow Grill, high up in Rockefeller Center, which has always presented a good deal of jazz. Goodman was now a grand old man, an emeritus figure, and he was frequently in the news. A party was given in January 1968 to celebrate the thirtieth anniversary of the Carnegie Hall concert, at which a considerable number of the people who had played at it were present.

He was beginning to age, and he continued to suffer from back problems. He liked to fish, he liked to garden, he enjoyed going to lunch with people who were sympathetic to him and enjoyed his conversation.[36] But he could not stop playing. Music was at the center of his existence; without it he was lost, wandering purposelessly through life. So he continued to put together bands, although these were mostly small groups which were easy to assemble for brief engagements.

Even Russ Connor admits, though, that "Benny's produce in the 1970s is not highly esteemed by Goodman's enthusiasts, and likely never will be compared favorably with his work in other decades by Goodman collectors."[37] His playing was simply not nearly as inventive as it had been, and there are even moments when his astonishing control falters, although these are rare. There is, of course, no reason why in his sixties Goodman should have played as well as he had in his twenties or even his forties: jazz is a young man's game. Furthermore, he was not surrounding himself with the best musicians he could find—the Charlie Christians, Bunny Berigans, Phil Woods—but with younger and less well-known players. Many of them were fine jazz musicians, and some, like Scott Hamilton and Warren Vaché, would go on to make their names in jazz; but the inspiration Goodman had derived from Berigan, Wilson and the others was often not there. At the time of the Russian tour Teddy Wilson told Bill Crow that one reason for continuing to play with Goodman was that "these jobs allow me to play with a class of musician I can't afford to hire myself."[38] That was less the case than it had been.

Then in February 1978, Alice Goodman suddenly died in their home in St. Maartens in the Caribbean at the age of seventy-two. Her body was returned to Connecticut, where there was a small private service. How Goodman felt was impossible to know. He said nothing publicly, and went out the next day to play a scheduled charity performance, on the grounds that Alice would not have wanted him to cancel it.[39]

He was now moving into his seventies, but still he would not stop. There were many reasons why he should have. John Bunch, who played with him until the last few years before his death, said, "Physically, he was failing. . . . He'd come out and say, 'Now the band's going to play, I'll be back in a little while,' and he'd go off, sit down, lie down. He'd do the second half, which would be real long. They'd get their money's worth. Sometimes it'd be an hour and fifteen minutes long."[40] But, Bunch adds, he would at times play wonderfully. He recalled one tour when Goodman "could hardly walk on the stage. One one of the sound checks we had to do, we were just fooling around. I started playing 'Runnin Wild' real fast on the piano, and the drums started doing it with me, and Benny started playing it. I'm going to tell you, it was unbelievable, it was so exciting. We were all saying, 'Hey, yeah, Benny, Benny that sounded great, nobody heard it except us and some stage hands, why don't we play it tonight?' He said, 'Well, okay.' But he never called it."[41]

Nor had demand for his services slackened. Even as late as 1977, *Down Beat's* John McDonough could say, "Goodman is the only bankable jazz star left who can pack a concert hall by himself. Basie would need a co-star. So would Herman, Kenton, maybe even Rich . . . but the Goodman mystique has not only survived, it's thrived."[42]

By the 1980s Goodman's problems with his health had increased. He was beginning to suffer from arthritis in his fingers, he had a chronically sore knee, and in November 1983, he decided to see a doctor, something he obviously should have done earlier. As soon as the results from the electrocardiogram tests were in he was rushed to a hospital, "while a team of surgeons strove to dissolve an embolism in his descending aorta."[43] In January 1984, Goodman went back to the hospital to have a pacemaker implanted. He spent a year away from music, recuperating in Connecticut and at St. Maartens, where he could do the swimming that eased his back. Carol Phillips said, "He was a courageous man and a magnificent patient." But, she added, "He tried the rocking chair and didn't like it."[44]

Early in 1985 Bill Hyland, an attorney and clarinetist who became one of Goodman's most trusted advisors and executor of his estate, mentioned to Goodman that a friend was wondering if Benny would play the wedding of his daughter. Much to everybody's surprise, Goodman decided to do it. It was just the sort of quiet, unpublicized event at which he could see what was left of his old skills. According to Connor, who has heard a tape of the event, "His playing is brilliant, effortless, faultless, inspiring . . . the sidemen are visibly impressed."[45]

Encouraged, Goodman began rehearsing with a big band, once again playing mainly the arrangements from the 1930s. The band played some broadcasts, and then, through 1986, a few concerts. Goodman was pleased with the orchestra and the way he himself was playing. He scheduled a concert tour with the group which would by fall take him to the West Coast. But he never played the tour.

On June 10, 1986, Russ Connor talked to Goodman by telephone and discovered Benny's speech to be "thick and hesitant."[46] The next day James T. Maher also talked with Goodman and concluded that he was not well.[47] He called Connor and both urged Benny to cut down on his activities. On June 12, Benny and Carol Phillips went out to a club called Mr. Sam's.[48] It was raining, and Goodman was having pains in his shoulder. Carol suggested that they go to a small apartment she kept in the east Seventies, which was nearby, but Goodman wanted to go home to his Sixty-sixth Street apartment. In the morning Phillips went to her office, the plan being that they were to go to Connecticut for the weekend. Goodman did some routine business, ate lunch and then went into his study to nap. Phillips, meanwhile, went back to her place to pick up some groceries which had been delivered there. She had only been there a short while when the phone rang. It was Goodman's housekeeper, who said, "There's something wrong, Miss Phillips." She rushed down to Sixty-sixth Street. "I went into Benny's [study] and he was sitting us, his clarinet next to him. There was some heartbeat." Phillips called the emergency number, but when she came back to the study Benny Goodman was dead. The Brahms Sonata opus #120 was on the music stand beside him.

Not long before his death, Goodman had arranged with Yale University to house his papers, the most valuable portion of which is some thousands of hours of music Goodman had made over the years in his private recording studio in Stamford and elsewhere. These are being issued, with the royalties going into a fund which will be used to house and catalogue Goodman's papers, which include pictures, about a thousand arrangements, awards, a few scrapbooks and some video as well as the audio tapes. However, Goodman made it clear that he wanted no ghost band of the kind that was put together after the deaths of Glenn Miller, the Dorsey brothers, Duke Ellington and Count Basie.

There will, however, be a lot of new music to come from Yale, record companies with unissued material and, undoubtedly, bootleg concerts and broadcasts. We will be hearing new music from Benny Goodman for years to come.

# 28
# The Legacy of
# Benny Goodman

It is not as easy to assess the place of Benny Goodman in the history of jazz as it is with some, like Armstrong and Charlie Parker, who were such overpowering improvisers that they drew everybody in behind them and changed the course of the music. As a jazz musician Goodman ranks a step behind the tiny group of musicians at the apex, a group which includes Armstrong, Parker, Ellington and perhaps Beiderbecke, Lester Young and John Coltrane. He belongs, rather, to a not much larger group, which in my judgment would include Teagarden, Miles Davis, Coleman Hawkins, Bill Evans, Billie Holiday, and perhaps a dozen others—every jazz fan will have his own list. Many will disagree, but I think the case can be made. For one thing, Goodman was probably the single most influential clarinetist in the history of jazz, and he was emulated by some very fine clarinetists indeed, among them Edmond Hall and Jimmy Hamilton. Hall said, "They don't come any better than Benny. . . . Benny's always been my favorite jazz musician,"[1] and Hamilton's debt to Goodman is evident everywhere in his playing. Goodman furthermore had one of the most awe-inspiring techniques in jazz, to be ranked with that of Art Tatum on his instrument. He was also one of the hardest swingers to play the music, and his work was rhythmically as varied as any of the other great improvisers. His primary weakness was the lack of coherence, the inability to construct long speeches. Thus, from a viewpoint of technique, ability to swing, and influence, it seems to me that Goodman has to be numbered among the greatest of jazz musicians, the first clarinet player in jazz.

But Benny Goodman stands out in jazz history not just as an improvising musician. For one thing, there are the small group recordings. They constitute a large and varied body of work which by themselves would have made Goodman an important figure in jazz. They are scintillating, sparkling, the bubbling champagne of jazz music. Despite the fact that they included a number of very great jazz musicians, it was Benny Goodman, and nobody else, who set the musical philosophy for these groups. He picked the musicians, he chose the material for them, and he shaped it according to his own ideas, and was, moreover, the major soloist with them, the leader in all senses. These groups reflect Goodman as much as Duke Ellington's orchestra reflected him, and they are intensely individual and instantly recognizable. They are one of the chief treasures of jazz music.

Finally, there were the big bands. As we have seen, many hands contributed to the making of the swing band which dominated popular music and jazz for fifteen years, and continues to have a life some fifty years later. Art Hickman, Ferde Grofé, Don Redman, Fletcher Henderson, Bill Challis, Benny Carter, Gene Gifford, Duke Ellington, Ben Pollack, Red Nichols, Glenn Miller, John Hammond and all the other musicians whose names are scattered through this book, added something to the mix. But it was Benny Goodman, in the years around 1935, who gathered up all that had gone before and set the form for swing music. Whiteman, Ellington, Pollack, Nichols, Casa Loma had been there first. But it was Goodman who found the form—the formula if you will—which captured the mass audience. He was the one who turned the jazz-based dance music of the 1920s into the dominating popular music of the next two decades. Writer Frank Norris said in 1938, "No other band of this quality has ever had such public acceptance. In the past year and a half it has sold more records, played longer runs and scored higher radio ratings than any band of its kind in the history of American popular music."[2]

It is my contention that the big band swing music of that period was the finest kind of popular music we have seen in centuries, rivaled perhaps only by the waltz music of the late nineteenth century. For one thing, it was carefully rehearsed with close attention to detail, and played expertly and at times brilliantly, by thoroughly trained musicians, many of whom were capable of playing in the best symphony orchestras. For another, it was harmonically richer than any other popular music I can think of, and it became more so as it educated American taste, to the point where by the mid-1940s big-band arrangers were using harmonies that could have been drawn from Mahler, Brahms and the twentieth-century modernists—and often were. For another, it employed a great deal of counterpoint—not as much as is found in, say, a Bach fugue or the early New Orleans dixieland—but far more than is customary in popular dance music. Finally, it was built on the very subtle and complex rhythmic scheme of jazz, a system so delicate that nobody has yet found a way to notate it.

Swing music was not, I submit, as great a musical form as, once again let us say, the European symphony of the eighteenth and nineteenth centuries. But it was a sophisticated and skillfully played music which at moments reached toward the highest levels. Benny Goodman was the man who found the way to it, and opened the door for the bands which rushed through the gap—among them Basie, Herman, Barnet, Lunceford, Berigan, Crosby, Webb, Shaw, and eventually Kenton, Raeburn and the modernists. How things would have turned out without Goodman is hard to say. But they would have been different.

# Notes

The following abbreviations are used in the notes. "Rutgers" refers to the Institute for Jazz Studies, Bradley Hall, Rutgers University, Newark, New Jersey. "Tulane" refers to the William Ransom Hogan Archive of Jazz, Howard-Tilton Library, Tulane University, New Orleans, Louisiana. "Yale" refers to the John Herrick Jackson Music Library, Yale University, New Haven, Connecticut. "KS" refers to Benny Goodman and Irving Kolodin, *The Kingdom of Swing* (New York: Stackpole Sons, 1939). "Connor" refers to D. Russell Connor, *Benny Goodman: Listen to His Legacy* (Metuchen, NJ: The Scarecrow Press, 1988).

## 1. The Family

1. Ray Ginger, *Age of Excess* (New York: Macmillan, 1963), 23.
2. Ibid., 313–14.
3. James Lincoln Collier, *The Reception of Jazz in America* (Brooklyn: Institute for Studies in American Music, 1988), 14.
4. *Down Beat*, Nov. 17, 1977, 14.
5. Benny Goodman and Irving Kolodin, *The Kingdom of Swing* (New York: Stackpole Sons, 1939).
6. Irving Cutler in *Ethnic Chicago*, Melvin G. Holli and Peter d'A. Jones (eds.), (Grand Rapids, MI: Eerdmans, 1984), 77.
7. Ibid.
8. Ibid., 81.
9. See Chicago City Directories.
10. Interviews with James T. Maher, Nov., Dec. 1987, Jan. 1988.
11. Ibid.
12. Steven Mintz and Susan Kellogg, *Domestic Revolutions: A Social History of American Family Life* (New York: The Free Press, 1988), 84–91.
13. *KS*, 17.
14. *KS*, 16.

15. *KS,* 17.
16. *KS,* 18.
17. Interview with Maher.
18. Interview with Helen Ward, Dec. 12, 1987.
19. *KS,* 19.
20. Interview with Maher.
21. Interview with Ward.
22. Interview with Maher.
23. Interview with Carol Phillips, April 29, 1988.
24. *KS,* 17.
25. Interview with Phillips.
26. *KS,* 17.
27. *KS,* 19.

## 2. The Musical Apprentice

1. *KS,* 20.
2. Robert H. Wiebe, *The Search for Order* (New York: Hill and Wang, 1967), 289.
3. James Lincoln Collier, *Louis Armstrong: An American Genius* (New York: Oxford, 1983), 38–39.
4. Stanley Dance, *The World of Swing* (New York: Da Capo, 1979), 265.
5. Robert H. Wiebe, *The Search for Order,* 120–21.
6. *KS,* 20–21.
7. Stanley Dance, *The World of Earl Hines* (New York: Scribner's, 1977), 193.
8. *KS,* 22.
9. Allen F. Davis and Mary Lynn McCrae, eds., *Eighty Years at Hull House* (Chicago: Quadrangle, 1969).
10. Ibid., 10.
11. *KS,* 22.
12. F. Geoffrey Rendall, *The Clarinet* (New York: Philosophical Library, 1954), 102.
13. I am indebted to clarinetist Robert Sparkman, with whom I discussed the subject of Boehm and Albert systems at length.
14. *Down Beat,* Nov. 17, 1977, 15.
15. *KS,* 27–28.
16. *Woodwind Magazine,* Nov. 1949, 3.
17. Lodged in Goodman archive at John Herrick Jackson Music Library, Yale University.
18. Collier, *Louis Armstrong: An American Genius,* 230–32.
19. See Collier, *The Reception of Jazz in America,* 7–8.
20. Undated clipping in Nick LaRocca scrapbooks, Hogan Archive of Jazz, Tulane University.
21. *KS,* 23.
22. Collier, *The Reception of Jazz in America,* 7.
23. *New Yorker,* Dec. 26, 1977.
24. Personal communication, from Grover Sales.

25. KS, 29.
26. Collier, The Reception of Jazz in America, 14.
27. KS, 23.
28. Dance, The World of Earl Hines, 193.
29. KS, 24.
30. Hull House Year Book for 1921, 35.
31. Oral history of Art Hodes, #2–46, Rutgers.
32. Dance, The World of Earl Hines, 193.
33. KS, 28.
34. Ibid., 29.
35. Ibid., 30.
36. Bud Freeman, You Don't Look Like a Musician (Detroit: Balamp, 1974), 28.
37. Oral history of Jimmy McPartland, #1–58, Rutgers.
38. Collier, The Reception of Jazz in America.
39. KS, 33–34.
40. Mintz and Kellogg, Domestic Revolutions, 84–85.
41. KS, 36–37.
42. Dempsey J. Travis, An Autobiography of Black Jazz (Chicago: Urban Research Institute, 1983), 25.
43. Illinois-Chicago Commission on Race Relations, The Negro in Chicago (New York: Arno Press and the New York Times, 1968), 323–24.
44. Dance, The World of Earl Hines, 48.
45. Oral history of Bud Freeman, #2–41, Rutgers.
46. Interview with Jess Stacy, April 29, 1987.
47. KS, chap. 2.
48. KS, 38–39.
49. KS, 45.
50. Freeman, You Don't Look Like a Musician, 40.

## 3. The Rise of the American Dance Band

1. Philip Van Doren Stern, The Beginnings of Art (New York: Four Winds Press, 1973), 175–76.
2. Down Beat, Dec. 15, 1940, 10.
3. Robert A. Woods and Albert J. Kennedy, Young Working Girls: A Summary of Evidence from Two Thousand Social Workers (Boston: Houghton Mifflin, 1913), 105–8.
4. Caroline and Charles H. Caffin, Dancing and Dancers of Today (New York: Da Capo, 1978), 256–69. Originally published in 1913. See also issues of the New York Times for the 1910–12 period.
5. Tom Stoddard, Jazz on the Barbary Coast (Chigwell, England: Storyville, 1982), 28.
6. New York Times, June 25, 1922, sec. 3, 8.
7. Tom Stoddard, Jazz on the Barbary Coast, 29.
8. Henry O. Osgood, So This Is Jazz (Boston: Little, Brown, 1926), 89–90.
9. Edward A. Berlin, Ragtime: A Musical and Cultural History (Berkeley: Univ. of California Press, 1980), 147.

10. *Music Journal*, April 1955, 23.
11. Oral history of Bill Challis, Rutgers.
12. Interview with James T. Maher, Dec. 1987.
13. San Francisco journalist E. T. Gleason, quoted by Maher in interview with Maher, Dec. 1987.
14. Stoddard, *Jazz On the Barbary Coast*, 132.
15. *American Mercury*, April 26, 1927, 385.
16. *Scribner's*, Dec. 1931, 594.
17. *International Musician*, Aug. 1953, 19.
18. *Etude*, July 1938, 425.
19. *Scribner's*, Dec. 1931, 594.
20. *Etude*, July 1938, 425.
21. *International Musician*, Aug. 1953, 19.
22. Ibid.
23. Stoddard, *Jazz On the Barbary Coast*, 32.
24. Ibid., 36.
25. *International Musician*, Aug. 1953, 19.
26. Stoddard, *Jazz On the Barbary Coast*, 127.
27. *International Musician*, Aug. 1953, 19.
28. Personal communication from Maher.
29. *Orchestra World*, March 1936, 6.
30. *American Mercury*, April 1926, 386–95.
31. *The Melody Maker*, Feb. 1926, 29–32.
32. Quoted by Maher, in interview.
33. *Down Beat*, Feb. 15, 1940, 12.
34. *The Clipper*, Feb. 7, 1923, 18.
35. *Orchestra World*, March 1936, 6.
36. Interview with Maher.
37. *Orchestra World*, March 1936, 6.
38. Thomas A. DeLong, *Pops: Paul Whiteman, King of Jazz* (Piscataway, NJ: New Century, 1983), 24–25.
39. Ibid., 36.
40. Letter from Abel Green to James T. Maher dated March 11, 1964.
41. DeLong, *Pops*, 59.
42. Unidentified clipping, LaRocca scrapbooks, Tulane.
43. *New York Times Book Review and Magazine*, Feb. 9, 1922, 8.
44. Tom Stoddard, *Jazz On the Barbary Coast*, 127.
45. *Down Beat*, Sept. 1940, 7.
46. Maher, personal communication.
47. DeLong, *Pops*, 61–63.
48. *The Clipper*, Jan. 4, 1924, 25.
49. *The Clipper*, Nov. 8, 1922, 28.
50. *The Clipper*, Nov. 15, 1922, 28.
51. *The Clipper*, Jan. 4, 1924, 25.
52. *New York Times*, Feb. 13, 1924.
53. *Atlantic*, August 1922, 182–89.
54. *The Bookman*, June 1928, 422.
55. James Lincoln Collier, *Duke Ellington* (New York: Oxford, 1987), 48.
56. Collier, *Louis Armstrong: An American Genius*, 128.

57. Arthur Lange, *Arranging for the Modern Dance Orchestra* (New York: Robbins Music, 1926).
58. *The ASCAP Biographical Dictionary* (New York: 1966), 419.
59. Lange, *Arranging for the Modern Dance Orchestra*, 211.
60. Liner notes, *Fletcher Henderson: First Impressions.* Decca DL79227.
61. Brochure for *Big Band Jazz*, Gunther Schuller and Martin Williams, unpaged.
62. Arnold Shaw, *The Jazz Age: Popular Music in the 1920s* (New York: Oxford, 1987), 46.
63. Richard M. Sudhalter and Philip R. Evans, *Bix, Man and Legend* (New Rochelle, NY: Arlington House, 1974), 185.
64. Interview with Maher, from his interview with Don Redman.

## 4. The Pollack Orchestra

1. Details of Pollack's early career are found in interviews with him appearing in *Down Beat*, Oct. 1936, 2; Nov. 1936, 11; Jan. 1937, 3; Feb. 1937, 7; March 1937, 15. See also John Chilton, *Stomp Off, Let's Go* (London: Jazz Book Service, 1983), 10–13.
2. *Down Beat*, Oct. 1936, 2.
3. Oral history of Bill Challis, #2–4, Rutgers.
4. Oral history of Jimmy McPartland, #1–69, Rutgers.
5. KS, 77.
6. *Down Beat*, Nov. 1936, 11.
7. KS, 66–68.
8. *Down Beat*, Jan. 1937, 3.
9. KS, 70–71.
10. Ibid.
11. John Chilton, *Stomp Off, Let's Go*, 10.
12. KS, 82.
13. Collier, *Louis Armstrong: An American Genius*, 167.
14. *Down Beat*, Jan. 1937, 4.
15. Oral history of Jimmy McPartland, #1–66, Rutgers.
16. Oral history of Bud Freeman, #38–40, Rutgers.
17. Radio interview with Charles Edward Smith, late 1940s, in author's files.
18. *Down Beat*, Dec. 1937, 7.
19. *Down Beat*, Jan. 1937, 4.
20. KS, 90.
21. Stanley Baron, *Benny: King of Swing* (New York: William Morrow, 1979), 19.
22. Connor, 6.
23. Oral history of Jimmy McPartland, #1–141, Rutgers.
24. Ibid., #1–69–70.
25. *Down Beat*, Jan. 1937, 4.
26. *Down Beat*, Feb. 1937, 7.
27. Ibid.
28. Ibid., 10.
29. Oral history of Jimmy McPartland, #1–68–70, Rutgers.

30. Ibid., #1–60.
31. *Down Beat*, Feb. 1937, 10.
32. Oral history of Jimmy McPartland, #1–70, Rutgers.
33. Details of the dissolution of the Pollack band can be found in John Chilton, *Stomp Off, Let's Go*, 11–14.
34. *New York Times*, June 9, 1971, unidentified clipping, Pollack Vertical File, Rutgers.
35. John Chilton, *Stomp Off, Let's Go*, 11.
36. Ibid., 11–12.
37. Charlie Barnet with Stanley Dance, *Those Swinging Years* (Baton Rouge: Louisiana State University Press, 1984), 14.
38. Oral history of Jimmy McPartland, #1–68, Rutgers.
39. Oral history of Bill Challis, #2–3, Rutgers.
40. *KS*, 94–95.
41. Ibid.

## 5. Influences on Goodman

1. In the 1940s Goodman gave many of his records to the Widener Library at Harvard. They have been examined by Grover Sales.
2. *New Yorker*, Dec. 26, 1977.
3. Unidentified news clipping of Berendsohn obituary, probably from a New Orleans newspaper.
4. Ibid.
5. Soards Directory, 1916.
6. Unidentified obituary, as for note 3.
7. *Down Beat*, unidentified clipping from John W. Miner Collection, Tulane.
8. Unidentified obituary, as for note 3.
9. *KS*, 29.
10. Jack Brymer, *Clarinet* (New York: Schirmer Books, 1976), 151–53.
11. Personal communication from Sparkman.
12. Stanley Dance, *World of Earl Hines*, 195.
13. *KS*, 33. Goodman said he heard Roppolo once; Stanley Dance, *The World of Swing*, 262, quotes Goodman as saying he never heard Roppolo in person.
14. *New Yorker*, Dec. 26, 1977, 41.
15. George Hoefer liner notes for *The Chicagoans*, Decca DL 79231.
16. Interview with Stacy.
17. Oral history of Bud Freeman, #86, Rutgers.
18. Lewis Porter, *Lester Young* (Boston: Twyane, 1985), 34–35.
19. H. O. Brunn, *The Story of the Original Dixieland Jazz Band* (Baton Rouge: Louisiana State University Press, 1960), 165.
20. LaRocca scrapbooks, Tulane.

## 6. The First Recordings

1. Interview with Sid Weiss, April 28, 1987.
2. *Down Beat*, July 1951, 3.

3. Interview on *Jazz Tonight*, Channel 13, 11:30, Oct. 22, 1981. Film in archives of John L. Fell.
4. *Down Beat*, July 1951, 2.
5. Ibid., 3.
6. *KS*, 110.
7. Connor, 3.
8. *The Melody Maker*, Dec. 17, 1949, 9.
9. Voice of America interview with Goodman, reprinted in *Down Beat*, Feb. 8, 1956, 13.
10. *Phonograph Monthly Review*, Nov. 1928, 71.

## 7. The Free Lance

1. Details of Klein's life from an interview with Mannie Klein, April 29, 1987.
2. Erik Barnouw, *A Tower in Babel: A History of Broadcasting in the United States* (New York: Oxford, 1966), 90.
3. Ibid., 91.
4. Ibid., 127.
5. Ibid., 186.
6. Ibid., 221.
7. Ibid., 224.
8. Roland Gelatt, *The Fabulous Phonograph 1877–1977* (New York: Collier, 1977), 255.
9. *Variety*, Nov. 12, 1930, 1.
10. Collier, *Duke Ellington*, 96.
11. Herb Sanford, *Tommy & Jimmy: The Dorsey Years* (New York: Da Capo, 1977. First published by Arlington House, 1972), 35–36.
12. Nat Shapiro and Nat Hentoff, *Hear Me Talkin' To Ya* (New York: Dover, 1966 repr. First published by Rinehart, 1955), 269.
13. Oral history of Jimmy McPartland, #1–70, Rutgers.
14. *KS*, 102.
15. Ibid., 103.
16. Ibid., 109.
17. Dance, *The World of Earl Hines*, 195.
18. Baron, *Benny: King of Swing*, 22.
19. *KS*, 115–16.
20. Ibid., 114.
21. Baron, *Benny: King of Swing*, 23.
22. *KS*, 114.
23. *KS*, 119.
24. Oral history of Bud Freeman, #2–46, Rutgers.
25. *Saturday Evening Post*, Dec. 18, 1954, 67.
26. Quoted by Mel Powell in interview, April 27, 1987.
27. *KS*, 120.

## 8. Enter John Hammond

1. *KS*, 117.
2. Baron, *Benny: King of Swing*, 24.
3. Connor, 93.
4. *Orchestra World*, May 1932, 19.
5. *The Melody Maker*, June 1932, 503–4.
6. Eric Hobsbawm, writing as Francis Newton, *The Jazz Scene* (New York: Monthly Review Press, 1960. Reprinted New York: Da Capo Press, 1975), 64.
7. *KS*, 122.
8. *Down Beat*, Feb. 8, 1956, 41.
9. Details of Hammond's family background and youth are in John Hammond with Irving Townsend, *John Hammond on Record* (New York: Summit Books, 1977).
10. Ibid., 15.
11. Ibid., 36.
12. Interviews with R. D. Darrell May 21, 1982 and Oct. 4, 1984.
13. Hammond, *John Hammond on Record*, 46.
14. Carl Van Vechten, *Nigger Heaven* (New York: Knopf, 1926).
15. Bruce Kellner, *Carl Van Vechten and the Irreverent Decades* (Norman: University of Oklahoma Press, 1968), passim.
16. *Vanity Fair*, July 1925, 52, 92; August 1925, 57, 86, 92; Oct. 1925, 46, 92, 98.
17. Unidentified clipping, Hammond vertical file, Rutgers.
18. Hammond, *John Hammond on Record*, 67.
19. *Down Beat*, Feb. 8, 1956, 11.
20. *New Masses*, March 2, 1937, 29.
21. John Hammond, *John Hammond on Record*, 122–23.
22. Collier, *The Reception of Jazz in America*, 71–73.
23. *The Nation*, April 26, 1933 and Dec. 20, 1933.
24. *New Masses*, April 20, 1937, 35–37; July 13, 1937, 27.
25. Otis Ferguson, *The Otis Ferguson Reader* (Highland Park, IL: December Press, 1982), 103.
26. *Harper's*, Sept. 1939, 436.
27. Ferguson, *The Otis Ferguson Reader*, 197.
28. *Harper's*, Sept. 1939, 436.
29. John Hammond, *John Hammond on Record*, 177.
30. Interview with Barney Josephson, fall 1975.
31. Collier, *Duke Ellington*, 244.
32. Oral history of Teddy Wilson, #2–29, Rutgers.
33. *Society Rag*, Sept. 1938, collected in Ferguson, *The Otis Ferguson Reader*, 97–103.
34. *Harper's*, Sept. 1939, 431–40.
35. *Newsweek*, Sept. 20, 1943, 108.
36. Hammond, *John Hammond on Record*, 108.
37. Ibid.
38. Hammond, *John Hammond on Record*, 108.

39. Details of this story are given in *John Hammond on Record*, 109, and in *KS*, 123.
40. Collier, *Duke Ellington*, 196.
41. Hammond, *John Hammond on Record*, 110.
42. *The Melody Maker*, Jan. 7, 1956, 3.
43. Details of this recording session are given in Hammond, *John Hammond on Record*, 109–12, and *KS*, 124–25.
44. Hammond, *John Hammond on Record*, 112.
45. *Down Beat*, Feb. 8, 1956, 41.
46. Ibid.
47. *Harper's*, Sept. 1939, 436.
48. Collier, *The Reception of Jazz in America*, 21.
49. John Chilton, *Billie's Blues* (New York: Stein and Day, 1975), 6.
50. Collier, *Duke Ellington*, 127.
51. Hammond, *John Hammond on Record*, 68.
52. Interviews with Maher.

## 9. The Free-Lance Recordings

1. Connor, 31.
2. *KS*, 112.
3. Arthur Rollini, *Thirty Years with the Big Bands* (Urbana, IL: Illinois University Press, 1987), passim.
4. Ibid., 13–22.
5. Walter C. Allen, *Hendersonia*, 119.
6. *KS*, 113.
7. Personal communication.
8. James Lincoln Collier, *The Making of Jazz* (Boston: Houghton Mifflin, 1978), 221.

## 10. Goodman Forms a Band

1. *KS*, 132.
2. For details of the development of the Casa Loma Orchestra, George Simon, *The Big Bands*, 4th ed. (New York: Schirmer, 1981), 117–26.
3. Maher, personal communication.
4. Baron, *Benny: The King of Swing*, 27–28.
5. *KS*, 130.
6. Hammond, *John Hammond on Record*, 140.
7. Maher, personal communication.
8. *Collier's*, Jan. 20, 1956, 27.
9. *Down Beat*, Oct. 19, 1955, 39.
10. Art Rollini, *Thirty Years with the Big Bands*, 34.
11. Pee Wee Erwin, as told to Warren W. Vaché, Sr., *This Horn for Hire: The Life and Career of Pee Wee Erwin* (Metuchen, NJ: The Scarecrow Press, 1987), 106.
12. *Down Beat*, Feb. 22, 1956, 11–12.

13. *KS*, 141.
14. Art Rollini, *Thirty Years with the Big Bands*, 34.
15. *Collier's*, Jan. 20, 1956, 27.
16. Art Rollini, *Thirty Years with the Big Bands*, 34.
17. *Down Beat*, Feb. 22, 1956, 11–12.
18. Art Rollini, *Thirty Years with the Big Bands*, 33.
19. *KS*, 142.
20. Art Rollini, *Thirty Years with the Big Bands*, 35.
21. *Down Beat*, Feb. 22, 1956, 11–12.
22. Allen, *Hendersonia*, 298.
23. *The Clipper*, Jan. 24, 1923, 30.
24. *New York Times*, May 31, 1924.
25. Ibid., Dec. 11, 1924, 2:5.
26. *Orchestra World*, Jan. 1926, 19.
27. Ibid., 1927, 3.
28. *Down Beat*, Oct. 1935, 1.
29. Allen, *Hendersonia*, 317.
30. Interviews with James T. Maher. Much of the material on the *Let's Dance* show comes from the Maher interviews.
31. *Down Beat*, Feb. 22, 1956, 11–12.
32. Maher, personal communication.
33. *New Yorker*, Dec. 26, 1977.
34. *Baron, Benny: King of Swing*, 29. John Hammond says $120 for the sidemen, "quadruple" for the leader, *Down Beat*, Feb. 22, 1956, 11–12.
35. Most of the material on Helen Ward is from an interview with her, Jan. 12, 1987.
36. Simon, *The Big Bands*, 208.
37. Oral History of Freeman, #2–20, Rutgers.
38. Interviews with Maher.
39. Interview with Mannie Klein, April 29, 1987.
40. The provenance of Goodman's arrangements, especially the early ones, is not always easy to work out. Walter C. Allen, in *Hendersonia*, 317–21 gives some attributions. The best source are the some 1200 Goodman arrangements at Yale, attributions for which are based on information supplied by Russ Connor, but reviewed by others.
41. Pee Wee Erwin, *This Horn for Hire*, 91.
42. *International Musician*, June 1987, 8.
43. Erwin, *This Horn for Hire*, 91.
44. Details of Fletcher Henderson's career can be found in Walter C. Allen, *Hendersonia*, passim.
45. Dicky Wells as told to Stanley Dance, *The Night People* (Boston: Crescendo, 1971), 24–25.
46. *KS*, 157.
47. Interviews with Maher.
48. *Down Beat*, Jan. 1935, 3.
49. *Metronome*, March 1935, 22.
50. George Simon, *The Big Bands*, 206.
51. Art Rollini, *Thirty Years with the Big Bands*, 40.
52. *KS*, 170, 183–84.
53. Interviews with Maher.

54. *KS*, 185–86, and Hammond, *John Hammond on Record*, 130.
55. Hammond, *John Hammond on Record*, 147.
56. *Toronto Daily Star*, May 27, 1965, 19.
57. *Harper's*, Sept. 1939, 437.


## 11.  The First Victor Records

1. Interview with Maxwell.
2. Interview with Weiss.
3. Simon, *The Big Bands*, 223.
4. Connor, 47.
5. Maher, personal communication.
6. Allen, *Hendersonia*, 321.
7. Sanford, *Tommy and Jimmy: The Dorsey Years*, 47–50.
8. Chilton, *Stomp Off, Let's Go*, 13.
9. Collier, *Duke Ellington*, 175, 180.
10. *Down Beat*, July 1935, 1.
11. Collier, *Louis Armstrong: An American Genius*, 249–69.
12. Interview with Hammond, 1982.
13. Collier, *Duke Ellington*, 87.
14. *Saturday Evening Post*, Dec. 18, 1954, 67.
15. Interview with Maxwell.
16. Interview with Stacy.
17. Oral history of Cootie Williams, #215–16, Rutgers.
18. Reported by Jimmy Maxwell in interview.
19. Interview with John Bunch, April 6, 1987.
20. Interview with Weiss.
21. Ibid.
22. Interview with Powell.
23. Ibid.
24. Interview with Maxwell.
25. Interview with Powell.
26. Interview with Bunch.
27. Interview with Powell.
28. Interview with Weiss.
29. Interview with Maxwell.
30. Reported by John Bunch in interview.
31. Interview with Maher.
32. Interview with Bunch.
33. *Down Beat*, Nov. 17, 1977, 14.


## 12.  Making It at the Palomar

1. Rollini, *Thirty Years with the Big Bands*, 242.
2. Erwin, *This Horn For Hire*, 111.
3. Hammond, *John Hammond on Record*, 143.
4. Most of the biographical information on Jess Stacy is from an interview with him, April 29, 1987.

5. *Down Beat*, July 11, 1957, 19.
6. Interview with Stacy.
7. Oral history of Bud Freeman, #2–2, Rutgers.
8. Interview with Stacy.
9. Ibid.
10. *New York Times*, Feb. 6, 1975.
11. Interview with Stacy.
12. Interview with Helen Dance, April 28, 1987.
13. Interview with Stacy.
14. Ferguson, *The Otis Ferguson Reader*, 90.
15. *Metronome*, Oct. 1943, 33.
16. Interview with Weiss, April 28, 1987.
17. Interview with Stacy.
18. *Down Beat*, July 1936, 8.
19. Connor, 307.
20. Interview with Maher.
21. Ibid.
22. Ibid.
23. *Down Beat*, August 1935, 4.
24. Interview with Stacy.
25. Connor, 126.
26. Paul G. Cressey, *The Taxi-Dance Hall* (New York: Greenwood Press, 1932), passim.
27. *KS*, 193–96.
28. Interview with Stacy.
29. Goodman, in *KS*, 196, says that it was Bunny Berigan's idea to split the band up, and he put a stop to it, but Rollini, *Thirty Years with the Big Bands*, 42, and Helen Ward in interview, both say that it happened as I have given it.
30. Rollini, *Thirty Years with the Big Bands*, 46.
31. *KS*, 198.
32. *Down Beat*, Jan. 12, 1951, 3.
33. Interview with Maher.
34. *Disques*, Sept. 1932, 290.
35. *KS*, 199.
36. Interview with Maher.
37. *New Yorker*, April 17, 1937, 35.
38. *Down Beat*, Dec. 1935, 12.
39. Rollini, *Thirty Years with the Big Bands*, 46.
40. Oral history of Bud Freeman, Rutgers.
41. Dance, *The World of Earl Hines*, 196.
42. Interview with Maher.
43. Unidentified clipping in Berigan vertical file, Rutgers.
44. Interview with Maxwell.
45. Interview with Stacy.
46. *Down Beat*, Jan. 12, 1951, 3.
47. Interview with Powell.
48. Dance, *The World of Earl Hines*, 196.
49. Interview with Maher.

### 13. Finally, Success

1. Interview with Maher.
2. *Chicago Sunday Tribune*, Nov. 3, 1935, otherwise unidentified clipping at Yale.
3. *Literary Digest*, Aug. 25, 1917, 28–29.
4. Collier, *Duke Ellington*, 149.
5. Information on Ashcraft from interview with Helen Oakley Dance, and John L. Fell, personal communication.
6. Interview with Helen Oakley Dance.
7. *Down Beat*, Oct. 1935, 7.
8. Interview with Helen Oakley Dance.
9. *Down Beat*, Dec.-Jan. 1935–36, 1.
10. Interview with Helen Oakley Dance.
11. *Down Beat*, Dec.-Jan. 1935–36, 1.
12. Ibid., April 1936, 1.
13. Collier, *The Reception of Jazz in America*, 22.
14. KS, 210.
15. Interview with Helen Oakley Dance.
16. Hammond, *John Hammond on Record*, 159.
17. Interview with Helen Oakley Dance.
18. Connor, 56.
19. Collier, *Louis Armstrong: An American Genius*, 76.
20. Whitney Balliett, *American Musicians* (New York: Oxford, 1986), 337.
21. Willie "The Lion" Smith with George Hoefer, *Music on My Mind* (New York: Da Capo, 1975, originally published by Doubleday, 1964), 4.
22. Charlie Barnet with Stanley Dance, *Those Swinging Years* (Baton Rouge: Louisiana State University Press, 1948), 58.
23. *Crescendo International*, April 1987, 21.
24. Interview with Helen Oakley Dance.
25. *Down Beat*, April 1936, 9.
26. Oral history of Jimmy Maxwell, #2–31, Rutgers.
27. Oral history of Teddy Wilson, #3–7–9, Rutgers.
28. *Saturday Evening Post*, Dec. 18, 1954, 33.
29. *Crescendo International*, April 1987, 21.
30. Oral history of Teddy Wilson, #3–5–7, Rutgers.
31. Ibid., 6.
32. Ibid., #1–46.
33. Interview with Leonard Feather, April 27, 1987.
34. Oral history of Jimmy Maxwell, #1–40, Rutgers.
35. *Saturday Evening Post*, Dec. 18, 1954, 33.
36. Details on Teddy Wilson are from his oral history at Rutgers. I am grateful to Alyn Shipton for access to an unpublished manuscript by Wilson.
37. Ibid., #1–18.
38. Ibid., #1–20.
39. Ibid., #1–34–5.
40. Hammond, *John Hammond on Record*, 113–14.

41. *New York Times Sunday Magazine*, April 14, 1974, 28–29.
42. *Time*, Jan. 20, 1936, 35.
43. *Down Beat*, May 1936, 9.
44. *KS*, 212.
45. Personal communication from Connor.
46. Rollini, *Thirty Years with the Big Bands*, 48.
47. Ibid., 52.
48. *Down Beat*, Oct. 19, 1955, 39.
49. *Orchestra World*, August 1936, 6.
50. Erwin, *This Horn for Hire*, 137–41.
51. Rollini, *Thirty Years with the Big Bands*, 52.
52. Ibid., 61.
53. Ibid., 53.
54. Details of Lionel Hampton's autobiography are from Dance, *The World of Swing*, 265–70.
55. Chris Albertson, *Bessie* (New York: Stein and Day, 1972), 75–76.
56. *Saturday Evening Post*, Dec. 18, 1954, 32.
57. Erwin, *This Horn for Hire*, 140.
58. Hammond, *John Hammond on Record*, 173.
59. Rollini, *Thirty Years with the Big Bands*, 53.
60. Interview with Maxwell.
61. Dance, *World of Swing*, 271.
62. *Saturday Evening Post*, Dec. 18, 1954, 32–33.
63. Rollini, *Thirty Years with the Big Bands*, 54.
64. John Chilton, *Who's Who of Jazz* (London: Chilton Book Company, 1972), 37.
65. Simon, *The Big Bands*, 209.
66. Ferguson, *The Otis Ferguson Reader*, 94.
67. Details of James's autobiography from the *New York Times*, July 6, 1983, sec. B, 8.
68. Ibid.
69. Rollini, *Thirty Years with the Big Bands*, 54–55.
70. Interview with Maxwell.
71. *Saturday Evening Post*, Dec. 18, 1954, 33.
72. Ibid., May 7, 1938, 22.
73. *New Yorker*, April 17, 1937.
74. *KS*, 219–20.
75. *Variety*, March 17, 1937, 43.
76. *Billboard*, March 6, 1937.

## 14.  The Swing-Band Phenomenon

1. *Down Beat*, Feb. 1936, 5.
2. See George Simon, *The Big Bands*, for details on the rise and decline of various of these bands.
3. Hammond, *John Hammond on Record*, 172.
4. Baron, *Benny: King of Swing*, passim.
5. Rollini, *Thirty Years with the Big Bands*, 56.

6. Cab Calloway and Bryant Rollins, *Of Minnie the Moocher and Me* (New York: Crowell, 1976), 263.
7. *Washington Tribune*, May 8, 1937.


## 15. The Victor Classics

1. Connor, personal communication.
2. Hammond, *John Hammond on Record*, 133.
3. Dance, *World of Swing*, 261.
4. Interview with Maher.
5. Ibid.
6. Erwin, *This Horn for Hire*, 85.
7. Autobiographical data on Harris from *Down Beat*, Oct. 1, 1943, 15.


## 16. The Star

1. *Variety*, March 24, 1937, Yale scrapbooks.
2. Interview with Helen Oakley Dance.
3. *Down Beat*, June 1937, 1.
4. Ibid., 2.
5. Ibid., 3.
6. *Down Beat*, Oct. 1937, 1.
7. Ibid.
8. *Radio Daily*, March 29, 1937, Yale scrapbooks.
9. *Herald Tribune*, Yale scrapbooks.
10. *Life*, Nov. 1, 1937, 120–24.
11. *New Yorker*, April 17, 1937, 27–34.
12. *Saturday Evening Post*, May 7, 1938, 22.
13. *Down Beat*, May 1937, 3.
14. *New Yorker*, April 17, 1935, 32.
15. *Down Beat*, May 1937, 1.
16. Rollini, *Thirty Years with the Big Bands*, 62.
17. Ibid., 62.
18. *Down Beat*, Feb. 1937, 4.
19. *The Melody Maker*, April 8, 1939, 2.
20. Oral history of Freeman, #2–40, Rutgers.
21. Interview with Helen Oakley Dance.
22. Oral history of Wilson, #2–27, Rutgers.
23. *Down Beat*, March 17, 1968, 20.
24. Interview with Weiss.
25. Interview with Bunch.
26. *Down Beat*, August 15, 1943, 1.
27. Simon, *The Big Bands*, 213–14.
28. *Saturday Evening Post*, Dec. 18, 1954, 67.
29. Interview with Helen Oakley Dance.
30. Interview with Maxwell.
31. Ibid.

32. Gene Lees Jazzletter, August 1986, 8.
33. Interview with Bunch.
34. Interview with Dance.
35. Interview with Phillips.
36. Interview with Maxwell.
37. Interview with Powell.
38. Dance, The World of Swing, 315.
39. Philadelphia Daily News, March 22, 1974, Yale scrapbooks.
40. Metronome, Oct. 1946, 18.
41. Interview with Powell.
42. Shapiro and Hentoff, Hear Me Talkin' To Ya, 321.
43. Barnet with Dance, Those Swinging Years, 186–87.
44. Interview with Maxwell.
45. Ibid.
46. Down Beat, Jan. 12, 1951, 1.

## 17. The Famous Carnegie Hall Concert

1. New York Times, Jan. 16, 1938, sec. 8, 21.
2. Samuel B. Charters and Leonard Kunstadt, Jazz: A History of the New York Scene (New York: Da Capo, 1984, originally published by Doubleday, 1962), 26.
3. Arnold Shaw, The Jazz Age: Popular Music in the 1920s (New York: Oxford, 1987), 47–53.
4. The New Grove Dictionary of American Music, 319.
5. Collier, Louis Armstrong: An American Genius, 94.
6. Collier, Duke Ellington, 157.
7. American Music Lover, June 1936, 63.
8. Liner notes by Irving Kolodin, Benny Goodman Carnegie Hall Jazz Concert, Columbia OSL-160.
9. The New Grove Dictionary of American Music, vol. II, 442.
10. New Yorker, Dec. 26, 1977, 34.
11. Wall Street Journal, Jan. 7, 1988.
12. Liner notes, Benny Goodman Carnegie Hall Jazz Concert, Columbia OSL-160.
13. Ibid.
14. Ibid.
15. Hammond, John Hammond on Record, 200.
16. New York Times, Jan. 16, 1938, sec. 8, 7.
17. Down Beat, Feb. 1938, 5.
18. New York Times, Jan. 17, 1938, 11.
19. New York Herald Tribune, Jan. 17, 1938, 7.
20. New York World Telegram, Jan. 17, 1938, 11.
21. New York Sun, Jan. 17, 1938, 15.
22. New York Herald Tribune, Jan. 17, 1938, 7.
23. New York Times, Jan. 17, 1938, 11.
24. New York Sun, Jan. 17, 1938, 15.
25. Otherwise unidentified clipping from New York Times, 1968, Yale.
26. Time, Jan. 24, 1938, 58.

27. *Down Beat*, Feb. 1938, 1.
28. Ibid., 6.
29. Connor, 80.
30. *New Yorker*, Dec. 26, 1977, 40.
31. *Down Beat*, June 28, 1938, 4.
32. *Collier's*, Feb. 25, 1939, 13.
33. Voice of America interview, reprinted in *Down Beat*, Feb. 8, 1956, 12.
34. Connor, personal communication.
35. Stanley Dance, *The World of Count Basie* (New York: Scribner's, 1980), 304.
36. *Down Beat*, April 1938, 6.
37. Connor, 83.
38. *Down Beat*, May 1938, 1.
39. *Down Beat*, June 1938, 1.
40. *Down Beat*, April 1938, 6.
41. *Down Beat*, May 1938, 1.
42. Interviews with Ward, Maher.
43. Simon, *The Big Bands*, 535.
44. Rollini, *Thirty Years with the Big Bands*, 58–59.
45. Interview with Ward.
46. Details of Freeman's youth from his oral history, #1–12, Rutgers.
47. Ann Banks (ed.), *First Person America* (New York: Knopf, 1980), 227.
48. Details of Tough's biography are from Freeman oral history, #52–60, Rutgers.
49. Interview with Weiss.
50. *Down Beat*, April 1938, 2.
51. Rollini, *Thirty Years with the Big Bands*, 66.
52. Ibid.
53. Interview with Powell.
54. Rollini, *Thirty Years with the Big Bands*, 67.
55. *Down Beat*, August 1939, 1.
56. *Down Beat*, Dec. 15, 1939, 19.
57. Allen, *Hendersonia*, 371.
58. *Metronome*, August 1939, 7.
59. Allen, *Hendersonia*, 372.
60. Simon, *The Big Bands*, 218.
61. Interview with Stacy.
62. Ferguson, *The Otis Ferguson Reader*, 87.
63. *Down Beat*, Nov. 17, 1977, 15.

## 18. The Carnegie Hall Band

1. Voice of America interview printed in *Down Beat*, Feb. 8, 1956, 12.
2. Oral history of Eddie Durham, #2–31, Rutgers.
3. Personal communication, Maher, Connor.
4. *The New Grove Dictionary of American Music*, vol. IV, 362.
5. Ibid., vol. I, 286.
6. See Hammond, *John Hammond on Record*, for details of this story.

7. Ibid., 176–77.
8. According to Connor, Goodman is probably playing tenor saxophone on the August 16, 1934, Columbia recording of "Take My Word," possibly in two other places, and definitely on a Sextet version of "Powerhouse" from September 14, 1937, which has been issued on LP.
9. Freeman, *You Don't Look Like a Musician*, 29.
10. *The Melody Maker*, April 8, 1939, 2.
11. Interview with Maher.
12. Maher, personal communication.
13. Connor, personal communication.
14. Simon, *The Big Bands*, 217.

## 19. The First Small-Group Recordings

1. Collier, *The Making of Jazz*, 299.
2. Winthrop Sargeant, *Jazz: Hot and Hybrid* (New York: Da Capo, 1975, originally published by Dutton, 1938), 58–60.
3. Unpublished manuscript.

## 20. The Columbia Band

1. *Down Beat*, Nov. 15, 1940, 2.
2. Neil Leonard, *Jazz and the White Americans* (Chicago: University of Chicago Press, 1962), 139.
3. *Variety*, April 28, 1937.
4. Leonard, *Jazz and the White Americans*, 89.
5. *New York Times*, May 19, 1937, 26.
6. *Down Beat*, Jan. 1938, 6.
7. Hammond, *John Hammond on Record*, 210.
8. Ibid., 144.
9. *Down Beat*, Dec. 15, 1939, 2.
10. Interview with Weiss.
11. Rollini, *Thirty Years with the Big Bands*, 69.
12. Details of Maxwell's biography from his oral history, Rutgers.
13. Ibid., #2–6.
14. Oral history of Eddie Sauter, #1–122, Rutgers.
15. Oral history of Maxwell, #2–14, Rutgers.
16. Details of Sauter's biography from his oral history, Rutgers.
17. Ibid., #1–64–5.
18. Ibid., #1–62.
19. Ibid., #1–83.
20. Ibid., #1–69–71.
21. Ibid.
22. *Metronome*, Nov. 1946, 19.
23. Oral history of Sauter, #1–132, Rutgers.
24. Interview with Maxwell.
25. Allen, *Hendersonia*, 371.
26. Oral history of Sauter, #1–112, Rutgers.

27. Ibid., #1–113.
28. Ibid., #1–84.
29. *Saturday Review*, May 17, 1958, 41–43.
30. Joel Williamson, *The Crucible of Race* (New York: Oxford, 1984), 401.
31. *Saturday Review*, May 17, 1958, 42.
32. Ibid., 43.
33. Ibid., 42–43.
34. Porter, *Lester Young*, 9.
35. Interview with Maxwell.
36. Oral history of Eddie Durham, #1–72, Rutgers.
37. Ibid., #2–82.
38. Hammond, *John Hammond on Record*, 223–26.
39. Allen, *Hendersonia*, 373.
40. *New Yorker*, May 20, 1972, 128–29.
41. Collier, *The Making of Jazz*, 348.
42. Connor, personal communication.
43. *Swing*, Nov. 1939, 6.
44. *Down Beat*, March 15, 1940, 1.
45. Connor, 112.
46. Ibid., 380.
47. Ibid.
48. Ibid.
49. For details of Williams's life and career, see Collier, *Duke Ellington*, 85–87.
50. For details of Williams's switch to Goodman, see ibid., 239–40.
51. Ibid.
52. Details of Powell's life and career are from interview with Powell.
53. Ibid.
54. Smith with Hoefer, *Music on My Mind*, 253.
55. *Down Beat*, Sept. 1, 1941, 16.
56. Interview with Stacy.
57. Interview with Powell.
58. Ibid.
59. Details of Catlett's life and career are from a manuscript by George Hoefer in Catlett vertical file, Rutgers.
60. Ibid., 6.
61. Ibid., 7.
62. Ibid., 1.
63. Ibid., 2.
64. Interview with Powell.
65. Hoefer ms. in note 59, 3.
66. Connor discusses the Catlett departure in detail, 125.
67. Simon, *The Big Bands*, 269–70.
68. *Chicago Sun*, Nov. 7, 1942.
69. Simon, *The Big Bands*, 223.
70. John L. Fell, personal communication.
71. Maher, personal communication.
72. Interview with Maxwell.

## 21. The First Columbia Recordings

1. Oral history of Eddie Durham, #22, Rutgers.
2. Interview with Powell.
3. Oral history of Eddie Sauter, #1–73–4, Rutgers.
4. Ibid., 111.
5. Interview with Maxwell.

## 22. The Sextet

1. New Yorker, May 20, 1972, 129.
2. Collier, Duke Ellington, 60.
3. Oral history of Eddie Durham, #2–81, Rutgers.
4. Connor, 113.

## 23. Marriage and Family

1. Ben J. Wattenberg and Richard M. Scammon, This U.S.A. (Garden City: Doubleday, 1965), 35.
2. Robert A. Woods and Albert J. Kennedy, Young Working Girls: A Summary of Evidence from Two Thousand Social Workers (Boston: Houghton Mifflin, 1913), 56–59.
3. Interview with Carol Phillips.
4. John Hammond, John Hammond on Record, 112.
5. Ibid., 140.
6. Interview with Maher.
7. The Melody Maker, April 8, 1939, 2.
8. Interview with Ward.
9. Hammond, John Hammond on Record, 24.
10. Ibid., 60.
11. Ibid., 18.
12. Ibid., 24.
13. The Melody Maker, Jan. 28, 1956, 4.
14. Ibid.
15. Interviews with Maher, Weiss, Ward.
16. Hammond, John Hammond on Record, 238.
17. Ibid.
18. Interview with Powell.
19. Hammond, John Hammond on Record, 60.
20. Interview with Mae Weiss, April 28, 1987.
21. Interview with Powell.
22. Hammond, John Hammond on Record, 12.
23. Interview with Stacy.
24. Interview with Maher.
25. Interview with Powell.
26. Rollini, Thirty Years with the Big Bands, 35.
27. Interview with Maher.

28. Interview with Powell.
29. Interview with Mae Weiss.
30. Interview with Maher.
31. Interview with Powell.

## 24. An Era Ends

1. *Variety*, April 28, 1937.
2. *Down Beat*, August 1, 1942, 1.
3. *Down Beat*, Oct. 1, 1943, 1.
4. *Down Beat*, April 15, 1942, 1.
5. *Down Beat*, Jan. 15, 1943, 1.
6. *Down Beat*, Oct. 15, 1942, 1.
7. *Down Beat*, June 1, 1942, 13.
8. *Metronome*, April 1943, 16.
9. *Down Beat*, July 5, 1943, 2.
10. Collier, *Louis Armstrong: An American Genius*, 221.
11. See Connor, 145 for details of this story.
12. See issues of *Metronome*, May 1943, 7; June 1943, 6; July 1943, 7, for details of this story.
13. *Metronome*, August 1943, 7.
14. Interview with Weiss.
15. Ibid.
16. Donald Russell Connor, *BG—Off the Record* (Fairless Hills, PA: Gaildonna, 1958), 210.
17. *Down Beat*, August 15, 1943, 2.
18. *Metronome*, October 1942, 8.
19. *Metronome*, May 1944, 42.
20. *Down Beat*, April 1, 1944, 1.
21. Connor, 155.
22. Oral history of Eddie Sauter, #130, Rutgers.
23. Ibid., 120.
24. *Down Beat*, Sept. 1, 1945, 11.
25. *Down Beat*, Feb. 1, 1945, 1.
26. *Metronome*, April 1945, 26.
27. *Metronome*, August 1945, 15.
28. *Down Beat*, August 1, 1945, 8.
29. *Metronome*, July 1945, 18.
30. *Down Beat*, July 1, 1945, 8.
31. *Metronome*, May 1946, 42.
32. *Metronome*, August 1946, 14.
33. *Metronome*, July 1946, 14.
34. *Down Beat*, Sept. 1, 1945, 1.
35. *Down Beat*, Jan. 1, 1946, 1.
36. *Down Beat*, Nov. 15, 1945, 1.
37. *Down Beat*, Jan. 1, 1946, 10.
38. *Down Beat*, May 15, 1944, 1.
39. *Down Beat*, May 1, 1944, 1.
40. *Down Beat*, July 1, 1946, 3.

41. *Down Beat*, August 12, 1946, 1, 12.
42. Ibid., 1.
43. *Down Beat*, August 26, 1946, 7.
44. *Down Beat*, Sept. 9, 1946, 1.
45. *Down Beat*, Nov. 18, 1946, 1, 4–5.
46. Ibid.
47. Ibid.
48. *Down Beat*, Dec. 2, 1946, 1.
49. *Washington Post*, Dec. 2, 1946.
50. Rollini, *Thirty Years with the Big Bands*, 121.
51. Interview with Stacy.
52. Chilton, *Who's Who of Jazz*, 210.
53. Collier, *Duke Ellington*, 127, 246.
54. See Collier, *The Making of Jazz*, for the rise of bop, 341–61.

## 25.  The Bop Band

1. See Collier, *The Making of Jazz*, 341–61, for discussion of the rise of bop.
2. Ross Russell, *Bird Lives!* (New York: Charter House, 1973), 135.
3. Collier, *Louis Armstrong: An American Genius*, 305.
4. Unidentified clipping in Yale scrapbooks.
5. *Down Beat*, July 26, 1966, 21.
6. Quoted in ibid.
7. Unsigned ms., probably by George Hoefer, in Goodman vertical file, Rutgers.
8. Brian Rust, *The American Record Label Book* (New Rochelle, NY: Arlington House, 1978), 57.
9. Interview with Weiss.
10. Interview with Bunch.
11. Ibid.
12. Interview with Stacy.
13. Interview with Powell.
14. Ibid.
15. *Down Beat*, April 9, 1964, 22.
16. Connor, 191.
17. Unidentified ms., probably by Hoefer, in Goodman vertical file, Rutgers.
18. Details of Hasselgard's biography from *Capitol News*, Feb. 1948, 7.
19. *Metronome*, Sept. 1948, 20–21.
20. *Down Beat*, July 26, 1966, 21.
21. Ibid.
22. Unidentified ms., probably by Hoefer, in Goodman vertical file, Rutgers.
23. Talk at International Association of Jazz Record Collectors' Convention, Culver City, Los Angeles, August 15, 1987. Tape in author's files.
24. Collier, *The Making of Jazz*, 400.
25. See note 23.
26. *The Melody Maker*, Jan. 1, 1949, 2.

27. See issues of *The Melody Maker*, May–July 1949 for details of this story.
28. Connor, 197.
29. *Down Beat*, July 26, 1966, 40.
30. Ibid.
31. Quoted in *Down Beat*, July 26, 1966, 40.
32. Ibid.
33. Ibid.

## 26. The Classical Goodman

1. *Down Beat*, Nov. 17, 1977, 42.
2. *KS*, 166.
3. Ibid., 167.
4. Ibid., 168.
5. Connor, 86.
6. Ferguson, *The Otis Ferguson Reader*, 81.
7. *Down Beat*, Nov. 17, 1977, 42.
8. Interview with Ernest Lumer.
9. Ibid.
10. *The Melody Maker*, Oct. 22, 1938.
11. Ibid.
12. *Sunday P.M.*, Dec. 8, 1940, otherwise unidentified clipping in author's files.
13. *New York Times*, Dec. 13, 1940, 28.
14. *New York Times*, Dec. 16, 1947, 47.
15. Simon, *The Big Bands*, 221.
16. *New York Times*, Nov. 19, 1946, 40.
17. *New York Times*, Dec. 16, 1947, 47.
18. *Down Beat*, May 7, 1952, 4.
19. *The Guardian*, Dec. 10, 1976.
20. Interview with Powell.
21. Interview with Lumer.

## 27. The Last Bands

1. *New Yorker*, Dec. 26, 1977, 40.
2. *Down Beat*, Dec. 31, 1952, 1.
3. Hammond, *John Hammond on Record*, 312–22.
4. Collier, *Louis Armstrong: An American Genius*, passim.
5. Hammond, *John Hammond on Record*, 312–13.
6. Ibid., 314.
7. Ibid., 315.
8. Collier, *Louis Armstrong: An American Genius*, 265–66.
9. Hammond, *John Hammond on Record*, 315.
10. Ibid., 316.
11. *Down Beat*, May 20, 1953, 1.
12. Hammond, *John Hammond on Record*, 322.
13. *Down Beat*, July 1, 1953, 1.

14. Hammond, *John Hammond on Record*, 316–17.
15. Shapiro and Hentoff, *Hear Me Talkin' To Ya*, 322.
16. Hammond, *John Hammond on Record*, 316, says that Goodman "staggered" on stage at Carnegie Hall during the tour with Armstrong; Canadian promoter Richard Flohil observed Benny to drink "two bottles of excellent French wine" before a concert in Toronto, according to a letter from Flohil in *Gene Lees Jazzletter*, July 1987, 2. Confidential sources say that Goodman was treated for problems with alcohol.
17. Interview with Weiss.
18. Interview with Maxwell.
19. *Gene Lees Jazzletter*, August 1986, 6.
20. Interview with Carol Phillips.
21. Interview with Bunch.
22. *Down Beat*, Jan. 12, 1951, 3.
23. Hammond, *John Hammond on Record*, 323–25.
24. Ibid., 323.
25. *Down Beat*, Oct. 19, 1955, 39.
26. Connor, 262.
27. Information on Russian jazz is based on trips to the U.S.S.R. in 1966 and 1985, which included many meetings with Russian musicians, critics and promoters.
28. *Gene Lees Jazzletter*, August 1986, 3.
29. Interview with Bunch.
30. *Gene Lees Jazzletter*, August 1986, Sept. 1986, Jan. 1987.
31. Avakian, personal communication.
32. *New York Times*, May 31, 1962.
33. Letter from Myssovsky to author, dated Nov. 30, 1987.
34. Ibid.
35. Connor, 241.
36. Interviews with Maher, Powell, Ward.
37. Connor, 297.
38. *Gene Lees Jazzletter*, Sept. 1986, 2.
39. Connor, 290.
40. Interview with Bunch.
41. Ibid.
42. *Down Beat*, Nov. 17, 1977, 14.
43. Connor, 307.
44. Interview with Phillips.
45. Connor, 308.
46. Connor, 315.
47. Interview with Maher.
48. Details of Goodman's death from interview with Phillips, and *New York Daily News*, June 14, 1986, 5. The versions are slightly different.

## 28.  The Legacy of Benny Goodman

1. *Metronome*, August 1945, 13.
2. *Saturday Evening Post*, May 7, 1938, 22.

# A Selected
# Discography

Because Benny Goodman's popularity has remained high, record companies have kept in print a huge amount of his work, with good samplings of cuts from all his periods. Central to any Goodman collection is the RCA box of sixteen records, called *Benny Goodman, The RCA Victor Years*. These records are also available in eight double albums, called *The Complete Benny Goodman*, vols. I–VIII. The Columbias have not been systematically reissued, but three volumes have been issued in the Columbia Jazz Masterpieces series, called simply *Benny Goodman*, vols. I–III. A good sampling of the Victor sides is available on *This Is Benny Goodman*, VPM-6040, a double album. There is single album sampling called "Benny Goodman and His Orchestra, Sing, Sing, Sing," in the Bluebird Treasury series. "Benny Goodman's Greatest" Col. CL 2483, is a good short selection of the Columbias.

Goodman's earlier work has been reissued on at least a score of albums, the bulk of them by Sunbeam, which has specialized in Goodman. Of particular interest are "Benny Goodman and the Whoopee Makers," Sunbeam SB-114; "Ben Pollack and His Orchestra," Sunbeam SB-136; and three volumes of airchecks from the *Let's Dance* show.

For the small groups, the French Black and White label has issued a complete set of the Victor small groups in its lengthy Jazz Tribune series, called *The Small Combinations*. For the Columbia Sextets, there is "Solo Flight: The Genius of Charlie Christian," G-30779. Columbia also has kept in print the Carnegie Hall concert; the current package is called "Benny Goodman Live at Carnegie Hall," and is also in the Jazz Masterpiece series. Finally, Musicmasters, in an arrangement with Yale University, is issuing both on LP and CD selections from the vast library of tapes Goodman left to Yale. This archive will continue to be mined, and there is as well an enormous body of other Goodman material in the hands of private collectors, some of which will come on the market in haphazard fashion over the years.

# Index

Downes, Olin, 40, 216–17
"Down Home Rag," 144–46
"Down South Camp Meeting," 134, 197, 244
"Dream," 326
Du Bois, W. E. B., 263
Duchin, Eddy, 189
Duckworth, George Arthur, 297–98, 350
"Duke's Idea," 287
Dunbar, Rudolph, 341
Dunham, Sonny, 123
Durham, Eddie, 46, 237, 261, 263–64, 278
Duvivier, George, 146, 351
Dylan, Bob, 95, 100

"Earl, The," 273–74, 283–84
"Early Autumn," 287
"East St. Louis Toodle-Oo," 287
Eberly, Bob, 319
"Eccentric," 151
Eckstine, Billy, 323, 332
Eddie Lang–Joe Venuti and Their All Star Orchestra, 115
"Egg Head," 336
Egstrom, Norma. See Lee, Peggy
"Egyptian-Ella," 113
Einstein, Albert, 218
Eldridge, Roy, 140, 172, 202, 203, 235, 251, 273, 353
Elitch's Gardens, 164, 179
Elizalde, Fred, 115
Ellington, Duke, 23, 31, 37, 79, 108; background, 41, 73, 322; and Goodman, 216, 310; and Hammond, 100, 104; influence, 360–62; musicianship, 14, 133, 149, 152–53, 156, 261; orchestra, 19, 58, 141, 167, 189, 228; popularity, 87, 114, 122, 150, 166, 258, 307, 316; songs, 117, 194, 236, 283, 286; style, 43, 47, 188–89, 236, 268–69, 283, 287, 291, 321, 352
Ellison, Ralph, 262–63
Elman, Ziggy, 190, 200, 222, 243, 278; background, 184–85; on Goodman, 210, 213; with Goodman, 195, 226, 245–46, 253, 267, 277–78, 346, 350–51
Engel, Carl, 40
England, 114, 127–28, 171
Erwin, Pee Wee, 125, 133, 134, 158, 169, 183–84, 195, 198, 244
Esquire, 225, 310
Etri, Bus, 264
Europe, James Reese, 30, 145; and the Clef Club Orchestra, 214
Evans, Bill, 360
Evans, Gil, 181, 183
Evans, Herschel, 190
"Everybody Step," 37, 39

"Everything I Have Is Yours," 130
Ewing, Annemarie, 216
"Exactly Like You," 184, 249

"Farewell Blues," 116
Fatool, Nick, 259, 288
Fazola, Irving, 53–54, 185, 202
Feather, Leonard, 175, 321, 334
Feld, Morey, 310, 313
Feldman, Vic, 354
Ferguson, Maynard, 321
Ferguson, Otis, 99–100, 161, 184, 227, 340
"Fidgety," 151
Fields, Dorothy, 51
Fields, Lew, 51
Fields, Shep, 189, 193
Fisher, Eddie, 165, 320
Fishkind, Arnold, 332
Fitzgerald, Ella, 131
Five Spot, 215
Flindt, Emil, 172
"Floyd's Guitar Blues" (record), 263–64
"Flying Home" (record), 288, 290
"For Dancers Only," 193
Foresythe, Reginald, 117, 147
Forrest, Helen, 266, 275
"Four Brothers," 282, 287
"Four or Five Times," 56, 65
Foyer, Bernie, 52
Free for All, 93
Freeman, Bud, 22, 25, 27, 42, 50–51, 66, 79, 85, 91, 117, 160, 167, 208, 222–26, 231, 240, 243, 313–14
Friar's Society Orchestra, 21, 64
Froeba, Frankie, 105, 145, 150, 159
"Froggie-Moore," 58
"Frolic Sam," 286
"Futuristic Rhythm," 55

Gabler, Milt, 140
Gale, Harry, 22
Garrison, Jimmy, 289
"Gee! But You're Swell," 196
Geller, Herb, 168, 184
Gennett Records, 19
Gershwin, George, 38, 57, 89–90, 255, 282
"Get Happy," 133, 201, 204
Getz, Stan, 72, 146, 240, 313–14, 327, 350–51
"Giant Steps," 79
Gifford, Gene, 46, 123, 151, 362
Gilbert, Gama, 216
Gilbertson, Gish, 315
Gillespie, Dizzy, 71, 215, 234, 288–89, 320–24, 326, 329–30, 334–35
"Gilly," 289–90
Gilmore, Patrick Sarsfield, 33
"Gimme a Pigfoot," 118

harmonic, 340; Tenderloin district, 29, 30, 34, 224
New Yorker, 206
New York Herald Tribune, 217
New York Sun, 217
New York Times, 29, 38, 214, 216, 341–42
New York World Telegram, 217
Newman, Joe, 356
Newsweek, 100
Newton, Frankie, 117, 173
"Nice Work If You Can Get It," 70
Nichols, Red, 41, 75–77, 96, 102, 122, 132, 221, 257, 305, 362; Goodman with, 77–81, 88–92, 112; and His Five Pennies, 40, 43, 67
Nigger Heaven, 96, 97
"Night Wind," 145
Niles, Abbe, 40
Nine-fifteen Revue, 89
"1937–38 Jazz Concert No. 2, The" (album), 345
"Nitwit Serenade," 144
Noble, Jiggs, 133
Noble, Ray, 328
Noone, Jimmie, 16, 64–68, 83, 155, 159, 162, 327, 331; influence of, 25, 116, 177, 247
Norman, Gene, 330
Norris, Frank, 206, 362
North, Alex, 342
Norvo, Mildred, 138
Norvo, Red, 146, 214, 225, 261, 339; and Goodman, 111, 117, 135, 139, 146, 177, 232, 310, 312–13, 327, 351
"Now's the Time," 336
Nunez, Alcide "Yellow," 293–94
"Nuthin' But," 37

Oakley, Helen. See Dance, Helen Oakley
Oak Park High School, 22, 224
Oberstein, Eli, 137
O'Brien, Floyd, 171
O'Connell, Helen, 319
"Ode to Billy Joe," 352
O'Farrill, Arturo "Chico," 333, 335
"Oh Baby!," 314
"Oh, Lady Be Good!," 250, 314–15
O'Keefe, Francis "Cork," 123
Oklahoma City, 262–63
"Old Black Joe," 238
Oliver, Joe, 113
Oliver, King, 18–19, 24–45, 39, 43, 214–15; arrangements, 58, 116, 119, 144; Creole Jazz Band, 40; Dixie Syncopators, 40
Olsen, George, 127, 257
"Omph Fah Fah," 314

124th Regiment Field Artillery Band, 21, 62
"One O'Clock Jump," 232, 241, 265, 286, 352, 355
"On Revival Day," 111
"On the Trail," 31
Onyx Club, 103, 214
"oooOO-OH-BOOM!," 240
"Opus 1/2," 249
Orchestra World, 35, 180
Original Creole Orchestra, 18
Original Dixieland Jass Band, 18–19, 25, 30, 61–62, 68, 86, 107, 159, 215, 219
Original Memphis Five, 38, 62, 68
Osborne, Will, 275
Osgood, Henry Osborne, 31
Osman, Sylvester "Vess," 124

"Paducah," 312
Page, Hot Lips, 168, 263
Page, Patti, 165, 320, 332
Page, Walter, 239, 241, 263, 293
Pal Joey, 279
Palomar, 164, 179, 183–84, 189, 352; Goodman at, 158, 166–67, 170, 180–81, 205, 215
Palumbo, Frank, 332
Panelli, Charlie, 19, 293
Paramount Theatre, 88, 163, 219, 230, 309, 313, 345, 351–52; Goodman at, 186–87, 190–91, 206, 271, 314
Parenti, Tony, 112
Park Central Hotel, 51–53, 55, 89
Parker, Charlie, 84, 140, 215, 288, 329, 332, 335–36; bebop, 320–22, 323, 327; style, 14, 72, 326, 360
Parlophone Records, 101–2
Pastor, Tony, 190, 226
Paul, Eddie, 88
Payne, Al, 127
"Peckin'," 232
"Pennies from Heaven," 203
Pennsylvania Hotel, Madhattan Room, 184–86, 206–7
"People," 352
Perkins, Francis D., 217
Pete Kelly's Blues (film), 275
Petrillo, James C., 304, 305
Philadelphia, 332
Phillips, Carol, 11, 296, 299, 348, 358–59
Phillips, Flip, 351
Phillips, Helen, 211
Phillips, Sam, 165
Phonograph Monthly Review, 83–84, 96
"Picasso," 247
"Pick-a-Rib," 245, 249, 255
"Pick Up Your Sins," 37